Selections from the Gutter

Selections from the Gutter

Jazz Portraits from 'The Jazz Record'

Edited by

Art Hodes and Chadwick Hansen

UNIVERSITY OF CALIFORNIA PRESS

Berkeley · Los Angeles · London

802871

University of California Press
Berkeley and Los Angeles, California
University of California Press, Ltd.
London, England
Copyright © 1977, by
The Regents of the University of California
ISBN 0–520–02999–2
Library of Congress Catalog Card Number: 75–7193
Printed in the United States of America

This book is for Thelma Hodes
and for Louise and Herbert Hansen

My music? It's people's music. It never had a color to distinguish it; it did have tints and hues. From the very beginning it was a happy marriage of varied cultures, but it came to us from the insides of a downtrodden race. My music is spirituals that speak of hope, promise, better ways. It's the blues. . . . Leadbelly singing "When you got chicken on your plate an you can't eat, you got the blues." It's the street corner washboard band . . . the jug band . . . the piano man keeping the left hand going as the right connects with a drink . . . the jazz band that hits you down the middle, inside . . . Muddy Waters saying goodnight to Sarah Vaughn (after she'd spent an evening in his place, listening) and reminding her, "Now, you all come back, 'cause this is where the sure-enough is." My music is from down home, my music is.

ART HODES, "My Music"
The Jazz Sheet, March-April 1969

This magazine speaks for the music and its musicians, to set down those things a horn itself cannot express, to bring alive the personalities listed on your record labels, and to encourage the musicians and those who like their work to keep playing the real and authentic jazz.

ART HODES, "A Jazz Note to You," 1945

Contents

PART 5: LEST WE FORGET

Preface

Art Hodes was born in Nikoliev, Russia, on November 14, 1904; his family moved to the United States when he was six months old. Raised on Chicago's tough West Side, he took piano lessons at Hull House and began gigging—playing occasional jobs—as a teenager. His first full-time job came in 1925 in the gangster-owned Rainbow Gardens. His advanced training in jazz came from many sources: from Wingy Manone, the New Orleans trumpet player with whom Hodes roomed and worked in the late twenties, and with whom he made his first recordings; from Louis Armstrong, to whom Wingy led him; but especially from the many blues pianists on Chicago's black South Side. "Chicago's South Side became my alma mater," Hodes once wrote. "I studied nightly." One is reminded by that line of Melville, another American artist who learned his art outside the academy, and his "a whale-ship was my Yale College and my Harvard."

Since his apprentice days he has had an extraordinarily full career. The list of musicians he has played with reads like a jazz hall of fame; they include Louis Armstrong, Eddie Condon, Sidney Bechet, Bix Beiderbecke, Bud Freeman, Pops Foster, Pee Wee Russell, Wingy Manone, Gene Krupa, Chippie Hill, and Bunk Johnson. He has played many of the best-known jazz clubs, including the Blue Note, the Brass Rail, Rupneck's, and Jazz Ltd. in Chicago, and Nick's, Jimmy Ryan's, the Stuyvesant Casino, and the Village Vanguard in New York. He has recorded for Decca, Mercury, and Victor among the majors and for many of those small companies which have done so much more than the so-called "majors" to keep jazz available to the record-buying public. The list of these is long and distinguished; it includes Blue Note, Commodore, Solo Art, Signature, Jazzology, Paramount, GHB, Delmar, and Storyville.

He has lectured and played at many colleges and universities, and has been more than willing to play high schools as well, putting up with the inconvenient hours and the minimal pay because he believes passionately in bringing jazz to people who have never had the opportunity to hear it before. (If it seems odd to suggest that most high school students have never had a chance to hear jazz, think about it for a moment. High school students get their music from the radio and from the local record store. Ninety-nine percent of the music available to them is popular music, plus a small amount of classical music; there is seldom any jazz.) I can remember hearing him for the first time at a high school assembly in Bronxville, New York, in the early forties.

He has taught jazz piano. In recent years he has made a number of television shows, chiefly for educational television, and one of them, *Plain Ol' Blues*, won him an Emmy. Currently he is doing concert tours with his own group for Columbia Artists.

Art Hodes

Hodes is a two-fisted pianist, which is to say that his left hand—his rhythm hand—is as authoritative as his right. He says that he developed it early, playing solo piano in clubs whose owners wouldn't hire a bass or drums, so that he had to be his own rhythm section. That authoritative left hand has served him well in solos, and has also made him one of the great band-pianists. For years he has been a leader both in name and in fact. He is also that rarity, an articulate musician, who speaks and writes as he plays, directly and with authority.

In the early forties he did a jazz record show for WNYC, New York City's public radio station. The letters and the phone calls from his audience gave him his first full view both of the public's ignorance of jazz and of its willingness to learn. So when Dale Curran, a printer and author of jazz fiction, approached him with the idea of starting a jazz

Art Hodes

magazine, Hodes was receptive, and from February 1943 to November 1947 the two of them edited *The Jazz Record*, Curran dropping out during the last year and Hodes carrying on with the help of Harold Hersey.

The initial aims were modest: the magazine was to be primarily a newsletter, telling the public where they could hear jazz, and acting as a medium of exchange for collectors of jazz records. But very early the magazine began to bridge the gap between the musicians and the public in another fundamental way—by telling the musicians' stories. This was done in part through the conventional technique of having a critic or aficionado do a biographical article. But more importantly, it was done in two ways no other magazine had ever tried. First, Hodes wrote his own autobiographical articles, and wrote them very well. Second, he persuaded other musicians to come to the office and tell their stories, while Curran, who could type as fast as the musicians talked, took down what they said. The result was an important body of oral history, created before that technique (or the term itself) was in general use among professional historians.

Hodes has felt for some time that these musicians' stories deserved a more permanent and accessible home than they found in the pages of the magazine. They find that home here, and they also gain by being gathered together out of the more ephemeral materials in the magazine. So gathered, they form an impressive composite portrait of the traditional jazz musician in the forties.

About the title—Art explains its general meaning in the last piece in the collection, but it has a specific meaning as well. *Selection from the Gutter* is the title of a blues he wrote when he was scuffling in New York, trying to make it at the end of the depression. When the late Dave Tough heard that title he liked it so well that he asked permission to use it as the title of the book in which he was to tell his own story—a book that never came out.

Many people have helped in the putting together of this anthology, but we would especially like to thank Carrie Louvar, of the American Civilization Program at the University of Iowa, who retyped several of the original articles, and Alain L. Hénon and Gene Tanke of the University of California Press, who proved to be sympathetic and helpful editors. The largest debt, of course, is to all the people who made *The Jazz Record* the magazine it was, and especially to all the musicians whose stories were told there.

CHADWICK HANSEN

University of Illinois at Chicago Circle

August 15, 1976

Introductions

Introducing . . .
The Jazz Record, 1943

by Art Hodes

On April 6th of last year, 11 a.m., Gene Williams, publisher of the now defunct *Jazz Information* magazine, sat with me in the reception hall of Station WNYC waiting for my audition for the position of Metropolitan Reviewer. Ralph Gleason, also of *J.I.*, had convinced me that I was the man for the job—that I could do it.

Their main argument was that if the job left open by Ralph Berton's moving to another station should fall into the wrong hands, jazz would suffer a setback.

And so I sat waiting for the audition. I was interviewed by the head man. I was tested over the mike, and accepted, and that same afternoon I did my first program.

Within two or three months I was doing the program alone. At first this was quite a task. To begin with I owned about one hundred and fifty records at that time. I borrowed a few records; I was loaned a discography. I began collecting.

And that's the story of my becoming a jazz commentator.

Which ties up with this magazine. Some months ago it dawned on me, through the mail I received from listeners and through talking to jazz enthusiasts, that the listeners to my program didn't know where to hear jazz played—that is, most of them—also, they didn't know where to get hold of the records they wanted. After the restrictions on shellac for recording, it became even more difficult. Meanwhile, some record stores took advantage of the situation and charged fantastic prices for beat records. Here I was devoting my time to passing the word along on jazz, and trying to keep it alive, and on the other hand a whole set of circumstances was doing a great harm and defeating my purpose.

About this time Dale Curran, who is a writer and jazz enthusiast, and also a printer, got to talking to me about a small publication on jazz. As several others had already told me I should do something along those lines—and as the need was there—we decided to publish a small semi-monthly magazine, with a two-fold purpose—

To keep jazz lovers informed as to where they could hear jazz played in person—and when I say jazz I speak in the broader sense in which the word has come to be accepted—I really should say, hot music.

Then, to help them get their hands on records. This problem we have met by starting a record exchange, columns devoted to records that collectors have for trade, for sale, or that they want. Through these columns you will meet other collectors, you will learn about records, about their history and value, and you will become an active collector yourself.

By the time this war is won there can be such a great number of jazz lovers and collectors that the recording companies will have to take our desires into consideration. And the result will be better musicians, better bands, better recordings.

One more point: as an active musician, taking a hand in a work of this sort, I hope to create a better understanding between musicians and their listening public.

3

Mr. Curran and myself realize the job we've taken on is no cinch. It means a lot of work. We also realize that others have failed before us, and that at no time, to our knowledge, has a jazz publication paid for itself. We have no financial backers, but there is a job to be done and we believe there's an audience, a public—waiting, wanting—a publication of this sort. Most of the young men who would have been willing and able to do the job are off to war. We want to do our share in building a better world to live in, and this is work we can do.

But we can't go on without your help, without your constant support. This is your magazine. Whether it fails or succeeds rests with you—we'll do our part.

The Jazz Record: The First Year, 1944

by Art Hodes and Dale Curran

This month *The Jazz Record* is a year old. We make that simple announcement with considerable pride. At any time, just surviving for a year is a big achievement for a jazz magazine; starting in wartime, fighting paper shortages and high prices and the general upheaval of all civilian life, it becomes a sort of miracle that we don't even understand ourselves. And if, beyond that, a magazine can grow and expand—that is really something to congratulate ourselves about.

A year ago, when No. 1 came off the press, it looked as though jazz and jazz literature were in a bad way. Many of our best jazz musicians were being unceremoniously dumped into the army where they had neither time nor opportunity to play; record collectors, critics and music lovers were going the same way. There seemed to be no time in a war-busy world for jazz, its players or its listeners. We felt then, and still feel, that there was danger of slipping back; that jazz, beginning to be accepted by serious students of music, might be driven underground by indifference, or ruined by commercialism.

A year ago there was not a single regularly published magazine in the jazz field. We knew that there was a large and eager public, record collectors, young (and not so young) enthusiasts of jazz, who wanted and needed a publication to keep the true spirit of jazz alive, to fight, however feebly, against commercialization of the music and commercial exploitation of its players. We had no illusions about making money; in fact, we had lively apprehensions of losing our shirts. We felt that if nobody else took on the job it was somehow our responsibility.

Within the first few months it became obvious that we had underestimated the job ahead of us. Starting with publication twice a month, and concentrating on the New York field, with news notes of local musicians and where to go to hear them, we found that our circulation was rapidly spreading out all over the United States; we found that what our readers wanted was a magazine that would cement together all the scattered jazz lovers of America and help them keep themselves on the right track. They didn't merely want to know where Joe Blow is playing now; they wanted to know more about Joe and his music, what he plays and why, where this music came from and where it is going.

So *The Jazz Record* grew. As soon as the increasing circulation permitted, it grew from eight pages to sixteen. It grew from a news-sheet to a general monthly magazine. It reached out to cover all possible angles of the world of jazz, living and recorded.

We discovered many things in this year. First, that the musicians themselves, creators of the music, are the best possible people to tell about it. We discovered that, given a little encouragement and stenographic help, such people as Kaiser Marshall, Jack Bland, Mezzrow, Davenport, had good stories to tell and could tell them well. We discovered new writers and critics—Alma Hubner, Fats Baker, Bob Aurthur, to name a few of the regular contributors.

We had help and encouragement from the established critics and writers, Hammond, Charles Edward Smith, etc. We were fortunate in adding Sergeant Avakian to our staff as record critic. Especially we are indebted to Sergeant Otto Hess for his fine series of photographic portraits that have made our covers into collectors items.

And so at the end of the year, the magazine is still alive, still growing, still going places. How about jazz itself in that year?

Jazz is doing all right. Possibly we had some small influence in helping it. In spite of war conditions, in spite of record shortages, jazz has had a good year. But there are dark spots, troubles in view. Too many good jazz musicians are out of jobs, in spite of the night-club boom and the general pick-up of interest in jazz. Too many corny record-jockeys are selling the public a synthetic and unintelligent substitute for jazz. Too many of the me-too boys are trying to climb on a bandwagon they neither love nor understand, knowing only that there must be money in anything so popular. We still have a big job to do, and with the continued support of our subscribers and advertisers, we are going ahead with it.

The Jazz Record Remembered, 1973

by Art Hodes

1943 was a good year, and New York City was where the happenings were taking place. Chicago had it but let it get away. Jazz had made the trip to the Windy City from New Orleans. You could hear it all then. King Oliver and Louis Armstrong. Johnny and Baby Dodds. Kid Ory. The New Orleans Rhythm Kings. The beat was there. But it didn't last, and by the '30s the spirited players had moved it on East.

The Big Apple wasn't "jazz" jumpin' but somehow or other a good share of the "le jazz hot" players managed to make it come together and hung in there. Harlem was a warm place; 52nd Street existed, and we had Greenwich Village. There actually were some places where a jazz man could play for a

listening audience without being back-up to a floor show.

For the first time in my life in jazz I found people who weren't players taking a hand in helping the music exist. Milt Gabler and Steve Smith had record stores and were issuing jazz recordings. The late Gene Williams, and his partner Ralph Gleason, were publishing a fine magazine, *Jazz Information*. Eddie Condon was promoting the music. There was a feeling that we weren't going to let our music dry up. So, when I was offered a radio program on Mayor LaGuardia's city station (WNYC), I grabbed it. No salary, no expenses; not even records. My backers and myself furnished all the ingredients except of course the turntable and the needle. So, for six afternoons weekly I talked about the music I loved, spun the records, and played some piano. I got some of our greatest jazz greats to contribute their talents. And within a short time I had gathered a tremendous listening audience.

It was during this period that a gentleman (Dale Curran) approached me with the idea of issuing a jazz periodical. Dale was a printer by trade and an editor by inclination. And he'd had two books published *(Piano In The Band,* and *Dupree Blues).* I was convinced there was a need for such a magazine, just reading the mail I was receiving from my many listeners. My audience wanted to know where to purchase the recordings I was featuring; where to hear the greats whose music I played, etc. There was a need to bring the music and musicians, and the public together.

February 15th, 1943, brought *The Jazz Record* into reality; our first issue. And from this very first issue we featured a jazz musician's picture on our cover, alternating Negro and White. Almost immediately, jazz lovers flocked to our help. John Hammond contributed our first article ("Is Duke Ellington Deserting Jazz?"). Mezzrow *(Really The Blues)* was our first "musician" writer. Now the doors opened. Bob Aurthur (now Robert Alan Aurthur) came on the board. Photographers Otto Hess and Charles Peterson sent us fine cover photos. And I began to write for the magazine quite regularly. But we needed more articles by the musicians themselves. And that became my big job. Here's how we worked it out.

I knew, of course, that most "le jazz hot" players don't "function" during the day; they recuperate. So "forget it" about asking them to write. What's the solution? We hit upon this: get a player to visit with you. When he's at ease, get him to tell his story. Dale could type away as fast as one could talk. So we got each tale word for word. Now we began to have a jazz mag of distinction. Some of the stories we got were worth our every effort.

Dale Curran really did yeoman duty. The editing, the mailing. But there was a satisfaction we both got. There was a war going on, and one doughboy in France would read *Jazz Record,* then re-mail it to a friend in the South Pacific area. At one point our English friends were handling some thousand mags an issue. Yeh, it was something worthwhile.

Eventually though, I lost my radio show. The (late) Mayor (LaGuardia) usually was on and off the air before my show appeared. But one afternoon his schedule varied. So he heard me announcing names of recordings, labels, companies etc. "Get that guy off the air; he's commercial." So I was warned. But when you're operating on a "no pay" budget you can't afford a secretary to handle your mail. Impossible answering all the inquiries. I had to do it on the air. Yes, there was a second time the Mayor heard the show. That had to affect our subscriptions. I'd lost a large audience. And after four years of *JR* with Dale Curran at the helm, he called it quits. So I struggled on one more year. The mag had lasted close to five years; some sixty issues. No regrets.

When I think that if it wasn't for *Jazz Record* quite a few of our greats in jazz would never had a word of their life's story recorded in words. Just the Cow Cow Davenport article alone is worth the time I put in. I just can't begin to name all the stories that I enjoy looking at once more. So much "straight from the mouth" talk. The thought occurs "would you do it again?" No question; push the clock back on the years and my answer has to be "of course." That, my friends, is the beauty of jazz and the players and what they have to say; especially when it comes out without hesitation; when it flows. For reading some of the enclosed is like listening to a "for real" jazz player render a chorus. It's like being in a jazz band; someone stomps off a tempo and you're into a tune. Now you know this jazz tune real well. Don't have to look at the sheet. You shut your eyes and improvise. It flows out. You're tellin' the truth.

1

The Facts of Life

by Art Hodes

It was primarily Art Hodes whose tastes and ideas set the tone of the magazine, and it will be Art who introduces many of the musicians whose stories are in the following sections. So we start with Art himself, and the pieces he wrote for the magazine. Some of them were written as a series called "The Facts of Life." Others were done as individual pieces, and appeared at random throughout the life of the magazine. Gathered together, they make a brief but impressive autobiography, full of the people, the places, and the music that made up one musician's life.

C.H.

The Rainbow Cafe

The first cafe I ever worked in was called the Rainbow Cafe. It was situated on West Madison Street in Chicago.

I believe I was nineteen years old, or less, when I started there. The place was a corner apartment, and you climbed about 25 stairs to get there, and there it was—no doors to open—the top of the stairs and the waiter got you seated.

This was about 1924 or '25, prohibition days. You got a drink if you were O.K. The place seated about 150, tops. Just a piano player all week, with a small band on Saturday, maybe, depending on the weekly business. Always two or more entertainers, girls who could mix and drink. In those days a gal singer mixed and drank or she found herself out of work. For the most part the pianist depended on his tips for his salary, or the bulk of it, and the gals split their tips with the piano player. A non-mixer never made much gold, so . . .

Well, my boss was one of Chicago's tough men. He was a big man in his way. He never spent much time in the joint, but left the running of it to his woman. She was my direct boss, and she treated me O.K. For that matter, so did he, but he had other businesses. I heard rumors of this and that but all I actually knew about was his gambling house. I had had the bad sense to try out the poker game once—and just once. And that's where I heard about the big boss' partner, The Greek, being able to drop $2,000 without flicking an eyelash. He was a crazy guy. I remember him racing me, my car going in third, his in second, down a boulevard, just at daylight. When he saw me beginning to draw away, he almost ran me into a tree on the sidewalk.

I remember auditioning for the job. My boss had two brothers who were musicians,

union men (my, how big that sounded to me then!). The boss was a bit musical himself. He owned an expensive guitar which he tuned like a ukelele, and sang some of the dirtiest lines I've ever heard.

Well, when he heard me play a bit, he said: "O.K. Start next week. Thirty-five bucks. Be here at nine o'clock."

The boss had taken a liking to my playing and besides he was saving fifteen a week by hiring me. So, although the entertainers squawked at first, because I couldn't transpose the popular tunes into their keys (I could only play in about four keys then) the boss kept me and let the entertainers groan. Little by little I learned to play in a few more keys and added numbers by memory. I stayed there eighteen months in all, and by the time I left, I knew the business pretty well.

Yes, I knew the business. That's what I want to tell you about—the business. Sure, you pick up a record and hear a wonderful chorus played. "Isn't it wonderful to be able to play like that!" It sure is. But there's a price we have to pay to get that way. We have to go through the mill. There are no geniuses, boy wonders, born artists. In all my playing days I never met one yet.

Let's get back to the Rainbow Cafe. Mind you, when I went to work there my folks hadn't as yet told me the facts of life. Don't get me wrong—I have the best parents in the world—but they didn't know about beer joints and dives and here's one thing they couldn't have told me about.

One night a bunch of the boys came into our cafe—the ruling mob of the day —gangsters, over a dozen of them. They sat down at a table with the gang boss at the head, ordered liquor (their own—our place was buying from them). They spotted me almost immediately as being green, so I was fed plenty of liquor—so I got plenty sick. But one thing I do remember—the boss' woman in tears. She had to serve them, and it was common gossip that that gang had taken care of her husband. It was just a sample of that fine sense of humor among that clique that I became better acquainted with as I went along.

At the time I took the job, I had never heard any real jazz on records or heard any colored musicians play in person. I had a habit of beating time with the side of my foot against the side of the piano. The boss told me: "You better quit beatin' my piano or I'll tie your foot up."

And I remember the first time anyone ever stole a tip from me. It was a good looking entertainer who was being chased quite a bit and by the right people. I saw her get a two dollar tip, and I watched her hand me fifty cents. I was fit to be tied. I'd never had any experience with anything dishonorable, and it came as a shock to me.

And so I got a bit calloused. I watched people get drunk, I saw a lot of night life. I got better acquainted with the piano. Singers began to like my playing. I got a bit relaxed, I began to look around, visited other joints, met the help.

Up to the time I got this job, I'd been playing a few Italian weddings, or week ends at dime-a-dance halls, or small parties —piano and drums—possibly saxophone added. I'd never come in contact with anything as commercial as what I was now doing. I'd sit at the piano from 9 p.m. to 4 a.m. A couple of times during the night I could sneak out to the boys' room. Not too often —the piano player had to keep the lull out of the joint. When it starts getting quiet in a cafe people get restless and leave. That's bad. So I learned to play without killing myself, and when a live one came in, a man with money, we all came to life. Song after song for him; the gals would come up and stuff the money in my pocket. At the Rainbow job I never used my salary. I bought a car, nice clothes, and was in the chips.

One experience there stands out vividly in my memory. Two young chaps, about 25 or so, came in one night and started picking up drinks at other people's tables and taking them away, claiming to be Federal agents. One was acting up, the other fellow was just

with him. Well, my boss and a few of his pals got there in a hurry. By that time there were just a few customers left, and they were shooed out and the door was locked. The boss went to work on this "agent," who, of course, turned out to be a phoney. Well, that's the first time I ever saw someone worked on. The boss got him in a corner and would kick him in the shins, and then when he'd bend over, straighten him up with his fists. It went on longer than I could stand. At the end of this unmerciful exhibition, he was thrown down the twenty-five steps; someone hauled him around the corner to the alley and left him there. His friend got away easy in comparison—just for being in bad company.

Musically, that place was swell for me. I learned lots of tunes, I developed my ear. It got so all a gal had to do was sing the melody to me once or twice and away we went. That was wonderful training. I began to hear harmonies I never knew existed. Before I left I was getting offers right and left to work other places.

Cafes in those days were about all alike. If it was a real class spot, it sported a five-piece band and an intermission piano player and singers. A floor show would consist of a M.C., a line of girls, the singers in the place—the band was strictly for background and a little dancing. Not much dancing—a boss can't make money with you out on the floor, away from the table. The entertainers were the important people in the place. The band was at the bottom of the ladder. The piano player was more important—we had our social status, you know. The first few days in a new place you'd feel like you weren't wanted. Everyone put on airs. If you were still there a week later you'd fall in place.

The first real band I heard was in a high-class cafe on Wabash Avenue. A friend of mine, a drummer named Harry Smith, had the band, and Joe Sullivan was playing piano in that band. I'd got a job playing for entertainers there. The band was getting sixty bucks a week; I was getting twenty-five. But when I took the job the boss told me: "If you make less than a hundred at any time, quit." I stayed there for several months and the first time I made less than a hundred dollars I quit. I used that as an excuse because I liked to move around and by then I was in demand.

I remember Sullivan and I having an argument because I played on the piano he used. He told me: "You're an entertainers' piano player—lay off my piano." At that time Joe was listening to Earl Hines at the Apex Club, but I'd still never heard a colored man play.

Everybody's in the Union

"If you want to get anywhere in the music business you'll have to join the union. Everybody who can play is in the union."

Although there were quite a few jobs floating around Chicago in the middle and late twenties that were non-union, the best jobs were unionized. I knew I'd have to get a union card, but I was afraid of the exam. I'd heard it was hard—they put up some tough music for you to read at sight! It was many years later that I found out it wasn't so; almost anyone with some bit of musical knowledge could join, whether they could read well or not. But at the time it was a major hurdle for me. Besides, I had to get up a sum of money that loomed large.

Well, I let the union business alone until I happened to be working a small roadhouse job in Hammond, Indiana. There I got nerve to take the exam. I'd played four bars of a waltz, when I was stopped. "O.K., fill out this card."

Back in Chicago I put in my Hammond card, applied for membership, and became "one of the boys." That was doing it the hard way.

Some time later I met Earl Murphy, who was then playing banjo. And when some drummer Murf knew was looking for a piano player who would go out of town on a summer resort job, Murf recommended me, and I went.

That was Delavan Lake, Wisconsin. And that's where I was introduced to jazz— to Armstrong, Dodds, Ory, Bix—a new world for me—through Murphy's record collection.

The drummer's name was Les; he was the leader. Les was crazy about the way I played waltzes, and he also liked my natural way of swinging. The other men, besides Murf, Les and myself, played violin, sax, and trumpet. They were all better "papermen" than I was, all had more schooling.

Almost immediately Murf got "on me" to listen to his Louis records and the way the rhythm played behind Louis. And he played Bix records. In a short while I'd bought some records of my own, and a vic., and I was studying jazz intensively.

And from then on I always had trouble of one sort or another with the men I worked with, first on that job and later on others. You see, in the Hot Fives that Louis made, he didn't use drums. And Miss Lil and the banjo, St. Cyr, had to carry the beat. The result was that Miss Lil had to play a lot of chords—"solid piano"—instead of "spreading out." Without thinking about this at the time, I started pounding out chords which knocked the drummer, Les, out of his mind. And many were the arguments that followed. One time I was even invited outside. I got out of that in a hurry. Coward? No, I wouldn't quite say that. Les was a war veteran and he told me that if I started with him it was for keeps—no holds barred. And I was still much of a kid.

But I kept playing that piano my way, except on those waltzes. We played plenty of those.

Lots of things happened to me on that job. Did you ever hear of a Dr. Clark who wrote a book called *How to Live and Eat for Health?* Somehow or other Murf and I discovered him (I think the violinist put us on his track). Anyway, it says in the book "meat and potatoes don't go together—drink 'steen glasses of water daily—eat this—don't eat that . . . " Murf and I became hypnotised by Dr. Clark, and more troubles appeared on this peaceful summer resort job. We started getting particular about what we were fed, stuck up our noses so to speak—and, well, all in all, people got a little uncomfortable out there. One thing, Murf and I were in the best of possible health—that was the healthiest period I can remember—but we could have found an easier solution.

The place where we worked, Delavan Gardens, was about two city blocks at the most from a beautiful lake. The working hours were short, the pay was good.

The dance hall could hold a thousand people and on Saturdays, did. That's when we'd have to "pep it up." That was the expression then. "Tiger Rag" was the order of the day—up to tempo—everybody on his feet.

We had a fellow on sax by the name of Baker who was a character if there ever was one. He could do less moving around than anyone I ever saw. He'd cross his feet, put his sax on one side and play. He had a good tone and knew his instrument. As I recall, though, he didn't have anything to say that I can remember— I mean musically, of course. He could get Les, the drummer, more exasperated that anyone. Saturday night, with the place going like mad, Baker would sit there and hardly move. Les, sitting behind him, would reach over with his drum stick and clip him sharply on the dome, hoping to get him to come to life and stand up and let it out. No, not Baker. He'd uncross his feet slowly and turn around slowly and look at Les, and turn back slowly and resume playing his way. Yes, Les had troubles with the band that summer—on top of living with his wife's family.

When I first heard the Hot Five records Louis knocked me out—his ideas, his thoughts—while the rest of the band didn't penetrate my skull. In fact, for a long time I couldn't understand Kid Ory, or that style of playing. It seemed rough and a bit harsh to me—then I only had ears for Louis. And Bix—I liked him immediately, but I could feel that he didn't have the rhythm behind him that Louis did. Many were the discussions we had then as to who was greater, Louis or Bix. I still hadn't heard any good piano on records. That came on my return to Chicago, when I heard Earl Hines on Jimmie Noone's band record "Sweet Lorraine." That was the first time I felt like I ought to give up playing. It happened to me many more times as the years rolled on.

Delavan Lake. Get up in the morning, go down to the lake—row, swim (I mean try), loaf around, listen to Murf's records, play cards—which reminds me . . .

Sometime during the summer two young chaps (one an athlete) who "knew Tesch," came over to our place and we got acquainted. They were staying a few miles away. They knew the "language" so well, and knew all the boys that I'd heard of but never met, that in no time I was hanging on to their every word, taking rides with them. It seemed we were friends.

Seemed is right. On a July 3rd evening they invited the band to their cottage. Nobody accepted but me. We listened to records and made plans for the next day. The 4th we got up and went out. They both had pistols, and I watched them shoot at targets. I wondered at the time about the guns, but didn't question them. I had to play a double-header, two sessions, the 4th. So they drove me back early.

The boys grabbed me when I got back. "Boy, wait till you see your room—man, oh, man!" Some one had robbed me of everything I had. That was one bum kick. And I had to work through that day. Someone told me about "the company I was keeping," but I stoutly defended them. Yes, and they kept running around with me all the following week. Helped pick new clothes for me. Some time later, after they had left, we read about them in the papers. They'd driven to some town and held up a shoeshine shop. A colored boy working there somehow grabbed one of their guns and shot one of the two, killed him. He was the one I liked most. The other got away, but was caught and sentenced to 40-odd years. Funny thing about that. They had two guns—one they forgot to reload. Probably since the 4th.

Well, I was so brought down by all this that I took to gambling with the natives and some of the boys in the band. And luck stood alongside of me all summer; I just couldn't lose. That turned out to be a lucky season for me. The boys got disgusted—it was fifty one night, eighty the next. I couldn't lose, nothing went wrong—they tried everything. They even threw a "special party" for me on my last night there. I won that night too. I bought new clothes, records, and came home with a pocket full of dough.

That job ended in an awful hurry for me. One day, at dinner, someone put one of those advertisements of "I used to be skinny like you but look at me now" under my plate. Well, I about blew my top, and walked out. So the leader came over to give me my notice. I guess I felt the same way he did, because I quit on the spot. They got Dave Rose to follow me in—*The* Dave Rose. I went back to Chi.

One more line about Delavan—at the close of the season the owners used to run a dance, a special affair, and split the proceeds with all the help. The band was back in Chicago by then, but made a special trip. It was considered worth while. Well, a couple of hours before dance time the boys discovered that Baker hadn't brought his sax along—only a bottle of gin. They had to drive to the factory, which was nearby, and get him one. What a character! Murf later got him a job that paid one and a quarter and that didn't faze him. He was late the first night.

It seemed I was always running into characters. Instead of meeting the right people and doing the right things, I'd get mixed up with the wrong people, the "fast set," and do the wrong things. Instead of taking the "Twilight in Turkey" route, it had to be "Gut Bucket" and "Yes, I'm in the Barrel."

Playing for Kicks

Funny thing, how Wingy Manone and I first met. I was introduced to him at the union hall in Chicago, and he immediately started talking big about who he was and what he'd done. I was very much unimpressed and left him with one of those "glad to have met you" routines that people go through with. But we met again.

This time he was looking for a pianist, and Ray Biondi was trying to help him find one. They finally fell into where I was working. They stood in the basement underneath the band and listened, and Ray tells me that when Wingy heard me play he said: "That's the man I want."

And so started a most important period in my life. In a short time we were roommates—then buddies—the best and closest of friends. We lived every minute of each day—and each day was a complete life in itself.

We checked in and were checked out of a hotel where the rent in itself was only eighteen bucks, and I was earning one hundred and twenty-five that week. Yet they kept some of our things in lieu of the bill we didn't pay. If you knew Wingy that wouldn't sound strange. He'd get on the phone and call all over the country. The Ford had to be washed, greased and delivered. We ate the best. Louis Armstrong was at the Savoy at that time, playing in Carroll Dickerson's band, and we were steady customers.

Wingy owned a victrola and a half dozen records, all by Louis, which he played and replayed. Anybody who was somebody stopped at our apartment at some time. The list would sound like a who's who in jazz.

THE JAZZ RECORD

ART HODES, *Publisher*

15c A COPY

No. 25 New York, N. Y. October, 1944

Wingy Manone

The main reason, the only one, was Wingy—his personality. He was a funny man and good kicks were plentiful around him.

Chicago was the home of jazz then. Red McKenzie was doing front office work at Brunswick, digging up talent. Freeman was trying to get started with his own band. Wingy had a band—Louis was at the Savoy—Hines was at the Grand Terrace. The South Side was jumping.

Wingy had a big bear coat that we both took turns wearing. Louis used to greet us with: "Who's the bear tonight?" Joe Oliver would drop in to see Louis regularly. Louis and the boys in the band kept a flat especially for themselves, to be able to drop in at all hours and relax. You know the conversation that takes place on the record by Armstrong called "Monday Date" where Louis says to Earl Hines: "I bet if you had a half pint of Mrs. Circha's gin . . . " (and I'm spelling her name the way it sounds, I've never seen it in print)—well, that was the name of the woman who kept the flat for the boys. For a half-buck you got a cream pitcher full of gin which was passed around as far as it would go. In those days that was what the boys drank.

Sometimes work wasn't too plentiful. Wingy had a connection up at M.C.A. for a while. Once he had two nights booked at the Aragon Ballroom, opposite Wayne King. That first night the King and his men were really hanging around us, paying homage; we really did it that night. Freeman, Krupa, O'Brien—an all-star big band. Wingy stood up in front and directed. Paul Mares stood in the wings and cheered us on. After the job we sat up all night talking about it, and listening to records. The next afternoon we

were a mess. Nobody felt like playing. That was one we fluffed.

Gee, it's funny, when you think back, how every one of us guys had that one thought in mind—music. Who'd ever have thought that so many of us would get involved in so many different directions? All we wanted to do was play our music the way we heard it inside, and none of us thought much about getting famous or making a lot of money. But after the crash of '29 it was just too much to try living on the remains. So most of us started looking for better pickings—and that's another story in itself.

I made one record with Wingy. That was the "Tryin' to Stop My Cryin'"—"Isn't There a Little Love" disc that had [Frank] Teschemacher on clarinet, Augie Schellange on drums, Ray Biondi on guitar, [George] Snurpus on tenor, myself on piano, Wingy on trumpet and doing the vocals. We rehearsed two days for the recording, and it was strictly a recording band; we never worked together as a band anywhere. Schellange really beat it out on drums. He was tending bar at some joint in Chicago's South Side, and we used that place to rehearse for the date. That was the best music that place ever had. We got to swinging so good at times that everyone would lay out but the drums and piano, and that good tempo would go on and on.

And I guess I'll always remember Wingy answering the phone one day. "Hello . . . No, this isn't Art . . . Yes, Art's working —with me . . . Yes, I'll tell him you called." And I was standing right there. And we could have used that money—we were both low. But we wanted to stick together, and play together, and nothing else was more important to us then.

Wingy, Louis and Me

I t was after I returned from Delavan Lake that a most interesting period in my life came about—my first encounter in person with the great Negro musicians. I was to become very well acquainted with Louis Armstrong, and to see quite a lot, and what was more important, hear a lot, of Earl Hines. I was to become friends with Zutty Singleton. Let me tell you about the Wingy Manone days.

I'd just met Wingy up at our union, in Chicago. I'd made friends, sort of, with a lot of musicians who congregated at the union hall three or more nights a week. There were at least three pool tables and sometimes as many as thirty card games going on at the old union, and leaders hired their men there. There was a real good feeling in that place although at times the boys got to arguing a bit. Well, I fell right in and was doing all right at about the time someone introduced me to Wingy, who was looking for a piano player. But it was later, when Ray Biondi brought him to the basement of a place I was working in and he heard me without knowing it—it was after that that I got acquainted with Wingy.

Augie Schellange, the New Orleans drummer, had gotten a job for a small band at a place on North Clark Street. I believe it was called the Breakfast Club. Later I know it became the Liberty Inn.

But to get back—Augie called Wingy—so Wingy and I went to work there. Also Boyce and Harvey Brown—five pieces. Harvey played guitar, Boyce alto sax. The band was swell. We enjoyed playing together. But it only lasted a short time. The fourth night on the job, about one hour after we'd come to work, Augie gets off the stand and starts packing up his drums, very quietly, without talking to anyone, with plenty of people in the place. No one wanted to ask Augie questions. He looked and acted, and talked, tough—and we just didn't want to bother him with questions. Well, when he got all packed he walked over to the boss and asked for his pay—and what was more, got it.

Well, we were mystified, and it took us awhile to find out what was wrong. Augie didn't like all the talking that was going on —on the stand and off the stand. On the stand he believed no talking was necessary at all. And off the stand—well, Boyce and Harvey were both interested in Yogi and Hindu philosophy; in fact, quite a few of the leading hot musicians in Chicago had gotten interested in it, and there was lots of discussion going on. Boyce and Harvey had talked about Yogi on the job, and Augie was a low down, gut bucket drummer who didn't know anything about "when you die your spirit, etc.," and unfortunately for us, musically, he'd happened to wander into a conversation between the two brothers and he got jumpy.

The guy could drum, and he loved to drum. For instance, when Wingy got the date to make four sides on Vocalion, Augie was tending bar at a Capone joint on Chicago's South Side. He had his set of drums set up there, and there was a piano. And that's where we rehearsed for the date. Although even before that, we'd played there—Wingy, Wade Foster on clarinet, Augie and I. At that time I still had much of my original style of playing. I'd only heard two pianists on records, the only two pianists to date who had made any impression on my style of playing—Hines and Miss Lil Armstrong. I'd fallen right in with Augie, and also with Wingy. Neither of them ever criticized me at any time. I remember asking Wingy at the record date how I should play when Tesch took his chorus, and Wingy answering, "Play like you always play."

Well, up there at Augie's bar we'd play music together with no listeners but our-

January 1947
No. 51   20¢

The Jazz Record

Wingy Manone

selves. And when it got good you'd probably see Wingy walking around patting the wall, and just Wade, Augie and me playing—and then just Augie and me, and nobody saying a word. Didn't want to break the spell—but when it did break, they'd come back in and we'd play a few and take it out. And then we'd sit around happylike and kid among ourselves.

Those were the days. The last thing we talked of was getting paid for playing. We wanted a job so we could keep playing together. Yeah, that didn't last long. Four days work, a few rehearsals and a few nights playing for our kicks—and a record date—and so long, Augie.

The date was a windy one. Wingy picked me up in his car. Away we went to Augie's place, where the rest of the gang was —Tesch, Snurps, Augie and Ray Biondi. We sat down and started playing, playing just anything. When the band really started sounding right, Wingy broke it up and away we went to the studio.

After the engineers had padded the bass drum with everything in sight, and after they had us seated just the way we wouldn't seat ourselves if we had anything to say about it, we started in. We fluffed very few sides. I think Wingy cleared his throat on one take—anyway, that was that.

After the date we saw less and less of each other. Augie, Snurps and Tesch all seemed to drift. We still saw plenty of Ray Biondi. Meanwhile Wingy and I had moved in together, first at a Near North Side hotel, where we did it up right—right till the last minute. I think we lasted two weeks there and they wound up holding our bags. And then we moved to the North Side proper —Lawrence Avenue, around some kids from New Orleans that Wingy knew, and in no time at all, I knew.

And the tales I heard from them about New Orleans, and different places, and Mardi Gras, and the musicians! In me they had a real listener. Anybody from New Orleans had a beat, could feel the music. I'd been led into a completely new world than the other I'd known at the union floor.

In the two years I lived with Wingy I don't believe I read one book. Our day was so packed with listening to music and playing music and going to see people from our world —mainly Louis Armstrong—that we had no time for reading; we didn't miss it—we didn't know books existed.

Right now I can't believe I could do it again. Each day was about the same, except as to the people we'd run into. Our house was the Mecca for all hot musicians who hit Chicago. Wingy had such personality, could be so funny, and above all, could really play then. He had a beat you couldn't get away from. If we had two blocks to walk, we'd walk it in time. Wingy would sing some song as we walked along and we'd both swing along in time. Never real obviously—yet at times Wingy would make himself very obvious. But those couple of years I lived with Wingy, we lived with a beat. Our mistress was music; we worshipped her as a god. In the morning when we'd start in on the vic till late at night when we were exhausted and had to sleep, we had but one desire—to play, to play better this minute than we had the last, to hear something played that would knock us out. I'd wake up with "Muskrat Ramble" going on the vic, and immediately I was back in time, walking to the music, dressing to it, and being walked out of the house.

We didn't get to go see people who would break the spell. Out to the Savoy Ballroom to hear Louis—the joint was always packed and it would take us minutes to get to the back where the bandstand was. But Louis would see us at once, and his face would light up—and we'd feel warm inside. And right after the set we'd go back with the band into the band room, and most likely Joe Oliver—King—would come in for his "visit," and there'd be a lot of good feeling in the room. And somebody would say something funny, and that would give Louis an opening and you couldn't beat Louis at being funny—not even Wingy. And we'd laugh through the whole intermission, and then slowly walk Louis back to the stand—and then we'd wait for the band to begin playing again—and for it to be Louis's turn to play. Man, the guy could really blow then.

Liberty Inn Drag

Somewhere in Philippines

Hello Art:

I guess you'll be plenty surprised to hear from me. I've been overseas for over 25 months and in the meantime I've been trying to keep tabs on you and some of the other boys that used to be around the old Liberty Inn. I got a card from Earl Wiley, from N.Y.C.—if you run into him say hello for me.

The first notice I saw on you was about a year ago, pictures that were taken at Ryan's by ¯some picture mag.—I can't remember which one. Yesterday I ran across another notice on you in *Pic*, and today I pick up a November *Band Leader,* and lo and behold I run across your column and the swell notice you got by Marie Desales. Man, I sure got a bang out of it. You sure are a sight for sore eyes; you haven't changed a bit, in fact I think you look better than the last time I saw you, which seems like ages.

I hear from Johnny McGovern quite often, giving me all the dirt from his and all the other joints around. He sent me a *Chi Nite Life* and when I got through reading it I have an awful let-down. The old gang that worked in the old place are all in the European Theatre—Red McCusak, Louie Monogue, Eddie Fischer, Al Petty and all the rest of them . . .

M/Sgt. George DeMura

* * *

The old gang—McGovern's Liberty Inn —Clark and Erie. On the corner; the news-stand right in front—do I remember? Something tugs at me everytime I look back so I keep my eyes forward and go on. But even though you try not to remember, you don't forget.

The news-stand—that reminds me of the newsboy, the crippled kid who peddled pa-

pers from joint to joint. One of the tough boys who hung around had found out that the guy who owned the stand had hit this kid because he was infringing on his territory. I was there when this bruiser walked up to the news-stand and engaged the owner in innocent conversation up till the appropriate moment, when he dragged out a foot of iron tubing from under his coat and started whacking the news man on the back and shoulders, and the afflicted one ran through the Liberty Inn like mad—and in a few days sold his stand and cleared out.

McGovern sure had a weakness for girlie pictures out in front, the more the merrier. You walked through the front door, a kitty-corner doorway, and into the saloon—a long bar, with tables alongside the wall and a piano behind the bar—a small affair. "Let's drop in and see Art (this is January, 1938)—he's working there in the afternoons."

Old Man McGovern was a sprightly white-haired man, and did he know the business! He didn't miss a bet. There was the time some guy came in for some innocent diversion, only he had about a grand on him (1,000 bucks to you). We had about six gals working there then, all sizes and all types. McGovern liked girls around. They worked on a percentage, so many drinks —phonies—("B's we called them) drunk a night, so much earned. Well, this unlucky guy comes in. I strike up a tune, some gay thing, and the big parade starts. First one gal sidles up to this fall guy; he doesn't give her a tumble. Then another, and still another. By this time he's downed several and is more amiable. Soon he latches on to one he likes. You know these girls could promise strange worlds with their eyes—it didn't pay to gaze too deeply. Well, he invites one of the gals to drink with him, and soon she's warming him up, and he buys me one—and then she invites one of her "girl friends" to join her—and pretty soon it's one big happy family, with our friend for the afternoon buying drinks for the house, about ten of us, and the drinks comin' so fast that nobody got a chance to really drink except, of course, our indiscreet friend.

And somehow he passed out and had to be assisted upstairs (the hotel was right next door—didn't even have to go out of the bar—connecting door—also owned by McGovern). And Mr. Grand was put to bed. And just before my shift was up, he awoke—refreshed, but very short of dough. Very short. He was very outspoken about it, but no one knew where it had strayed, except—"Remember, you were buyin' everybody drinks—remember?" And so he started drinking again, and fell off one of the stools. This time the dishwasher helped him up, but somehow his hand got caught in this man's pocket. But the man with the grand (minus) wasn't *that* drunk. He put up a squawk. So there was nothing for Old Man McGovern to do but fire the dishwasher. So he got his hat and coat on and with his head hanging low, walked out—out, past the front window to the side door that also led back of the bar (partitioned off) to the kitchen, where I later saw him back at work, washing dishes.

Yes, the Liberty Inn was an education. But it was more than that. If you were one of them (and if you worked for them you were) then you knew where to go if you needed help, any kind of help, from brain to brawn.

But let's not stand out at the bar—let's go in.

The first time I saw the Liberty Inn was when it was called the Breakfast Club, during prohibition days. That was when Wingy, Augie Schellange, the Brown boys and myself worked there for a short time, a matter of weeks. Later on Johnny Lane, a fine clarinetist in the Rappolo-Noone tradition, got the job for a small band, not being able to handle it for a while, turned it over to his friend Gibby Eurton, a good 4-to-the-bar guitarist, who in turn grabbed me. I recommended Earl Wiley, and we then looked up Bennie Moylan, and the four of us started there. Wiley stayed there for at least ten years, I guess, while we drifted back and forth. Chicago, by the way, rewarded Lane for his ability by granting him—oblivion. It is

truly spoken, "A prophet is without honor in his own home town."

The back room, cafe, part of the Inn could seat somewhere in the vicinity of one hundred people. Music would start at 10 p.m. The band would play a short dance, then the pianist in the band rolled a small piano onto the middle of the dance floor and a couple of entertainers would make the rounds of the tables, and come back with the folded money—if they were lucky—of which you'd get your share. Half—if you keep your eyes on them. As I was developing the habit of playing with my eyes shut so as to concentrate better on my music, quite often I lost out in the other department, and often got ribbed by the help about being a "sucker." Well, after playing for the singers, you dragged the piano back and played another dance. This went on 'til the show started. Then, of course, you played the show. The show was a killer—one singer, one comedian (the M.C.) and four strip girls. The place did good business, everything moved along at a given pace, but all in all it was a grind for the man at the piano.

The McGoverns were a fighting Irish clan and asked odds from no one. There was the time a tall husky Texan refused to pay the bill and started to fight about it. First Johnny and then Jim McGovern and then McCusak and a couple of others battled him from his table clear across the dance floor during the middle of the show with the light on full blast. They battled and bustled him right through the door that led to the bar, and so into the men's room where the bill was collected. The porter mopped the blood on the dance floor and the show proceeded as scheduled. The show must go on—and it did.

And once a disgruntled customer threw a brick through the front window and ran. Johnny, who by the way was about 5 feet 10 and weighed in the neighborhood of 140 pounds, chased him clear to Chicago Avenue, about four blocks, and about a hundred feet from a police station caught up with him and—well, that was that.

But the funny one was when some tough gal was gettin' too cantankerous for comfort, so she was handed a Mickey—or Michael. Now, to you who don't know what a Michael is (and are there any who don't?) a mickey is a pill that works wonders with a stomach—any stomach, for example, a horse's tummy. It's a neutralizer—it makes a sissy out of a killer. This gal was handed a Mickey (and by the way, that's an art in itself, handing a party a Mickey without them getting wise to the fact). The bathrooms were then crowded with people so that when Mr. Mickey started to work, there was no—well, the result was that this female ran out into the nearest alley and was not heard of since.

And there was the time the fellows in the band chipped in for a jug and sent Eddie Condon's brother Pat after it. And when we next heard from him he was in Australia.

Yes, there'll be stories told about the Liberty Inn wherever any of its many friends get together and start reminiscing. All wasn't blood and thunder, either. Underneath the surface there was a heart of gold. McGovern's Liberty Inn was the last of the bucket-of-blood joints that we read about in the history of many a town—New Orleans, for instance. The Inn was unique because it kept running and being itself at a time when all other places had lost all identity—had just become upholstered sewers. Zurke came in there once and played a mess of piano. One time it was Marty Marsala, Wingy, Louis Prima and Paul Mares all playing together—four trumpets. The drinks were practically free to the help. Dave Tough, who at that time had no use for the kind of company he now keeps, often came in. One time Earl Wiley, decid-

ing he needed a vacation, got Tough to sub for him for a night and went up to his room in the hotel and downed a few fast ones. All was well until a knock on the door brought a message that "You'd better come down —your sub is drunker than you are." Maybe I shouldn't tell tales out of school—after all I was part of all that. And I was no better or worse than any of the rest of the boys. We were all part and parcel of the whole thing.

Oh, well . . . Looking back, a pleasure I rarely afford myself, I'd say that the Liberty Inn was an education—an education you don't get in schools. But I wouldn't have missed it for the world. And talking about the world, who's fighting this war to make this universe a better place to live in but the boys from—yes, the Liberty Inn—George De-Mura, McCusak, Louis Monogue, Fischer, Petty.

That's Eddie Fischer, the singing waiter. He could put over a song. "Gee, but I'd give the world to see—that Old Gang of Mine." Spin my Decca recording of "Liberty Inn Drag"—shut your eyes and turn back the years, ten of them. There's Johnny popping out from around the bandstand. You hear him say: "Come on, fellers—let's get goin'—what is this, a sanatorium? Did you fellers come here to rest? Let's have some action."

Jam Session

"Bix is in the house."

The word had passed all around and the next any of us knew a spotlight had been played on his table and finally found him, and it continued to glare on Bix til he consented to play, although it took a good deal of applauding to get him finally to play—not that Bix had to be coaxed—he was there to get his kicks, not to sit in.

But the public (and at that time we, the musicians themselves, were most of the pub-

lic) was not to be denied. Bix got up and wandered over to the bandstand.

The place was "My Cellar" on State near Lake Street. Sam Beers owned that joint, if I remember correctly. Wingy Manone had the band—and I wasn't in it. In fact we weren't speaking at the moment. Forget just why.

But when Bix got up to play, Wingy came over to me and asked me to sit in. Wingy's piano player just didn't know the tunes.

So I sat in with Bix, and we jammed 'til early morn when Boze relieved Bix. I remember Bob Conselman was on drums. When we'd stop to rest Bix would fool around a little at the piano. No one made a sound 'til we'd finished playing. Then the house resounded with applause.

How many more times I've gone with musicians somewhere to jam I can't recall. They were many, I know. Back in Chicago we didn't go long without playing. Sometimes one of the boys would know of some place that didn't have music and he'd arrange with the boss for us to play that night. The boss probably thought we were all crazy for playing for nothing and sometimes he'd pay for a lot of drinks to encourage us to keep on going, and a few customers would request tunes that had to be gotten around, and it would depend on the mood you were in how you'd get around to playing them.

But usually the public we jammed for —was ourselves.

Back in '38, when I came to New York City, I came up against a situation that had to be solved. I wanted to play—and there was no place to play at; none that I knew. In New York it was all business. If you went somewhere and waited around awhile, you might get asked to play. Then again you might not, and I just had to play.

I tried organizing a few of us from Chi, and we tried doing the same thing we'd done in Chi. The first place we jammed at they had a band, so a few of us relieved a few of the boys in the band. But it didn't work so good for me. The drummer and I couldn't get together. With me it's either you're in time or you're not in time. Let me quote my friend Zutty Singleton, the drummer. "Art, so many guys can play when the beat ain't there, but man, I can't do a thing 'til everyone is right in it. Then I can play."

I tried it again at a few more joints 'til I gave it up as a bad job. New York City musicians weren't interested in going out to jam where they wouldn't be seen. I found out that the town changed your way of thinking. That even the boys who'd come here at about the same time as I had were drifting from our Chicago ways to New York ways—mainly, not worrying about playing so much but worrying about making connections and getting on, or something.

One day a clarinet player by the name of LeRoy Smith called me up, and I met him at a joint he told me of, the Ross Tavern, 51st and 6th Avenue. He introduced me to Jimmie Ross who was a friend of George Zack the pianist. Jimmie told me, "Boy, anytime you want to play come down here and play." "Here" was the Ross Tavern basement, a dreary place, rafters above, a cat that chased after the water bugs, the toilets that the patrons above would have to use, and the chef's haven. But I loved it—a piano to play with no one to bother you. I made use of it at once.

Every day I'd make the trip to Jimmy's basement—alone. Sometimes the chef's helper would request a couple of tunes, and sometimes he'd make me a nice sandwich. Sometimes it was Jimmie himself I'd play for; then again Jimmie would bring a few choice customers down to hear me. Or a drunk might wander from the toilet. But it was a haven.

I came and I played. The thing lasted the best part of a winter. When it finally got around to Dan Qualey and then to the *Jazz Information* gang, Gene Williams, Ralph Gleason and Herman Rosenberg, the exact date I don't know. But that gang came to listen, and they brought life into that cellar. Stella Brooks, Herbie Dell, George Zack, Meade Lux Lewis, others, sat in on Ross's old upright. The drinks would flow, whoever had the money would pay. Everything got quiet while the music went on—talk about your playing for keeps.

But Ross Tavern is another story. Did you ever hear a modern jam session? I've played at quite a few of them and I've heard many more, but I can't for the life of me understand what goes on in the listener's mind. A trumpet player will take a chorus and immediately at the finish will receive a round of applause. Mind you it isn't the end of the number; in fact the applause will run into the next man's chorus. It reminds me of people at a picture theatre when something funny is said and everyone laughs so loud that you miss part of the dialogue that follows. Anyway, the trumpet player will get a big hand—many times the chorus he played wasn't exceptionally good, and many times a man will play an exceptionally good chorus and not get any applause; and I've even heard the house resound with applause after a drum chorus in which the drummer got all out of time with himself.

I've come to the conclusion that the jam sessions of today and yesterday differ. Yesterday's jam session would have made a good recording. No collector of jazz would buy a recording of a session as you hear it today. Oh, there are good choruses produced, undoubtedly, but the whole thing in itself, no. A jam session today has come to mean an atmosphere of excitement, you can feel it as you enter the room. It doesn't mean good jazz. You play for the crowd, and they demand effort, sweat. They want to be "sent."

Now let me ask you one question. If you went to hear a symphony would you applaud for a clarinet player after he made a fine run or a cadenza? You wouldn't think of doing that. You'd wait most naturally till the whole performance was finished and then applaud.

No, I'm afraid that the jam session today hasn't anything in common with the jam session of yesterday. I have a feeling that you could run a prize-fight or a football or baseball game right after a jam session and lose hardly any of your audience.

I don't dislike jam sessions as they are today. There's definitely a place for them in our world. At the same time I'd like to see in existence a different kind of jam session, the kind we musicians knew in Chicago —Freeman, Tesch, Mezzrow, Wingy, Muggsy, Bix—we all knew them. I remember one night at the Liberty Inn, Paul

Mares, Wingy and Marty Marsala and Louis Prima fresh from New Orleans, a trumpet cuttin' session, we jammed for kicks, the crowd be damned. It was New York that taught me that the customer is always right and you have to please the people, but darn it, that's one lesson I haven't learned well.

And it was New York that taught me to hold my head up and keep trying and fighting for my beliefs. That's one thing we didn't learn elsewhere—we, the jazz men, hot men, that left Chicago and came to New York City in the twenties and the thirties. For New York is Condon, Pee Wee, Gabler, Nick's, *Jazz Information*, Decca, Bluebird, Ryan's, Ross Tavern, Solo Art, radio, transcriptions, so many things—and jam sessions—The Vanguard, Kelly's, Ryan's, Carnegie Hall, Newspaper Guild, Town Hall. We learned our jazz in Chicago, but we had to come to New York City to be able to pursue jazz as a livelihood. And how many of us boys have looked to the jam session at one time or another for that mighty dollar to live on. Plenty that I know. Hate it? No, I could never hate the jam session of today. We get the kind of government we deserve. We get the kind of music we're ready for. When we're all ready to sit down real quietly to an evening of non-violent listening to jazz we'll get the real thing. The musicians haven't forgotten "how."

But 'til then I give you the modern day jam session. May it continue.

Cops

We were talking about policemen. Some chap had returned a purse he'd found, only to be nabbed by two of our "finest," and released five hours later. I thought that anyone reading that certainly wouldn't be driven to honesty. But then, maybe it's because of some experiences I'd had. I lived with a policeman for several months. He was a good egg. He was a southerner and could do a swell jig. We got along well together—except when he'd drink. Oh, he was OK. But he was too big—and very strong. And if he wanted to emphasize a point, I'd find myself six feet away, merely by his friendly way of pointing a finger at me.

Of course, that don't compare to the time Wiley, Murphy, and I wound up in a bar, opening time in the morn, imbibing, and talking "hot" music. And Wiley got emphatic and I went through the front glass door.

No, it wasn't one of several experiences I had casually encountered in my heyday. Now I remember. It was Calumet City, Illinois —dates I forget—But the town was still open, or like they now say (check me if I've fallen behind since yesterday): "Man, it was jumpin'."

I never, to my knowledge, saw the town in the daytime. I got there just ahead of being on time for work. And my especial place to be was a corner bar and back room. Chicago had taught me long ago not to look around too much. Go to work, do your job; have your fun, but be careful not to pick on the boss' girl, or any other gals of his close friends, relatives, friends of his friends, or even a fifth cousin of his mother-in-law. You just didn't do that. I did it once, but I always had to learn the hard way—Skip it.

But this joint. You know who hung out there? Frank Melrose and George Zack—and a couple of guys came in or worked there, that weren't bad. No, man, we got some good sounds out in that room. Of course, I don't know what the critics would say about it if it had been recorded. But the boys who played the music and the customers were the only critics in those days. You see what I mean, we were happy—and mostly broke. Frank would come in and play some piano; then I'd play. And if it got good, Frank would run home for his fiddle and sit in. He didn't do bad, we got our kicks.

Gettin' back to the law, one day it was kinda slow. Someone had a brainstorm that it'd be a good idea to march out the door, around the corner, and back in the side door, Salvation Army style, drums, clarinet, cymbals, and trumpet, goin' full blast on a march. No sooner thought than did. Ta-da-da de da-di-da-da—C-C-B flat-A-A—A flat-A. What's the name of that anyway? Well, we got around the corner and about to the side door, when two cops grabbed us. "What the h . . . do you think you're doin'?" And boy they went on, and we were scared. Inside they marched us, and told our woman-boss

off. But she could take it, and hand it out too. That was a stand-off. Then we found out that our boss' late husband had run into a bad dose of lead, and she'd soured on the cops, and the feeling was mutual.

So the nite wore on and it was time to hit for home. Bert Lawrence, the drummer, was driving this night, and I was riding with him. We noticed a squad car eye us as we drove away, but we didn't give it much thought. We'd had a good night of kicks, except for a bad moment, and we were tired. Let's go home. So we came to South Chicago, and then it happened. First we heard angry sirens screaming at us. Then a squad car pulled up along side and ran us to the curb. Another pulled up behind us. Heavily armed police (and I do mean they were carrying everything but a tank gun) circled in on us. We were told to get out, hands in the air. We did, gingerly. We were frisked—that was a disappointment. So they went to work on Bert's roadster and like to tore it apart. Looking for what? Let me tell you.

"What did you do with 'em? Come on, talk. Where'd you ditch 'em?" Well, man, you know what they are looking for? Guns! Some other cops had called in to be on the look-out for two dangerous characters who'd just stuck up a bank, or something. "Be on your guard; take no chances; they're dangerous." So help me, that's the truth. But we didn't find it out right away. No sir, there's a ritual to this. I was directed to a back seat in one car; Bert to the other. I sat between two giants, both holding shotguns (maybe they were rifles; anyway, they looked big). No word was spoken. We drove to the station. Into a cell I was pushed and four citizen-protectors joined me. The questions came fast; the same ones. "What did we do with the guns?" You know, it took us one hour to convince the cops of one thing? That maybe we were musicians and maybe they should invest one nickel and check with Calumet City. "Maybe it's a joke." And that's how we got out. "All right, get the h . . . out of here and beat it." No "Excuse the mistake, buddy." We were darn lucky we hadn't picked up a few lumps.

You know, we wound up doing a good deed for the city's automobile club. Yes, sir, we discovered a way to get to Calumet City without driving anywhere near that police station.

Taxi Dance Hall

T en cents a dance—that's what they pay me—do re do re do sol—" July 1941—Dick Donohoe and I living on West 90th Street, New York—Short of dough, as usual. You remember Dick? Plays trumpet and a little fiddle; arranges; a valuable man in any band, especially where there's more than one horn needed. Worked with Goodman's band when they played Chi, or was it Milwaukee? Don't remember. Anyway, Dick gets lucky and gets a 25 buckeroo job—I mean a week—at a dance hall, dime a dance—over on East 14th Street—joint called the Diana. I believe it's closed now. Boy oh boy, some joint. It said on the window "Learn to dance—Special attention given to beginners." No sense goin' into that angle of this tale; it'll only be deleted by the censors. Special attention—hm—. But I guess that's what draws all the men there; fugitives from the lonely hearts club. Being out of work and very short on that filthy stuff I'm supposed to be stuffed with, if (according to the great minds) I was any good at all, I had plenty time on my hands. So I wandered down to the Diana and dug the music, and the goin's on. The music was sad. Two choruses was all you got for your dime—no more. "Get your tickets, girls." If the customer was "enjoying" his dance lesson, he'd keep the same partner; if not, he'd change. Dick and the boys kept grinding it out—an hour and a half work—ten minutes intermission. Dick had his jug handy so that his nerves would hold up. Boy, he sure needed it on that job; waltzes, tangos, rhumbas, what nots. I sat in, just so as I could keep my hands in playing shape—a hell of a price to pay.

Come to think of it, I once had a dancing school job, but oh so different. The idea was the same but not the music. This was in '31—Chicago—The Capitol Dancing School —Randolph and State—4th floor. Tony de

Lancey was the boss man; a well bred college man at that. And he knew how to pack the place. He had the prettiest chicks in Chi working for him. Bud Freeman had the band there before I got the job. Dave Tough, the ex-dixielander, was on drums; Tut Soper was his pianist. For some reason I can't figure out, the boss got himself sold on me and gave me the job. Opening nite he presented me with a basket of flowers that topped me in height, and then made a speech about his new band. What an opening. Four piece band. I had Le Roy Smith on clarinet, Earl Wiley on drums, and Earl Murphy on banjo and guitar. Le Roy played a cornet style on his clarinet. And that rhythm section really moved along. The joint was jammed. The boss bought us a gallon of wine and that set the pace from then on in. We got so fixed that first night that Murf finally broke all his banjo strings tryin' to play as loud as the rest of us and had to play his guitar. He hated that, 'cause in that quartet you couldn't hear it. All of a sudden, from behind me, I heard what sounded like a pistol shot. So did the boss. Out he ran from his office with his two pearl handled revolvers unholstered, ready. And what do we see? Murphy holding his guitar, its neck broken, dangling. He'd gotten so mad at the damn thing that he busted it on the piano bench. We calmed him down, brought him into the office and set the jug by his side and played out the night with three pieces.

That was an exciting job for Murf. He was attractive to women (he didn't exactly hate that) and in that joint it meant he could pitch a ball. He did. But it wasn't long before some customer got peeved at him over some chick. It got back to Earl that this guy was out to get him. So Murf took to wearing a gun; a small affair. We kidded him about it. "At a time when all the gangsters are ditching their rods you go to carrying one," etc. Then one night the unexpected happened. While Murphy was having a bite to eat downstairs, his pistol fell out of his pocket and someone told the cops. The next I knew about it Tony De Lancey said to me, "Just got a call from the station; Murf's been picked up with a rod." We rushed over to the jailhouse and Tony used his influence. He had enough in his pocket to choke a horse, if you know what I mean. Murf was back on the stand the next night, owing the boss his life. As it turned out tho, he came out in front on that deal. 'Cause when the job folded on us (as jobs do) we all had at least $100.00 comin' to us in salary, which we never got.

For the most part Chicago musicians acted as if this band just didn't exist. You'd think they'd flock to hear something good; they didn't. Union musicians, as a rule, are very clannish. Because we weren't, we were outcasts; a happy feeling. That's one thing we hot men can look back on; years that weren't wasted hanging around with the wrong gang just to be "in." But Wingy Manone dropped in on us, listened to the band, then said, "Hell, you guys don't need a trumpet." Dave Tough was another constant visitor.

After we'd been on the job a while Le Roy decided to leave and we got Bennie Moylan to join the group; the man with that wonderful voice and own style of tenor playing. It was about that time that the boss decided to spread out and go into the night club business. That was the beginning of the end. He started pouring his winnings into his losings and it wasn't long before we were behind in pay; way behind. Came the day that we all decided this couldn't go on any longer. Because we couldn't induce Tony to come up with some gold dust something had to be done. But what? We finally hit on a solution. Saturday night, when the joint filled up with customers, I was to call the boss up at the Kentucky Club (that was the name of his ill fated nitery) and tell him to instruct the cashier to give us some back salary or else; or

else we'd quit right there and then. Boy, did you ever hear a telephone rattling? This one did. He blew his top. He talked to me; argued; cajoled; finally threatened me with a ride. I stuck to my guns, but so did he. His answer was "no dough." Well, no doughee, no playee.

Up to that stand I marched, told the fellows to pack up on the double (and they didn't waste a second) and got Wiley to give me a roll on his drums. The astonished customers gathered around me as I announced our withdrawal from bankruptcy. I believe I also threw in a few words on the 14 freedoms. And out we went. We stayed under cover that night and the next. Early Monday morning I went to my union to explain the situation. Mr. De Lancey was there. Nothing happened. We'd lost the job and we didn't get our back pay. But it finally turned out bad for Tony too. The dancing school couldn't support both itself and the nite club and within a few months both closed down.

A few years later Tony and I met in a lunch room; talked about old times like good friends and reminisced about what might have been. I'll always remember the music we played. Certain originals I've recently recorded for Blue Note were part of our nightly repertoire. Also such tunes as "Dr. Jazz," "Shoe Shiners Drag," "Kansas City Stomps," "King Porter," "I'm Gonna Gitcha," "Original Dixieland One-Step" and others. We didn't play music with our eyes on the clock. Those customers never knew what tune would hit them next. This was one joint where the customer was never right. We didn't bother to learn the pop tunes of the day and we didn't play any tunes we thought weren't any good. We developed a set of deaf ears and went on our merry way. I tell you we didn't have good business sense. But come to think of it, the funny thing about this was that the joint remained packed every night and people danced; actually danced to jazz and liked it.

Big Bands: I

My friends have often asked me, "why do you stay out of big bands?" Oh, I don't mean my musician friends; they know why. Take Muggsy for example; he's been at Nick's for over a year with a small group. Before that he had a big band of his own. No sign of him weakening. Max Kaminsky hasn't joined anyone since he came back from the Pacific after serving under that warrior-leader Artie Shaw. And at press time I see that Sidney Bechet is still not joining anyone. What goes? Admittedly, the leader of a band is an honored person, and name bands bring in the moola. But what about the sidemen; the employees; the party of the second part? Is it or isn't it worth while being a member of a large orchestra? Well, here's my story.

I'd been out on the road with the Wolverines Orchestra, touring the east. The time, the late twenties. This was Dick Voynow's band. He owned the name "Wolverines." Of course Bix had a lot to do with the fact that the title now was a valuable piece of property. But that's how it is. Bix had left and Dick signed with M.C.A. who sent Voynow down to some point in Texas to take over the Smith Ballew band. Am I gettin' too involved? Let me explain. Smith Ballew had a band of his own but no job. The Music Corporation of America, through one of its representatives, offered Smith work if he'd allow Voynow to front the band. It goes like this. Joe Public will pay to see Dick Voynow and his Wolverines 'cause they've heard of him. But outside of Texas, Mr. Ballew was unknown. So a deal is consummated. Everybody is happy. M.C.A. is doing business. Dick V. has a band and is cashing in. Smith gets a bonus in the way of a good salary, and the boys are working. One happy family.

In case, dear readers, this comes to you as a surprise, let me tell you that it's not an uncommon practice with booking agents. Anyway, I found that the reason I'd got the job was because of a fist fight between Smith's pianist and Dick, who was formerly a pianist himself. The day I joined the band, at rehearsal, Voynow said to me, "I don't care how much piano you play or whether you're a good or bad sight reader. What I want from you is plenty of oompah piano." Perhaps you don't know what oom-pah piano is? Well, ask any of the alumni or faculty of (or at) Nick's in the Village; or dig Nick in person at the piano. But just in case you live elsewhere, oom-pah means accentuating the after beat. Back in those days drummers played much more softly and bands depended on a strong afterbeat from the pianist for the extra rhythm they needed. O.K. Let's go on; I made it. I had me a ball in that band. A wonderful bunch of guys; good company. It was kicks for me, traveling and seeing the country.

"After the Ball Was Over." What a title. Well, this lasted about four months. The band broke up and I landed right back in Chicago with exactly one week's pay in my pocket. No, I was gettin' a fair shake as far as salary was concerned. But every night after work, somehow or other, the boys would get me into a card game, and brother this bunch knew 'em all. I used to be considered a pretty fair gambler myself (eh, Murphy?) but this gang never gave me a chance to get set. As soon as I'd learn one game they'd switch me on to another. I learned more card games that summer!

The band bust up because of two leaders in one orchestra. There always was an undercurrent of dissatisfaction, and what with Smith having his wife along for the tour, it wasn't long before an open feud broke out. It used to strike me funny. Smith was over 6 feet tall while his frau was a little bit of a gal, but possessed, man, what fire. One day the band had a meeting and the fellows voted to stick to S.B. I went along with the boys. So here I was, with some big band experience, back in Chicago. It didn't set bad on me at the time. I got the cure a bit later. I believe it was Johnny Craig who got me the job with Doc Rudder's band out at the Cocoanut Grove. This was fun too. Doc played tenor; we had trumpet, trombone, three saxes and a rhythm section. Wonderful guy, Doc; a dentist by the way. Every time Bud Freeman visited us Doc would get him to sit in, listen to a set, then pack his horn and go home. We liked Doc so well that in spite of the fact that the pay wasn't hittin' us regular we stuck with him. I remember the time that the bass player and I got up enough nerve to tackle the "front office." We actually barged in and asked for our money. Suffice it to say, we learned our lesson there and then. The bosses accused us of being Communists. We shut up and went back to work. Rather go without pay than be called that.

One day they had a meeting in the front office and it was decided that what the place needed was new leadership. The minds hired Henri Lishon. There's the guy I blame. He was responsible for curing me of big bands. Thanks, Henri. I suppose you'd like to know how it happened. It came fast. Henri L. called a rehearsal. Somebody's always calling rehearsals; more jobs lost that way. Mr. L. had his own ideas, his own arrangements and his own tenor saxophonist (to replace Doc) who doubled on fiddle, thereby giving us the added distinction of having a string section. Mr. Lishon also played the y-o-lin. After rehearsing waltzes, and sweet tunes 'til they came out of my ears, I got off my stool, went to the rear of the hall and sat down. Mr. L. didn't dare challenge me on that; the house considered me too valuable a piece of property to fire. I just sat and watched the deba-

cle. When those two fiddles got to playing it sure sounded sad. But I didn't reach bottom 'til Lishon called out "let's try the 'Tiger Rag' arrangement." That was it. He had the whole front line stand up. The tempo he beat off was fast. Everything held together fairly well, even tho the arrangement stunk, until the band came to the final "go" choruses. This was the masterpiece. You know the tune; remember the part that says "Hold that Tiger . . . hold that Tiger." Well in this chorus, Henri had the saxes blowing two bars of music and the horns the next two, and what with the brass section pointing their instruments at the sax section for one bar and in the opposite direction the next, and the saxes doing likewise, and the music getting louder and faster and all six of the boys standing up on their chairs in a grand finale gesture, well, I almost fell out of mine in a fit of laughter. After that the blowoff just naturally had to come. We were having a snack together when Mr. Lishon started telling Floyd O'Brien how to play his trombone. That was too much for me. I blew my top. After I got thru expressing my views on leaders in general, and on the violin as an instrument in a dance band, especially a hot band, there was nothin' left for me to do but leave.

'Course all that happened years ago. Things may have changed since then. But somehow or other I don't feel inclined to experiment. I'm out of it and it feels good. Now I'm not advising anybody else not to join a big band. No sir. I'm just talkin' 'bout myself. I feel like the character Bert Williams sang about on a Columbia disc titled "Somebody Else." It seems there'd been a shooting and the cops were on the way. It was essential that the police find someone there with the corpus delecti when they arrived. And Bert says, "Now the man who stays behind a hero will be; yes sir, somebody else; not me."

Big Bands: II

I don't think I'll forget April the 11th for a while, because that's the day Eddie Condon called me up and got me involved with a big band.

Eddie and I joined Joe Marsala and his seventeen-piece production for a week at Loew's State—Loew's Nose, as Eddie called it. We did 29 shows, an hour and ten minutes each show. We played the same music all week; we heard the same jokes. One I won't forget very easily: "I wasn't born here but I'll sure die here."

A human being is a wonderful thing to be able to survive an experience such as ours. First show, 12:08. Five saxophones, six brass—a production number—a vocal number—a dance team—three other numbers, the last one with a "Are You from Dixie" finish—curtain. Enter the the comedian—a ten-minute skit—another band number—another comedian—a harp solo—more comedy—speech about Eddie winning the Down Beat award for being the best guitarist. (Note: friend of mine, on leaving theatre, overhears a couple: "The best guitarist, and all he does is sit there . . .")

Eddie, they should know how hard that was to do—"just sit there." Just sit there and hear the same gags, play the same arrangements. Five saxes, who spent lots of time practicing in between shows, reaching for high notes, maybe a squeak now and then. One would break out on a Coleman Hawkins kick, then the other; then a clarinet would come in—just clean fun.

We got a lot of sleep between shows. Here goes that buzzer—"On stage." We're off again; the 3:27 show. "Well, after this one we'll have a drink."

The band was made up very well. "Six brass," one of them tells me. All I hear is one trumpet. I wonder what the other two are doing all through the show. "Take your bow, Eddie." He's having a hard time staying awake, trying to keep two jobs, Nick's and Loew's.

Two down, two to go. We eat. Maybe Hackett, Wettling or Brunis drop in. Or Amy Lee, George Hoefer. They don't have to tell us what it sounds like—we know. But they tell us anyway. "It doesn't sound real bad. It's just because you're not used to it, Art. Don't forget, you haven't been with a big band for years." Thank God.

Making a Record

Say, has anyone ever told you what it feels like, making a record? Sometimes I wonder how anyone can make a good record.

In the first place, records are almost always made at the worst possible hour for the musician. For example, "Liberty Inn Drag" was recorded at a 9 a.m. session. I don't have to tell any of you who have seen us in action what a musician feels like that early in the middle of the night. Then of course there are at least five "experts" around to see that everything goes right. The rhythm section is never seated in away to help the band, but in the best possible manner to help the engineer.

The room itself is my idea of a good place not to get excited in. Now, then, if you must take into account how everyone's nerves are at about 9 a.m., and how they hadn't improved any when the master you played good on was spoiled by someone sneezing—and remember there's no bar in the studio—you have a perfect set-up for a nervous breakdown.

Instead, someone picks your record as one of the best of the year. There's a phenomenon I've never exactly understood.

Another thing I've never figured out is:

sometimes a guy thinks he's playing his head off, and nothing happens. Then, when he's just fighting his instrument and not seeming to get anywhere, the ceiling comes down with applause. Really it shakes our faith in our reasoning—although I think I've read somewhere or other that we weren't supposed to have very much of that left.

But getting back to the records. A few months after the records are released you pick up a trade magazine and read where "in the second chorus the clarinet takes a soft melodic phrase and plays a beautiful subtonic tonal poem, blending the heavy rhythms of the bass horn with the intricate phrasings of the savage muted trumpet" . . . and gentlemen, that alone should stamp him as the best clarinetist of all time.

I really didn't mean to go into all that, but somebody asked me why I don't review records in *The Jazz Record.*

Enlightenment— Through Radio

I had to get up at 7:30 a.m. so as to be awake and ready for this big moment of mine—still I snoozed a little more but didn't breakfast. I was at C.B.S. on time; it was an awfully cold day and that time of the morning is murder for one of us jazz men. Still, it had to be done.

I walked into the studio, saw I knew the bass player. Yes, there was a thirteen-piece band there, rehearsing little bits of material—sounded good—but where they had to swing, bad. The leader told me he didn't have any music for me and I got worried that I didn't belong and that it was going to be another one of those things. Because I had time, I went across the street for breakfast and got to feeling good. Back I marched.

Meanwhile the orchestra had rehearsed a harmonica player, not bad at all—a girl singer, a man singer—and about 12:45 the director and the actors—Eddie Dowling and others—marched in. The sound effect man got busy and a C.B.S. announcer was there, and all in all about thirty people assembled. I was fighting my cold, two handkerchiefs were well used by now. Someone handed me a script and looking through it I found my name. A relief—I was in it. Rehearsal started.

Wide Horizons—that was the name of all this mess. An actor asks Eddie Dowling, "What are my wide horizons? Here I am in New Guinea, a soldier—was going to be a dentist—now what? What's it all about?" We soon learn. It's about a young man who wanted to build planes, and though his father discouraged him, he stuck to his beliefs and made it—but big—American boy makes good—from poor boy to millionaire. And what are we doing in the play? Well, we're all swell entertainers who gave up our all to work for this man in his plane factory. And when the boys come back we'll be glad to give them these jobs back, and unemployment will be solved, and we'll all live happily ever after. That was the play.

But to me that wasn't the play. The play was going on all around us—we were the play, every one assembled here on a cold day, drawn by one thing—money. All from different worlds; I was going to play a little jazz; the band was earning a dollar; the producer was gambling on an idea.

The script unfolded, and we got down to a part where it said "When a fellow has a terrific idea he'll find money," and there a little trouble developed.

The orchestra leader had to dig up music that was appropriate "money finding music," and the first five items he displayed didn't hit right. The producer got short of temper, the band leader got hot under the collar, the cast started looking at the leader—everyone thought "What a dope! Anyone could have done better than that." The script was tackled again. Came time for the band, and they'd slow it up. It's pretty hard to get thirteen men to act as one when they don't know exactly what's going on. The producer started losing patience. He tried eliminating the music part wherever possible. The leader would holler "Will you wait just a minute while we go over this," or else "Just listen to this," and the pressure on him grew. Finally one of the fiddlers, who was contractor for the band, called a ten minute intermission.

When the band got back the fun began. The producer said something to the leader and he exploded, threw his baton down, asserted himself. I could tell what had happened—the boys had given the leader a good bracing up. "You don't have to take all that crap . . . Who the hell does he think he's talkin' to?" Anyway, the leader blew off, and demanded respect—and by the way, got it.

By this time it was announced that we'd do it once all the way through as a dress rehearsal. Actually this was it. You see, they never tell you in transcriptions when they're cutting the real thing, for fear you'll get nervous.

When you don't expect it, you're actually making a recording which is the "one" you were hired for.

Well, everything just went along, with just a fair performance being turned in on the script, and the two singles doing their songs just all right.

Came my turn—I was supposed to play "Pistol Packin' Papa." "We also have with us Art Hodes—Art is from the El Segundo plant—a great professional entertainer who gave up a lucrative career to pinch-hit on a war job—whose boogie-woogie recordings, etc. . . . Will now play 'Pistol Packin' . . .'" Well, I'd talked my way out of the Pistol thing into "St. Louis Blues," so I started in at a fast pace, with just enough St. Louis to justify myself and into the blues. I'd determined I'd wake them up and I did. It was one of my good days. You know people love technique—"Just look at his fingers flyin' over the keyboard! . . . Oh, boy, he's hot!" I'd been practicing hard, and I mixed the real thing with the showy. The band played one chord at the end, and the beat was there. The rest of the show moved on in animation. They came to life; the pace was stepped up, and finally it came to its end.

The producer rushed out from behind his glass cage and hollered: "That was it! That was it—we did it, we cut it!" Everyone acted surprised, but relieved—I know I was. I was saying to myself just before, "Just my luck, I play good when it doesn't mean anything," and now here it was—we'd done it, and done with it.

The producer was acting like an excited boy—"We did it, we did it! . . . Great!" He went up to the orchestra leader and hugged him (just think of it, a half hour before they were hating each other at about 400 miles an hour). "You did a swell job, Joe," etc., etc. Happy days are here again.

Finally the producer smiled at me —actually. Before that he'd acted like I wasn't there at all. And his secretary knew me by name now.

It was now 4 p.m. I'd been there five hours. Seemed like a year. I grabbed a subway and two fast drinks the minute I got out of the train—and two more after a block's walk—and grabbed a fast one at home. Just to get drunk, and not to think about the play. Oh, I don't mean the script; I mean this play we live, these hours we waste, this silliness we engage in.

Blues for Bennie

first met Bennie Moylan on the train, going to a job in Racine, Wisconsin. His appearance didn't startle me—and at that time I always carried a lot of chip on my shoulder anyway. He was around my height, 5-10½, full of face in a lean sort of manner, nice smile. Jack Daly, a guitar player, introduced us.

We were four characters on that job. Moylan played sax, clarinet, a little trumpet, and sang. Jack Daly played guitar, and fooled around a bit on piano during intermissions. Sleepy Kaplan played drums, myself on piano.

Sleepy really earned that name—talk about a guy moving around slow! We'd decided to play cards one night after work; Sleepy said he'd take a shower and be right out. After about an hour of waiting we gave up. But what kills me is the night I called him up for a job, and his dad answered the phone. I asked, "Is Sleepy there?" He answered: "There's nobody slipping here!" in a real heavy Jewish Brogue.

Bennie tried to play tenor sax like Louis was playing trumpet at that time—which was about 1930. He honked on it, got a tone like Pee Wee gets on clarinet, only considerably heavier. And he sang beautifully. Crosby reminds me of Bennie only Bennie was hearing Louis all the time, and that's what would come out of him.

There's not much I can remember about that job in Racine except playing and listening to records and drinking.

After that job in Racine we came back to Chi and Bennie and I would hang out together. I had the use of a small organ—you know, the kind arrangers work out on, or the kind the Salvation Army uses—and I'd become pretty good at it. It's not an easy instrument to play on, with a beat. Bennie and I would stay home, or visit friends, and play. Once we went out on a strip of sand—you

could stretch it a bit and call it a beach—and sat and played till we were scared off by the cops.

Time passed—I got a job at a dancing school—that is, a joint where fellows came in to get acquainted or make dates with the gals. The last thing anyone does at a dancing school is worry about the art of dancing. I took Earl Wiley with me on drums, Earl Murphy on banjo, Leroy Smith on clarinet (and he played all the jazz tunes of Oliver and Jelly Roll like you would on trumpet —melody clarinet). When Leroy left us, Bennie joined us. I vaguely remember Wingy hanging around, Dave Tough sitting in. The job ended too soon again.

And then Murphy got us a job at a spot about thirty miles out of Chi. A lot of swanky people came there. Someone drove us out there and we played for the boss. We had a band—besides playing as much music as any four pieces I've heard would produce, Bennie sang, Wiley could do a dance, soft-shoe, that would kill us. Murphy sang—and I'd written a song for a gangster that was very popular among that set. And when the boss found out I was the author—I sang plenty too—it was a dirty ditty—we were in. Ask me about it some time when we're alone.

After an audition the boss gave us all we wanted to eat and drink, also $100 to get a car, so we could drive there and back. Oh, yes, we were hired. We got a good salary, all we wanted to eat and drink. That's how it was when we started.

But how we could drink! In a few days the bartenders couldn't take it. So new rules were laid down. A pint of gin when we got there, a pint of gin on the way home; in between a few drinks at the bar. Mind you, we were up there playing when we had to. One night we were all packed up, in the car ready to drive off, when a few of the boss' cronies came in, wanting to hear my song.

We got out the banjo and gave it to them right out in the yard, chorus after chorus. And he paid off, and we all split.

But that ride home! Going there we wouldn't fight much about who drove the car we all owned, but coming back everyone was a race track driver. And shortly I developed a bad set of nerves. We had a couple of close calls that I'd like to forget.

One day our place was held up. We were all on the stand playing when it happened. I found out later the hoodlums broke the doorman's head a bit, and ruined the chap's arm just to impress us. And then one of them slid across the dance floor up to the band with a gun pointed at us. "Get off and lay down, face forward." Needless to say, we did.

We'd just drawn fifty bucks to pay the union with, and Bennie had it in his pocket. "Get up!" The band got up. "Empty your pockets." Then Bennie did something I'll always remember. "Man, we ain't got nothing—we're musicians, we're always broke—man, you know that . . ." The hood sort of laughed and passed us by, but went down the line and took every one else's bank roll. Also, they escorted a couple of girls out of the washroom. Those guys meant business. They also took everyone's car keys. It was a mess. All we could do was step to the bar and drink—on the house. And I wrote another verse to my tune about "Did you ever meet the hold-up man—well, into this cafe he ran, pointed his gun, get off your—off the stand." After that the band was really set with the boss; we could have had anything.

But like all good things it came to an end. We started taking advantage a bit; we'd be late, and that would murder the boss. Once we had to lay Bennie off for four days, "rest him up a bit," figuring he'd need the job and would behave when he got back.

So we got Bud Freeman to take his place, just to help us out. But Bud wasn't happy in our sort of band. He heard notes, harmonies, we didn't play. And as for us, well—Bud was no Benny Moylan, Bud made pretty runs and knew his horn, but Bennie was Louis on Gut

Bucket. Bennie honked on his tenor, he had a whiskey tone. He was in a groove that couldn't be mistaken. We sent for Bennie to come back.

Three fellows in the band—all but me —had Irish in them, and you've heard of the fighting Irish. Well, when it got so bad that we took to talking of fighting between ourselves (this is all the way home, of course), and when Wiley pushed me through a plate glass door, just while emphasizing a point, I decided I needed a rest. Tut Soper took my place. But pretty soon I was back, too—and pretty soon we lost that job.

I worked on a couple more jobs with Bennie. One, during the depression, paid us all of $10 a week, and our drinks. And the only reason I mention it is because the second night we were there, the boss called us over and told us we'd have to make other arrangements about the drink department.

The other job is a story in itself that I'll sit down and tell you about some day.

Too bad Bennie never recorded. Bennie and I made a few of the ten-cent variety of records while we were in Racine, but they warped on me and though I tried my damnedest to dub them, it was impossible.

I believe Bennie died at 27. He was in the hospital but wouldn't stay put; got out of bed saying, "Man, I'm not sick!" He was too strong to stay in bed; but it licked him; Bennie went.

So you want to talk of tenor sax giants—so you go out and hear someone running up and down the scale, or play "Body and Soul," and you say "Oh, my God!" Well, we said that, ten, fifteen years ago, when you had to be damn good before one of the boys said that about you.

Some time, when you catch Dave Tough drinking and being himself, ask him about Bennie Moylan. Or else ask Earl Murphy. You'll hear about a guy who could make you cry when he sang, and turn around and play you some low down music on his sax (rubber bands and string attached) like you won't hear being played anywhere today.

Blues for the Dago

The Boss—"Dago" Lawrence Mangano—Stopped Slugs in Chicago—Back in 1927 He Liked Jazz

So they shot the Dago! The man who refused to wear the crown (king of the underworld). They put 200 slugs in him and five bullets—and he lived seven and a half hours. After they'd pumped lead into him once he got out of his car and started after them, pure instinct, but they weren't taking chances. They circled the block and came back to finish up. They did.

Of course I was sad when I read it—"Chicago Gangster Killed" the headlines screamed. And of course the politicos will get busy and "clean up" the town now. So a few thousand musicians, entertainers, bartenders and waiters will be thrown out of work "temporarily."

No doubt the Dago had it coming. The law of the mob seems to be "kill or be killed." It was his turn. And fifty-four is a long time to live if you're a gangster. I just can't forget him so easily because he was my first boss. He gave me my first steady job. He was a musician at heart; he had brothers who were professional musicians. Remember the time that . . .

It was the dead of winter. Man, it used to get awfully cold in Chicago. And boy, you sure could freeze in that town. This was Halsted Street, where Blue Island Avenue runs into Harrison. Somewhere in that neighborhood Mangano operated a night club. Tonight it was full, people getting drunk and celebrating—upstairs, unknown to the customers (many of them) was a gambling joint. You could lose plenty up there. Johnny Craig (a drummer) and myself were playing downstairs—"I've grown so lonesome —thinking of you—thinking of you"—when all of a sudden, pop-pop—the Fourth of July, pistols and all. And me with my back turned! Man, I was scared. I ducked. Some guy celebrating, shooting at the ceiling, and it was made of tin. Those gamblers upstairs must have done some moving around.

Well, this celebrater couldn't have shot all his bullets away when the Dago came out of the kitchen, fit to be tied, picked up a heavy water bottle, walked up to this guy with the gun in his hand, and stretched him cold with one blow on the top of his skull. And if it hadn't been for some gal pleading with the Dago to let him be, Lawrence would have kicked and beat him to pieces—he was that mad.

Well, after it was all over two dicks—plain clothes men—came in, walked straight into the kitchen, stayed there about ten minutes, and then walked out into the night. Later I found out (the talk gets around, you know) that it had cost the boss fifty bucks apiece to "keep it quiet."

And how about the time we were all leaving the Rainbow Gardens, four a.m., when three hoods jumped the boss. He fought them single handed all over the sidewalk until they beat it, one by one. And when someone asked him why he didn't use his gun, the Dago said: "Waste lead on them punks?"

Then there was the time the Dago grabbed the colored porter from behind, and he gave a yell and two handfuls of change (he'd just come back from an errand) went flying all over the place. We screamed 'til exhausted.

Yea, the Dago led a full life. Pretty women, plenty to drink and his banjo, tuned ukelele style. His favorite tune was "It's Tight Like That" and I who have heard thousands of verses still remember one of his—unfit to print.

His day was an era of lawlessness —policemen that could be paid off; politicians that could be bought; opposition that was done away with. Jazz lived and flourished in that atmosphere. The New Orleans Rhythm Kings, King Oliver, Johnny Dodds, George Mitchell, Louis Armstrong—Lincoln Gardens, Friar's Inn, Kelly's Stables—all buried away in the past—a glorious past —when the boss man went for the real jazz. "What is this, a morgue? Jazz it up!" O.K., Dago. I'll bet he'd a loved to have a real jazz band play at his funeral. All hail the King —the King is dead.

Blues for Nick and Tricky Sam

During the past month two men took their turn at the plate and both struck out. Nick Rongetti and Tricky Sam Nanton have gone the way of all flesh. One man supported jazz; the other played it. There'll be yards of wordage spilled on both now that they're gone. Which seems to be a human failing. Few of us receive homage due while we're still alive and kicking.

I never met Tricky Sam but I heard plenty of him on discs. He was great. I'll have to leave it to others that knew him to write of him. But I did know Nick fairly well. Not like Pee Wee, Muggsy and Hackett knew him. They say that Pee Wee Russell is unemotional, 'cept when playing; that he stammers and that one can't make head or tail out of his conversation. Me, I don't believe it. Yet, even if it is true, his eyes gave him away when he told me the sad news. They were kind of dewy.

Maybe Nick wasn't the guy you could love like a brother. Still I'd like to lay you a bet that there were certain musicians that were helped more by Nick than they were by their family or closest friends. But the big thing he did was that he founded a home for jazz music during the dark ages; the lean years.

When I reached New York City in '38 one of my most immediate problems was to find a place to "sit in and play." I didn't have a piano and I just had to keep my fingers in shape. At that time the Spirits of Rhythm were holding down the intermission job at Nick's. I managed to sit in one time and after that I was set. But not solid, man. I had to fight for that seat. You see, Nick loved to play piano and every chance he could steal from his business he did. He really got a kick out of playing. Hey, Phil Featheringill (calling Session Records), remember the time you and I were at Nick's and he was playing and you asked me who he was 'cause you wanted to record him? Remember? Yes, Nick's face would light up when that music was in there. Still he never turned me down when I asked him if I could sit in. Never.

I remember when Fats Waller dropped in and the purple carpet came out; Fats was king and Nick led him to the throne. N.R. didn't draw the color line in his tastes. A great pianist always rated at Nick's. I don't think there's any sense in rattling off the list of greats that found employment at 10th and 7th. You remember them as well as I do. During the years that no other spot in this whole country featured jazz, Nick did. There were times when he couldn't meet his payroll. That was when he could have changed his policy; maybe featured mickey-mouse music or girlie acts or any of a dozen different ideas that were thrown at him. Only he didn't.

Which brings to mind the night a famous swing(?) vocalist was visiting the bistro and suddenly broke into song. Nick jumped up like he'd been shot. "What's goin' on here anyway?" he asked. Somebody told him about the great honor that was being paid him. Nick shouted "I don't care who he is; if he wants to sing let him go outside." And that was that. Yes the man Rongetti was stuck on our kind of music. Stuck on it and by it. In all my travels I never met a cafe owner who did as much for jazz as Nick did.

Well, why go on? The "who-bit-you-harry's" have all been written and by much better writers than this person. But before I fold up let me tell you one thing. There's enough good (I mean great) musicians, gone

to that place that we all have to go sometime, to form several great bands. Make no mistake about that. Morton, Oliver, Noone; Ladnier, Dodds, Nanton; Bix. There's Bessie Smith to do the vocals. On bass there's Blanton, Patterson and Steve Smith; Charlie Christian on guitar. There's plenty of good music there. But every band must have a place to play and someone to run it. Well they're all set now. They've got a guy that loves to hear it as much as they love to play it. They've got Nick Rongetti.

Blues for 52nd Street

Did you ever hear of the Keyboard Club? Well, you're one up on me if you have, 'cause up to the time I was asked to go in there, the name meant nothing to me. But that's not

unusual. On the street places come and go. Almost every club on 52nd Street has had several changes of names. As far as the boys in the know care, the street is bounded by

The Last go-round at Ryan's: A Milt Gabler jam session, 1942. Jack Bland, Eddie Condon, Max Kaminsky, Zutty Singleton, Sidney Bechet, Marty Marsala, Frank Orchard, Sandy Williams, Lips Page, Joe Sullivan, Happy Cauldwell, Brad Gowans, Pee Wee Russell, Bill King.

Art Hodes and his Chicagoans, New York, March 22, 1944. Left to Right: Sid Jacobs, bass; Rod Cless, clarinet; Jack Bland, guitar; Danny Alvin, drums; Ray Coniff, trombone; Max Kaminsky, trumpet; Art Hodes, piano.

the White Rose just off the corner of 6th and 52nd, and the Keyboard. The One Rose, as Rod Cless used to call it, is a saloon where we stop for that opening and closing drink as well as the few or many we may find we need that night to get through it safely. As you turn the corner you see a long line of old four story houses; mostly furnished rooms. The first club you hit is the Three Deuces. After that it's the Downbeat, the Spotlight, and finally the Keyboard. Across the street, on the corner within a great big fenced off cemented lot, the Douglas Aircraft people have on exhibition a great four-motor job. One of those planes of tomorrow. For two bits you can climb up and stare and the visitors really do. A couple of doors past is the Onyx Club and then comes Ryan's. That's it. Swing Street. Every club has its doorman who on Saturday night turns out to be the barker. "Step right in folks; the show starts right away. Hear the world's greatest jazz singer, Billie Holiday," etc., etc. It reminds you of the circus. Those guys hustle trade.

Any one of these clubs are about big enough to turn around in. Outside of Ryan's none feature dancing. The prices are up there and if you think you can stand around one minute without ordering you're in for a surprise. The bartender grabs you in about the same manner that a dice game man will reach out with his long stick and pull in the money. With each room holding tops 100 people and name stars pulling down hundreds of dollars for their week's stint, they have to operate that way. The few other business places on the street seem oddly out of place. The Chinese restaurant is changing hands. The bartender at the Rose is taking it over soon. I guess he'll pull a lot of trade away with him. Most of the colored boys hang there. But then at Reilly's the opposite is true. So everyone's happy.

Funny how the boss at the Keyboard happened to get in this racket. Knocked me out when I heard the story. You may have heard of Charlie Bourne. He's a pianist and a darn good one. No, not a jazzman. If you like music you'd take to him. Usually he can store away a lot of wet stuff during the course of a night's work. Charlie can go. Anyway, Tommy, the boss, is nuts about the classics. He's running some sort of successful engineering firm when he bumps into Charlie. From then on in he's a Charlie Bourne fan. Picks him up every time he falls. Takes him home and straightens him out. Goes to hear him wherever he plays. Well, one time Charlie disappears from all known haunts for three days and when the bossman finally finds him he's a mess. So Tommy packs him off upstate where T's brother lives and they straighten him out. Then they get him a job and in no time he's got the natives piano conscious. The place finally climbs up to doing four grand every week from about $500 before C.B. That makes Tommy think. Why not get a spot in New York and do it for myself? And so it happens. Charlie opens with all the trimmings and fanfare. Only it don't last. The flesh is weak. When customers mistakenly ask Charlie to play some boogie woogie he tells them to go next door. He conducts himself like a high priced artist that don't help the till (the register, you know). Well, why lengthen it out? Business falls off and there comes the parting of ways. That's how come Wild Bill's in there now. It accounts for my job too.

Wild Bill's got himself a young band. Some of his boys did an army stint with Bill. They're all nice guys and with Bill in there blowing it sounds pretty good. The Wild One doesn't pull his punches you know. Opening nite was a honey. Milt Gabler and Brunis took over; mostly Brunis. It sounded like old home week. Plenty of action at George's end of the bar. Dizzy Gillespie came in and listened. They tell me he's a nice guy. I'd give a lot to know what he thought. In fact I'd like to know what all the boys on the street think of this foreign invasion. Brunis on one side and Bill on the other. Sacrilege!

They're beginning to tear down part of the street. Before long it's all slated to go, I hear. Gotta make room for more Rockefeller Center, I guess. I suppose it'll look prettier then. Those big buildings are such impressive structures. Run right up to the sky. But where will the street run? Maybe you don't care for sideshows. In that case you won't miss it. I will though. Rubbing shoulders with the boys at the White Rose; Big Sid Catlett, Billie Holiday and her big dog. Must cost plenty to feed him. Lips Page a'talkin'; Red Allen and Higgy; Sandy Williams, Mezz, Kaiser. Those Sunday afternoon gatherings when Milt's sessions were still the thing. A lot of things went in to make up that good feeling you get when you think of the street. Most of it happened a long time before those signs outside of certain places appeared, which read "King of the Esquire Poll," etc. I guess I just don't like polls. Maybe it's because I never won on one of those things. Could be. I came close once tho. Close to the bottom. Somebody made a mistake and my name slipped in. The History of Swing Street would make swell reading, but who is there who could write it? Certainly not me. Well, drink up fellows. Here's to a street. Long may it be remembered.

2

Beginnings—Blues, Boogie-Woogie and Ragtime

Before jazz there was black piano, and guitar and vocal music—blues, and a special kind of blues with an eight-to-the-bar bass figure, called boogie-woogie, and ragtime. There are articles on all of these in Part Two, including the only published writings of Cow Cow Davenport, and including also a remarkable series of reminiscences of Bessie Smith, three by musicians and one by Carl Van Vechten, the writer and photographer who played so large a part in the Harlem Renaissance.

One article in this section, on Scott Joplin, illustrates almost perfectly the cultural gap between the musician and the jazz fan on the one hand and the general public on the other. Today we are in the midst of a ragtime revival, and the music of Scott Joplin, the classic ragtime composer, is selling better on phonograph records than that of any other classical composer. But in November 1947, when R. J. Carew's article appeared and *The Jazz Record* carried

Joplin's picture on its cover, Joplin's name and Joplin's music had been forgotten by almost all Americans. The only exceptions were a few musicians and a few of the more dedicated fans in the small audience for traditional jazz.   C.H.

Play It, Mr. Piano Man

Close your eyes and imagine a time before TV and juke box entertainment. When every bar, every corner saloon had somethin' goin'. Some kind of music. Mostly a piano man. Depending on what part of the city you were in, the music would vary from hot to sweet. From barrelhouse to honky-tonk to "cry-in-your-beer" ballads. Then again, out on the South Side of Chicago there were rent parties; flats; apartments that were turned into "musicales" any given night, but mostly on weekends. Thats where you heard what I call "the real thing." Man talks to you at the piano.

Saturday night; could be "cross the street from the rib-joint." There's that big 'lectric player that you can pump, but mostly someone is at the keyboard layin' down the truth. That cat's cookin'. I hear someone shout, "Play it Mr. Piano Man." And then when it really gets good you hear a voice from way over there, shout "Turn out the lights an' call the law." Sometimes a cat would come in and set up his drums; depending on who was in the house. But there'd be the kitty and we'd all throw somethin' in. But mostly that "professor" took care of all the music in that flat. There'd be singin'; sure. But Mr. Piano Man kept it rollin'. That's what I hear now when I listen to Pete Johnson on his recording "Roll 'em Pete." That left hand would agitate and you could feel the room jump. That was the time of the two-fisted piano player. Had to make it on your own. No drums and bass a'sittin' down to support you. It was all your gig.

You know somethin'? We (our country) produced some greats. Pine Top Smith! What a beautiful style; what a message. Cow Cow Davenport; and he was an original. The Boogie Woogie Boys (Ammons, Johnson, Lewis). They burn you up. Hersal Thomas, Wesley Wallace. So many others. Sit down at a piano and tell your story. One man could take care of a whole room. 'Course we're talkin' about Negroes playing for a Negro audience. Everybody with everybody. All one language. No mikes; no amps; you made it strictly on your own. Yeh! We had a day, and we had an age. Well, the giants been here an' gone. We have recordings, and we have stories.   A.H.

Mr. Davenport (Cow Cow to You)

It was one of those collectors, Herb Abramson (later he became part of Atlantic Records) who brought Cow Cow Davenport to my attention. Herb had been very helpful to me and my Metropolitan Review program, a radio show I conducted over New York City's own station, WNYC, six afternoons weekly. Brother, I needed help. Cow Cow, piano-man and song-writer. He was on the bottom, looking for a hand-up. The newspaper *PM* sent a photographer over and someone did a piece on the whole bit, and it appeared (pic 'n all) in print. That led to other collectors getting interested; if nothin' else it gave Cow Cow heart to go on; stick with it. Davenport didn't hang around New York for long, but in the time he was there he made his presence felt. Eventually a collector (I believe it was George Avakian) beat the drums for Cow Cow and ASCAP gave him a membership which led to some sort of income.

Certainly Cow Cow Davenport created a style that must be considered original. It was a boogie-woogie style and was a mood that moved me. No doubt about it; Cow Cow Davenport brought something to jazz. And having seen him in action I can add to his pluses; he was a showman.   A. H.

Cow Cow and the Boogie-Woogie

by Cow Cow Davenport

The word "Boogie" was derived from our old grandmothers' use of the word meaning the devil. When the kids broke the rules in any way such as fighting, running away or disobeying in any way we were told that the "Boogie man" was going to get us. The blues was considered bad music as it usually alluded to love affairs. In those days, only the lowest class of people in the towns, or people who were known to be without self-respect, would dare to be heard singing the blues.

So whenever I'd get a chance I would slip away from my home to practice on some neighbor's piano and tried to play a blue tune, at the same time thinking of what my parents would think if they could hear me, and what they would say to me, I called my music "Boogie" music.

In 1917, before the First World War, there were several dances in vogue, namely: "walkin' the dog," "jazz dance," and "ballin' the jack," that were used in dance halls; other dances resembling the rhumba or "scraunch," etc., which were done in the honky-tonks, joints where nice people did not go. I gave the name of "Boogie-Woogie."

When I began playing the "Cow Cow Blues," I was trying to imitate a train, and originally called them the "Railroad Blues." I was trying to get in a part where the switchman (with many of whom I had a personal acquaintance) boarded the train from the

cow-catcher or the front of the train. The word "cow" somehow stuck with me and subconsciously, in a theatre, I once ended my song with "Nobody here can do what Papa Cow Cow can do." The audience immediately picked up the song and those who liked the number were anxious to get acquainted with me. After the show they would walk up addressing me as "Papa Cow Cow," and from then on I have been called by such a moniker.

Charles "Cow Cow" Davenport

Mama Don't 'low No Music

by Cow Cow Davenport

When I was a boy down in Alabama, the people who played music played only guitars. The guitars were carried swung on the neck with a long string, and people called them easy riders. My father didn't like that idea of his son being an easy rider so he wouldn't let me learn music. In those days the musicians had all the girls, and daddy despised it; so he didn't allow me to play in his house. He had purchased a piano, though. My mother was pianist for a church they organized. My mother admired me because I could play, and my daddy hated me because I could play. He was going to make out of me what he wanted me to be, that was a preacher. He sent me to Selma University, a Baptist college in Alabama.

At that school I could play piano like I wanted to. Naturally, I'm a piano player. I'd get invitations to all the socials, and I would play. At that time they didn't allow them to dance. But they would march up a breeze. Quite naturally with my old ragtime playing, when they'd get to corners they'd kind of shake themselves. So one reception we had the professor didn't allow me to play that music either. There's where the idea came for "Mama Don't 'low No Music Playin' Here."

After I came out of school I was too large to work so I wouldn't go home. Papa always said you got to work for your living. So I drifted to Birmingham. That was the largest town around my community. There I was first hired as a piano player, in a place down on 18th Street. Then I began to hear other people play. There weren't so many competitors at that time. By me not knowing music I had to make up the stuff to play. The others would get interested in me and gang around the piano.

I left Birmingham with a carnival show. The man who got me the job, Bob Davis, was the first man who ever showed me one key to the other, A-flat to C-sharp—before that I didn't know but one key, and they called me a one-key piano player. Bob Davis needed a piano player to play the show. I could always play for myself but couldn't play for anybody else. Quite naturally with women I had to learn different keys. He'd sit down and hum the show over to me and the different keys the girls sing in. That was a great day's work for me, to learn to play in those different keys. At that time it wasn't very many people knew music so when they found another piano player that was the end of me. They didn't want to fire me because I'd been with them. But I could sing, so I got on the stage, started to sing my own songs. And I began to write songs I wanted to sing. Those conditions in the south caused me to write the "Jim Crow Blues."

After I left there I began to wander around, found me a girl then, so we formed a team, and called it Davenport and Carr —Dora Carr. I started working with the T.O.B.A. [Theatre Owners Booking Association; a black vaudeville circuit] so me and Dora found something together. She had a nice voice, and I wanted to learn to sing. So I began to write the music for her to sing.

So in traveling over the circuit we came to New Orleans, and we laid off there. That gave me time to get around to the sporting districts, and I began to sing and play around in those places. I heard Louis Armstrong play trumpet one morning, waking me up; he was selling coal, you know. He came to my attention because he had such a clear tone. At that time Clarence Williams and William [A.J.] Piron were trying to get started publishing music, their own tunes. Piron really had a good band at that time, and we happened to meet. Mr. Peer, a talent scout from New York, heard me play, and he asked me to go to New York. I had never been to New York, didn't know anything about it. I asked him what he wanted me to do. He said "Sing the

songs as you sang last night." I knew it took lots of money to live in New York, so I said, "Give me some money." Generously he gave me a hundred—the first hundred dollars I ever had in my life. So I came to New York.

Well, Clarence Williams had made his way up here too by then. I went directly to the Okeh company, and they sent me to Clarence. I began to record my numbers, and Clarence began to publish them. The first was "You Might Pizen Me"; I made that with Dora Carr. We were the first to make doubles in America. After we made the records—we hadn't been used to having much and didn't have sense enough to think of royalties—I got two or three hundred dollars. Then we had to go back home and show off. I showed off Dora too much, somebody took her away from me. I asked her to come back to New York and she refused. Dora having money and me having money, I soon spent out. When I spent out she put me out. So I went and got me a room and started writing. I was trying to write the "Cow Cow Blues." "Lord, I woke up this morning, my gal was gone." That was the creation of the "Cow Cow Blues." There was a piano roll company in Cincinnati by the name of Vocal Style. So I worried the man to get him to hear my blues. Mr. Miller decided he'd let me cut it on piano rolls. He didn't know whether it was good or bad, didn't know if it would sell, and neither did I. I said, "Give 'em to me, I'll sell 'em myself." I carried them to several music stores, and they didn't know what it was all about. A music store on 6th Street told me they wouldn't give me 75¢ for a hundred of them. So I went from house to house with my "Cow Cow Blues." At that time they gave me 4¢ for each roll sold, royalty. The manufacturer gave me 50-50 until payment was made for making them. Then he said, "If you can sell them I can sell them," and put them in the catalog. They began to circulate. I used to demonstrate them everywhere I played. I carried 50 or 100 rolls all the time in my trunk. Then I'd play and sing them. I'd ask the audience, "If you like them I got them here and can sell them to you." That's the way the "Cow Cow Blues" started.

So I drifted back to New York. Thinking I'd get some protection, Clarence Williams published it. I was exclusive on Okeh at that time, 1923. So I played them and Dora Carr sang them. She came back to me after I started making money. We had a contract; this was before Butterbeans and Susie. It was the first recording of boogie-woogie.

So I left New York again on the little small time. I played from one theatre to another. I happened to hit in Pittsburgh at the Star Theatre on Wylie Avenue. Being a piano player I would go around to all the honky tonks in town. I went with a friend of mine to the Sachem Alley, and there I found Pine Top Smith. He had heard my "Cow Cow Blues," wanted to meet me. He sat down playing, didn't know what he was playing, so I said, "Boy, look here, you sure have got a mean boogie-woogie." Pine Top didn't know what he was playing nohow. I began to tell him what it was, then he tried to sing it. He could never rhyme it together, just said "Come up here, gal, to this piano . . . playing my boogie-woogie." That's where the name boogie-woogie derived from.

So I wrote in to Chicago to Mayo Williams, who was selecting talent for Vocalion. I said I heard a boy play mean boogie-woogie. Pine Top went to Chicago and made recordings. I met him in Chicago when I went back there. He had made five or six numbers and he was just getting paid off for the songs he had made. He gave me a swell time, carried me out to his house, and he tried to pay me for getting him on records. I wouldn't accept it. He put ten dollars in my pocket anyhow. I think Pine Top had never had any money either at that time, the way he was giving it away to me. So I took the ten; he wouldn't let me spend anything; he spent all his money, so glad I put him on records. At that time I told Pine Top he was a nice looking, smooth little black fellow, all the women crazy about him. I told him not to go around in places so much because the men hated him. He looked good; you can't last long if you look good. I gave him the best advice before I left Chicago. Told him to be careful, take his wife with him, and keep out of trouble. But he didn't do it. He got killed, accidentally, and that was the end of him.

I mooched along till I thought of the "Mooch Piddle." I made a record of that for Vocalion. Mooching along, running from place to place, playing down in Birmingham, I met a man named Harry Charles, a scout for Paramount. I got a quartet together, I was trying to get somebody to sing my material. They disappointed me; only three of them came to Chicago with me. I was playing accompaniment and they would sing spirituals. So I had to find another tenor after I got to Chicago. I went to all the hotels where performers stayed, and asked for a tenor. That's where I found Sam Thread. I had the date all set with Paramount and he came along and filled out on recording with me. After we got through I didn't want to go south again, so we stayed around Chicago. My kind of playing wasn't accepted at that time any place but honky tonks. The only one left out of the quartet was Sam. So I told Sam, "Get something together." So we go up to Brunswick. That's when I wrote "I'll Be Glad When You're Dead, You Rascal You." Trying to make Sam as an artist, they advertised him. That's how the song got away from me. The advertising made Sam and the song, but I'm the man who wrote it.

I went to Vocalion then, and I began to succeed a little in the music I was writing, through Mr. Mayo Williams. I began to write things for Sam, and pulled out that number, "Mama Don't 'Low No Easy Riders Here." So Half-Pint Jaxon was going to record this song for me for the new Brunswick. I gave him the words written out on a piece of paper. It had never been recorded before, and he forgot the words. He started to jive with the musicians, saying "Mama don't 'low no drum playing, no piano playing, no Cow Cow piano here" and so on; you can hear it on one of the Brunswick records.

At that time we weren't much salesmen on songs, people didn't know us. I didn't think we could sell the songs either, or put them with people like Armstrong who had names. I didn't know the value of my songs; I would just sell it, and anything they gave me was all right. After leaving Chicago I got lucky. Paramount owed me about $3,000 for royalties on songs I'd written. I met a woman named Iva Smith, so she and I got together; I had money and didn't know what to do with it. So we organized a big show together. That was just before the toughest depression. Paramount owed me $3,000, so I bought a bus and had it charged to them. We traveled from Chicago to Kansas City in the bus, played the old Lincoln Theatre on 18th with our show. We went in on a 50-50 basis, but the man was excited and gave me $1300 for the show. Wasn't that a lift? I had money enough to pay my people off and everything.

We left Kansas City and started down south again. From there to Tulsa, Oklahoma, to Dallas, and then things began to break bad. I began to lose my money. All I had was invested in my show, and I tried to keep on. People didn't have enough money to come to see it. My last stop was in Mobile. I didn't have enough money to pay expenses; I had to borrow some money from somebody, so I started to pawn my bus. I would put it up for security. So I pawned my bus too many times; down south they put you in jail for that. They caught me and gave me six months in Camp Kilby, out from Montgomery. It gave me a chance to think. All my show folks left, bus gone and me in prison. I couldn't do any farm work, in fact I couldn't do anything. I had never worked before. After I got my whippings they decided I couldn't work. They put me with the old men as a gardener. Naturally I sat down on the ground. I caught pneumonia. It must have settled in my right arm. When I got out of Camp Kilby I went to Tallahassee, Florida, and joined Haeg's circus, which was coming up this way. I worked with them as a minstrel until they crossed the Mason-Dixon line; then I saw they were going back and I quit that show.

I stopped in Cleveland with my sister Martha. I had just got up from that pneumonia and I had practically lost the use of my right hand, so she tried to help me. After I began to get back to life, I began to play just a little, so I started leaving home. Runs up on a girl named Peggy Taylor, who had a little old show at the Grand Central Theatre on Central Avenue in Cleveland. She was a performer, did a dance with snakes, something I didn't know anything about at that time. When you see shows, you always want to join them. So I go in and tell her who I am. She didn't have a comedian and she asked me to help her. She was single, too. So we got together. She had a nice house and gave me a room. I began to write to J. Mayo Williams to get back into recording.

In 1937 the Elks had a big convention in Cleveland. I didn't have but $50, but Peggy asked me to do her a favor. She had a tent and everything and she had an idea how she could make money with those snakes. My

sister had that $50; I go and ask her for it. She said, "All right, take it, go, throw it away anyhow!" Peggy got permission to put up her tent where she worked on the inside, and that was how I got to be the spieler, with snakes. I got a cowboy hat and went on the front to talk. We made about $20 a day, so I told her, "I think you got something." I got in touch with her agent and they booked us into Cincinnati at the Cotton Club.

Traveling was a lot of trouble; I had snakes and didn't want people to know it. I'd get a room; the people would come to see the show, see Peggy dance, and then they would put us out. At one place the lady sat up until we came home from the show and said, "You people get out!"

We bought a trailer and car to travel with. So we mooched on through Ohio, playing through the summer in a tent. So many people had us arrested about those snakes that we would first get a room and camp the trailer in the backyard. But folks found out and had the police raid us and take them away. I decided we better get a house. So that's how we got to Cleveland. My wife, Peggy Taylor, went to work for the city as a playground attendant, taking care of smart kids. She has been there seven years, still working. She is Director of Playgrounds now, very successful, so I can't bring her away.

I began to get in touch with Williams again, and began to write more stuff. I formed a band playing around Cleveland after we decided to live there. The boys in that band thought I was full of stuff, they didn't want to learn what I told them. I made an appointment with Decca, in 1939, and they sent for me with a car. The boys all had excuses why they didn't want to go to New York with me. So as the car was there and I had the material, I came to New York alone. That's where I found Sam Price, at the Woodside Hotel. I asked him to play for me and he did. Then he formed his own band and began to use my material. We made five records then—"That'll Get It," "The Jive Is Here," and others. I sang, Sam Price played piano.

So I go back to Cleveland and pick up a colored paper, the *Chicago Examiner*, and see where Sam Price is down at Cafe Society in New York imitating Cow Cow Davenport. So I began to think. I came back to New

York. I go up to William Morris' office and he booked me into the Plantation Club in Nashville, Tennessee. I guess they must have thought I was the imitation. I went for four weeks but they only used me a week. Sam Price had just left and he must have been using my material. So I went back to Cleveland and waited a while.

Now I'm in New York. I just cut eight sides for the Comet Record Company. I'm wandering around, trying to get some work.

The Blues in His Heart

by Jasper Wood

It has always seemed a shame to me to see the way that Cow Cow Davenport has been treated. Because the last few years have really seen Cow Cow kicked around.

First let's go back a few years. Cow Cow was trying to get into ASCAP on the strength of having written "I'll Be Glad When You're Dead You Rascal You" and "Cow Cow Blues" and many many others. But there was no one to help him out (as in the case of Meade Lux Lewis) so Cow Cow is still on the outside looking in. The difficulty in Cow Cow's case (as with so many other race artists of the 20's) is that the recording directors in those days got you the record job but had you sign a paper releasing all rights to whatever original tunes you did. A lot of the (at the time) friends of the recording artists built up big books in this manner, entered the publishing business and are now well heeled. But not so the many recording artists of that period, especially Cow Cow Davenport.

About five years ago when Julian Krawcheck and I were running the Hot Club of Cleveland we had Cow Cow come down and play for us. At that time he was working in a defense plant. He played the blues in the old and real manner and not many of the fellows (or gals) cared for his music. It was too much real blues for them to be impressed. They liked Wilson and boys of that ilk. But Cow Cow came back to the next session, and brought along his wife. Well Cow Cow played the blues and his wife sang some really filthy lyrics and the crowd went nuts,

really nuts. And afterwards Mrs. Davenport sold little dime-store Kewpie dolls with banners reading The Hot Club of Cleveland.

I spent several nights at Cow Cow's room interviewing him for a story that I did for Steve Smith's *Hot Record Society Rag*. Well, the *Rag* folded shortly after and the story never saw print. Don Haynes did get a short piece in *Jazz Information* around that time, however.

It was during this time that Cow Cow was trying to get modern—"Get back into the swing of things, today," was the way he phrased it. We went out into the hall outside his room where there was an old upright and he played some of his new compositions for me. One was called "Jump, Little Jitterbug." It was competent riff composing, but it really stank, my friends. I had to get away fast. It was too much to sit there and hear an old, forgotten master of the blues play that way and try to make the compromise (the big sell-out) so that he could go on making his living by playing the piano. But that was the way things were in Cleveland in the late thirties.

I didn't get to see Cow Cow again—soon he left for New York. Art Hodes had him up to play on his radio show one day. Cow Cow's hands were in bad shape. They had been bruised this way and that by the defense plant work. Art says now, "One thing that I was really proud of on my radio show was that I had the best of the piano players. I had Sullivan a couple of times, and James P.

Johnson, and Cow Cow Davenport." That was about the only real recognition Cow Cow has had in many a year.

Then one day a few weeks ago, I walked past the Musical Bar on Playhouse Square in Cleveland and there was a photograph in the window of Art and Cow Cow (taken during the radio show). He opened that day. I wasn't able to get down for three or four nights to catch the show. But I did get there as soon as possible. I walked past the long bar and into the back room. Teddy Wilson runs were flowing out of a large gold encrusted piano. But I couldn't see the gray-haired (close-clipped) Cow Cow around anywhere. I went back up to the front bar and found the manager. "Where's Cow Cow Davenport?" I asked.

"You'll find him out at Thompson Products, working in the defense plant," was the reply.

"There's a picture of him in the window. I thought that he was playing here," I said.

"He started here the first of the week. But I had to yank him out of the show. He might have a name but I can't use him. Plays too old fashioned for me. The crowd didn't like his stuff. So I put in a guy who sounds like Teddy Wilson."

"Nuts to you, brother," I said, and walked out of the place.

So that is the way that one of the great blues pianists has been treated for the last several years. It is a sin to watch the thing happen. Maybe there isn't any market for old time blues piano. At least not for an old man like Cow Cow Davenport. But he was robbed of what should have been an income that he could have retired on. So what is there to do but work in a defense plant long enough to make a little money and put a little aside and then come out and try again? It's a tough grind, making money playing the blues. Cow Cow hasn't taken to the bottle, yet. He lives a clean and respectable life. But, brother, it breaks your heart to see the story out.

But thanks again for that shot on the radio, Art. And the picture too. It added a little lustre to the life of one of the greatest blues men of all time.

Rag Alley Story

by Rudi Blesh

Last January my friend Jimmy Ernst wrote to Montana Taylor to inquire about the lost years (1928 to 1946) in the life of the great barrel house pianist, years in which his whereabouts and his fate were an unsolved mystery of the jazz world. Montana replied as follows:

Dear Mr. Ernst:

Received your letter, was more than glad to hear from you. In my small way I am going to try and explain myself and my feelings to you, about "piano playing," and what I have done in the seventeen years I have not played. Started playing at the age of eighteen at and around Chicago and Indianapolis, for rent parties.

Played at Goosie Lee's "Rock House" in Indianapolis for two dollars a night. Enjoyed it very much. I made my first recording in 1928 in Chicago, for the company Vocalion. It was "Detroit Rocks" and also "Montana Blues." Think I received a pretty rotten deal as I never got any royalties; me not knowing much about the recording business I did not get my just deserts. I became very discouraged and refused to play any more. In 1936 I came to Cleveland, just knocked about doing nothing. In the years 1942 and 1943, certain magazines carried my name and the names of my recordings.

Charlie Cow Cow Davenport had seen them and located me to give me the informa-

JAZZ RECORD

25c

April 1947

No. 54

Montana Taylor (Montage by Jimmy Ernst)

tion. *He told me about Rudi Blesh and how he wanted the original Barrel House Blues. In March, 1946, Cow Cow Davenport went, with myself, to Chicago and made a few more recordings.*

Please give Art Hodes my regards and tell him to please get in touch with me. Once in a while I get a chance to play at a rent party, but very seldom.

Arthur "Montana" Taylor

The cryptic understatement of this letter tells—more eloquently than a thousand words—of the tragic predicament that the creative folk and jazz artist has faced in America for the last twenty years. The men and women who gave the world the most significant and challenging musical development of this century were literally beaten down into oblivion during what might have been their most fruitful years.

Some (like Muggsy Spanier, Kid Ory and Art Hodes) fought on against the dollar sign that took the place of the clef sign in music. Credit that to sheer guts, for the fight looked hopeless until the last year or so. Others (like Bunk Johnson, Montana, Chippie Hill and Hociel Thomas) were no less courageous but they had only the weapon of passive resistance, the last right left to them, that of refusing to play or sing except in the way they knew to be right. Such a battle, however unequal, is never hopeless—the seeming accidents that have helped some of these great artists, looked at with perspective, are perhaps, not accidents at all.

It seemed an accident when Cow Cow told me (in December, 1945) of Montana's whereabouts. But it was no accident that Montana (from his early records) had been a bright legend of my musical life.

So I took the next train to Cleveland; went straight to Cow Cow's address on Scovill Avenue in the heart of that appalling slum district that says to you if you have ears "Here is what you get in America if you're black."

In a few minutes Montana came in. Short but strongly muscled and dark of skin, everything about him is quiet: his dress, his gliding way of walking, and his soft voice. His words are few and rather uncommunicative but all the time his presence spreads electrically throughout the room, a personal dynamism that I find impossible to describe. Sitting down without being asked, he began to play:

"The Detroit Rocks" and "Indiana Avenue Stomp" (he calls it "Montana's Blues"). Something wonderful happened. The simple but tragically beautiful minor chords were saying something and in the compressed, instant revelation of great art I knew all about Montana Taylor's lost years. None of the dates, none of the events, but the *feel* of that wasted time in Montana's own heart.

Suddenly he began to sing:

Along about the break of day
Oh, baby, I said about the break of day
I felt the pillow where you used to lay . . .

Then, humming a few bars, he began to whistle the lonesome "long and short" of a far away train in the night: "I don't know where it's from; I don't know where it's going; but it's taking my baby away."

Turning on the stool he began to talk.

"I was born in 1903 in Butte, Montana —that's where I got my name. My father had the Silver City Club there, a cabaret, and we lived in back. The gambling was upstairs.

"I was six or seven when we left and went to Chicago. In about a year we moved to Indianapolis. When I was about sixteen I began to play piano. There were two brothers, Tom and Phil Harding—they could really play the blues. Each one had a piece and I learned it, like I learned from 'Funky Five' and 'Slick' and Jimmy Collins. All those boys played all around Indianapolis and Hammond. All the rest of the stuff I made up myself.

"It was about 1923 when I began to play for keeps. There was a dive—corner of Indiana Avenue and Rag Alley in Indianapolis —called The Hole in the Wall. I made my first money there. Then I began playing at rent parties, too, around Senate Avenue and on Blake Street.

"I was playing one day in a music store on Indiana Avenue when Guernsey walked in. He was the record company's talent scout and he signed me up. Then I went over to Chicago and recorded six numbers but two never got issued."

A few dollars for recording and then the depression came and the bottom dropped out of jazz music. Even Bessie Smith's records scarcely sold. Seventeen lost years and Montana is in Chicago again, in a recording studio way up in the Opera House building. Montana doesn't want to rehearse very much. He seems impatient to record as if this were a ritual that would wipe out the dead past time.

So here's my chance to test my recording theories. A new sort of "balance" that is not the studio sort of thing that, after all, is only a convention to which we're accustomed. No, a liveness, a sense of "presence" that will make the player seem to be in the room with each one who plays his record. And, above all, the relaxation of playing as the artist feels it; get all the inspiration in and take a little mistake or two as a part of the real inventive process.

You test a little and then tell the engineers, "Take down everything that happens at 33⅓." And you go out into the studio with your pianist and let him play while you sit on a stool with a stop watch and signal when it's time for the last chorus. It's as simple as that—if you have a great artist.

You begin at 2:30 and at 3:05 Montana is through. You've cut seven masters on this one day, and the engineers come rushing out. Excited? They can't believe it happened, not after the three hour sessions they put in day after day with the swing bands to get one master, maybe.

But there they are, seven of them being played back while Montana sits alone with his head in his hands and just listens. Then you name the ones that just happened there with no names: the one that Montana hummed and whistled *has* to be called "In The Bottom"; a slow drag sounds to Montana "the way you feel" " 'Fo' Day"; another is named "Rag Alley Drag" to commemorate Montana's first job.

So you have the records—a few precious minutes of the great art of a man who—given the chance—could pour it out endlessly for all who would listen. That's something you do for posterity and for those who, today, have the time and the will to listen to soft, clipped tones, to rhythmic chords, so jubilant yet so deeply sad; to music that speaks ever so quietly something that we need very much to hear amidst the roar of machinery and the clamors of war or armed peace. You can pay Montana a little royalty now and then and hope that seventeen years shall have given the world enough time to catch up with a great artist of our day.

Little Brother

We were doing a date (recently; '73-'74) for a Modern Art Gallery in dear ole Chi; Brother and I. . . . So we got to talking; and L. B. reminded me that "you used to come hear me way back when" . . . and of course I remembered . . . for it was during the time I was just comin' up. . . .

I call it my Wingy (Manone) years. I was actually going to school (looking back that's what it was); for Wingy and I lived for jazz; around it, into it; every day . .·. I guess it was Louis Armstrong who steered us into the barbeque place. We'd asked him for the name and address of a good place to get some ribs. Anyway, as I remember it, that was the first (and in Wingy's case, the last) time we found ourselves out to 48th and State. A real, broken-down frame store, with a small counter to eat at; a few tables to sit at, plus an old-time juke box and a big upright electric piano. Yeh! I used to put my nickels in and the music came out black. What wonderful times. The food was the greatest; those ribs and pies. Man . . . But I'd come there for a different kind of food. That's where I learned the blues.

On a week-end there'd always be live music; some kind of a trio; then maybe just a piano-man. And that's when I first heard Little Brother. Yeh, I sat and I heard; I listened. You ask me where I went to school? There's where it was. I became a fixture . . . didn't matter if I just had the fare to get there; I was there . . . Sometimes with others; most times alone. I was drawn like by a magnet. Papa Couch usually played the drums. And I recall a sax-man. And of course "the kitty"; a catch-the-money contraption that you were asked to feed. It no doubt was a good part of the musicians' salary. That's where I first met (and heard) Little Brother Montgomery.

L. B. gets to go abroad quite a bit. They send for him to play festivals; blues concerts. It's somethin' to watch him operate with that left hand. That's his "boogie-woogie hand." Sure, Brother does vocals now; and he writes originals too. But for me, it's that sound he creates at the piano. Yeh, and he's had a stroke; in his left hand. But no matter; he still plays. He's found a way to operate. You see, that's his thing . . .   A.H.

Little Brother

by Eurreal Montgomery

Eurreal Montgomery, the one called Little Brother Montgomery, was born at Kentwood, Louisiana, on May 17, 1907. His father and mother was the father and mother of ten children, five girls and five boys; one girl and one boy died which left eight children living—Leon, Eurreal, Joe and Tollie; the girls were Olema, Aris, Ella and Willie Belle. The father of Little Brother's family is named Harper Montgomery and mother is Dicy Montgomery.

When he was six years old he could play the piano. His father owned a piano when Little Brother could first remember. Now the whole family of Little Brother's sisters and brothers could play piano also. His father was a cornet player at that time, his mother was an organ player. So when Little Brother was eleven years old he ran away from home. Little Brother Montgomery went to school at Tangipahoa Parish Training School located at Kentwood, which was his home, before running away. So he ran away at the age of eleven, a small boy.

First job was at Holten, La. Next job he had was at Platman, La. Next job he had was at Fariday, La., at the Royal Garden, and next Vicksburg, Miss., at Prenes Theater. So when Little Brother was eighteen years old he had a band at Gulfport, Miss. He left the South on a tour with Clarence Desdune's orchestra of New Orleans, and came to Omaha, Nebraska. That is where he quit the band and started his recording career.

He came to Chicago and started working for Paramount Recording Co., located at Grafton, Wisconsin. His first numbers were "St. Louis Woman" and "Borrowed Love Blues," with Irene Scruggs. With Irene he made "Vicksburg Blues," "No Special Rider Blues," "Louisiana Blues" and lots of others; "Shreveport," "Farewell," "Farish Street Jive," "West Texas Blues," "Out West Blues," "Never Go Wrong Blues," "I Love You Baby But You Don't Mean Me No Good," "Something Keep Worrying Me Blues," "Black Boy Blues." "Jam Jam Blues," with Minnie Hicks; "I'm All Right Now" and "That's All For You," with Joe McCoy.

Preserve Genuine Early Ragtime

by S. Brunson Campbell

Genuine early Ragtime and New Orleans Dixieland Jazz music must be propagated by musicians here in America for it is the only genuine American music we have.

I was an early ragtime pianist, and about the only white pianist alive who had a solid contact with the early Negro pianists and composers of that era, have been doing my bit to help preserve it for the last three years.

One of the great Negro pianists and composers of the early ragtime era was Scott Joplin, ragtime's perfecter. He and Otis Saunders, Joplin's pal and also a fine pianist, taught me to play the "Maple Leaf Rag" while I was in my early teens. It came about this way. In the later part of 1898 I met Otis Saunders in Oklahoma City, Oklahoma, and he started me to play the "Maple Leaf Rag" from pen and ink manuscript. A few months later I meet Scott Joplin in Sedalia, Missouri, a very black Negro, about five feet seven inches, solid built, and a neat dresser, and musically very studious, and a sight reader. Saunders, Arthur Marshall, Scott Hayden, Louis Chauvin, and many of the early Negro pianists and composers of ragtime made Sedalia, Missouri, their headquarters. It was in Sedalia, Missouri, ragtime was born, not in St. Louis as so many writers on the subject claim.

I think I am the only old white ragtime pianist, who played ragtime that had that something the Negro had, as you will notice in my piano recording of the "Maple Leaf Rag." Of the two Negroes who taught me to play the "Maple Leaf Rag," Otis Saunders was the more even tempered. Joplin while a very fine teacher, was a little hot headed at times. My early association with these early Negro greats of ragtime gave me the opportunity to capture the Negro's musical soul in playing ragtime up to 1908; I could hold my own playing ragtime piano with those early Negro pianists.

In those days we early ragtime pianists played on old battered square pianos. Some were inlaid with mother-of-pearl, and none I ever played on were in tune. Of course we had the first uprights to play on, some with mandolin attachments and some of them would be pretty much out of tune, with quick action, just right down our alley for playing ragtime. True ragtime should be played fairly slow. Even that early lots of us rocked the bass and walked it. You just don't hear any real ragtime any more, played in the original way. Some of the modern styling of the old numbers makes us old timers pull our hair. We did not have the spots to play in, in those early days of ragtime that paid real big salaries like the musicians have today, but we made it possible for today's musicians to enjoy the fruits of our labor. We played in saloons, clubs, dance halls, pool halls and cigar stands, theaters, steamboats, road shows, minstrels, etc. In every city of any size, you could find some of the best ragtime pianists on the "Row or Line." A buck a night, tips and beers, and a place to flop, was about tops, for the average pianists. Spots like the Everleigh Club in Chicago, Illinois, and others, of course, paid well. We all had plenty of excitement, for it was truly the Gay 90's and Early 1900's. So you musicians commence to brush up on good old Joplin Rags—and real New Orleans Dixieland Jazz. Play on, Bunk Johnson and Kid Ory; lead the way *back*.

They All Had It

by S. Brunson Campbell

Of the early Negro pianists, composers of ragtime in the '90s, it can be said that each one had a distinctiveness about him that stood out. Joplin, Tom Turpin, Louis Chauvin, Scott Hayden, James Scott, Arthur Marshall, Tony Williams, Tony Jackson, Jelly Roll Morton, Otis Saunders—all had what we call "it." Take Otis Saunders for example.

Otis was a very fine pianist and a very technical musician with a fine musical education and a fine singer with a beautiful baritone voice. He was very light in color, about five feet six inches in height, a very neat and stylish dresser and very handsome. The colored ladies were all crazy about Otis, and that seemed to be his failing —women. They seemed to keep him well supplied with money, but if he needed money quick he would write a "rag" and sell it to some Negro pianist for whatever he could get.

I first met Otis Saunders in Oklahoma City in 1898, when I was just a kid. He had followed a colored girl from Sedalia, Missouri, with whom he was really in love, and who was also a fine pianist, and was playing piano in the red-light district of that city. Otis also got a job in the district, and in about two or three weeks they made up and returned to Sedalia. Otis was very active, giving advice to the early Negro pianists and composers of ragtime in Sedalia in the '90s. He was Scott Joplin's pal, and Scott Joplin very seldom did anything in a musical way without first consulting Otis.

In those early Sedalia days of ragtime, while Otis was a little younger than Joplin, he knew his music. But in a few short years Joplin progressed musically far above Saunders and the rest of the early Negro composers, and kept progressing right up to his death in 1917 at the age of 49.

When Otis Saunders entertained with his singing and piano playing, you were struck by his pleasing performance and his wonderful personality. He was a gentleman. But if need be, he could be rough. I don't think the true story will ever be written about this wonderful true pioneer of ragtime. The man who could furnish that story was his pal Scott Joplin, the perfecter of ragtime.

Surely Otis Saunders had that musical quality called "it." I would like to see the big American bands like Harry James, Benny Goodman, Ellington, Paul Whiteman, Benny Carter, Lionel Hampton, and smaller bands, as well as known name pianists and musicians, record and play some of Scott Joplin's and Tom Turpin's old original ragtime numbers. If you can't get them, I have them, and I would be more than pleased to loan them to any reliable band or artist who would guarantee to use them—but with the understanding that they are to be played as written. I would like to ask this question of the leaders of our great American jazz orchestras: Where would you be today, if it had not been for such Negro composers and pianists of ragtime as Tom Turpin, Scott Joplin, Louis Chauvin, James Scott, Scott Hayden, Tony Jackson, Jelly Roll Morton—the Negro musicians who had "it."

Scott Joplin

by R. J. Carew

Scott Joplin was born on November 24, 1868, in Texarkana, Texas. His father, who played the violin, wanted the boy to follow a trade or profession, but Scott, becoming fascinated with the piano, refused to yield to parental pressure, and left home to make a living as an itinerant player. There seems to be no record of young Joplin's activities until 1895, when he was a member of the Texas Medley Quartette, a traveling group that got as far as Rochester, New York, where two songs by Joplin were published. In 1896 Joplin compositions were published in Temple, Texas, indicating his return to his home state. The next place we find Scott Joplin is in Sedalia, Missouri, where he probably landed in 1897, and from that time his progress is pretty well recorded by his musical activities.

During the 1890's a revolutionary change took place in American music. Popular music and dancing took on a much livelier tempo; the two-step came in, the cake walk became popular, and syncopation came increasingly into popular music. There is little doubt that the changes taking place were caused largely by the fact that Negroes were acquiring greater opportunities to present their accomplishments in person to the public; they were dancing their own dances to their own music, and writing their own songs. The light syncopation of the cake walk prepared the way for genuine Negro ragtime. Ragtime, of course, was played before it got into print, and as an itinerant Negro pianist, Scott Joplin doubtless was familiar with it from its humble beginnings. He claimed to have composed an early cake walk, and his distinctive style of playing in a Sedalia gambling saloon attracted attention. Accepting advice, he studied music at the George R. Smith College for colored people, thus preparing himself for the vital part he was to play in American music. Conditions and the fates combined to make the time and place propitious: a musical revolution was under way; Joplin was thoroughly familiar with the old and the new forms; Sedalia, Missouri, was a "wide open" Mecca for Negro players, pioneering and exchanging ideas along the new lines, men like Otis Saunders, Scott Hayden, Arthur Marshall and others; and publishers had begun to see the possibilities in publication. Sedalia merits the name Cradle of Ragtime.

Joplin sold his first rag, "Original Rags," to Carl Hoffman of Kansas City, Missouri, who published it in 1899. That same year he contacted John Stark and Son of Sedalia, then preparing to move to St. Louis, and got a five-year contract with them on the merit they saw in "Maple Leaf Rag," "Sunflower Slow Drag" and "Swipesy," then in manuscript form. The "Maple Leaf" and "Swipesy" were published in Sedalia, after which the Stark firm moved to St. Louis, soon to be followed by Joplin. The Starks became The Classic Rag House, and Joplin took the title King of the Ragtime Writers. Success encouraged expansion, and in 1904 John Stark opened an office in New York City, and again Joplin followed, making the metropolis his headquarters from then on. Joplin's output of high class rags did not diminish to any extent until about 1910, when he seems to have concentrated on his opera, "Treemonisha." In New York Joplin confined his work almost entirely to composing and teaching, whereas in earlier years his music was in constant demand for parties, balls, entertainments, etc. It has been commented that Joplin was not the best of the St. Louis players, on which point we have no argument; however, we have it on good authority that his piano was completely adequate wherever he played. There is no argument, however, as to the superior quality of his ragtime compositions, and it is noteworthy that his earliest

NOV. 1947
No. 60
25¢

JAZZ RECORD

SCOTT JOPLIN
"Mr. Ragtime"

Scott Joplin

efforts stand up with anything he wrote later. "Original Rags" is a fine number, and the "Maple Leaf Rag" has never been been surpassed. He believed in ragtime, and judging by his output, he kept his aims high. His failure to see "Treemonisha" performed successfully in public probably had an adverse effect on his declining health. He died in 1917 in New York, where his widow, Mrs. Lottie Joplin still survives him.

Ragtime constitutes a very definite and important phase of the American musical revolution. When it appeared on the scene, it gave a lift to the music of the times; its infectious vigor and hilarity refreshed the tired musical spirit, and gave zest to the occasion. To say that Scott Joplin was the King of the Ragtime Writers is not to disparage others; there were many other writers who wrote many fine rags. But no other writer was so prolific and uniformly good over such a length of time, nor gave expression to such a diversity of ideas. It was probably because of Joplin's sincerity and belief in himself that his rags are the best and most consistent that appeared over the twenty years that ragtime reigned supreme. Embodying practically every use of syncopation, they deserve the attention of every lover of American music, and the student will find pleasure and profit in going over them seriously.

It is not enough to say that Scott Joplin left his mark on American music. The influence is stronger than that. It was with prophetic inspiration that the Stark Music Company advertised:

Here is the genius whose spirit, though diluted, was filtered through thousands of cheap songs and vain imitations.

COMPOSITIONS OF
SCOTT JOPLIN
Rags

1899 Original Rags (Arranged by Chas. N. Daniels)
1899 Maple Leaf Rag
1901 Peacherine Rag
1901 The Easy Winners
1902 A Breeze from Alabama
1902 Elite Syncopations
1902 The Strenuous Life
1902 The Entertainer
1902 The Ragtime Dance (Song, words and music by Joplin)
1903 Weeping Willow
1903 Palm Leaf Rag

1904 The Favorite
1904 The Chrysanthemum
1904 The Sycamore
1904 The Cascades
1905 Eugenia
1907 The Nonpareil
1907 Gladiolus Rag
1907 Search-Light Rag
1907 Rose Leaf Rag
1908 Fig Leaf
1908 School of Ragtime (Exercises and instructions)
1908 Pine Apple Rag
1908 Sugar Cane
1909 Paragon Rag
1909 Wall Street Rag
1909 Country Club
1909 Solace (A Mexican Serenade)
1909 Euphonic Sounds
1910 Stoptime Rag
1912 Scott Joplin's New Rag
1914 Magnetic Rag
1917 Reflection Rag

Operas
1903 A Guest of Honor (Unpublished and probably lost)
1911 Treemonisha—Opera in three acts.

Ragtime Waltzes
1905 Bethena—A Concert Waltz
1909 Pleasant Moments

Songs Written to Joplin Rags
1903 Maple Leaf Rag (Words by Sydney Brown)
1910 Pine Apple Rag (Words by Joe Snyder)

Rags Writtin in Collaboration
1900 Swipesy (Arthur Marshall)
1901 Sunflower Slow Drag (Scott Hayden)
1903 Something Doing (Scott Hayden)
1907 Heliotrope Bouquet (Louis Chauvin)
1907 Lily Queen (Arthur Marshall)
1911 Felicity Rag (Scott Hayden)
1913 Kismet Rag (Scott Hayden)

Miscellaneous
1895 A Picture of Her Face (Waltz Song)
1895 Please Say You Will (Waltz Song)
1896 The Crush Collision March
1896 Combination March
1896 Harmony Club Waltz
1901 Augustan Club Waltzes
1902 March Majestic (6/8 March)
1902 Cleopha (Two-step)
1905 Rosebud March (6/8 March)
1905 Binks Waltz
1906 Antoinette (6/8 March)

Music Written by Joplin for Songs by Others
1901 I'm Thinking of My Pickaninny Days (Words by Henry Jackson)
1903 Little Black Baby (Words by Louise Armstrong Bristol)
1905 Sarah Dear (Ragtime song, words by Henry Jackson)

1907 When Your Hair Is Like the Snow (Words by
Owen Spendthrift)

Arrangements by Joplin
1907 Snoring Sampson (Ragtime song by Harry
LaMertha)
1908 Sensation Rag, by Joseph F. Lamb

Unverified
1905 Leola (Two-step)

It is believed that the above list is complete and correct. We will welcome any additions or comments.

Big Bill

Big Bill Broonzy? Did I know him? Man, that was a blues-man. . . . Sure I knew him; well. . . . We worked the Village Vanguard in New York City. Still remember Wild Bill (Davison), Big Bill and me sharing a fifth. I was low man on the totem pole; and after Big B. lowered that jug and I seen where "the waters" had receded, that was it. No, I'll go it alone. But that was just part of knowing Bill. We made music together. And how can I forget his verse "when you're white, you all right . . . when you're brown, stick aroun' . . . but when you black, get in back; way back." An' the time we both played a concert in Chicago. . . .

And after the concert, we gathered at my brother-in-law's apartment. Chuck (Wright) always told me that anytime I was in town to "make my home your home." There was Big Bill and his wife Rose. Man, she could really cook up a storm! Talk about red beans and rice! With a ham bone added. Hm . . . Doc Evans brought his horn (cornet); that front room was filled with talent. So naturally we blew; and Bill sang some. It began to get warm. Turn on the air-conditioner (yeh, we opened some windows). It was early . . . like 11 p.m. on a Friday night. It was gettin' good when the knock hit the door. The Po-lice; someone had called the law. They were polite but firm. "You have to stop the noise." It was the same "noise" Bill and I had just made in Carnegie Hall. . . .   A.H.

Baby, I Done Got Wise

by William "Big Bill" Broonzy

The first time I tried to play anything was in 1914. It was a home-made fiddle and I couldn't play it right away. That was in Arkansaw near where the Mississippi and Arkansaw rivers came together. I had first heard a home-made fiddle played by a blues singer we knew as See See Rider. Don't know his name—everybody called him just See See Rider, because he used to sing a blues by that name. Later on Ma Rainey made a record of that tune, but I first heard it down around my home. I never saw anyone else play a home-made fiddle except See See Rider. He was born and raised in Redale, Arkansaw, and he played for everybody around there. Hearing him made me want to do something too.

Me and a boy named Louis made a fiddle and guitar from wooden boxes we got from the commissary. The neck was a broomstick and we'd get broken strings from See See Rider and patch them up. I made me a bow out of hickory wood by bending it and leaving it to dry. We'd cut a tree with an axe and go back the next day for rosin. I kept the fiddle hid because my old man and woman didn't want me to play it. Me and Louis would play every chance we got and one day a man heard us and took us to his house to play a piece. He liked it and said he'd get us a good fiddle and guitar. He sent to Sears-Roebuck in Chicago but it was a long time before I could play a regular fiddle. My home-made fiddle had only two strings and I played two strings on the new one fine, but it took a while to learn to use all four strings. After I could play it, I couldn't tune it. We used to go on picnics and barbecues and I'd play my fiddle, with Louis on guitar and a bass player named Jerry Sanders. But my brother-in-law would have to go along to tune the fiddle.

The first job I had playing music in a public place was in Little Rock. That was after I got out of the army in March 1919 and lasted until February, 1920. Then I went to Chicago and got a job as yard-man for the Pullman Company. I didn't play any for a few years until I met Charlie Jackson in 1924. He found out I could play a fiddle and had me come around. John Thomas, Theodore Edwards and Charlie were all playing then on the West Side. Later on I played guitar on a record for Teddy Edwards and the tunes were "Barbecue Blues" and "Louise Louise Blues."

Charlie first got me started on guitar at that time and showed me how to make chords, and I played around a little with John Thomas. Charlie was a well-known recording artist at that time and he got me to go to Mayo Williams, who was working for Paramount then. John Thomas and I auditioned two numbers for Williams—"Big Bill Blues" and "House Rent Stomp"—but he said we didn't play well enough. I guess it

wasn't very good because I was just starting on guitar. I had my job for the Pullman Company and only played once in a while at house parties. We made those two numbers for Williams later on though. That was in 1926 and when we got to the studio, Aletha Dickerson, who was Williams' secretary, asked me my name. I told her, "William Lee Conley Broonzy," and she said, "For Christ's sake, we can't get all that on the label." She said she'd think of a name for me and later on when she wanted me for something she said, "Come here, Big Boy." That gave her the idea to call me Big Bill and that's the way I've been known ever since. I think I recorded six sides for the Paramount Company, but the first was "Big Bill Blues" and "House Rent Stomp."

There were a lot of good guitar players and blues singers around Chicago in those days and I knew all of them from playing around at different places. Shorty George recorded the first guitar blues of my knowing. Barbecue Bob was one of the first too—I met him around Chicago. I worked with Georgia Tom about that time—he was the leader of the Hokum Boys and wrote all their tunes, and when we made a record, we'd use a tune that they made, like "Somebody's Been Using That Thing." One day in 1930, we all piled into a Ford and drove to New York. There was Georgia Tom and I, a girl named Mozelle, Lester Melrose—he was the manager of the record company—and two members of the Hokum Boys, Arthur Pettis and Frank Brandswell. They sang but they didn't play and we made records like "Come On In," where Mozelle, Tom and I sang and Tom played piano and I played guitar. We also made records for the Starr Piano Company in Richmond, Indiana, with Georgia Tom on piano. Later on I made records there with Black Bob on piano. Georgia Tom's name was Thomas A. Dorsey and he was on a lot of records, including all of Tampa Red's, until he quit for the church about 1933.

All this time I was working during the day and they'd pay me to play at night. I was making records too and we'd all get together in the recording studio. I always went around to watch when Ma Rainey was recording. Maybe I'd be making records in one studio and Ma in another and others would be there, like Blind Blake, Charlie Jackson, Blind Lemon Jefferson and Leroy Carr. I never worked with him but I think Leroy Carr was the greatest blues singer I heard in my life. I knew him from seeing him around and listening to him and he was the best guy you ever met. He played piano on all his records and usually worked with Scrapper Blackwell. He really could sing the blues and he couldn't have been more than 30 when he died.

My first personal appearance in Chicago was in 1932. I mean in a public place and playing music for a living. None of us would ever make enough money just playing music. I had to have my day job and play music at night. Friends who were interested in us would pick us out for jobs for parties and maybe in small taverns, like Ruby Gatewood's and Johnson's Tavern. The biggest was in theaters. I played off and on at the Regal, Savoy and Indiana Theaters and once for four nights at the Morson Hotel. One fellow had sort of a political job but I don't remember his name. They treated us swell but it never lasted long. I had my family in Chicago to take care of and bought a home for my mother in Arkansaw. I couldn't do that on music alone.

I'll never forget one party I was on in Chicago. It was a musicians' party at 1112 South Washburn Street. It was free for musicians and the others had to pay. Pinkie Thomas gave the party—she was the landlady of the building—and I went over with Blind Percy. He was a guitar player and I picked him up at his house and took him over. He was really blind and had to be led up the stairs. There were eight rooms and all full of people and everyone cutting up. In those days we used to keep the front rooms dark and lamps in the other rooms. The front door was locked and the musicians used to be in the rear room nearest to the back exit if anything happened. We all had a good time until about twelve o'clock when two guys got to fighting. Then everybody got into the fight and I headed for the door. I got out of there pretty fast but when I got down to the street I remembered about Blind Percy. I started back up the stairs. Somebody said, "You can't go back up there," and I said, "I can't leave a blind man up there in all that fighting." He said, "There's Percy sitting over there on the sidewalk." I don't know how he got out but he was the first one out when the fighting started. So then we headed for the alley-way

to the courtyard in back of the apartment. They used to hang the whiskey out the window and we went after it. A couple of others had the same idea but when we went around, they thought we were the police and ran away, so we got the gallon. By the time the police came, everybody was out, even two guys who had their legs broken, but they picked them up later in a hospital. Windows and lamps were broken and they found a lot of knives laying around and they caught the landlady and her daughter. There was a deaf and dumb girl at that party and before the fight was over, she was talking that night. She is still in Chicago and now when I see her, I can get close and understand what she's saying, but not before that night.

The first big chance I had was in 1939, when John Hammond was down through Chicago and he wrote me a letter to come to New York. I played in Carnegie Hall and then Cafe Society for a week. Ida Cox was there and Josh White and Sonny Terry and everybody treated us very well. But I wanted to be with my family so after a while I went back to Chicago. I had a job in a foundry then. I came back to New York again in 1940 to play another concert at Carnegie Hall and Cafe Society, but went right back home again. I was home most of the time after that until 1945, except for a couple of tours in 1941. I was on the road then with Lil Green, playing guitar for her, with a piano and bass player. We'd be on the road for six weeks and home for two, until she decided to make a change. It was on one of those last trips that I met my wife and married her sixteen days later on June 7, 1941. We had lived in Chicago ever since until this year, when I got connected with Joe Glaser and he brought me to New York.

I think I must have made about 200 sides under my own name and many others with other artists. Robert Brown—that's Washboard Sam—is my half-brother and I played on all his records. I used to write some numbers, and arrange others, for him, and many times he'd play his washboard on my records. I played guitar on all of Jazz Gillum's records, and he played his French Harp, which sounds like a harmonica, on some of my numbers, like "Key to the Highway." I worked with many others, including Sonny Boy Williamson, the Yas Yas Girl (Merline Johnson), all of Lil Green's records before

1945, and on some of Roosevelt Sykes.

My own records are on Banner, Melotone, Perfect, two for Victor, and many on Vocalion and Okeh, besides the Paramount and Champion. All my numbers are ones I wrote out myself except a few, like "Shake 'Em On Down," which is Bukka White's number, and "My Gal Is Gone," which was written by Tampa Red. On "Key to the Highway," the tune is mine and the words were written by Charlie Segar. I made a few numbers like "Mistreatin' Mama Blues" and "Oh Yes" by myself, but on most of the records there are other artists accompanying me. Buster Bennett played tenor on a lot of them and sometimes there'd be a trumpet or clarinet, or maybe piano and bass or piano and washboard, besides my own guitar. I worked with many fine piano players after the early records with Georgia Tom. Aletha Dickerson played piano for me and Black Bob played on some early Melotones and Perfects, like "Cherry Hill," "Seven 'Leven" and "Match Box Blues." After that I worked with Blind John (John Davis), who I think is the best all-around piano player I ever recorded with. But my favorite piano player and the one who worked on all my records from 1936 until he died on Feb. 18, 1940, was Joshua Alt-

heimer. He played a boogie-woogie style and he seemed just right for me. I think he was the best blues piano player I ever heard. He wasn't very big and he couldn't have been very strong because he died when he was only 30. Josh played for other artists too, like Washboard Sam and the Yas Yas Girl. I know two numbers he made with Johnny Temple were "Louise Blues" and "Beale Street Sheik." Of my numbers, he liked "Looking Up At Dawn," but his favorite number, and also my favorite number with him is "My Last Goodbye to You." Some other favorites of mine are, "Your Time Now," "Done Got Wise," "Just a Dream" and "Truckin' Little Mama," all made with Josh. We made some that were never released, like "Rock Me Baby" and "Hit the Right Lick," because the studio said they were too suggestive. I made them again later on with Memphis Slim on piano, and "Rock Me Baby" is now called "Rockin' Chair Blues."

After Josh died, I used Blind John, Memphis Slim (Peter Chatham), Horace Malcomb and on my last date on Feb. 19 and 24, 1945, Big Maceo played piano. None of the last ones have been released as yet.

Memories of Bessie Smith

by Carl Van Vechten

Bessie Smith spent most of her youth singing in the Deep South, where, when she felt like it, she could fill a big tent with colored people from all the surrounding farms and towns, but she made a profusion of records and I was very early aware of these. I had boxes and boxes of them which I played and played in the early 'twenties and everybody who came to my apartment was invited

to hear them. As a matter of fact, musicians arriving from Europe called on me especially to listen to these records. Eventually I deposited them with the James Weldon Johnson Memorial Collection of Negro Arts and Letters which I founded in the Yale University Library, together with the records of that other great Blues singer, Clara Smith, and the early records of Ethel Waters, one of

JAZZ RECORD

SEPT.
1947
No. 58
25¢

Bessie Smith

which, "Maybe Not At All," concludes with Ethel imitating the styles and personalities and tones of the two great Smith girls, who were *not* sisters.

It was not, however, until Thanksgiving Day night, 1925 when she was appearing at the Orpheum Theatre in Newark, that I actually had my first opportunity to hear Bessie Smith sing on the stage. My friend, Leigh Whipper, who will easily be recalled as the Crabmeat Man in Porgy, was manager of this theatre at this epoch and he had saved a box for me and my party on this occasion, no mean feat as the auditorium held as many persons as could reasonably be jammed into it. I must say all of us enjoyed a mood of the highest anticipatory expectation. It would be no exaggeration to assert that we felt as we might have felt before going to a Salzburg Festival to hear Lilli Lehmann sing Donna Anna in "Don Giovanni."

We arrived about ten and not much later Bessie Smith made her appearance. She was at this time the size of Fay Templeton in her Weber and Fields days, which means very large, and she wore a crimson satin robe, sweeping up from her trim ankles, and embroidered in multicolored sequins in designs. Her face was beautiful with the rich ripe beauty of southern darkness, a deep bronze brown, matching the bronze of her bare arms, walking slowly to the footlights, to the accompaniment of the wailing, muted brasses, the monotonous African pounding of the drum, the dromedary glide of the pianist's fingers over the responsive keys, she began her strange, rhythmic rites in a voice full of shouting and moaning and praying and suffering, a wild, rough, Ethiopian voice, harsh and volcanic, but seductive and sensuous too, released between rouged lips and the whitest of teeth, the singer swaying slightly to the beat, as is the Negro custom:

"Yo' brag to women I was yo' fool, so den I got dose sobbin' hahted Blues." Celebrating her unfortunate love adventures, the Blues are the Negro's prayer to a cruel Cupid.

Now, inspired partly by the expressive words, partly by the stumbling strain of the accompaniment, partly by the powerfully magnetic personality of this elemental conjure woman with her plangent African voice, quivering with passion and pain, sounding as if it had been developed at the sources of the Nile, the black and blue-black crowd, notable

for the absence of mulattoes, burst into hysterical, semi-religious shrieks of sorrow and lamentation. Amens rent the air. Little nervous giggles, like the shattering of Venetian glass, shocked our nerves. When Bessie proclaimed, "It's true I loves you, but I won't take mistreatment any mo' " a girl sitting beneath our box called, "Dat's right! Say it, sister!"

After the curtain had fallen, Leigh Whipper guided us back stage where he introduced us to Bessie Smith and this proved to be exactly the same experience that meeting any great interpreter is likely to be: we paid our homages humbly and she accepted them with just the right amount of deference. I believe I kissed her hand. I hope I did.

A few years later, Porter Grainger brought her to my apartment on West Fifty-Fifth Street. Fania Marinoff and I were throwing a party. George Gershwin was there and Marguerite d'Alvarez and Constance Collier, possibly Adele Astaire. The drawing room was well-filled with sophisticated listeners. Before she could sing, Bessie wanted a drink. She asked for a glass of straight gin, and with one gulp she downed a glass holding nearly a pint. Then, with a burning cigarette depending from one corner of her mouth, she got down to the Blues, really down to 'em, with Porter at the piano. I am quite certain that anybody who was present that night will never forget it. This was no actress; no imitator of a woman's woes; there was no pretence. It was the real thing: a woman cutting her heart open with a knife until it was exposed for us all to see, so that we suffered as she suffered, exposed with a rhythmic ferocity, indeed, which could hardly be borne. In my own experience, this was Bessie Smith's greatest performance.

Again, she came to my apartment on Fifty-Fifth Street in February 1936, a year or two before her tragic death in Memphis, brought this time by my friend Al Moore, so that I might photograph her. She was making one of her final appearances (although we were not aware of this fact) at a downtown night club and she came to see me between shows, cold sober and in a quiet reflective mood. She could scarcely have been more amiable or co-operative. She was agreeable to all my suggestions and even made changes of dress. Of course, on this occasion she did not sing, but I got nearer to her real personality than I ever had before and the photographs, perhaps, are the only adequate record of her true appearance and manner that exist.

It is pretty generally forgotten that Bessie made a film of the "St. Louis Blues." It is a short and so poignantly effective that it was not immediately acceptable to the wider moving picture public, as the characters were sordid and the story relentless in its depiction of the way men and women who are in and out of love behave, but it is a wonderful

memorial to the artistry of Bessie Smith and, if a copy of this film can be discovered, it should be revived to prove what a great singer she was and what a great actress she might have been, given the opportunity. Anybody in the future who sees this film (and hears it) will be able to understand in some degree how we felt in that room in West Fifty-Fifth Street, when cigarette depending but never falling from one corner of her mouth, she moaned: "Duh wo'khouse ez up on a long lonesome road."

Bessie Smith

by Art Hodes

It was dead of winter. Cold, man, like it only can get cold, icy, in dear old Chi. Not that it made any difference. I still made my merry way, looking, seeking out all the colored music I could find. Night time, of course; whoever went looking for it in the day! So I found myself alone, walking the streets on the South Side. Just to hear a colored man whistling a blues, paid off. Not like today, with some Tin Pan Alley tune coming from the lips. No, man, this was still the real thing. But look here; isn't that Stepin Fetchit advertised at this theatre? Darned if it ain't. But that below it; man, I'm in luck today. If I ain't dreamin' that's Bessie Smith. Let's go.

Inside, it was the picture that was on. Not a damn thing about it I can remember. All I know is I waited it out. There it goes, finished.

And now the orchestra climbs into the pit, the overture, and that was a honey; and there's Stepin Fetchit. There's a guy that surprised me. I'd always pictured him as a guy that moves slower than slow. That was his Hollywood character. This must be a different guy. Funny? He had me roaring. But I was in for a treat. Evidently I had caught the first show of the week. The band

and the actor weren't exactly together but Mr. S. sure straightened that in a hurry. Talk about a guy doing his act and rehearsing the band at the same time, this guy was it. How he improvised. Instead of blowing his top when the music went wrong, he called loudly for a phone and the prop man brought it out. He got on the phone and called, guess who? The orchestra leader, and in a sweet professional way, yet never losing his audience, he straightened him out on what had to be, and what wasn't. It was my first and most impressive lesson in stagecraft. And that audience was right with him; they didn't miss a trick. It was sure somethin' to hear.

Now comes the big hush. Just the piano goin'. It's the blues. Somethin' tightens up in me. Man, what will she look like? I ain't ever seen her before.

Then I hear her voice and, gosh, I know this is it . . . my lucky day. I'm hearing the best and I'm seeing her, too. There she is. Resplendent is the word, the only one that can describe her. Of course, she ain't beautiful, altho she is to me. A white, shimmering evening gown, a great big woman and she completely dominates the stage and the whole house when she sings the "Yellow Dog Blues." Ah! I don't know, she just reaches out and grabs and holds me. There's no explainin' her singing, her voice. She don't need a mike; she don't use one. I ain't sure if them damn nuisances had put in their appearance in that year. Everybody can hear her. This gal sings from the heart. She never lets me get away from her once. As she sings she walks slowly around the stage. Her head, sort of bowed. From where I'm sittin' I'm not sure whether she even has her eyes open. On and on, number after number, the same hush, the great performance, the deafening applause. We won't let her stop. What a woman. If she has any faults, like the big head, or prima donna, it doesn't seep through. You just don't get that feeling from her. You just know you're listening to the greatest blues singer you've ever heard.

Outside it's still cold. I don't know when I get up to go and I'm sure I'm not sure where I'm goin'; just walkin'. But there's a record playin' back somethin' that was recorded; recorded in my head. There's that one woman's voice, "Oh, you easy rider, why don't you hurry back home . . . " So help me, I still hear it.

Really the Blues

by Milton (Mezz) Mezzrow

"When I was a-nothin' but a child," Bessie Smith sang this first line on a Columbia record, "Reckless Blues," (No. 14056-D, Master No. 140242), with Fred Longshaw on the organ and Louis Armstrong on the cornet. This is one of the finest recordings Bessie ever made. She sings it in her own relaxed way. Her incomparably expressive voice, so full of soul and warmth, is here displayed at its best.

You cannot teach style but Bessie's art should be studied in the schools for the everlasting contribution which it has made to our music. As originally written the first line of "Reckless Blues" was, "When I was nothing but a child." Bessie adds the word "a" and leaves off the "g" in the line that follows, as a result of which the phrase has a more musical flavor and an open throat when sung. She embellishes the text to bring out her natural feeling for cadence, as when a whole note appeared in the music without color and had a very flat and abrupt ending, thereby giving the whole sentence a powerful, emotional impact. (i.e., the words "a" and "child" in the first line).

"Reckless Blues" is another proof of the high artistic level of the blues and jazz. As Leopold Stokowski has said, although perhaps not in these exact words, jazz is the only authentic and original American music and it serves to revitalize the whole stream of musical development, not only in our country but everywhere. In the classical school, the beginner is taught to make embellishments called the Gruppetto or Turn, the Mordant, or Trill. These are used mostly in Italian music and it is mainly one of the reasons most classical music lovers and musicians like Italian music more than the German or French music. To them, German music is profound and serious; French music, too dramatic. But Italian music is supposed to have a more free and facile nature to its song mostly because of its ornaments.

Well, you can rest assured that Bessie didn't get her ornamentation from any school other than that of hard knocks and oppression.

To begin the second chorus, the way she ornaments the word "now" (the first word of the second chorus) shows the great feeling she could give to a single word with a flexibility of voice that would put any opera singer to shame, were she to try and duplicate it. Bessie also starts a new melodic line to break up the monotony of repetition on the twelve bar blues, making it more interesting and putting the correct emphasis on the words that tell the story. In each of the other lines there is the same execution of lyrical ornamentation, the examples of which I will leave for you to detect for yourself. This is a good ear training and will help you look for the things that are the most important to know about the blues and jazz.

As for Fred Longshaw and Louis Armstrong, there is far more than I can say in the allotted limitations of time and space, so I will defer that for a later day—unless you write in to *Jazz Record* and request it at once! I don't mean this as in commercial correspondence tabulation because I don't get paid for this mess, so 'til I hear from you, "Stay with it ole man, you got to git."

I Remember the Queen

by Zutty Singleton

Yes, I remember Miss Bessie Smith, the Queen of the Blues Singers, for it was my pleasure to play for her when she came to New Orleans to appear at the Lyric Theater. That was around 1922, when I was with John Robichaux' orchestra. She came to New Orleans about four times a year, and every time she appeared it was a sell-out. She always had a bigger line at the box-office than any performer in New Orleans.

At that time her stage set-up was like the old-time recording studios, with the old-fashioned horn. And she would explain to the audience how she made records, and sing the tunes she had recorded, like "Gulf Coast Blues," "Aggravatin' Papa," "Baby Won't You Please Come Home," and a whole gang of tunes. Everything she sang was blues. She had a way of taking the popular tunes of the time and singing them like the blues.

I remember she had a beautiful dress she wore for the big show (usually the last day). It was white, but when the electricians turned a certain kind of spotlight on it, Bessie's dress would shine with beautiful colors which the special light brought out. With the dress she wore a big headdress—like the Queen of Sheba—and she *was* the queen. What a sight

. . . every inch a woman, a magnificent woman.

Miss Bessie (I always called her that, because when I used to talk to her backstage, I could never get up enough nerve to call her just "Bessie") always waited until she got to New Orleans to have her music straightened out. In traveling around, parts would get lost or mixed up, and she trusted old John Robichaux to fix up her arrangements. At that time Robichaux had Picou on clarinet, Johnny Lindsay, trombone, Miss Margaret (I can't remember her last name) on piano, Andrew Kimball, trumpet, and myself on drums.

Bessie's musical director, Fred Longshaw, was with her several times, and he would be in the pit with us, and cue us on her music.

Now, if everything went all right, Bessie was the nicest woman you ever saw. But, man, if things went wrong she was really rough. Bessie was a good woman though. She was real close to God, very religious. She always mentioned the Lord's Name. That's why her blues seemed almost like hymns. Everybody liked her, and any performer on a bill with her was always proud to be on the same show with her. She was a charitable woman, too, always giving something to the kids around the theater. And how she could sing. She always wanted the music soft . . . she didn't like loud music, and she brought out those blues right from the heart. Bessie was a big woman, and she carried herself in a way to demand respect. She was always well-groomed, and graceful in the movements of her hands and arms and body. No wonder everybody loved to watch her and listen to her sing.

New Orleans certainly loved her. Boudreau and Bennett, the managers of the Lyric Theater were always so happy when she came to play their theater. They would have a big party for her on the stage, with shrimp, sea food and other New Orleans dishes. She told me once, too, that it was always a pleasure for her to play in New Orleans. And she showed us she appreciated our music, too. Because even though she always came on in the headline spot, which was next to closing, Miss Bessie would always come down to stand in the wings and catch our overture.

Yes, I remember Bessie Smith, the Queen of the Blues, and man, I'm sure sorry for the folks who missed seeing and hearing her. You don't know what you missed by not seeing and hearing the Queen in person.

3

New Orleans and All That Jazz

What can you say about this section, except that these are the fathers; these are the men who made traditional jazz? After three articles on New Orleans in the early days, we have divided these into two groups: musicians who made their mark early, in the first jazz age, the twenties, and those who came from the same generation of musicians, but had to wait until the New Orleans Revival of the forties to achieve something of the recognition they deserved.

C.H.

New Orleans Trumpeters

by Cy Shain

Papa Mutt Carey, a tall, strapping titan of jazz, laid his trumpet on the table and chatted amiably about "the old days" in New Orleans when jazz activity was at its height. Now playing with the newly revived Kid Ory Creole Band in Hollywood, Mutt has recently resumed a brilliant career in jazz.

A grey-haired man of fifty-five today, Papa Mutt played in the famous street parades, band contests and all day picnics which marked the Crescent City's hectic jazz days. A New Orleans member of the Tuxedo, Eagle, Superior and Kid Ory Bands, Mutt Carey was generally acknowledged one of the four leading trumpet men in the city of jazz's birthplace during the early 1900s. Titled the "Blues King" of New Orleans at one time, Mutt earned his honor in competition with the other leading musicians of the time.

Having known the greats in jazz; having engaged in cutting contests with them on the streets of New Orleans, Papa Mutt was qualified to judge them as perhaps few men living today.

His deep-pocketed brown eyes staring seriously at me as I asked him my first question. "Who was the greatest trumpet player in jazz?"

"Louis Armstrong," he answered emphatically, "there's no question there! Louis played from his heart and soul—and he did that for everything. You see," he went on to explain, "he tried to make a picture out of every number he was playing to show you just what it meant.

"Louis had ideas, enough technique to bring out what he wanted to say and a terrific lip. You know when the ideas struck him he had the technique to bring it out right there on the horn.

"When I left New Orleans Louis was just a beginner. He had just gotten out of the Waif's Home and he was a coming trumpet man then.

"I remember once when Louis came out to Lincoln Park in New Orleans to listen to the Kid Ory Band. I was playing trumpet with the Kid then and I let Louis sit on my chair. Now at that time I was the 'Blues King' of New Orleans and when Louis played that day, he played more blues than I ever heard in my life. It never did strike my mind that blues could be interpreted so many different ways. Everytime he played a chorus it was different and you knew it was the blues—yes, it was all blues what I mean.

"When he got through playing the blues I kidded him a little. I told him, 'Louis, you keep playing that horn and someday you'll be a great man.' I always admired him from the start.

"I gave Freddie Keppard and Joe Oliver credit too," Papa Mutt said speaking about the two other impressive trumpet men, "They were great boys but there's no one who ever came close to Louis. No, Louis was ahead by a mile!

"Louis makes you feel the number and that's what counts. A man who does something from the heart and makes you feel it, is great. You see, Louis does that for everything. And one thing, Louis never rehearsed a blues number; he played them just as he felt at the time he was up there on the stand.

"Louis sings just like he plays. I think Louis proves the idea and theory which holds that if you can't sing it, you can't play it. When I'm improvising, I'm singing in my mind. I sing what I feel and then try to reproduce it on the horn."

Mutt Carey went on to speak of Louis' style of playing. "Louis' tone is so big and he fills all those notes—there is no splitting them when he plays. There's nothing freakish about Louis' horn. He fingers what he wants to play and there are no accidents in the notes he brings out.

"You know, it's a pleasure just to hear Louis tune up. Why just warming up he blows such a variety of things that it is a wonder to the ears, and a real pleasure.

"Louis set the pace for the whole world for trumpet players. Joe and Freddie did their bit but they never could teach Louis. God knows both of them were good but what the heck man, they could never teach Louis."

King Joe Oliver, whose band really set the Windy City of Chicago on its jazz listening ears, next came under discussion and observation. By way of introduction to his comments on Joe, Papa Mutt spoke briefly about New Orleans musicianship.

"In New Orleans all the boys came up the hard way. The musicianship was a little poor. You see, the average boy tried to learn by himself because there were either no teachers or they couldn't afford music lessons.

"John Robichaux's Band, the Tuxedo Band and the Superior Band lived strictly up to music but they were about the only ones in New Orleans to do so. Joe Oliver had a few numbers that were on sheets of music, but he got away from it as quickly as he could. You see, Joe was no great reader.

"Joe Oliver was very strong. He was the greatest freak trumpet player I ever knew. He did most of his playing with cups, glasses, buckets and mutes. He was the best gut bucket man I ever heard. I called him freak because the sounds he made were not made by the valves but through these artificial devices. In contrast, Louis played everything through the horn.

"Joe and I were the first ones to introduce these mutes and things. We were both freak trumpet men. Some writers claimed I was the first one to use mutes and buckets but it wasn't so. I got to give Joe Oliver credit for introducing them.

"Joe could make his horn sound like a holy roller meeting," Papa Mutt said in admiration. "God, what that man could do with his horn!"

Joe Oliver, who died in 1940, left a batch of records cut in the 1920s. Collector's items today, there is a great demand for them amongst jazz lovers. Papa Mutt Carey spoke about Joe's discs.

"I'll tell you something about Joe's records. I haven't heard a single one that comes close to sounding like Joe's playing in person. I don't know what it was but I'll tell you the truth, I don't believe that it is Joe playing on the records sometimes. It never has sounded to me much like Joe."

Recalling an experience involving Oliver's tour to San Francisco, Mutt said, "Joe's band followed me into San Francisco and it didn't go over because I had come there first with cups and buckets and the people thought Joe was imitating me. Joe and I used to get a kick out of that whenever we talked about it. He sure got his laughs from it," Mutt Carey said and chuckled.

"What about Freddie Keppard?" I asked.

"At one time," Mutt answered, "Freddie had New Orleans all sewed up. He was the king—yes he wore the crown. Then Louis got in and killed the whole bunch of them. Freddie really used to play good. He could have been as big as Louis since he had the first chance to make records but he didn't want to do it because he was afraid that other musicians would steal his stuff.

"When Freddie got on the street, it was the king on the street, Louis will tell you that. Keppard was the first man I ran into in a band battle, and it was just my hard luck to run into the king. We had a big audience on the street. It was on Howard and Villere Street in New Orleans. The crowd knew I was a younger musician and they gave me a big hand mostly to encourage me. It certainly was an experience for me I'll never forget.

"Freddie had a lot of ideas and a big tone too. When he hit a note you knew it was hit. I mean he had a beautiful tone and he played with so much feeling too. Yes, he had everything; he was ready in every respect. Keppard could play any kind of song good. Technique, attack, tone, and ideas were all there. He didn't have very much formal musical education but he sure was a natural musician. All you had to do was play a number for him once and he had it . . . he was a natural!

"When Freddie got to playing he'd get devilish sometimes and he'd 'neigh' on the trumpet like a horse but he was no freak man like Joe Oliver. Freddie was a trumpet player anyway you'd grab him. He could play sweet and then he could play hot. He'd play sweet sometimes and then turn around and knock the socks off you with something hot."

Papa Mutt picked up his trumpet and fingered the valves for a minute. He turned to me and said, "There was another good trumpet man in New Orleans. His name was Manuel Perez. Manuel Perez was a good musician as well as a fine trumpet man. He was a better musician than Joe or Freddie. Perez could fit into any kind of musical outfit.

"Perez was powerful and he stuck mostly to the legitimate side of the horn. He never was a hot man and he never professed to be one. His attack was great and he hit the notes just as they should be played.

"Buddy Petit," Mutt said, continuing his survey of New Orleans trumpet players, "was a boy who had the ideas like Louis but he let the liquor get the best of him. He never was as powerful as Louis but he sure had ideas and feeling. He was no high note man either. He used to say, 'Why make the note way up there when you could play it down in the middle register.' Buddy always had a way of getting out of a hole when he was improvising.

"Bunk Johnson deserves credit for what he used to do," Mutt reflected. "He had marvelous ideas and I used to like to hear him play. He wasn't quite the drive man that Joe and Freddie were, however. he always stayed behind the beat instead of getting out there in the lead like those other men. Bunk was good, and he was solid when he was playing. Bunk had plenty of competition on his way up and he never was the king down there.

"When you come right down to it, the man who started the big noise in jazz was Buddy Bolden. Yes, he was a powerful trumpet player and a good one too. I didn't have a chance to hear him too much but I sure heard a lot about him. He deserves credit for starting it all."

Kid Ory nodded to Papa Mutt Carey that it was time to begin the next set. Mutt excused himself and went to the bandstand to occupy the trumpet seat. I sat and listened to Mutt's playing which furnished me with a musical illustration of the traditions, and styles that he had been talking about. "The good old days" must have been great!

Jazz Music of the Gay 90's

by John A. Provenzano

Hello Art—Am sending a little memo of the old red-light district days; I am sure it is before your time and a great many more of your gang. Those were hectic days, and not the easy ones of today. Hope you understand article as it is typed in a hurry with a missing link; imagine playing your sax or piano without being able to blow the key (C) that is sticking on my old typewriter.

Well, will just give you a brief description in order to acquaint you with the writer. My career started in 1902, on a bugle. Born in 1890, I was eight years old when I acquired a lip, and learned from the phonograph pieces like "My Josephina My Jo," and "Old Faithful, Somebody's Waiting for Me." I bought a guitar, all patched up, and was the youngest of our old French Market serenaders, 1904, the year of the Russo-Japanese war. I bought a cornet with the help of a seasoned jazzman, and we got stuck with an E-flat and didn't know it until Emanuel Perez, the finest boy who ever blew a horn, discovered the mistake. I decided to keep on pumping the E-flat in parades; and use the B-flat for dance work.

I played with every white band in New Orleans, and knew all of the old time Negro boys personally. My concern is for Emanuel Perez, the man who got the sweetest tone ever on a cornet. He is not a well man anymore; this article is for you gratis, but if you want to make a small contribution for our old time friend, Perez, it would please me more than sending me 100 dollars for myself.

Your friend,
JOHNNY A. PROVENZANO,
Jazzland's Only E-Flat Trumpeter.

NEW ORLEANS TENDERLOIN

New Orleans, the mecca of music, good, bad and indifferent—jazz, fake, ragtime, raddy, and now called swing, was born in the city of fun. Visitors came for Mardi Gras, good food, fine drinks, the delicious coffee, and a stroll through the red-light district where jazz and not opera predominated, where the blues were played as blues, and not like the blues of today, where "Tiger Rag," "Clarinet Marmalade," "Milneburg Joys" and "High Society" were played as is, and not butchered like today from hordes of arrangers (poor old Tiger). The once pretty but fading prostitutes in their doorways behind half closed blinds calling you as you passed . . . you just looked and kept going. Someone would try and get smart at times and venture a wise crack —then the fun started, the invectives she hurled at him starting from his grandpa. The visitor if wise would move on, and move fast or else.

As you walked further towards the elite section that comprised Basin Street, Iberville, Franklin and part of St. Louis, the better-class cafes could be discerned. No more the ear-splitting blast of a cornet, augmented by the screech of some clarinetist who was perhaps just beginning, nor the off beats of the drums with the discords of guitar and bass that actually made you jumpy. As you approached the better-class joints, you took a deep breath—no more polluted air and ugly-looking women enticing you in. At last you are away and safe, the wail of a trombone

still rings in your ear, but in a few minutes you hear the sweet refrain of a slow number you are familiar with. You can easily distinguish the sweet tone of the cornet augmented by the variations of the clarinet, and then the rhythm section is clearly heard as you get closer and closer. You know you are listening to real babies, men who have had to climb the ladder the hard way but have made good. You go from one place to another and find that only for a difference in tempo or style the music is trumps. Why not? In one band you may find the clarinet wizard, Alphonse Picou, playing side by side with the one and only silver-tone boy, Emanuel Perez, who critics of the jazz world have failed to mention as one of the trumpeters of jazz days —yes, Emanuel Perez, the boy who shone in parades, at prize fights, on moonlight dances at Milneburg, the boy who was the first to bring the crying effect on his cornet. Emanuel Perez, who never bragged about his playing, but was willing to show white or Negro boy what he knew. Yes, the same Emanuel who went out of his way for others with no selfish thought, today is down and out, forgotten by the jazz world, yes, forgotten by the very race he was proud to be known by, but not forgotten by this writer, who knew them all, and knew the merits of them, be they white or colored.

As you visited further you must have seen and heard that tireless and fiery trumpeter Freddie Keppard; what a mean horn this baby played! The women say his style was irresistible, supported by clarinetists like Noone, Freddie Bechet, Big Eye Louis, and others as good, not forgetting the real baby of jazz, George Baquet. What more could one expect of flawless harmony with boys like these playing together from time to time with different bands.

Did we leave out something? Yes, but not for long; forgetting to bring Joe King Oliver into the picture is like closing Storyville and throwing the key away. Because Bad-Eye Joseph Oliver with his little short toy-looking cornet made his debut in the red-light, and had the best of them popping when it came to special rhythm. Emanuel Perez had tone, control and a fine technique. Freddie Keppard was fiery, tireless and made a band what it was. Bunk Johnson, the marvel of all time jazzers, is still good and was good as they came. Mutt Carey, Celestin, Allen, and many others were in the A class of jazz—but only one march king ever existed. That was King Oliver, from the old red-light district of New Orleans; the first man to improvise march tempo in jazz. No other than this same Joe Oliver, who with the rest of the class-A jazzmen went to fame and fortune; from the

hovels of the red-light district these jazzmen reached the four corners of the globe—dance halls, speakeasies, night clubs, royalty, society (yes, high society)—and oblivion, for some through wine, women and song. But jazz still lives, if only as a memory of the '90s.

"Mardi Gras, Chic la Pai"

by John A. Provenzano

"**M**ardi graw, chic la pai, run away, tra la la—Chineeman, monkey nose, jump the fence and stole my clothes!"

If you happened to be one of the lucky visitors in old New Orleans during our Mardi Gras celebration this 1946 era, and if you heard the familiar cry of "Mardi graw, chic la pai" being shouted by the children to the comic maskers, and you didn't know the meaning of the words, just go back to the Mardi Gras of the 1927 era. Some old-timers of the French Quarter still remember this cry, and they in turn imparted it to their youngsters. We do know it originated there, but who was the author is not known, and a search in old time files failed to find anything.

As I stand on the steps of the New Orleans Public Library waiting for the floats to come out of Calliope Street to take their places just around the corner of beautiful St. Charles Avenue, I see people, people and more people—one would think all the people of the city came to Canal Street. But that isn't so, and a good thing at that, because as wide as Canal Street is, and almost 12 squares in length, it is so crowded that one can hardly breathe. And this is no taking in the sardine-packed crowd lining both sides of St. Charles Ave., from Canal to Washington Avenue.

As the first float comes sneaking like a silent ghost from the den to pick up her crew of torch bearers, for the most part big stalwart brawny Negroes, the antics of these fun-loving comedians gives a big percentage of the color to our ever magnificent parades. As the floats appear suddenly from the dark the parade director, with his assistant, who happened to be yours truly in the latter part of the 1920's, will call out the name or number of band assigned to each respective float. Usually from 18 to 20 floats are in a parade. As far as I can remember from forty years of jazz music and carnival parades, the music contract, according to Music Director Braun and later Benny Mars, whom I assisted, called for a band to each float. But at no time did we have that many bands. Memories of 1909 to 1913 came to mind—as band after band fell in line, you could hear the director with a large megaphone on these very steps calling out "Jack Laine No. 1 band, Provenzano, No. 5, Fisher, No. 8" and so on. The assistant in the meantime with sheet in hand was checking the number of men assigned to each band. They had no more than 14 men, some had ten. A few of the out-of-town colleges and local schools had bands numbering well over 40, but a good 14-piece jazz band composed of "naturals" would make the school bands and some of the commercial bands look silly with their style of raddy march rhythm.

And now the crew of Momus has again started the ball rolling for Mardi Gras parades that will last the whole week, until March 5th, Mardi Gras night. From now on it will be continuous merrymaking, day after day, for our visitors and for the natives. Some have saved all year to have enough to spend on Mardi Gras day. Despite some shortages the last few years, New Orleans doesn't look like a place where anyone will want for food or drink. Restaurants seem to be holding their own; despite war prices the food isn't high unless you really want something special. Beautiful whiteway Bourbon Street, the Broadway of the Vieux Carré, leaves an impression one will never forget. All the way from Iberville to St. Ann one can dine, dance, and be merry—it is one continuous row of bright lights, eats, delicious drinks and music, music, music—some of it passable, some of it fair, some is just terrible. Only one original jazzman of the early '90s represented—it is Fats Pichon at the piano. Fats was good and still is good, and draws the fans with his inimitable style of original jazz music.

The white and Negro bands of yesterday are but a memory—Brunis, Christian, Fisher, Brown, Giardina, Laine, Schilling and others made history, supplemented by the cream of the crop of Negro orchestras like the Manuel Perez 1915 aggregation, the Tuxedo 1916, the Original Creole of 1912, with that dynamic Fred Keppard on cornet and George Baquet on the black stick. Today, strolling through this beautiful section, you wonder what people would say if one of your own original white or Negro dance bands of old could be brought back just for a one night stand. The men who made and played their stuff are fast fading—there will be no substitute, the original man left only a memory; no one can imitate our language. You have tried it but you failed, so play on in your mechanical style if you will. Tonight I heard you coming around the Lee Circle tooting "High Society." Memories went back to when we, the original loud and lousy bunch of 1902, 1903, 1909, on a memorable cold, sleety, windy Mardi Gras with only a five-man band, wet to the skin, had the nerve to play "High Society" as we rounded the bend at Lee Circle. Old General Lee on the top of his monument must have said: "Here comes the original jazz men of New Orleans—yes, they are good, but only nutsies would play in this kind of weather."

Yes, and nuts did play on that memorable day of cold and wind. The jazz men who finished that parade will never forget it; today many are on the sidelines waiting for the floats to pass. We know this is one of the best carnivals we have ever had. But one thing will be missing, the original New Orleans jazz men of old. Carnival with its Rex and the King of the Zulus will come to us every year, perhaps more spectacular as the years go by. But the days of "High Society," "Tiger Rag" and "Didn't He Ramble," and the inimitable "March of the Four Winds," will be only a memory.

Louis Armstrong

There was a time in the late twenties when Louis Armstrong could have been elected Mayor of the South Side (Chicago); he was that popular. Of course the South Side never (officially) had a mayor. But if there was such an office Satchmo could have filled it; he was loved. I can still see him being carried clear across the dance floor of that huge Savoy Ballroom by his cheering fans. Tell me; when's the last time you saw a jazz musician carried on the shoulders of his fans? Never happens. When Louis picked up his trumpet and blew he was "callin' his children home." That man could blow no wrong. And what a warm person to be around. What a sense of humor. He could turn most any remark into a laugh. Like the time . . .

I was in the bandroom with Manone. King Oliver, the band-leading trumpet-man from New Orleans, who'd preceded Satch up north and thus broke ground; then sent for "little" Louis, writing him that "you can put your stinkin' feet in my bed anytime," was in attendance. No jealousy; Louis had the crown now. We were hangin' in there; hangin' on his words. Someone passed a drink around and one cat remarked "There's sediment in the bottom of that glass." Armstrong caught that remark and quickly quipped "I don't know what that means but that's what he said-he-meant."

We had driven from 4800 North (Lawrence Ave.) to 4800 South. It was cold like only Chicago could get cold. Money was apparent by its scarcity; we had one overcoat between us. You could mistake it for a bearskin; Wingy and I took turns wearing it. Louis never missed a cue. I can still hear his greeting. "Who's the bear tonight?"

How does one estimate Louis Armstrong's contribution to jazz? By what yardstick? What he did for jazz? Well, that's one side of the story; consider that African date where some 100,000 people gathered to hear Louis. Dig! 100,000! As Edmond Hall (the clarinetist in that particular Armstrong band) put it, "unbelievable." Or the fact that when our country's reputation, politically, was riding a low ebb, an English newspaper said (after one concert appearance in England by L.A.) "Thank you Louis Armstrong for blowing the foul air out." Of course, you know Satchmo got to be known as "Ambassador Armstrong." What a good-will ambassador. His political speeches were preached through his horn.

But that's just part of the Armstrong story. Take a look at the story he left on recordings! From the days of the Hot Five on to his "Louis Armstrong Plays W. C. Handy." Man, who can equal that contribution. No one; no single artist in jazz comes close to Armstrong in jazz productivity. And what he had to say (musically) will live on and on. It's timeless.

Think of the doors he opened for other trumpet players! The work he created for his group and the many groups that followed in his footsteps. No, the job of estimating Louis Armstrong's contribution to jazz and its players is beyond me. Just personally, if there hadn't been a Louis Armstrong it would have been much harder for the likes of me in jazz. I've got to recall the year when trad-jazz was taking a beating from one writer in particular plus this character's "writer-believers." At that time it was being said (by this group) that our (my) kind of jazz had gone out with button shoes. One citadel of this "new" jazz was a club titled Bop City. Someone booked Armstrong into this club and he proceeded to break all existing records. That gave all and sundry pause to think and re-evaluate.

Yeh! I can get quiet and hear some of the things he blew. Phrases come back to me. Louis Armstrong; there was a giant. . . .   A.H.

Mr. Armstrong and Mr. Robbins

An Interview Between Fred Robbins and Louis Armstrong, Over Station WHN, January 26, 1944

Transcribed by Lorraine Lion

Fred: We have here, scholars, none other than the greatest of all trumpet men and jazz singers, a man who has risen to greater heights than any other jazz musician, a man whose fame and whose genius are comparable to the most distinguished genius in classical music . . . our good friend Louis "Satchmo" Armstrong . . . glad to see you, Pops.

Louis: Hello there, Fred, how's everything?

Fred: Well, that was a fine opening, Louis, riffing along to our theme, "Jam Session," and this time we've got you up here for 23 minutes solid.

Louis: That's right, it's a pleasure.

Fred: It's a pleasure indeed, and how are we going to cover everything you've done in the 43 years that you've made such a tremendous name for yourself, in 23 minutes?

Louis: Man, you goin' 'way back, ain't you?

Fred: Going to go 'way back when you were a firecracker baby, July 4th, 1900.

Louis: How 'bout that. . . .

Fred: That's when he first saw the light of day, 'way back down in New Orleans. And Louis, just going to review briefly your early life when you used to sell charcoal to the lovers of Creole cuisine on the old coal-cart pulled by the mule . . . remember it?

Louis: Do I remember it? Just like yesterday.

Fred: And I guess you used to sing as you sold that charcoal.

Louis: Yeah, that was the good ol' days, you know, we used to work all day, you know, wrasslin' with the mules and then we'd get our quartet together at night, you know, and go all 'round the town and pass the hat and we're through for the night . . . I was singin' tenor in that quartet by the way.

Fred: Tenor?

Louis: Yes I was . . .

Fred: Man, how your voice has changed.

Louis: I was 13 years old, you know, as you mature your voice "heavens up"—

Fred: I see, that's almost like being a boy soprano at one time.

Louis: I'm tellin' you, I usta really chirp, usta put my hand behind my ear, you know, an' sing right out. I usta hold that end down theah.

Fred: I know you were an orphan, Louis, and I know you played in the boys' home down in New Orleans in the brass band, so well, in fact, that you finally got some professional jobs and 'member reading that you used to slip into the tonk where Bunk Johnson was playing, tried to play blues on his horn. How 'bout that?

Louis: Yeah, that was the ol' Eagle Hall down in New Orleans where the Bunk Johnson Orchestra usta play. They usta . . . all the bands usta have seven pieces, ya know . . . we didn't use pianos in those days, just guitar, bass, an' then cornet, clarinet, trombone, drums an' I'm tellin' ya, sounds jus' like one of these big bands nowadays, ya

boys, of all nationalities . . . some of them couldn't speak English but they could read . . .

Fred: They all felt that international language though, didn't they Louis?

Louis: Thas' what I mean, an' they know records an' a whole lot of things, see what I mean, an' anything I wanted to tell them an' they didn't dig me, why I had a saxophone player in my band could speak 8 languages . . .

Fred: Ooooh brother . . .

Louis: So I jus' tell him, hip this cat to what I want him to do . . .

Fred: Hip that French cat to what I want, hip that Belgian cat . . .

Louis: Ya know like we do sometimes—'luk out theah, you' ya know, to the band or somethin' . . . well, I did that one time an' all the boys run off the stand . . . ya gotta watch that, ya know . . .

Fred: You couldn't say 'look out there' . . . attention.

Louis: Yeah, toute suite . . .

Fred: Oh that's a very funny incident Louis.

Louis: Yeah, it turned out alright, we toured all over Europe.

Fred: I know you played for the King of England, many times, twelve times—right?

Louis: Yeah, we did alright, yeah he was right theah, waved at him a lot of times . . .

Fred: You certainly have some wonderful memories to look back on, Louis . . .

Louis: Played for the King of Belgium . . . an' we went all up to Norway there an' gave four concerts, four days an' I made over twenty some odd thousand dollars in four days.

Fred: And then you came back to this country?

Louis: Well, I went back to England, then I came back.

Fred: Then you came back and have been here ever since . . . your fame has gone up tremendously and it's never come down.

Louis: Oh yeah, I've been doin' alright . . . can't squawk at aaaalllll.

Fred: Well now, Louis, we're going to talk a little bit about your style. I want to find out what influence the late, great blues singer Bessie Smith had on your style, both in singing and playing horn.

Louis: Well, I tell ya, Bessie usta thrill me at all times, it's the way she could phrase a note in her blues, a certain somethin' in her voice that no other blues singer could get an' I usta, I jus' look at her, and I usta make a lot of records with her too, ya know. There's one blues there, oh, it jus' knocks me out, what is it . . . "Sobbin' Blues?" an' "St. Louis Blues."

Fred: Of course, you made "St. Louis" all by yourself too . . .

Louis: Yeah, but I made one with her ya know, with a muted trumpet, an' I'm tellin' ya, she usta jus' thrill me.

Fred: She was a great artist.

Louis: She had really music in her soul an' felt everythin' she did . . . she was inspiring an' I want to be in theah jus' like her, ya know what I mean, 'cause she was so sincere with her music.

Fred: Well, that was a wonderful person to take after, no doubt about that . . .

Louis: Ooooh yeahhh, that's too bad we had to lose her.

Fred: Yes, it certainly was a tragedy but it's a great thing to have an inspiration like that, Louis . . . I know you had a lot to do with Joe Smith too who played a lot of blues with Bessie.

Louis: Yeah, he did . . . he was that boy who could get so much music out of a plunger an' a trumpet an' he had a tone, ya know, a beautiful tone in front . . . an' I always admire tone . . . ya know what I mean. From the old school, that was the first thing we would teach was tonation.

Fred: Tonation and that is so prevalent, so predominant in your style today.

Louis: It's very essential. And Joe Smith was another wonderful musician. He could do more with a plunger . . . make it sound jus' like a human voice.

Fred: Who today is the greatest exponent of that plunger on a trumpet?

Louis: Well, les' see now, I don't hear very many boys, not to that extent, the way Joe Smith usta use it, ya know, a lot of the boys play in sections and things like that . . .

Fred: I know Tricky Sam does all right on trombone.

Louis: Well yeah, oh, you mean "Mushmouth" the Duke?

Fred: I mean "Mushmouth" the Duke.

Louis: Well, yeah, he's in there . . . he's right.

Fred: He certainly is, that boy plays a fine lot of trombone.

Louis: Yes he does . . . It was Joe Smith usta take a whole chorus, ya know, that's swing lead, straight lead . . . jus' a regular solo, jus' like somebody would be singin' an' it was different. Now there's Bubber Miley was another great man . . . an' Cootie.

Fred: And Cootie . . . and LOUIS . . .

Louis: Yeah, well I mean . . .

Fred: Now don't forget Louis . . .

Louis: I'm not much with a plunger, mannnnn . . .

Fred: I know you're not a plunger man, you don't need that plunger . . .

Louis: Well, I mean, I like it at times, but I don't have time to git to mine . . . I'm standin' out theah ya know an' I probably have somethin' else to do, ya know . . . it's all understood. That's why I like my public, they begin to dig me as the years go on an' they kinda understan' my efforts.

Fred: Well Louis, you know your fans number in the millions and millions and millions . . .

Louis: Yeah, that's right an' I like 'em all too . . . I think we're doin' alright.

Fred: Of course, Bunk Johnson was a good friend of yours . . .

Louis: Yeah, he's a good ol' pioneer . . . of course nobody probably don't realize what a grand musician Bunk was 30 years ago . . . he was a wonderful man. An' jus' to show ya, all those boys was playin' at the same time . . . there's Bunk, King Oliver, Freddie Keppard, Manuel Perez, all the great fellows . . . an' everyone of them had their different styles an' they were great . . . wasn't that somethin'?

Fred: That certainly is . . . and they were all in the New Orleans vein, even though they interpreted it differently.

Louis: Sometime all of them would meet on the same corner an' it was awful . . . blowin' at each other, ya know, advertising for different things . . .

Fred: How many of them are alive today, Louis?

Louis: Well, Bunk is alive . . .

Fred: I know, he just made some records.

Louis: Les' see, Freddie Keppard's gone . . . an' you never heard of "Sugar Johnnie?" That's another trumpet player, well he's gone . . . I think Bunk is about the only one, an' you know he's around his sixties an' still doin' alright. Manuel Perez, yeah, he's livin' but

he's makin' cigars . . . he's happier when he's makin' cigars.

Fred: Louis, I wanted to ask you something . . . why did you give up the cornet for the trumpet back in 1926 . . . when fellows like Bix and Spanier and Rex always played cornet and still do . . .

Louis: Well, I'd a had my cornet today, but I happened to be in a symphony orchestra in 1925 in Chicago at the Vendome Theatre where I was playin' . . . from the Vendome I'd go to the Sunset, ya know, one of Mr. Joe Glaser's cabarets at that time, that was my manager . . . well, the orchestra leader, he came to me one intermission, he said now, he didn't say he wanted to drag me, but I mean, he said, well all the res' of the trumpets have long trumpets, see, an' he was sayin', I know you hate to get rid of your cornet, see, but it jus' look *so bad* sittin' up theah with the res' of the boys . . . It was a long time gettin' usta that trumpet, but . . . I did . . . ya know, yeah, I like the cornet though, I did.

Fred: Do you still ever play it?

Louis: Not any more. I gave it away to a little youngster in the Waif's Home, ya know, in New Orleans.

Fred: I know you go back there every year, Louis, don't you?

Louis: Yeah, I usta go down there and give the boys the horn that I finish up with.

Fred: The horn that you use of this year, you give it to the . . .

Louis: The one that's mos' promisin'.

Fred: That's a touching thing.

Louis: Yeah, it was nice . . . they appreciate it, an' they always have a good little band out theah, ya know . . .

Fred: And how do you feel when you go back to that old orphanage?

Louis: Feel at home, tell the truth, because I spend the whole day out theah an' have dinner an' everythin' with the boys. We have games . . . they have a big picture of me out theah an' the firs' ol' cornet that I learned on, an' I always bring some of the boys from the band so that they could witness that, ya know . . . some of the boys from up Nawth . . . when I go down South, I let 'em witness that.

Fred: Someday Louis, that Waif's Home is going to be a shrine.

Louis: Well, guess so . . . I'll never stop goin' theah, I'll tell you that. Even the judge was theah one day, I mean, they had all the 'ficials out theah one day, a big affair ya know, an' oh, it was wunnerful.

Fred: That's the big thing of the year, when old "Satchmo" comes back home . . .

Louis: Sho', I went down there an' bought them a radio so they could hear the programs when I was playin' at the Suburban Gardens for four months, an' every night they catch the programs an' I dedicate a tune to 'em . . . it's good spirit, after all. An' Mister Jones, he's still the same fellow, he looks jus' as young as he did when I was theah an' it's been over 20 yeahs ago.

Fred: And he was the head of the school when you were a little boy.

Louis: An' he's still theah, an' he tells me, 'listen heah, boy, I'll still spank ya.'

Fred: And what do you say to him?

Louis: Okeh, Mr. Jones, Okeh . . . Okeh.

Fred: Ah, he certainly must be proud of you, Louis.

Louis: He was the first one at the dance when we were playin' there . . . an' he'd point to me an' say 'That's my boy'—

Fred: Louis, how did you start scat singing? You know there's a story around that you forgot the words one day at a recording session and you just started to scat right from there. Is that true?

Louis: Oh yeah, that was a recording of "Heebie Jeebies," see, but it happened, ya know, well a case of presence of mind, see, but when we were kids goin' to school we usta always hum riffs and different things, say f'rinstance we followed a parade or a funeral, ya know, they always had bands to take the body to the cemetery an' then comin' back they swing, see, "Didn't He Ramble" or somethin' like that. Well, if it's a riff one of the instruments would play that would interest us, why we'd hum it to the other one—'Did you hear that riff son, Bum Bum Da De, Da De Da Da Da'—ya know what I mean? Well, thas' the way we went on for years, now when this recording comes up in Chicago an' this new number at the time, "Heebie Jeebies," I dropped the words, there wasn't any use in spoilin' this master, so I just went in there and started scattin' an' they kep' it. Well, they say that was the beginnin' of scat.

Fred: Well, it is Louis, it is, and there have been many, many guys since then who have been scattin'.

Louis: Well, I made some awful riffs there . . . there's that Leo Watson, he'll scat you out of the place if you don't watch it . . .

Fred: And I notice that your trumpet style is very similar . . .

Louis: Yeah, well thas' what I'm sayin', we make the same riffs that a horn would . . . thas' the way I sing now, yeah, sing the same thing I make on the trumpet.

Fred: Louis it was a wonderful tribute to you, a marvelous tribute at the Metropolitan in the All-American Jazz Concert when you were the star of the night, both number one on trumpet, number one in the vocal department.

Louis: Well, to me it was jus' a pleasure to be aroun' the boys, ya know what I mean, 'cause boys jammin' an' contestin' an' all that, I don't know, I just feel that I shouldn't be bothered with all that now.

Fred: I don't blame you, doesn't mean anything . . .

Louis: Well, I wouldn't do it anyway, so it's jus' a matter of all that happiness for me jus' to be aroun' all those cats and the good ol' musicians of the good ol' days, an' I thought it was nice, ya know . . .

Fred: And of course, it loses some of the elements of jazz. It loses the element of looseness and ease . . .

Louis: Well, everybody's gonna tighten up an' ya know, it's jus' one of them things.

Fred: Jazz has to be fresh and spontaneous, it's not supposed to be rehearsed . . .

Louis: The best way to catch a jam session is catch a bunch of musicians that doesn't know that anyone's listenin' to them, ya know, unaware, ya know, say we're sittin' aroun' the room jus' playin' for our own pleasure. But if somebody's sittin' aroun', like at rehearsals, ya see a lot of fellows sittin' aroun', they think it's alright, but they doin' the musicians a lot of harm . . . lot of times they try somethin' they wouldn't, because they figger this guy is sittin' out theah, he . . . oh, oh, ya know, one of them things . . . but when you catch a bunch of musicians jammin' all by themselves thas' when you really hear 'em. Like the boys always say 'You oughta catch ol' Satchmo' in his dressin' room when he's warmin' up . . . you liable to hear me playin' 'Cavaleria Rusticana' . . .

Fred: Come again with that Louis . . . well, to sum up, your improvisations on trumpet show a wealth of ideas and inspiration that really, any other guy looks so small in contrast, Louis, and I know that you still hit that F or G above high C with fulness and roundness and your tonal quality is really something. There's more power there than any other jazz horn man.

Louis: Yeah, I'm satisfied with my work . . .

Fred: It's full, it's majestic, it's polished and at the same time it's soothing and moving and emotional and I think more important is your feeling for jazz which has given you so much fame. Just a single bar or note has such intensity and rhythm that you really become a living example of the music and you have such great ideas, such relaxed playing, such tremendous tone that it's so impressive, that to compare you with any other musician is like comparing the Empire State Building with an old wooden shack . . . and of course that old voice of yours . . .

Louis: Yeah, well you know, Pops, I jus' like to play my horn right anyway, ya know, an' then like I said, the rudiments of jazz can always be there if you play it right . . . then if sometimes you're in the spirit an' you're up to par, ya want to pitch in there with a little extra jive, well, so much the better, but try to keep your work at least up to par.

Fred: Louis, do you think jazz will ever regain the freshness and the spontaneity and the naturalness of the music as it was played down in New Orleans?

Louis: It will, but there's always goin' to be some kind of an addition nowadays to polish it up, see, they couldn't afford to play jazz as rough as they did way back in the days of Buddy Bolden and King Oliver when he was a youngster . . . they couldn't do it . . . .They wouldn't appreciate it, it's gotta be smoothed out some kinda way . . .

Fred: Well, I hope it keeps its freshness . . .

Louis: Well, I mean, if you listened to a whole lot of them records way back theah, ya know what I mean, an' you'd say yourself, 'gee, a little modern arrangement of that would really fix that number up.'

Fred: That's true, but you don't mean to say that the stuff should be written down or anything like that, do you?

Louis: Well, lot of times it's necessary to write some things down so you won't fergit it . . .

Fred: The rough arrangement . . .

Louis: Yeah, not to the extent that you just want to write everything you play, but sometime it's good to jot down a little somethin' . . . an' remin' you of it . . . I don't know, I jus' like them full harmonies . . . well, by singin' in the quartet makes me have that yen.

Fred: I see, tell me Louis, what are your plans? I know you're organizing another band, I just heard you in rehearsal up there at Nola and I know you're going up to Canada for a series of one-nighters . . .

Louis: Then we go to Boston.

Fred: You coming back to make some records?

Louis: I believe we will, I'm supposed to go over and see a man, Mr. Kapp, today and get together on some tunes.

Fred: Well, I want to thank you a million for coming up, 'Satch.' You've been wonderful this afternoon and in closing I want to tell the cats as a final tribute to you, that you can say that your personality has saturated all of jazz and without you I'm just wondering what jazz would have come to be. I think it's going to take the world many years, Louis, to realize just what you've given it, so best of luck to you 'Satchmo' and thanks a lot for coming up . . . take care.

When Armstrong Came to New York

by Kaiser Marshall

In the winter of 1924 I was with Fletcher Henderson's band in New York, and we were one of the top bands at that time. We had a nice location and we were really in the money. It was at that time that Henderson sent for Louis Armstrong to come out from Chicago and join us.

We had a nine-piece band, which was the standard thing in those days. Whiteman, Olsen and all the others carried nine pieces, and only Lopez had more than nine men. The regular set-up was two saxes, two trumpets, one trombone, banjo, piano, drums and tuba. Fletcher wanted to try using three trumpets, and that was why he sent for Louis.

I remember the day that Louis showed up for rehearsal. We were up at the Happy Rhone Club, a night club at 143rd Street and Lenox Avenue that we used for rehearsals. The band was up on the stand waiting when he got there, and Louis walked across the floor. He had on big thick-soled shoes, the kind that policemen wear, and he came walking across the floor, clump-clump, and grinned and said hello to all the boys.

He got his seat and opened the book for the third trumpet. Now, Fletcher Henderson's book wasn't one that just anybody could open up and read at sight. He had a lot of difficult arrangements there, ones he made himself, and his brother Horace, and Don Redman, and some outside arrangers, including a man from Goldkette's outfit. They were pretty fancy arrangements, and although Louis was a good reader at that time, he had a little trouble at first. He would make a mistake, and jump up and say: "Man, what is that thing?" Then everybody laughed

and Louis would sit down and play it right the next time. After he made one mistake he didn't make it again.

We got along fine at the rehearsal that day, and at night we came on down to the Roseland Ballroom at 51st Street and Broadway. Everything went fine on the job. Louis played mighty well, and the more he got a chance to read that music the better he was. He was always a good showman.

Thursday night was vaudeville night at the Roseland. We used to have different acts all the time; George Raft used to do the Charleston with a little colored kid; I remember that Ruby Keeler, Al Jolson's wife, used to do her tap-dancing once in a while and always knock off the prizes. Bing Crosby was with Whiteman's Rhythm Boys then, and he used to come in and listen nightly. The master of ceremonies used to line the acts up and hold the money over a performer's head; the prize was awarded according to how much applause each one got. We used to have some good acts, too, sometimes big headliners, singers and dancers, came in on the show.

One Thursday night the program was short; the producer hadn't lined up enough acts, and it left the show pretty short. Louis used to mug around on some of the songs we played, so we got the idea he ought to get out and sing in the show. It took a lot of persuading, but he finally said he'd do it.

The stage was one of those sliding things that came right out from under the bandstand to the dance floor when the show was going on. We got Louis out on the stage and he did "Everybody Loves My Baby, But My Baby Don't Love Nobody But Me." He sang it and he played it on the trumpet; the crowd surely

THE JAZZ RECORD

PUBLISHED SEMI-MONTHLY

15c
A COPY

No. 1   February 15, 1943

Kaiser Marshall

went for it. He had the idea he wasn't in competition for the prize, but they made him come out and line up with the other acts, and when they held the money over his head the applause was so loud that there wasn't any question about it; he just walked off with first prize. From then on they used to cry for Louis every Thursday night, and he would play his horn and sing his songs.

Before Louis came East we had what you could call a swing band, even back in those days. Louis just fell right in with our style. We used to have a lot of sax background stuff in the arrangements, and a good solid rhythm section, with the horns out in front, and it sounded good. Sometimes we used bass saxes; Coleman Hawkins and Don Redman played bass sometimes, and Buster Bailey played baritone sax. Sometimes we used Queenaphones; a little instrument you never see any more, something like a toy instrument, although it cost more, and its tone was somewhere in the reed section.

For making records we sometimes added an extra sax, and for some dates we used only a small part of the band. Fletcher had a recording contract with Columbia, but we used to make records under another name, any old name at all, like Dixie Stompers and so on, for other companies. We recorded for Harmony, Regal, Paramount, and some others. When we played accompaniments for singers like Bessie Smith, Clara Smith, Ethel Waters and Ida Cox, we would break the band up into little units and switch around, using one trumpet, then clarinet and trombone, bass sax, and so on, with the rhythm section.

Louis stayed with the band about a year and a half. We got along fine, because everybody liked him and he was a fine fellow to have around. As I said, we were in the money then, with a location job, plenty of recording dates, and other things. Sometimes after we finished at the Roseland we'd go up to Harlem and play from two to three in the morning; it meant twenty-five dollars a man just for that hour of playing. We'd go to the Manhattan, Renaissance Casino, or over to Brooklyn to the Arcadia. We all lived high;

we were a top band and we had top wardrobes. The boys used to wear English walking suits that cost a hundred-ten dollars, seven-dollar spats and eighteen-dollar shoes. Things were good in those days.

Louis never went around much then. He was working hard and saving his money. At first he liked New York, but later he wanted to go back to Chicago, to be near his wife, settle down and organize his own band. He used to write his wife every day.

When he first came we kidded him a lot about his thick-soled shoes and his long drawers. He had to take so much about those drawers that he finally said to me, "All right, I'll take them off, but if I catch cold in the winter time I'll blame it on you."

While he was with our band Louis monkeyed around with trombone once in a while, but he never really played it, and I know he never played it on any recording session with us.

He finally decided to leave. Mr. Becker, the manager at Roseland, liked Louis so much that he loaned him a thousand dollars to buy himself a home in Chicago and start his band. A few years later Louis Armstrong was back in New York making records under his own name. In 1928 he got some of us together for a record date—Jack Teagarden on trombone, Happy Cauldwell on sax, Joe Sullivan on piano, Eddie Lang on guitar, and myself on drums. We had been working the night before and the record date was for eight in the morning, so we didn't bother about going to bed; I rode the boys around in my car in the early morning hours and we had breakfast about six so we could get to the studio at eight. We took a gallon jug of whiskey with us.

After we recorded that number the studio man came around with his list to write down the usual information, composer, name of tune and so on. He asked Louis what the tune was called, and Louis said "I don't know!" Then he looked around and saw the empty jug sitting in the middle of the floor and he said: "Man we sure knocked that jug—you call it 'Knockin' a Jug.'" And that's the name that went on the record.

Fred Moore

If you've ever seen Freddie Moore roll his eyes, go into his act, you book him; get him on stage and no one's goin' to steal a scene when he's around. He's funny. You know, Freddie and I wrote a number "Blues 'n Booze" where he sings "Mama, Mama, Mama . . . Why do you snore so loud (and this line repeats)" followed by the tag-line . . . "You may be a little woman but you sound just like a great big crowd." Fred wrote that lyric.

Moore played drums like so few do now a days. He kept time and he worked at swing. No flashy choruses but he did have an act. Sticks seemingly would be thrown in the air as one appeared in his mouth and others were switched from hand to hand as Freddie kept playing. All the time those eyes were rolling. Funny cat. I guess I got him to play the washboard. We were working at the Village Vanguard in New York City and I'd dug it out that Fred had played the washboard at one time. Moore was willing but he needed thimbles. And in the '40s they weren't the easiest thing to procure. The war had made such items a bit rare. But that was solved when my dad, a tinsmith by trade, made a set for Freddie. It was really somethin' to hear Moore take off on that washboard. He made beats like you thought he was a dancer.

One of our last dates together was in Chicago. An agent had booked us as a team at a South-Side bistro. Moore and Hodes. We opened on a Friday night; the house was half-full. We went on (a back-of-the-bar stage) and the audience dug us. Got a big hand. Then, as we were going off, the bartender said to me "the boss wants to see you". . . . So I walked over and this man was mad. He was burning. Though he'd signed our contract he hadn't known (at least so he said) that we were "a mixed" group. Nothing would do but for us to "get out of here right now." You can imagine how drug we were. This was '57 and up north; how can that be. But it was. So Fred packed and we walked out. It was a corner spot and as we turned the corner I saw a downstairs saloon. "Come on Freddie, I'll buy you a drink." I just wanted him to feel better. So we went in. After a taste we got to talkin' to the bartender and it turned out that both places we'd been in were owned by the same man. It was perfectly aw rite for us to have a drink downstairs and around the corner.   A.H.

King Oliver's Last Tour

by Fred Moore

When King Oliver called a rehearsal, whatever time he called it for, three o'clock or four, everybody knew they had to be there on time. Because the King would walk in with the music on his arm and his gun in the bosom of his coat. He would throw everything down on the table and look around to see if everybody was there. Then he would pick up his gun and ask "Is everybody here?" Everybody reported yes, we were there,

Fred Moore

then he would put his gun back on the table, and the rehearsal would go on.

That was back in 1931. The King was 51 years old then. Dave Nelson was arranger and trumpet at that time, and he kept telling the King about me, so he asked Nelson to bring me around. I had been in New York a while, and I guess I was a pretty fair tempo man, so I was hired. The King put his arrangements in front of me and I had to play them. He had about 150 arrangements. The band had eleven men. Hank Duncan played piano for rehearsals and recording. Don Frye was with the band too; he had three or four piano players.

We went on a tour by bus, jumped from New York to Wichita, Kansas, where we played the Eltorian ball room. Oliver had a contract for three months, but when we got there he didn't want to play his recording arrangements; the manager didn't go for that, so we were only there three weeks. From there we went to Ft. Worth, Texas, following Louis Armstrong on the same tour. Louis was getting $1.25 admission ahead of us, and Oliver was getting $1. We toured St. Louis, Kansas City, and smaller places, playing ball-rooms, both white and colored. But business was poor and the band started to break up. We finally got stranded in Kansas City when there were no more bookings.

It was a good band; the trouble was that managers wanted some particular thing and the King wouldn't do it. Bookers got to hear about that, and there was no work for us. They wanted to send us to New Orleans for a date that Louis Armstrong had got and couldn't fill; the King wanted more money than Louis, so no date. I stayed in Kansas City for a while and got a chance to make gigs, club dates. Finally the King took the whole band back to Wichita, but he took sick there. After about three months we started scrabbling around to get back to New York the best way we could, every man for himself. The King had money tied up in the banks (this was the bank holiday of 1932) but it was messed up so he couldn't get at it.

That whole tour lasted about six months. When we could get into a town, the first thing everybody did was look for a room and a place to eat. When we went to eat the King would order his, double portions. He wouldn't drink a glass of milk, but a quart bottle. A small steak, King would order double. Not three slices of bread, but a whole loaf. He was crazy about Boston baked beans and hot dogs.

He took a liking to me, and made me kind of a right-hand man. For rehearsals, I would round up the men and so on, like a straw-boss. Dave Nelson did all the arranging. When the tour broke up, Dave took all the arrangements back with him to New York, because the King never did pay him for them. He still has them.

When we made records, the King didn't play. His lip was bad and he had trouble with his teeth. Every time we made a recording, when it came to the play-back, the man would say, "Sorry, there was one note you tried to make, couldn't make it." After he tried one or two more playbacks, the King would have Ward Pinkett or Nelson do it. Sometimes we had Red Allen too.

I first learned to play drums when I was only twelve years old. I left home then and went to a place called New Bern, in North Carolina. I would go around to dance halls and the drummer let me sit in. I had pretty good tempo, but I couldn't execute much with my hands. I never took lessons, just watched the guy. I stayed there about five years, working in a meat market, delivering packages on a bicycle. They only had dances three nights a week. Then I got a chance to travel. I was band-boy with the A. G. Allen Minstrels. I took care of the coats for the band men, and played the drums in the street parade.

We would hit a town at 9 or 10 in the morning, traveling in our Pullman car, the whole company. The fellows who put up the tents, the canvas boys, would sleep in the possum-belly, the space under the car. We would sleep and eat on the car; the men brought their wives and girls along, and the wives would do the laundry. First thing, the boys put the tents up, and our parade would come off at 12:30. The band would lead the parade, with the entertainers, dancers and comedians out in front of it. I wore a high silk hat, long red coat, and wing collar. After three or four miles of parade, that collar would sweat down. The boss of the show would ride in a rented car ahead or behind the parade, with somebody in the car spieling about the show that night. At the big corner of town the band would make a circle and play a concert.

I got tired of traveling, so down in Birmingham I quit the show. I got a job in the Frolic Theatre for $7 a week, room and board, playing drums in the pit. I got all my experience there. We played all the acts. Sometimes we would have a rehearsal at 9 a.m. We had to rehearse every show Sunday night when it came in, and the people were tired from traveling, so they would start again Monday morning. If the show brought their own piano and drummer, the boss would send me to play a picture theatre. I would go around about 9:30 before the house opened and watch the picture and study the cue sheet that always came with pictures then. When somebody got hit, bam! Thunder and lightning, a roll on the bass drum, and a rim shot when some guy would shoot somebody. Then I used to go back-stage and watch the comedians on the TOBA [Theatre Owners Booking Association: a black vaudeville circuit] time, and started to learn to dance in my spare time after the show was over.

William Benbow's show called the Charleston Dandies came through, and I joined it. Our first date was in Chattanooga, next Atlanta, then to New Orleans and to Havana. We were in Havana six months. I had trouble when I got there; a boy named Rastus, a sensation drummer, very fast was there ahead of us. One thing about Havana,

we got paid every night, eight dollars; it was the law down there. When we came back I quit the show at Miami, our first stop. I had a little money saved up, so I went to St. Louis and started working around with Charlie Creath, playing club dates. This was in 1927.

I first joined the union there. It cost me $15. They just had a little light test; had three notes on the blackboard, away back, then put something over one eye and asked me what the notes were. I would say, "eighth note, quarter note, whole note." They gave me a sheet and said: "Make with the snare drum." So I made it. Something easy, I think it was compound triplets. "All right come over and give me the money." There were two unions in St. Louis; this was colored.

After that I left for my old stomping ground, back in Birmingham. I only stayed there three weeks. Everybody said: "Boy, why don't you go to New York, see what you can do?" I went up to Detroit and was there five months with my own band, seven pieces, at the Savoy night club. Then I gave that band up and came to New York.

My first job in New York was with Wilbur Sweatman at the Lafayette Theatre. He used to play his act, playing three clarinets at one time, his special number was "The Rosary." I made $90 that week, doubling, playing Sweatman's act and playing the show with the big band. I joined the New York union; the first week I worked I gave the union man $54 but I couldn't join right then. I had to learn how to play rhumbas and tangos, the hard way. I went to work in a dancing school, dime a dance, and was there for four years. Then I went with King Oliver.

After the Oliver tour I decided to get a trio. I had Don Frye and Pete Brown, and we were at the Victoria Cafe, 141st and 7th Avenue, for four years. We had Harlem sewed up. We finally gave it up and joined John Kirby. We were the first Kirby band when he was at the Onyx Club. But after he got a start he wanted to make changes, so he got his own boys, Spencer and Bailey and the others. I hung around the Street a while, and the next job was with Lem Johnson, sixteen weeks at Kelly's Stables. They closed without notice, and I got disheartened and started doing club dates.

Then this year I was down one Sunday to hear a jam session at Ryan's, and sat in, and Art Hodes dug me then. I made a few club dates with him. Also went on one of Eddie Condon's shows at Carnegie Hall. Then when Art opened at the Vanguard he told me he had a steady job for me.

We worked up some numbers using a washboard. I learned how to play washboard back in 1925, down in Norfolk. There was a boy there named Washboard and he really

could play. You use thimbles, and have a cow-bell and two cymbals fastened to the board. Cut off one of the legs to hold it against your chest, and on the other leg put an extension and a cross-piece to sit on. For a fast number you can really beat out rhythm on it.

The King's Nephew

by Dave Nelson
(As related to Danny Barker)

My first job was in 1925 with Marie Lucas at the Lincoln Gardens in Chicago. Then I was featured trumpeter with Jelly Roll Morton's band on the M.C.A. circuit. From there I played with Richard M. Jones and then I formed my own combination in 1927 and played at the Dreamland in Chicago. After that I played club dates with King Oliver and also made records with Richard M. Jones on a record called the Paramount, and also recorded with Ida Cox and Ma Rainey.

With my own combo, we played at a little club called the Pioneer, a few doors away from the Dreamland. After that I worked at the Apex Club with Jimmy Noone, and we also played the Apollo on 47th Street in Chicago. We went on the road, with my own combo and Mike's Merry-Makers. I came to New York in 1929 and played with Luis Russell at the Roseland and Cotton Club. Then I rejoined King Oliver and organized his New York band that recorded on Victor label.

At this time I wrote my first two hits which were "Boogie-Woogie" and "Mule Face Blues." I also arranged these hits. Others I wrote at that time were "Edna," "Too Late," "I Want You Just For Myself," and "Stop Crying." All these tunes were recorded with Oliver's band.

I then organized my own band which was booked by Irving Mills. The men in this band

were: Danny Barker, guitar; Sam Allen, piano; Simon Marrero, bass; Gerald Hopsin, drums; I played trumpet; Melvin Herbert, Clarence Berton and Wilbur DeParis, trombones; Buster Bailey, Glenn Pacque and Charlie Frazier, saxes. This was the first Blue Rhythm Band. We also recorded on Victor label under the name of Dave Nelson and the King's Men. Then we left Mills and went on Mae West's show, *The Constant Sinner*. After that we played dance engagements in and out of New York with Ella Fitzgerald at the Savoy Ballroom, Laurel Gardens, N.J., Continental Ballroom in New Jersey, Palace Ballroom in Brooklyn, Hotspot Ballroom in Milford, Conn., Essex Hotel, Nest Club in Harlem on 133rd Street, Swing Rendezvous, Elks, Town Tapers Club, Apollo Theatre, and also played a show with Buck and Bubbles in Troy, N.Y. Other spots were the Pelham Heath Inn, Roebling Ballroom, Alhambra Theatre and the Cedar Theatre in Brooklyn.

My first instrument was violin, my mother and father both played piano. One of my sisters plays organ in one of the largest churches in Chicago, Ebenezer Baptist Church.

When I was a kid there was such a great demand for musicians that a cat named Freddie asked me to join his band and play trombone (which he would purchase from a hock shop). When I told him I couldn't play trombone he said, "Man, just hold it and blow one big loud note."

At one of King Oliver's recording sessions, we had a saxophone player named Paul Whiteman. He weighed about 230 pounds. As King Oliver was playing his trumpet solo with his eyes closed, this big sax player was standing in front of him. King Oliver opened his eyes and saw him and said, "Man, sit down, you look like a damned circus tent standing up there. How you expect that mike to pick up this music with you in the way?" Every time a man hit a bad note, the whole band would holler "Jesus!"

I also wrote and arranged due to the inspiration Richard M. Jones gave me; he showed me how to put down my first note. Afterwards I took lessons from Mae Hood, the late Victor Herbert arranger, and also from Clarence Hall, who went to school with Paderewski.

Jelly Roll Morton

I wonder who it was told me that story 'bout Jelly; how he'd carry a little mirror with him on the bandstand and set it so he could dig everything that was going on with the bandsmen. Then when some cat thought to put him on, Jelly would turn around and point at the wising-off character and say, "O.K. buddy, you just got your two." In musicians' language that means in two weeks you're out of a job.

Morton must have been something. You can't underestimate the man. Sure, if you've never heard his "Mamie's Blues" . . . "This is the first-est blues I ever heard . . . She could hardly play anything else but she sure could play this. . . . " And Jelly puts it down so beautifully; no wasted motion or notes. The skill is absorbed by the message. He tells the story of a woman who's keepin' a man . . . "If you can't give a dollar, give me a lousy dime." Maybe you heard some of Morton's jazz band recordings? "The Chant," "Black Bottom Stomp," "Beale Street"? This artist produced some of the greatest sides of the times. As far as I'm concerned Jelly Roll Morton was to the small band what Ellington was to the large. Jelly could play a tune, then visualize it being played by a small band, and when he got a record date that tune would get played as he heard it (inside) and he'd have to write music, and on the date, to play it. So his renditions have stood the test of time. They sound just as good to these ears today.

Jelly the piano player? Before you form any judgment give a listen to something he cut very shortly before he passed on; a rendition he titled "Fingerbuster." You hear that and then you tell me he couldn't play. As a piano player I would hate to have to follow this bit onstage. As to Morton the writer, the author of "The Pearls," "Grandpa's Spells," "King Porter Stomp," etc., there never has been any disagreement; he stands amongst the "aloners." In my book, he was a jazz giant.

Years ago I had me a band, and we had a library of tunes, and among 'em, Jelly Roll's were our favorites. "Shoe Shiner's Drag," "Kansas City Stomp," "Wolverine"; you name them; great music. Now I realize, re-reading his letter to Mr. Ripley that when Morton talks about himself and blows his own horn he's telling the truth. This cat was head and shoulders above his competitors in his day; we still haven't caught up in deserved appreciation of his contributions. His playing was as positive as some of the statements you will read. His bands were the best; he only used top jazz players. If I was asked to pick the 12 most important people in jazz, of all time, I would most certainly include Jelly Roll Morton.   A.H.

Ferdinand "Jelly Roll" Morton

Mostly About Morton

by Omer Simeon

I first met Jelly Roll in Chicago while I was with Charlie Elgar. That was Charlie Elgar's Creole Band and we played mostly in Milwaukee. Somebody around Chicago had recommended me to Jelly Roll and he asked me to come down to make some records. We used to go to his home for rehearsals and the first time I was there, he handed me a piece called "Mama Nita," which had a pretty hard clarinet part. I guess he was testing me out and I knew he was pleased when I read it off at first sight. We rehearsed that tune but never did record it.

Walter Melrose brought all the music down from his music store. Morton was working for Melrose then and the pieces we played were mostly all stock arrangements Jelly had made up and published by Melrose. Jelly marked out parts we liked and he always had his manuscripts there and his pencils and he was always writing and changing little parts. Art Hodes reminds me of Jelly Roll the way he rehearses and records—pencil, paper and manuscripts and jotting down changes here and there. Jelly left our solos up to us but the backgrounds, harmony and licks were all in his arrangements. He was easy to work for and he always explained everything he wanted. He reminded me of a guy like Dizzy Dean—but he could back up anything he said. Every one liked to pick arguments with him because they liked to hear him talk and argue. Later on in New York, when swing was becoming popular, Chick Webb used to kid him—told him he didn't know anything about jazz and asked him about New Orleans. That would start him off about being the pioneer of jazz. He was always talking about New Orleans; about Buddy Bolden, Frankie Dusen, Buddy Petit, Tony Jackson—he could take off their mannerisms on a job and he was always a comedian. It was hard to keep up with him—he could talk 24 hours in a row.

We would have a couple of rehearsals at Jelly's house before the date and Melrose would pay us $5.00 a man. That's the only time I ever got paid for a rehearsal. Then we'd go around to the Victor studio on the North Side for the recording and he'd pay us $15.00 a side, which was more than scale in those days. Technicians set the stage for the date—Jelly had to take orders there for a change—and all this time I was commuting from Milwaukee. I was with Elgar until 1927, playing at the Riverview Ballroom and the Wisconsin Roof Garden. Elgar was very popular around Milwaukee. He had a large band for that time—about twelve pieces. Darnell Howard was with him and Cliff King played clarinet. Joe Sudler was with him and he was a good trumpet player. I was playing alto and clarinet and later on I got a soprano sax so I had three instruments to carry around. We had to play dance music but Elgar featured a lot of rags and other tunes like "High Society" and "Clarinet Marmalade." We never recorded though.

Melrose spared no expense for a record date—anything Jelly Roll wanted he got. Melrose worshipped him like a king. Jelly was great for effects as on "Sidewalk Blues" and "Steamboat Stomp" and later on like the opening on "Kansas City Stomp." I had never heard anything played like that before. Jelly thought it up and anything he needed for his effects, Melrose would go out and get it. For the second date he got Darnell Howard and Barney Bigard in for the trio effect he wanted on two of the sides. I played all the clarinet part and Howard and Bigard just sat there and held their clarinets except for the few strains Jelly wanted them to play. He had a Klaxon horn for "Sidewalk Blues" and I think it was Marty Bloom—Melrose's partner—who did the whistling. It was supposed to be a cop's whistle and Jelly took off the cop and Johnny St. Cyr did the other talking. They did the talking on "Steamboat Stomp" too. Bloom was the sound effects man. I remember on the second date, Melrose walked in with a bottle of scotch. We usually had a bottle around as the dates would be early in the morning and we had to get our spirits up. Anyway, Jelly had two drinks and we had to stop the session for a while and open all the windows so he could get some air. He wasn't much of a drinking man. Melrose sure got a big kick out of that.

I was still commuting from Milwaukee when the third date came up in December, 1926. On "Someday Sweetheart" I took a solo chorus on bass clarinet. Jelly wanted it and Melrose rented one somewhere. Took a little time to get familiar with it and I didn't like it too much. Jelly was always fond of effects and wanted to be different. He was always trying to find something different and whatever he wanted, we would have to do. He was fussy on introductions and endings and he always wanted the ensemble his way but he never interfered with the solo work. He'd tell us where he wanted the solo or break but the rest was up to us. Some more of Jelly's effects cropped up on the third date. He had two violins on "Someday Sweetheart" and I think one of them may have been Darnell Howard. He was quite prominent at that time on violin as well as on sax and clarinet. On "Original Jelly Roll Blues," Johnny St. Cyr played a guitar and the drummer used castanets to give a Spanish style effect. Jelly was sure full of ideas and he used them. I remember on "Dr. Jazz," the long note I played wasn't in the stock arrangement. Jelly liked it and had Melrose put it in the orchestration.

I didn't see Jelly again around Chicago. I played with Elgar a while after that and left him to go with King Oliver. I had one record date with Oliver in Chicago when we made "Willie the Weeper," "Black Snake Blues," "Every Tub," and "Showboat Shuffle." I took the soprano sax solo on "Willie the Weeper." Shortly after, we went to New York with Oliver, where we made a few more records. Also had a record date with Eddie Lang,

Oliver and Clarence Williams at a studio in Washington Square but can't remember the tunes. The Oliver band didn't stick together long in New York. Ory was first to leave, then Barney Bigard and I went back west, where I played again with Elgar at the Eagle Ballroom in Milwaukee. I left him late in 1927 and went back to New York with Luis Russell, where we played at the Nest Cafe. Andy Anderson was on trumpet.

In June, 1928, Walter Melrose came to the Nest and asked me to make another record date with Jelly. Jelly had come to New York and had a band at the Rose Danceland. All the boys on the date were in his band and I was the only outsider. Russell Procope was playing sax and clarinet at the ballroom but Jelly wanted me to play on the date. Ward Pinkett, Geechie Fields and the Benford Brothers were all in his band. Pinkett was a fine trumpet player, sometimes the way he played was a lot like Mitch. All the tunes were rehearsed at the Rose Danceland—"Georgia Swing," "Kansas City Stomp" and the others and he wanted to make a trio side too. He said Dodds had been making a lot of records and Benny Goodman was starting in and with everybody soloing, he wanted to give me a chance to show myself. He wanted me to work in his band too but I didn't go until fall and then only worked one week. He paid me $75.00 a week and wanted me to stay but the job was a taxi-dance hall and it was too hard. We'd play for fifty minutes in a row and the rest ten minutes. I had a chance to work for Erskine Tate in his pit band at the Metropolitan Theater in Chicago and could be with my family there. That was good experience too as I had to play all kinds of music with Tate.

I saw Jelly a couple of more times but never played with him again. Once on a one nighter with Earl Hines' band somewhere in Maryland, Jelly came over to see me. The last time I saw Jelly was in Washington at the Howard Theater. He came back stage and said he was going to organize a band again and wanted me to come with him. He had a club in Washington then and wanted to cook me some red beans and rice. I'm sorry now that I couldn't make it.

"Oh, Mr. Jelly!"

by Charles Edward Smith

"I've been working on some plans. I wish you'd come in with me on this. I got an idea it's big, very big." The curtains on the U Street windows stirred gently and the warm damp air of the Washington summer billowed in upon us, hanging like a vapour over the bare tabletops in the too-brightly lit room. Jelly smiled tentatively as though not quite sure one would fall in with his plans. "I considered this proposition a long time," he added.

The smile was characteristic of Jelly. Maybe not the Mr. Jelly Lord of the 1920's when a Cadillac and a diamond-filled tooth were understatement, but still Mr. Jelly Lord, even though only a small handful of the jazz world knew, or cared, that he was alive. It was that smile and not the big talk that was Jelly.

Ten years before he had been on top. A long decade! Poverty, illness and at times a pessimism that amounted to premonition. He had known poverty before, in the hard and hopeless environment of the Gulf Coast. But something held him up in those days, no matter how hard the luck came. He was young and the world was still his jug. He could play pool on the side (whether well or

Bluebird Recording date, September, 1939. Sidney Bechet, Sidney DeParis, Zutty Singleton, Albert Nicholas, Jelly Roll Morton, Happy Cauldwell, Lawrence Lucie.

badly didn't matter) and he could make his way from honky tonk to honky tonk, confident that when he reached St. Louis he could "take" everyone but Tony Jackson.

Jelly helped to build a world, only to find, in his last years, that there seemed to be no place for him in it. That was how it was when he came to that upstairs cabaret on U Street where most of his own customers didn't know who he was. His own tunes had been pirated or were used without benefit to him for at that time he was still fighting for his ASCAP button. He had no band and no offers for solo work. So he mixed malicious drinks in the back room for a generally lethargic clientele.

The sell-out guys in jazz, meanwhile were getting ahead. Jelly tried to convince himself that commercialism in music and music-making was artistic; he quoted, almost verbatim, the notion of some music magazines that, ironically, have fought and still fight all that Jelly stands for in jazz. Because no one with Jelly's sincerity and background could actually go commercial.

The conviction wasn't real but there were times when he tried to make it stick. In such moods born of his failure in worldly terms, he would come up with pseudo-pop songs and grandiose ideas, such as the one he proposed to me that hot July night. We would, he explained, plan a series of Juke Box recordings. That was where the money was. Fifty thousand Juke Boxes couldn't be wrong!

I thought of the Juke Box there on U Street and what had happened to it during the course of my Washington sojourn. At first there were few records of any merit in it. Then the influence of a small circle of Washington jazz fans began to tell and the neighborhood kids didn't know what to make of it; they complained about the corny old tunes on the Juke Box—"Wolverine Blues," "Beale Street Blues," "Honky Tonk Train," "The Pearls."

And Jelly was torn again. What the kids wanted was not jazz. "They don't know nothing about jazz," Jelly would say emphatically. But they represented "public." Ten minutes later Jelly would play one of his new "pop" songs, watching one for its effect. "Ain't it a kind of pretty thing?"—and you could see Jelly clutching for straws so that it was hard to say, what one had to say, "Jelly, I like the old tunes best. You know that. And you could do more like them."

Once in a while, if he felt especially bad, he would mutter, "No one wants that stuff any more." But his hands would be on the keyboard, feeling for the past. And in those moments he forgot the little compensations with which he'd tried to push aside the big frustrations. Apologetically, he would loosen the patterned tie on the starched striped shirt. "Man, I believe it's warm tonight," and Mr. Jelly Lord smiled, with that world again in a jug and the stopper in his hand. That was generally time for a drink for his friends and a sip of sherry for himself. "I can't drink, you know." Then: "What's that, one of the old ones? Well, this is no doubt one of the oldest, this one has whiskers." That way the evening got ripe and the unknowing customers, if any were present looked on, cynically ignorant but aware that Mr. Jelly Lord was not to be tampered with.

Without always being conscious of it, that small group of Washington jazz fans who encouraged Jelly, helped him immeasurably to resume his title and place in jazz. "I don't know what I'd do if a few friends didn't drop in. People don't know the old jazz any more." So it was good to talk old times and say flatteringly, "Your friend really knows. Say, listen to him talk about Buddy Bolden." Then Jelly would go back to the piano again.

I recall evenings with mixed groups (that were permissible in so few places in Washington), a bunch of us gathered about the spinet-piano, Jelly tossing off blues verses and goading Sterling Brown of Howard University into singing a few. I can remember Jelly telling a crowded, fidgety Union benefit audience, most of whom wanted to dance, that he would enlighten them with a resume of jazz history, beginning with Buddy Bolden. Many members of the exclusive Jelly Roll Club, such as Nesuhi Ertegun, I knew of then only by hearsay. Jelly was increasingly proud of his fans. One day at the Howard Theatre I corraled Sidney Bechet and we went up the creaking stairs. Jelly's wife happened to be in the place and the effusive greetings in Creole put New Orleans on the map all over again.

There was a lot more of that, all helping Jelly to realize once more his place in jazz and helping to undo some of the damage to his ego. And for those people Jelly's wistful and wishful build-up ("Inventor of Jazz, Stomps and Swing") fell away; he was able to think of himself, as they thought of him, a great jazz pianist and composer, a great jazz pioneer.

That's the way it was when Jelly recorded his amazing documentary series for the Library of Congress. If it irks connoisseurs that these records are not yet available to the public, it might be some consolation to consider that without them Jelly would not have been prepared to do his own best memorial, the General album. His fingers were often stiff and his heart wasn't pumping the way it should, yet many times during the period Jelly remarked how good it felt to play that way. The studio was a small room off a corridor behind the Music Section of the Library of Congress. When he was warmed up he played with all his oldtime fervor. That was the way he felt when he made his piano solo of "Wolverine Blues." I thought of his own explanation of his style:

"My theory is to never dischord the melody. Always have the melody going some kind of way, and of course your background should always be with perfect harmony, and what is known today as riffs, meaning figures—musically speaking, it is figures." His head was over the keyboard now, his right hand reaching for the treble. He said, "Oh, Mr. Jelly!"

I left Washington in August, 1939, and went up to Yaddo, Saratoga Springs, to do some writing. While there I got a note from Alan Lomax telling me that Gordon Mercer might like to do an album of Jelly's piano and singing, and that he had recommended that I supervise and do the booklet.

Shortly thereafter I received a letter from Jelly. There was, he informed me, "a subject of mutual benefit," that he hoped I would discuss with him at my convenience. This was also characteristically Jelly—the letter, I mean. It was formal, couched in a stiff and naively elegant English. And if it concerned business, as did this, it invariably had an air of mystery about it. Had I not heard from Alan and Gordon, I might have anticipated a new campaign against the Juke Boxes.

By the time the album project was a settled thing, Gordon Mercer was with General and we had the facilities of the Reeves Sound Studios to work with. This was a wonderful break, as was the whole-hearted cooperation given us. But before we went into the studio I had several sessions with Jelly at his place in Harlem. The money we would get out of it would obviously not compensate for the work involved so we decided to have a hell of a good time and do an album that would be an honest projection of Jelly and his background.

The way we worked it out was necessarily informal. Usually Jelly sat at the grand piano but if he didn't feel up to playing (and being in extremely ill health, he often didn't) we sat and talked and I took notes. After a couple of hours of this Mrs. Morton would bring on shrimps and rice, or something else that recalled New Orleans. Once Jelly excused himself before meal-time and I realized that on occasion he had had a hand in the cooking, as he often had had in Washington when his friends dropped into the cabaret.

We settled on the tunes right there in that apartment off upper Seventh Avenue. When we walked into the studio we had the album in order, backings and all, with a couple of substitutes on hand in the event we had to fight it out. We didn't. The album went through as planned. The tests thrown out (none of them accessible now) consisted of an infamous "Tiger Rag," an equally infamous "Animal Ball," and a "Sporting House Rag" that didn't come off. We used as many as four waxes on certain sides, because Jelly was really ill at this time, and we took a few sessions to complete the job. At Jelly's request I sat in the studio with him as he recorded and I thought at the time I was going through at least as many crises as he was. On "Winin' Boy Blues," for example, he closed his eyes on the humming passage. The clock was climbing up towards the three-minute mark. Gordon and the engineers motioned me frantically to nudge Jelly. I didn't. It was too good. Besides, I didn't dare. Jelly opened his eyes slowly and murmured "Oh, Mamie," as the number came to its close.

In making up the album Jelly and I put "Mamie's Blues" first. An official of the company nodded his agreement. It was the right thing to do. It wasn't commercially sensible because a number like that would not *sell* the album, he said. "Mamie's Blues" was listened to in Harlem by a younger-generation pianist and Mrs. Morton repeated his remark, "Yeah," he had said, "but why does he play that one-finger piano?" Jelly's face darkened and he said to his wife, "Don't you know when to keep quiet?" Then he shut up himself, and looked a little old and tired. A week later *Time* magazine devoted its music column to Jelly's beautiful blues about a certain Mamie Desdume, who played a walking bass and had two fingers missing from her left hand.

Baby Dodds

I guess I was lucky. When I start thinkin' about the select drummers I've worked with, that has to be the right word. Of course I was choosey. Work with enough bangers that should have been selling shoelaces and pencils instead (or stuck to violin). Boy, I used to come home a-swearin' about guys who owned drums and didn't have the slightest idea of a beat; keeping time, or swinging. I've had me some miserable hours. But then again, to sort of make up for it, there's been the good ones. The drummers like Baby Dodds.

Man, we had a together-ness goin'. The three of us (Pops Foster, string bass) "were" a rhythm section. You know somethin'? You hear a guy play, an' you just sit there and you can't believe it. That was my feelin' when I heard Johnny and Baby (Dodds) at Kelly's Stables in Chicago. It was a warm summer night. I didn't have the bread to go in the joint, so I sat across the street on the curb and listened. I'd been in Kelly's before so I could picture the set-up. The piano player at one end of the bandstand and the drums at the other. Impossible! How can you spread out a rhythm section and still it cooks? Man! Wow! I just get my jollies a'sittin' there, listenin'. That was the greatest small band (and I don't like that word but at that moment that's how I felt). That's what music was all about. God, if I could ever play with that kind of set-up. . . .

So here it was; maybe fifteen years later. . . . And I got the trio at Jimmy Ryan's. It's Baby, Cecil (Scott; sax, clarinet) and me. Plus we have Chippie Hill doing vocals. Man, how good can you have it? And then, later on I got this gig at the Ole South, and now its Baby, Cecil, Pops Foster; plus we have a trumpet and trombone (Goodwin and Lugg). 'Course, these kind of kick jobs don't last too long. I suppose if it did I couldn't stand it.

But now that I think of it, if I try to tell you about Baby D. I'm lost. What was he like? Sure, I can describe him . . . I'd say around 5'5", 160 lbs? Sort of roundish. Nice smile (most the times). Never met his wife so I can't tell you about that part of his life (if he had that part). Sociable. But at the drums he was serious. You'd better be in there with him or you'd know about it. An honest performer. . . . A.H.

"Oh, Play That Thing"

by Warren "Baby" Dodds

I tried hard to play that tin flute I bought but I finally had to turn it over to Johnny. He played it fine and I backed him up with home-made drums made by punching holes in a tin can and using chair rounds for sticks. Those were my first drums and Johnny and I had a lot of fun playing together at home.

I was born in New Orleans on the day before Christmas, one of four boys and four girls. All our family liked music—Dad was a deacon and could sing and we had a family quartet. Mother played the melodeon and my sisters all played the organ and harmonicas. Johnny was a couple of years older than I was and we palled around when we were kids. He was good on the tin flute so there was nothing for me to do but back him up.

Johnny was already playing a clarinet before I got my first set of drums. Dad wouldn't buy them for me because he said there was too much noise in the house. I finally got a rope bass drum and picked up a snare, and after a while we had a full set, all from pawn shops and it only cost me four or five dollars. We had a quartet which Willie Hightower got together and we thought a lot of that band. We'd rehearse every Wednesday afternoon over at Willie's house and he worked for an ice-cream company so we'd always have ice cream to eat when we got through. We had a lot of fun playing around and we even played for house parties. Roy Palmer would be there sometimes and he showed us how to play.

My first job was in the Fewclothes Cabaret on the corner of Basin Street and Iberville with Roy Palmer, Sidney Desvigne and Walter Decou on piano. After that I played in Manuel Manetta's band at the Villa Cafe, with Eddie Atkins on trombone, and then moved across the street to the 101 Ranch where Baby Ridgeley was in the band. Then I went back to Willie Hightower in a small band playing uptown, which was called the American Stars. All this time I was taking lessons and got myself a better set of drums. After Roy Palmer gave me my first pointers, I took regular lessons, first from Louis Cottrell and Dave Perkins and my last teacher was Walter Grundy.

After leaving the American Stars, I played with Bunk Johnson for the first time, in Frankie Dusen's Eagle Band. Then up to Lincoln Park with John Robichaux, which was my favorite band in New Orleans. He had a drummer named MacMurray who used a single head snare drum and I liked it so much I got one for myself. About that time I used to sit in with Armand Piron's band. His drummer was called "Rabbit" and I got a lot of pointers from him and also from Arnold DePas. Rabbit used to go on the road a lot playing shows with Ma Rainey and he was a swell drummer. At this time my brother Johnny was playing in Kid Ory's band with a trumpet player called "Chif" and I'd go over sometimes and sit in. They'd get me mad by making believe I couldn't play. One by one they'd walk off the stand and leave me sitting there by myself.

After I left Dusen (my first street parade job was with Frankie Dusen's band), I joined the Tuxedo Band playing at Jack Sheen's roadhouse. Sonny Celestin was the leader with Baby Ridgeley on trombone, Bontan on guitar and bass and Lorenzo Tio, Jr. clarinet. That was my longest job in New Orleans and it was there I developed my shimmy beat. It was during the war and a French soldier came into the place and he had never heard that kind of music before. He just stood still in the middle of the dance floor and shook his body to the music, and I imitated him. He laughed and gave me money to keep it up. Everybody in the crowd liked it and then they'd call for it every night so I kept it up.

The Jazz Record

20c

No. 44

May, 1946

Baby Dodds

Tio played a marvelous clarinet. He was big and good looking with features like a Mexican. He was very comical and always playing practical jokes. Sonny used to sleep on the stand and as soon as it was time for intermission, his head would drop and he was asleep. One night Tio got a piece of paper and tied it to the back of the chair and set fire to it. Sonny would get so mad he would want to murder Tio but he could never catch him.

I was still working at Sheen's when I got a chance to play in Fate Marable's band on the Strekfus line. Pops Foster was in the band and he wanted me to come in. The boat would be tied up in New Orleans for seven months and sailing the rest of the time. We'd draw big crowds all week in New Orleans, but especially on Sundays. Bontan came out to hear the band and one Sunday he brought his nephew Zutty (Zutty Singleton). Zutty was only a kid then and he asked his uncle, "When will I ever play drums like that?" So after his uncle put him through school, he bought him a set of drums and got him started.

We were out to get Louis Armstrong away from Ory's band and we finally got him. Louis replaced Joe Oliver in Ory's band when Joe went to the coast and Joe had taken Chif's place. Ory was furious. After we got Louis, we had some band. The crowd had its own favorites—Louis would have a crowd in front of him and I'd have my crowd. I was on the end and my admirers could get all around me. It caused great competition. It was a great band but it was hard work. Fate would call a rehearsal every day and he made us read and read fast. We'd rehearse a new number once and then in front of a packed house at night, he'd pull the new number on us. It was tough but it made us alert and made musicians out of us. The owners were musicians too and they had ideas for the band. Just before I left, the boss wanted us to play "toddle-time." That's the same thing everybody's playing today—four beats to the measure—but I couldn't get it right away. I wouldn't play it then and it wasn't until later that I learned it. Louis and I left at the same time and that broke up the band but while we were together, it was the best band on the boats. The drums set the time for the music and everybody else just fell into that time and it was a smooth band. Strekfus used to tell his other bands to come over and watch us and

they had to do it. One time, when we were playing the *St. Paul*, Dewey Jackson had the band on the *J.S.* with "Red" Muse on drums, and the boss told me, "Go over and hear a real drummer."

Red caught me one night though. He was playing at the Chauffeur's Club in a trio with Charlie Creath and a piano player. Louis, Fate and I went down there one night to see the band and sit in and while we were watching the band, some of the crowd saw us and called for us to play. Well Louis did all right but I really ran into something. We sat down and played a number and I was just playing straight rhythm and didn't try any fancy stuff. But when Red got back up there, he put on a show, throwing his sticks up in the air and doing all kinds of tricks, and I didn't expect anything like that. I wasn't exactly new at the game, but at that time I went in more for straight time, and Red knew more tricks than I did. So the only thing I could do was get out of there and Louis saw me leaving and he yelled, "Hey, Pops, I'm going too." I got back at Red later on when he came over to visit us, but he was a fine drummer, one of the best on the boats.

One day, I think it was in 1920, we were going up the river and a fellow came aboard and came over to us with a suitcase. He started to tell us about three quarts of liquor he had and at that time, it was all hush-hush, as it was bootleg stuff and it came pretty high. So Fate, Louis and I made a deal with him for the suitcase. He was asking $75.00 which made 25 apiece but when the time came to get up the money Louis and Fate paid him but I was broke. Well, I had the laugh on them, because when they opened the suitcase, there were three bricks wrapped up.

After leaving Fate's band, I went back to New Orleans and it wasn't long before I got a telegram from King Oliver to come out to San Francisco. Ory and my brother were out there too but the job we had only lasted two weeks. Then I gigged round a while with Ory and Mutt Carey. Johnny and Joe didn't play much then because they both had money, so they didn't care about working hard. Another reason Johnny wanted to stay home was because Johnny, Jr. was born out there about that time. Paper money was scarce then and we used to get paid off in silver dollars and it was heavy to carry around.

Then Joe got a chance to go to Chicago to

play at the Lincoln Gardens. We had union trouble and it was about a month before we were set. After we had been playing there about a month, Joe sent for Louis to come up. I was pleased because I had a chance to work with Louis again. Our music was appreciated in Chicago and it made you free and easy. We played so much music that I dreamed about it at night and woke up thinking about it. All the musicians used to come around and watch, and leaders like Whiteman, Paul Ash and Lombardo couldn't see how we did it.

We used to make up many of the numbers we used. The whole band had a hand in them. On "Dippermouth," everybody made up his own part—Johnny made up his clarinet part and Joe his three choruses and the drum and wood-block parts I made up. We never played "Dippermouth" before with the shouting in it until we went to Richmond, Indiana, to make the records for Gennett. There had always been a drum break for me right after the trumpet choruses, but this day I forgot to make it. Bill Johnson saw I wasn't going to make it and called out, "Oh, play that thing," and everybody liked it so much, we always made it that way after that.

In 1924 the band broke up. Four of us stayed together and went over to Freddie Keppard's band at Kelly's Stables. That was Dutrey, Bill Johnson, Johnny and I, but I only stayed there about three months. It wasn't long after we joined, that Keppard had some kind of an argument with Kelly and Johnny got the band and got Natty Dominique to take Keppard's place. When I left I went over to Willie Hightower, who had come up from New Orleans with his wife. He had a good band with his wife playing piano and I stayed with him until 1926. Then I joined Hugh Swift and we played at the Evergreen Golf Club. Roy Palmer was in that band too, and Mac McKendricks on guitar and Ray Smith on piano. Hugh was a good straight trumpet player and his wife was also a good musician. She played trombone but not in the band. I was with the band about a year and it helped me to get a rounded experience. We played at Jeffrey's Tavern at 84th and Jeffrey and we did a lot of concert and semi-classical work. We broadcast every Sunday from 4:30 until 5 and we had to play numbers like "Over the Waves," "Waters Of the Minnetonka" and the "Hungarian Rhap-

sody." I have had to play all kinds of music in my life and Hugh Swift's band helped me a lot.

Next I played with Charlie Elgar at the Savoy Ballroom, but there's a story to how I got that job. Christian had the job with Elgar and when he left to go on the police force, Zutty Singleton was supposed to take his place, and I was just starting a job in a pit band. I met Zutty on the street and when I told him about the theater job, he wanted to take it. That was fine with me as I would rather work a dance job and Zutty liked the theater work. Bob Shoffner and Manuel Perez were playing with Elgar then and across from us at the Savoy was Clarence Black's band with Tubby Hall and Louis Armstrong. So Louis and I were together again, even though we were playing in different bands.

The Elgar band had a trick number at that time, which they used to pull on all new drummers and it caught all of them until I got there. I guess I was lucky though because I didn't know what they were trying to do. Everybody in that band had a big book of music with all the numbers written up and the first night I went in, they gave me my book and the trick number was buried in the middle. They called for the number right away and I finally found the sheet and set it up, and I was wondering why all the band was looking at me. In the middle of the number, the music calls for a cymbal solo, and when the rest of the band stopped, I played right along. After it was over, everybody shook hands with me and said I was the first man to make it. I thought I had done something wrong when Elgar started to come over to talk to me, but he said Swift had told him I was good, and now he knew it after that solo and he said, "Baby, you don't need to read that music, just beat those drums any way you want."

Then in 1928 I went back to Kelly's Stables in Johnny's band. Natty Dominique, Dutrey and Charlie Alexander on piano were in that band and it lasted until 1930. During that time Johnny had some dates to make records for Victor, and before that we made records with Louis while I was still at the Savoy, playing opposite Louis. On Johnny's dates, sometimes we'd use Dutrey on trombone and sometimes Ory and on some of the records I played washboard instead of drums. I didn't like the washboard because it was harder work than drumming, but whenever the studio wanted it, I made it.

After Kelly's Stables, the same band played in a basement cabaret at 18th and Indiana and it was there that Teschemacher and others used to come and sit in. Tesch was in there for the last time about a week before he was killed. Then we moved to the K-9 Club and the "29" Club at 47th and Dearborn and the Plantation at 51st and Michigan, playing all together about three years at those places. We were at the Plantation when Oliver came through on a tour with a bus-full of kids and he asked me to join his band. That was the first time he had asked me since 1924 but I wouldn't leave Johnny. Then we moved to the Stable—not Kelly's Stables—at Devon and Broadway in December 1934 and played there through 1935. I was sick for a while in '35 and had to lay off and while I was out they told the band if I didn't get back, they would lose the job, because so many people were asking for me. I still wasn't strong but was able to get back and play so we could keep our jobs. After that we played again at the "29" Club and the Plantation; until 1938. During 1939 Johnny got sick and couldn't play steady, and in 1940 I had the contract for the job, and when Johnny played, he worked under me. The place was called the "9750" Club and all week we had only Dominique and I and Leo Montgomery on piano, with Johnny coming in on Saturday nights.

In 1940 I retired from music to run my business, which I had managed off and on since 1928. I thought I had lost it a couple of times in the depression but the Fair in Chicago in 1933 pulled it through and it's been going good ever since. After I lost my brother in 1940, everybody wanted me but I finally went with Jimmy Noone. Another job was at Tin Pan Alley with Laura Rucker. Before that I almost lost my drums when the Three Deuces burned down on New Year's morning. I was there with Lonnie Johnson and Fred Reed on piano. It was a funny combination when Lonnie and I were there alone on Fred's night off, but the drums and guitar worked good together. Anyhow,' after we got through on New Year's Eve, 1940, I was home sleeping and didn't know until the next day that our union president rushed down there and got my drums out of the place. I only lost one drum-stick.

I didn't do much after that until 1944 when I was in New Orleans on a vacation and Bill Russell asked me to make some records. I went back to Chicago and before Bill sent for me, I was sick again, but I was better in time to go down and make the records in August. Then in May, 1945, I went down again to make more records for Bill. It was then that we made the brass band sides and those are the ones I want to hear. I went back to Chicago again and in September, Bill wrote me a letter to come to New York with Bunk Johnson's Band.

Pops Foster

My man Pops. I still can't realize it that he was here an' gone. Like it was only yesterday we did a show (TV) together; no big rehearsal. Just a "run-through." Pops showed me how he liked to play "Just a Closer Walk with Thee" and did it his way. I remember (on camera) that he played some phrase that had me smilin'; and Pops caught it, turned to me and said "I didn't teach you everything" (meaning of course, that he had more tricks up his sleeves).

You go back; flip the years 'ago.' There was this gig I had in Long Island (N.Y.). Pops asked me "Are you sure there's a bass there?" He wanted to avoid lugging his axe all that way if it wasn't necessary. And I told him "Pops, its a high-school; they got lots of basses." Course, what I didn't think of was Sunday, and the band-room was locked. Well, I'd brought my son Bob along; so Pops carried him here and there and everywhere on his shoulder. Showed him the town. Yeh, he got paid and Bob never forgot it. . . .

Man, you hear bass players strugglin' and sweatin' away tryin' to get the job done, and Pops did it so easy. And even in his last years he could give the next (to him) generation lessons. He walked that bass. I still remember that gig I had in Pennsy, where I brought the band from the Ole South down to State College. Bechet was our added feature attraction. It was an 8-hour drive; and we started right after we'd finished work that a.m. So you know the shape we were in when we got there. The students met us in N.Y.C. and did the driving. Plus they entertained. Pops and Baby were in one car, and Sidney (Bechet) and I in another. Boy, when they arrived, they were feelin' no pain. But good old Bechet; the professional. We had a job to play and he made them take baths and sweat it out. What a show they did that night.

And now I remember the story I want to lay on you. For Pops asked me (on the program) "Where did you go? I haven't seen you in 19 years, not since the time I stood you outside, in the alley, to cool off. It was winter, I remember, but I knew you wouldn't freeze. You had so much anti-freeze in you." (Pops describes that incident in his book.) So I answered with a question. "Pops, do you remember that State College gig? Member coming home on the bus?" Then I went on . . . as I remember it. . . .

Sidney Bechet, Pops and I took a bus home while Baby (Dodds), Henry Goodwin and George Lugg stayed around there 'bout three more days (again, as I later got the story, they tried to solve the Negro problem). . . . Anyway, after a bit, Sidney B. and I slept but Pops got involved in chatter. Last I looked he was sharing a taste and talking to a sailor. Well, the bus landed us in the Big Apple (N.Y.C.) and we got off. First thing I paid Bechet and then I started to pay Pops off. I guess he was countin' out loud for the next thing I heard was Bechet saying "You ole s. of a b. where did you leave your teeth?" Man, that was funny. Evidently, Pops got to drinkin' and his teeth got heavy. So he took 'em out (plate) and laid them down in the seat. Well, we ran ourselves down to several stations, a'lookin' for Pops' teeth, but some joker must have picked 'em up for a gag.

So, when Pops reminded me of how he had left me, back in N.Y.C. 'yars' ago, I countered with the teeth story and ended with the punch line . . . "Pops, what does a guy tell his wife when he gets home from a gig with no teeth?"   A.H.

Forty-Eight Years on the String Bass

by Pops Foster

A lot of people think I'm older than I am. That's what Mr. Hersey said when he started putting some of my thoughts down on paper. Fact is, I was born the 19th of May, 1892, on a sugar plantation about 68 miles north of New Orleans. I played around Donaldsonville, a nearby town, with my brother, Willy Foster, at every entertainment the school

Pops Foster

gave. My sister, Elizabeth, played with us, too. At that time Willy played guitar, my sister, mandolin, and I played cello.

How I happened to go to New Orleans was that my brother went to work there and my mother took me down to see him around 1902 or '03 during the Mardi Gras parade. Ma's still there and doing fine. She's in her later eighties. She speaks seven different languages and I can't speak one good one.

I played with my first little band by the name of the Rozeales Orchestra in 1907. My brother had bought me a string bass to get me off the cello. I didn't want to play anything. All I liked was the ponies. I'd bought myself a three-legged horse that always came in last. Then he died on me so I kept on snapping the strings. From Rozeales I hung around with little three-piece bands.

In 1908 I went into the Magnolia Band. We worked together for about a year. It was in demand all over town even though it was just a bunch of kids. Then King Oliver came along and wanted us to play some dates with him. He had a book thicker than the Good Book with nothing but dates in it.

"This is the guy we need in the band," was what we said, and so we took King in. We're still waiting to play even the first date that Joe Oliver—that's what we called him then—had in his book.

But the band jumped sky high the minute he joined us so we made a few changes to liven up the group in the way it was done in those days. You just left a letter under the door of the guy who was to be fired. No two weeks notice! The guy would wake up in the morning and find he was out. Like as not it didn't worry him any—he'd soon be playing with some other band.

Freddie Keppard's brother, Louis, was the manager of the Magnolias. There was Honore Dutrey, Emile Bigard, and a kid on the drums named Chris.

We had a date for a dance in Homer, Louisiana, and we got invited for dinner. King ate so much that the man made us pay for the meal. At times he used to get three bottles of milk and about fifteen hamburgers. A hamburger in those days was really King size. He also topped off his supper with a dozen bananas for a nickle.

In later years I was with the Ory band, Jack Carey's band and the Spanish Fort band. Then Peter Bocage and Captain Johnny of the Riverboat Line asked me to come on the boats. This was when the yellow fever hit New Orleans. We worked only awhile before they shut everything down.

But we were back on the boats by the middle of 1918. The men in that band were Fate Marable, Peter Bocage, Frank Dusen, Alexander Lewis, Johnny St. Cyr, Dave Jones, Charley McCurtis, Emanuel Perez. This was the first band. The second band was myself, Fate Marable, Johnny St. Cyr, Baby Dodds, Sam Dutrey, Dave Jones, Joe Howard, William Ridgely and Louis Armstrong. This was the first colored band that ever played in St. Louis for a white dance. We had guards around the music stand but we didn't even know they were there until the season closed. We never had any trouble.

I've been a long way since then with my antique playing.

I came to New York in 1929 and have played with all the present day jazz greats.

It's been nice going. I'd like to have a few more years rompin' the big fiddle.

The Blues for Jimmy

by Vincent McHugh

All that February it rained, a maddening cold pour that made the royal palms look like draggletail ballet dancers. You walked down Hollywood Boulevard to the white banner with Jimmy Noone's name on it, and down the headlong pitch of the stairs into a big, damp joint like an abandoned automobile showroom, with pillars, a curved bar in the middle, and a bandstand inside the bar. There were always scads of soldiers and sailors dancing with the funny rag dolls they use for girls in Hollywood, and quieter people who came for the music but didn't always have their boots laced up. What with Ida James, Helen Humes and Gladys Palmer, the amount of bouncing female vitality on the stand warmed the dreary place up a little. But you were waiting.

Then Jimmy, coming out along the far wall, walking easily with a kind of thoughtful composure. His Roman senator's head, the firm, egg-shaped torso in the blue suit, made him look like a good courtroom lawyer. He would climb up on the stand, nod to a couple of friends, play a ripple or two, and stamp it off. The young bass player would mug and twirl his blond fiddle on its axis, the pianist did flashy stuff, and the drummer would get excited and keep tapping a cymbal in a very bad and busy way behind one of Jimmy's choruses.

But the choruses were coming out. The fine choruses—as fine as any on the too-few records from the Apex Club days, and before, to "The Blues Jumped a Rabbit." It didn't much matter what they were: a melodious pop called "My Heart Tells Me" or the signature, "Sweet Lorraine," done all the way through. That mellow, round, easy, warm New Orleans tone, given a slight whiskey-sour edge by the long Chicago influence. The whippoorwill wail, and the whippoorwill double-stopping that was like a trademark.

The glide up or down to a note and the deft mixture of melodic phrases with agile runs. The almost classical sense of form that could hang a chorus in the air and give it its own light shape and balance. All the wonderful, unshowy elegance and finesse of the thing. Some of it pleased you because it was so perfectly in the New Orleans clarinet tradition, but all of it was Jimmy.

That Wednesday in April he died. He was happy, except for the usual thing about a contract and a chiseling manager. He'd had it hard, very hard, for a while in Chicago. They said his music was old-fashioned. But now it was coming out all right. He got up that morning feeling fine and said to his wife that he'd either have to get a haircut or carry a violin case to work. Then he went into the bathroom and in a few minutes she heard him thump against the wall. When she went in and touched him he was dead, and after the doctor came and she was sure he was dead she had him carried out so that the children wouldn't know.

But they asked, and at first she told them he'd been taken to the hospital. She took Jimmy, Junior, his son, for a long walk. She said that his daddy had been taken to a hospital but they couldn't do anything for him. Then why didn't they take him to another hospital? Because he's dead, Jimmy's wife said. You won't see your daddy any more. The boy took it hard. But he was a good daddy, Mrs. Noone said after a while. He left you his diamond ring and his gold watch and his clarinet. Only a good daddy would do that. He wanted you to grow up and play the clarinet like him.

That Wednesday night the band of New Orleans veterans Jimmy had played with moved into the white Lescaze studio on Sunset Boulevard and played the blues for Jimmy. Many people heard Orson Welles speak the grave and tender promises of the Twenty-Third Psalm. But only a few people could see Kid Ory's face as he blew the long phrases of lament, or Zutty's big shoulders bowed and crying over the drums. Gone from Iberville, gone from Calumet. Yes, gone from Iberville, gone from Calumet. I won't see you baby, but you know I won't forget.

That Saturday they buried him from the very modern and correct mortuary on Jefferson Boulevard, off Central Avenue. Forty or fifty people in the straight white pews of the Georgian funeral chapel. The music of a Hammond organ flowed through the room and a warm Negro contralto with a silvery vibrato sang "Just A-Wearyin' for You." A young white sailor sat there crying with his face up. Nobody knew who he was. Some of Jimmy's friends got up and said that he had been a good man and a fine musician. The preacher, who had a North Carolina accent, said some musicians didn't talk very well. They didn't need to. They talked with their music, and that was what made people love them. He said David was a musician too.

Someone parted the gray curtains in the front of the room and Jimmy's face lay there. The casket and the wall behind him and the floor all around were covered with the abundant flowers of the Los Angeles spring: roses and lilies, stocks, gardenias, jonquils. People came out row by row—Nappy Lamare, Matty Matlock, Marge Singleton, Joe Sullivan, Gladys Palmer—and went up and looked at him. The last to come out were the bearers in the front row. The boys from Jimmy's band at the club. Tall, gray Papa Mutt and the small, graying Kid Ory. Dooley Wilson and Bud Scott. Zutty Singleton, walking softly. There was the unbearable crying of a woman behind the looped curtains as people went out into the pale sunlight under the glistening pepper trees.

A motorcycle escort led the line of cars to Evergreen Cemetery. An open, sandy slope, pale green, with two or three big palms in the distance, under the warm blue sky. They had hung a tarpaulin on the cyclone fence behind the grave. The eight bearers lifted the coffin, Zutty's big shoulders at the forward end cradling it down in the ruts. People formed up in twos behind, like the second line of a New Orleans funeral. The undertaker prayed and they stood a moment in the listening sunlight. The wind had spilled a few loose flowers off the casket. Some of the women picked them up and put them into their handbags as they walked away.

A Tribute to Joe Darensbourg

by John Wittwer

I first met Joe Darensbourg six or seven years ago when I got a job playing piano in a honky-tonk outside the city limits of Seattle. It was a three piece band, alto sax, drums, and piano; I got the job through the drummer. At first I thought Joe was Italian, or maybe Greek, but I found out later that he was a Creole. At that time I still hadn't gone overboard for New Orleans music, but as soon as I heard Joe play a few numbers, I knew that here was something special, even if it was on an alto sax. I worked that job for a while without ever hearing Joe play clarinet—it was in hock, or lost, or something, but I got to like Joe and his playing; he had had a very colorful life, and in his soft

Louisiana accent he told me many stories of his adventures, all true, too, and the time he asked Bessie Smith for a date and she told him, "Run along, sonny, you're too young for me."

Well, I took another job and lost track of Joe for a while. I would see him now and then, but I didn't hear him play and we didn't work together. Then, about three years later, I wandered into an after hour joint just off Seattle's Jackson Street, and there was Joe in another three piece band. He said, "Hi Wittwer, come on, sit in." I said, "Let's play 'Ballin' the Jack.' " He picked up a clarinet, and when we finished I realized that Joe was even better than I thought he was. For an hour or so we played a lot of tunes like that—tunes that Joe used to play and had forgotten he knew—tunes that I had learned from records. After the place closed I took Joe home in my car; we talked and chatted, and it was then I discovered that he knew Kid Ory and had even played with him and Mutt Carey in Los Angeles in the twenties.

At this time I had known Dr. Exner for quite a while, and the next day I excitedly told him the details of the great find, a real New Orleans clarinetist in Seattle! Well, nothing special happened for a while; then I finally got a chance to put a band into the China Pheasant, a night club, and a pretty dicty one at that. At first Joe couldn't play with us; he was on a steady job that paid him a lot more than I could, because it was an after hour joint with a big kitty. However, Dr. Exner and I were resolved to work toward getting recognition for Joe, and the first step was to get him out of the grind outfit he was playing in and get him into a jazz band where we, and others, could really appreciate him. Finally, after I badgered him for a while, Joe decided to play in my band.

My band was certainly no great shakes as a jazz band; the shortage of musicians was terrible. I couldn't find a good trombone player at all, so I took up the trombone and supplied that deficiency as well as I could. I would play piano most of the way through a tune and then jump to trombone for the last ensemble choruses. There weren't any musicians in town who knew anything about New Orleans jazz, but I managed to find some who turned out pretty good.—Keith Purvis, the drummer, in particular. Keith was playing in a kid swing band (he was only sixteen) and

Joe Darensbourg and Johnny Wittwer

although he was fooled by the modern jumping jive cats he had a pretty good beat, and after a few months of intensive listening to the Dodds brothers, Bunk, Louis, Ory, Lewis, etc. at the Doc's house and mine, he naturally realized that this was the best kind of music, as would any intelligent person, and his playing improved accordingly. He especially liked Dodds on the Morton trio of *Mr. Jelly Lord*, and he patterned his playing that way. He and I both thought it was much better to work on getting a fine relaxed brush beat than to fool around with a lot of woodblocks and stuff and forget the beat. I never did manage to find a good trumpet player except when I met Bob Scobey, who was with the Lu Watters band before he went into the Army; Scobey was in a band stationed in Seattle. After I ran into him, he played with us often; he is a wonderful trumpet player, and greatly under-rated; he plays a pure, non-exhibitionistic Joe Oliver style.

All this time Joe, Keith, Bob and I were constant visitors at the Doc's house, to listen to his fine collection and to jam. Well, after Keith got to playing good the Doc said that he sure would like to record us. He thought Joe was too good to keep under wraps and that everybody ought to hear him; and I guess he liked my playing too. We got together and made the four trio sides. That was October, 1944, and my band was still playing every night. After we made the trio sides I took a week off and came to Los Angeles to hear Ory at the Tip-Toe Inn. Ory was playing fine, although most of the time he played bass; Buster Wilson and Alton Redd supplied fine rhythm and fine vocals, but the trumpet player did not fit in at all.

After I met Ory and got to talking to him, he wanted to know how Joe was and how he was playing; I told him, and he told me a lot about Joe when they used to work together. I was much impressed with the way Ory sounded (I had never heard him in person before), and I thought how fine it would be to hear Joe and Ory together, with Papa Mutt. So, when I went back to Seattle I told the Doc my adventures and we both realized that we sure as hell ought to have some records of Ory's band with Joe. Ory was happy about the whole thing, so Joe came down and played at the Tip-Toe Inn for a while in place of the trumpet player, and then the records were made. (My band broke up ignominiously; we were playing way too much jazz for the society crowd.)

Anyone who had bought the Crescents naturally wanted more records of the band, playing the good tunes, and Dr. Exner was no exception. He thought the Crescents were terrific; his main interest was in doing a favor for Joe and for jazz lovers,—nobody else would have recorded Joe, because Joe had been in Seattle so long and nobody knew about him.

Dr. Exner and I have been hoping for a long time that sooner or later people will realize that Joe Darensbourg belongs in the great New Orleans tradition, that he is in the same class with the other great clarinetists. The fortunate people who have heard Joe with Ory's band at the Jade in Hollywood know how good he is; he is used to playing with the guys now and has been playing gorgeous stuff night after night.

Incidentally, the records bear Dr. Exner's name because Joe and I and the fans in Seattle insisted on it; we thought he deserved that much credit at least, because these records are going to take their place in the recorded history of the best music of the Negro and Creole musicians of New Orleans.

May, 1917—May, 1947

Few dates in jazz history are of greater importance than that day in May, 1917—exactly thirty years ago when five young men piled into Victor's New York studio with their instruments and arranged themselves in front of a strange looking acoustic recording apparatus. When they finished playing on that momentous occasion, jazz was on its way to immortality. We pay our respects to those five men who called themselves "The Original Dixieland Jazz Band."

The first two sides that Nick LaRocca, Larry Shields, Eddie Edwards, Henry Ragas, and Tony Sbarbaro cut in May, 1917, were "Livery Stable Blues" and "Dixieland Jass One-step." So popular was this first recording that it led to many more. Eddie Edwards is somewhat stouter now, his hair whiter and sparser. It was a curious experience for many of us, who consider ourselves grownup, when Edwards and Tony Sbarbaro appeared at a recent New York jazz concert. Eddie talked about the old times. His simple, direct words told of the turbulent Chicago days, success in New York, recording and night-spot dates. They had played that kind of music ever since they were kids. They adored and imitated jazz men then, the way youngsters of our time regard their screen idols. The name "Reisenweber's" can still be discerned on a building around Columbus Circle. It was there that The Original Dixieland Jazz Band had one of its most successful engagements. Reisenweber's doesn't exist today. Neither does the group that brought jazz to New York.

JIMMY ERNST

Once Upon a Time

by Eddie Edwards

Thirty years is a long time, and that, to the month, is exactly how long it's been since the Original Dixieland Band set the musical world on its ear by the band's first recording. There's a story wrapped around it that I'd like to tell.

In 1916 the band left New Orleans and went to Chicago to play a few cafe jobs. We had Nick LaRocca on trumpet, Larry Shields on clarinet, myself on trombone, Henry Ragas on piano, and Tony Spargo (Sbarbaro) on drums. Till the time we hit Chicago we'd never used the word jazz in connection with the band, because it had nasty connotations. But one of our bosses, Harry James (no relation to the musical James family) thought that it would be a good word. It would make people wonder what it was all about.

We were very successful in Chicago, but always in the back of my mind was the thought that we had to get to New York. Since I was also the manager of the band I wrote dozens of letters to agents and cafe owners there but never got an answer. Then one night, after a year in Chicago—we were working at the Casino Gardens—the crowd from the touring Ziegfeld Follies came in the place. I remember there was Eddie Cantor, Bert Williams, W. C. Fields, and Fanny Brice. Later Al Jolson came in with a big New York agent, Max Hart, who heard the band and immediately offered us a booking.

Most of the boys didn't want to leave Chicago. Larry Shields had once been there with an act, and he really had a tough time. We were making forty dollars a week at the Casino Gardens, and Larry convinced the rest of the band that we shouldn't leave. But when Max Hart gave us the chance, I couldn't see turning it down. So we came to Reisenweber's on a three-week engagement. We didn't leave for quite a while.

At first it was very tough. No one knew what we were doing. The people would neither applaud nor dance to the music. Some critics rapped the band very badly, but then others, progressive writers, convinced the public that here was something new that should at least be heard. The press did a great deal to make us. Another thing that helped a lot was the fact that show people started coming in. Professional dancers like Clayton and Powell came around and showed the customers how to dance to the music. Then the craze started.

Our first offer for recording came in early 1917 from Columbia. We went up to make two sides. But there it was the same old story. No one knew what we were trying to do, and the date was sabotaged. They were building shelves in the studio and kept hammering away while we tried to play. Also in the middle of cutting a side people kept running in and out, causing all kinds of confusion. The sides were never released. A short while later Victor picked us up, and we made our first release, "Livery Stable Blues" and "Original Dixieland One-Step." The recording director on that date was a young unknown assistant, Charles Souey. He did such a wonderful job with the band that he soon became top recording expert for Victor and later was sent to London to straighten out H. M. V.

In those days you blew into a four-foot horn with an eight-inch bell on the end. The horn led to the receiving wax. You couldn't play tests back, and we cut three masters of each tune to make sure that one would be good. With this horn you couldn't use a bass drum, which vibrated too much, or a snare drum, which came out blurred. Tony Spargo had to beat only on the cow bells, wood blocks, and sides of the drums. As a result, a

MAY 1947
No.55

25¢

JAZZ RECORD

THE ORIGINAL DIXIELAND JAZZ BAND

The Original Dixieland Jazz Band. Tony Sbarbaro, drums; Henry Ragas, piano; Larry Shields, clarinet; Eddie Edwards, trombone; Nick LaRocca, trumpet

great many drummers were influenced who heard only the record and didn't realize that the bass and snares were integral parts of Dixieland drumming.

Victor made the two sides as only novelties and didn't want us anymore. So we made another deal with Columbia to make another record. When it was released it was such a good seller that Victor called us back and made the series that are now so famous.

After we left Reisenweber's we played the Keith Vaudeville Circuit and then went to London to work a musical, *Joybells*. While in London we held three jobs at the same time. The Prince of Wales used to come into the Bond Club almost every night to hear us play. One time Shields and Spargo tried to crash Buckingham Palace and almost got shot. They just wanted to see the King.

Following a year and a half in London we came back to New York for another year and a half at the Folies Bergère. That takes us up to 1921, and in the summer of that year we played a season at Atlantic City. Then started the first of many road tours and one-night stands.

Today the boys are spread out all over the country. Shields is on the coast, Spargo lives in Queens and is doing society work, LaRocca is back in New Orleans, and I'm jobbing around New York. Our original piano player, Ragas, died while we were at Reisenweber's and we took on Russell Robinson who is out in California now.

Before we left New Orleans the first time, we tried to get Emile Christian to come along as cornetist. But Emile was playing parades at three dollars a parade and didn't want to leave all that good money. We also tried to get Tony Parenti for clarinetist but he was too young at the time, and Larry took the job. An interesting point is that although the band is known by many people as Nick LaRocca's Original Dixieland Band, it was actually the first cooperative band that I know of. We worked it that way to cut down in dissension. No one made any more than anyone else.

Yes, thirty years is a long time, and jazz has come a long way since we made that first Victor record. I have a complete set of the records we made, but I don't think I've played them more than three times. I like to think and talk about the band, though. Those were fine times, and we had a lot of fun.

Kid Ory

When I first heard Louis Armstrong (and it was on recordings) I was fascinated with the star; the soloist. Looking back, I can compare this first listening to my first viewing of a football game. All I could see was the ball carrier. Much later I heard of the players who sprung the carrier free; here was more to the game than the one fellow carrying the ball and making the touchdown. So, as I listened and listened to jazz recordings I found there was more to the music than just the soloist; much more. There was the clarinetist, weaving around the melody horn, and there was the trombonist, making the necessary fills. They were all essential (equally) to this New Orleans jazz music that was capturing my ears.

In jazz, if you're a player, eventually you'll meet all the other performers in your business; well, not all. Some may wander to the west coast as you travel east. This happened to me; I spent the years in New York City and Chicago at about the same time Kid Ory was homing in Los Angeles. We never met; I can't talk about the man. But I know his music; I know his musical thinking. I read him loud and clear. For without a doubt, here is the top tail-gate trombonist in jazz; there may be others, equally great or greater but they never came to the front an' center as did Ory. So when I heard the Armstrong Hot Five recordings I heard Ory; I listened and listened to his "Muskrat Ramble" (for years this, his own tune, was No. 2 on the Dixieland Hit Parade); I heard him. I feel like I know the man. In my book there is no other reason for blowing trombone in a dixie-style combo but to lay it in there; Kid Ory knew how; he still does.

A.H.

Kid Ory

by Alma Hubner

I

Edward "Kid" Ory was born on Christmas Day, 1889, at La Place, Louisiana. Little did his parents suspect that their Christmas bundle of joy would turn out to be the greatest trombone pioneer in jazz history. The word *jazz* was unknown in 1889, not even Buddy Bolden had come into prominence at that time. It was still a world of minstrelsy and the French Opera. Kid is of Creole origin, that interesting mixture of the African and French race so common to Louisiana, particularly New Orleans. He doesn't possess any of the characteristics of the Negro (physical or cultural) outside of an unusually good humor and an extraordinary musical instinct.

Kid Ory was able to speak the Creole *patois* from his very early youth. Only recently he resurrected his *patois* on a recording for Nesuhi Ertegun's and Marili Morden's Crescent label, "Creole Song," in which he sings a delightful jumble of exotic speech which reveals traces of French, Spanish, English and African dialects.

At 11 Kid was leader of a string quintet, in which he and four other neighborhood kids played for kicks. They manufactured their own instruments out of pieces of tin, cork, wood and strings of varied kinds. This group became so proficient that it was hired for dances and all sorts of town festivities. The money that the kids received for their playing was saved for buying professional instruments.

Trombones always fascinated Kid, he loved the way they showed off on brass band street parades. Consequently, as soon as he accumulated enough money, he purchased a trombone on one of his occasional trips to New Orleans. It was on one of those trips that Kid first met the famous barber of Franklin Street, the renowned trumpeter Buddy Bolden. They became good friends. Often "King" Bolden would invite Kid to sit in with his band, he did so consistently during

Kid Ory's Band, California, 1922. Ory, Trombone; Papa Mutt Carey, trumpet; Fred Washington, piano; Bud Scott, banjo; Pops Foster, bass and tuba.

1905-'10, the years that saw the Bolden Band at its peak. Sitting in with Bolden's boys Kid was able to familiarize himself with the style of trombonist Frankie Dusen, one of the outstanding early New Orleans trombone players along with George Filhe and Zue Robertson. During these years, and later, Kid was also taking legitimate trombone lessons from one of the prominent New Orleans instructors.

In 1911 La Place witnessed a migration of the Ory troupe to New Orleans. Kid and his boys found many jobs in Storyville cabarets during 1911-18. At the time Kid was one of the most popular leaders of the town, his band could be heard everywhere: at funerals, street parades, lawn parties and even on advertising wagons. One of Kid's most popular bands in 1915 included such men as King Oliver, cornet; Sidney Bechet, clarinet; Louis Keppard, guitar, and Henry Morton, drums.

The successful roamings of Jelly Roll Morton (California), Freddy Keppard (Chicago) and others caused some unrest in Kid Ory's mind. Storyville was closed down by the authorities in 1918 and King Oliver left for Chicago. Kid decided to do some exploring on his own and set off towards California. In 1919 he called his New Orleans gang to join him in California. They remained in Los Angeles, playing city night spots as well as the suburbs, until 1924. It is strange that fate should choose Los Angeles, the city where he began his long musical career, as the place where Kid has come to achieve his greatest success. Now he can play real New Orleans jazz in a commercial night club without having requests for the "Missouri Waltz," or "Frenesi," it's strictly "Muskrat Ramble," "High Society" and "Fidgety Feet" all the way through.

According to the information given in *The Jazz Record Book*, Ory was the first to record New Orleans Negro jazz. It was in Los Angeles, in 1921, that Kid Ory's Brownskinned Band recorded for Spikes Brothers, music publishers. The record was issued under the pseudonym "Spikes Seven Pods of Pepper Orchestra," it included the following personnel: Mutt Carey, cornet; Kid Ory, trombone; Dink Johnson, clarinet; Fred Washington, piano; Ed Garland, bass and Ben Borders, drums. The tunes recorded were "Ory's Creole Trombone" and "Society

Blues." Charles Edward Smith stated (*The Jazz Record Book*) that's Ory's playing on this early version of his celebrated creation is a match for the later one (1927) recorded with Armstrong's Hot Seven. It seems almost incredible that today, twenty-four years after, two of the men in this historic group are actually playing with Kid Ory in Hollywood. There must exist strong ties of friendship and musical respect between Kid, Mutt Carey and Ed Garland. For Mutt Carey, though he is unaware of it, is undoubtedly one of the greatest trumpet players in jazz. When he is properly recorded there will be many who will agree with me after hearing him. Papa Mutt is such a friendly, modest fellow that when I asked him to autograph a picture he wrote down "From Pops Mutt" then chuckled and said: "I better put 'Carey' down or you won't know who it is." You could say that Ory's actual band is made up entirely of friends. Carey and Garland have been friends of his along the years. Buster Wilson played with Kid during his sojourn in California in the early 20's. Bud Scott and Kid were pals in King Oliver's band in Chicago. Even Minor Hall had known Kid during his youth in New Orleans.

California was undergoing a jazz invasion in 1921, what with Kid Ory's Brownskinned Band playing in Los Angeles, King Oliver's Creole Jazz Band and Jelly Roll Morton touring theaters and ballrooms throughout the state. Ory then re-encountered his friend Joe Oliver, whom he was later to join in Chicago. It was in 1924, to be exact, that Kid Ory arrived in Chicago. Business was slack in California so his band broke up, even Jelly Roll Morton deserted California for Chicago in '24. It was also in that year that Louis Armstrong abandoned King Oliver's band in Chicago, organizing his own group with Lil Armstrong. So when Kid blew in from California looking forlorn and feeling lonesome his friend Louis caught hold of him and incorporated him into the Armstrong troupe. Louis soon left for New York to join Fletcher Henderson's band so Kid was left to look out for himself. He became part of King Oliver's band that same year, in which he played until 1927. From 1924 to '27 the Oliver band could be heard mostly at the South Side's Plantation Cafè, situated in what the jazz enthusiasts denominate "Chicago's hot corner": 35th Street and Calumet. King Oliver's Dixie

Syncopators recorded many sides for the Vocalion label with the following personnel: Joe Oliver and Bob Shoffner, cornets; Kid Ory, trombone; Barney Bigard, Darnell Howard, Albert Nicholas, reeds; Luis Russell, piano; Bud Scott, banjo; Bert Cobb, tuba and Paul Barbarin, drums. Ory plays magnificently on numbers such as "Tack Annie," "Jackass Blues," "West End Blues," "Sugarfoot Stomp" and "Snag It." The last two numbers were re-issued, the first on UHCA and the second on the Brunswick Collectors Series, "Riverboat Jazz" album. These numbers were recorded in 1926.

II

The years 1925-'27 saw Kid Ory practically living at Chicago's recording studios. It was at this time that he waxed 90 percent of the discs that have made him famous. To start off with we should recall the magnificent recordings he made with Louis Armstrong's Hot Five (1925-26) and Hot Seven (1927). With the Hot Seven he recorded classics like "Ory's Creole Trombone," "Twelfth Street Rag," "Potato Head Blues" and "S.O.L. Blues" which alone set him off as the most outstanding jazz trombonist on record. His records with the Hot Five are too numerous to mention, but we might as well list "Muskrat Ramble" as *the* number that has won him most acclaim. Kid composed "Muskrat Ramble" in 1926 and recorded it the same year. The title has often appeared as Muskat instead of Muskrat. When interviewing Kid I asked him which of the two was correct, he replied: "I originally titled the number Muskrat Ramble because I had thought of a little muskrat rambling around and the music seemed to illustrate the idea. When the number was published by Melrose in Chicago he thought that the name 'Muskrat' wasn't nice, so he blotted out the 'r' and called it 'Muskat,' which doesn't come anywhere near a muskrat."

In 1926 Kid also recorded with Luis Russell's Heebie Jeebie Stompers and with the New Orleans Wanderers. The latter group was brought together by Lil Armstrong for a recording date, it included such jazz aces as George Mitchell, Kid Ory, Johnny Dodds, Stump Evans, Buddy St. Cyr and Lil herself on piano. Four sides were made, two of which have been re-issued by UHCA, they

are "Perdido Street Blues" and "Gatemouth." The Hot Five recorded two amazing sides in '26 for Vocalion under the pseudonym Lill's Hot Shots: "Georgia Bo Bo" and "Drop That Sack." Both were re-issued this year in the Brunswick Collectors Series "Louis Armstrong" album. Ory's solo on "Drop That Sack" is perhaps the greatest he has ever recorded. Had he never waxed a single number besides "Drop That Sack," it alone would be sufficient to distinguish him as one of the most outstanding jazz trombonists of all time.

Ory's association with Jelly Roll Morton during 1926 resulted in a number of the most exciting jazz recordings ever made, the Red Hot Peppers sides for Bluebird. It is apparent that Ory did not appear on all of the Red Hot Peppers discs as the personnel for some is still unknown, however, his presence on at least ten sides has been ascertained. Of these, "Cannon Ball Blues," "Black Bottom Stomp" and "Dead Man Blues" should be mentioned for brilliant trombone improvisations. The George Mitchell-Kid Ory-Omer Simeon combination on the Red Hot Peppers recordings is as unique as the Armstrong-Ory-Dodds triumvirate.

King Oliver's band broke up in 1927 and Luis Russell retained most of the musicians to organize a new band, soon leaving Chicago for the East. Kid did not join Russell because he wished to remain in Chicago. In 1928 he played with Dave Peyton's Symphonic Syncopators which at one time harbored both King Oliver and Pops Foster. In rapid succession he was with Clarence Black (1928-29) and with the Chicago Vagabonds. Then came the great financial crisis that shook the United States, the effects of which so few could estimate at the time. Jobs for musicians became scarce in the Windy City so Kid decided to return to sunny California. He was heard playing with different bands around Los Angeles until 1931, then retired from music to take up chicken ranching with his brother. So absorbed was he in the mysteries of the chicken coop that he had almost entirely forgotten his music. In 1938 his brother's sudden death and the spectacular upsurge of "swing" induced him to return to jazz. His composition "Muskrat Ramble" was successfully published at the time, this injected the required stamina into Kid's veins and he started writing again with renewed vigor. Proof of his prolific work of these years is the large number of new compositions that his new band plays at the Jade Palace. Perhaps in a few years we'll "discover" new jazz classics after the fashion of "Ory's Creole Trombone" and "Muskrat Ramble."

In 1942 Kid played trombone and doubled on string bass in Barney Bigard's band at the Club Capri in Los Angeles. It was his first public appearance with a band since 1931. He was heard frequently in Hollywood jam sessions, where you often expected Mickey Rooney to pop up at the wrong time and borrow your instrument for a laugh. Through the efforts of Rudi Blesh, Kid was able to appear at the Bunk Johnson jazz concerts held in San Francisco's Geary Theater in 1948. These concerts were sponsored by the San Francisco Museum of Modern Art. In 1944 Kid could be heard every Wednesday night on Orson Welles' broadcasts. In the Spring of that year he broadcast from San Francisco for California's Standard Oil Co., which produced a radio series on American music, the New Orleans part being handled by Ory and a group of Crescent City old-timers. The Orson Welles programs featured the following personnel: Mutt Carey, trumpet; Kid Ory, trombone; Jimmie Noone, clarinet; Buster Wilson, piano; Bud Scott, guitar; Ed Garland, bass, and Zutty Singleton, drums. Jimmy Noone's unexpected death in April ('44) left the group minus a clarinetist so Wade Whaley (whom George Avakian seems to rate highly) was called on to take Jimmie's place. Ory headed this same group for the Standard Oil broadcasts.

It was also in 1944 that Kid waxed the Crescent records that everybody is raving about. The band included the same men who are actually playing with Ory in Hollywood, with the exception of Omer Simeon, who played clarinet on the date, and drummer Alton Redd. The tunes cut were "South," "Creole Song," "Blues for Jimmy" and "Get Out of Here." The success of these records was so great that in a short while the Jazz Man Record Shop sold out its entire supply and wasn't able to re-press any right away due to shellac shortage.

On April 1, 1945, Kid Ory and his Creole Jazz Band went into the Jade Palace. I think that a letter I received from Marili Morden best describes the story of Kid's success, so I shall quote a paragraph: "It is now quite impossible to have anything resembling solitude when listening to Kid Ory's Band—as a matter of fact, one is lucky to get a seat within listening distance. Yes, the place is really packed, particularly on week-ends when the crowd stands two deep at the bar. And so many people have been telling me for months past that the band was fine but wouldn't draw enough business for anyone to risk hiring them. Other night club owners, who previously had every opportunity to hire them, are now trying to lure them away from the Jade. Of course, Ory won't leave, being a man of his word. He'll be here at least another four months, barring the usual unforeseen circumstances of war, etc." This letter was written June 25th, barely over two months after Kid's opening at the Jade Palace. I would like to add that the band has been recorded by Decca for the benefit of those who don't live within taxi-distance of Hollywood's Jade Palace.

Many have said that Kid Ory's new band is the best jazz band that has existed since 1927, many might disagree but I think so too. There is no explanation for it except that it is jazz played in its purest form. It is genuine. It is relaxed. It is carefree, sincere and in good taste. It is New Orleans! There are many who say also that Kid is playing more and better now, with a profounder feeling and a greater depth to his playing, than he was 20 years ago.

You might say that Ory's boys improvise with the enthusiasm of the Hot Seven, the freshness and dynamic characteristics of the Red Hot Peppers and the great musical attributes of King Oliver's Creole Jazz Band. All this without surface noise. It is a *dream band*. Could there be anything finer? Jazz fans of "the righteous stuff" are rejoicing the world over because Kid Ory is back to stay and with him New Orleans jazz.

Folk Jazz

I can remember Bunk Johnson coming to New York City; opening night at the Stuyvesant Casino, a Jewish catering hall on the East Side . . . sometime in the mid-forties. I didn't miss a night of that band's engagement . . . seven-piece band. They'd play a tune like "Tiger Rag" at a real easy danceable tempo; and the dancers would be out there on the floor, and it would be so good, that they'd do an encore; same tune, same tempo . . . and hold that audience . . . never seen anything like it. Bunk was musical; anything he played, he could sing. . . . In fact, his music sang itself out of him into his horn. He was somethin' to watch too, for Bunk was natural; he'd feel like goin' to sleep and it didn't matter; he'd sleep right on the bandstand . . . in front of everybody, in the same chair he'd been blowin' in. Some one called Wild Bill Davison to rush over and sub; Bill doesn't blow soft . . . you can hear him. Bunk just slept through the rest of the evening . . . it was somethin' to see. Yeh, but that was a band to remember; they had a sound all their own . . . fresh-like. I always felt I'd rather hear the band than sit in and play in it; it was like hearing something primitive and not wanting to spoil it or change it; just enjoy it.

A.H.

A Letter from Bunk

Bunk Johnson, the almost legendary trumpet player of the early New Orleans days, is now living in New Iberia, Louisiana, and times are hard. The following letter was received by Isidore Schoenberg, fifteen-year-old New York jazz enthusiast, and speaks for itself. Mr. Schoenberg is interested in doing anything he can to help Bunk get started again. Anyone who would like to help can do so by getting in touch with Schoenberg at 80 East 7th Street, New York, or with Bunk Johnson direct at the address below—EDITORS.

511 Providence Street
New Iberia, La.

Dear Mr. Isidore:

Just a few lines to let you hear from me, and also to let you know that I am feeling a lot better at this present time, and hope that this letter will find you and your dear family well and enjoying the very best of happiness.

Now I did enjoy your very fine letter that you wrote to me, and it made me feel about

Bunk Johnson

thirty years younger, when I was in my prime and really could make a band go, but . . .

Now I have gotten to be an old man, but I can yet play a mean trumpet. Now I have been down sick for three long months, and unable to help myself, but any way, God is good to me and I'm back up on my feet once more.

And I do hope to stay up, so I can get a job of some kind, as I do not have any money at all to live off and have been down sick and no job at all; so you know just what shape I'm in, and it is real cold here and I do not have the money to buy me coal or wood at this present.

Now, Mr. Isidore, the 27th of December I passed my 63rd year; now I was born December the 27th, 1879, so you know by that I have been here a long long time, and I do wish that I can make 63 more, so you please write me when you have a little spare time so I will know if you received my little picture. Good day and good luck to you.

Sincerely yours,

WILLIE (BUNK) JOHNSON.

Jam Session with Bunk

by Lewis Eaton

One of the finest things in jazz happened to New York last Sunday and I was very fortunate to be there when it happened.

I had heard Sunday morning that Bunk Johnson was in town and verified it thru collectors in the know. He had been here since Friday and was scheduled to play at Gabler's session at Ryan's, so I made it a point to get out there early. Arriving about 4 o'clock, my wife and I decided to have a couple in the White Rose. We had no more than ordered our drinks when she spotted Bechet going by. I turned in time to see that Bunk was with him so out I went. Catching up to them, I greeted Sidney and invited them in for a drink as it was very early (I never expected to see musicians show up an hour in advance for a session). Bechet called Bunk, who had courteously waited two or three steps away while we were talking, and introduced us. Acknowledging the introduction, I told Bunk I had been looking forward for a long time to shaking his hand. He smiled in genuine pleasure.

He readily consented to go back to the White Rose with us and shortly after introducing him to Marge, Bechet joined us also. I guess we were there for about three quarters of an hour, before Bechet left first as he was scheduled to go on, and we promised to bring Bunk over in a few minutes. But for the time we were there, it was a great pleasure to visit with Bunk. He was one of the finest gentlemen I've ever met, both in his speech and his manners, and not at all an illiterate black man from Iberia, La., as might be gathered from previous stories. He mentioned going to college, I think at Tuskegee Institute. He has a family of twelve, eleven of which are living and all have finished their education, with the exception of the youngest girl who is still in college. His second wife is Maude Baquet, sister of Geo. Baquet, N. O. clarinet player who recorded with Jelly Roll. Of the eleven children, six boys are in the service and he was hoping to meet one of his sons, who is stationed in Boston at present. Some of his children are musically inclined, the son in Boston being a fine piano player, Bunk says.

I asked many questions about music in New Orleans, as that is my favorite. Bunk had worked recently with George Lewis, Jim Robinson and others. He didn't recall running into Herb Morand, who is supposed to be back in N. O. He said he didn't have too much time to look around. If he played in N. O., he'd travel to town for the job and leave for home directly after. And his work wasn't all music. He showed me his hands, which are tough and calloused from driving a truck and trailer to make a living.

Knowing he worked with Buddy Bolden, I asked him how Buddy compared with Oliver and Keppard. Bunk said Bolden was the greatest with the exception of Louis Armstrong. The conversation got around to Louis quite a few times and I could tell Bunk is very proud of "his boy Louis." He taught Keppard and Oliver also but Louis is his boy. Bechet seemed to think that Louis was out of town Sunday, having closed at the Zanzibar, and Bunk agreed he must be, otherwise Louis would surely come over to see him. He also mentioned teaching Ladnier and others I can't remember, mostly N. O. boys who stayed home. He likes Punch and Lee Collins and saw both in Chicago recently. Says they're playing well but drinking too much. Whisky got them all he says, but he's still going strong. Old Bunk is the only one who can take it according to him and I was reminded of Jelly Roll's lack of modesty, although Bunk isn't the braggart Morton was. Not far from it though.

I didn't quite understand his connection with the Victor company years ago. He says he was supposed to come up to New York and record for Victor and it must have been about the time Bechet, Hines and Rex Stewart made their records. He has some feeling about Rex, possibly he was shunted out of the Victor job by him, but he says he'd like to meet him some day. At the time Bunk says he was supposed to record many original tunes, which he still has. Different people have tried to get him to part with the music, but he's guarding them at his home, like the shrewd business man he is. He must have mentioned fifteen titles of songs he has, all originals—rags, stomps and blues.

Anyhow, all good things must end. Quite a few musicians had been in to get a drink and say hello, Jack Crystal came in and left to start the session and took Bechet and shortly after, over we went with Bunk. Met Gene Williams and a couple of others on the way and had quite a time getting Bunk thru the mob of musicians on the street, all of whom wanted to meet and talk to Bunk, most of

them a little in awe of the great man. To all who met him, Bunk would say he was an old man of 65, but he came up to N. Y. to show the boys he was down but not out, "and when I start to play you'll see where Louis got his stuff, although Louis plays it up and I play it down." A wonderful character, confident of his ability to show the boys, but still a little nervous with all the acclaim.

Finally in Ryan's, a set was in progress and Jack Crystal came over and told Bunk that Pete Brown would go on next and Bunk would play the third set. Meanwhile Bunk fingered his cornet and finally got out a mute, stuck it in the end, and standing in front of the telephone booths in the rear, started to blow softly with the boys in the band. Only a few right in front of him could hear him but we knew we were in for a treat. Gene and Rudi Blesh and I were around him all the time, sort of a self-appointed body-guard. Some people were afraid Bunk might drink too much and not be able to play. After a while, the second set started and we went down front. Bunk went into the men's room, giving me his cornet to watch and wading through more musicians. Louis Metcalf was down from uptown and seemed particularly impressed with Bunk. I saw him again after Bunk played and he was enthusiastic about Bunk's phrasing and ideas. Pretty soon Bunk was there again, and took the mouthpiece off his horn and tried it a couple of times.

Finally the time came and the announcement named Hank Duncan, Kaiser Marshall, Pops Foster, Sidney Bechet, Sandy Williams and Bunk. Jack Crystal said it was a great privilege to have Bunk here and Bunk spoke into the mike, as if he had been doing it for years. Bunk was fine on the first set but on the whole it was nothing to brag about, a couple of players messing around. One of the numbers was "Confessin'," probably to help people see the resemblance to Louis. The best kicks came in Bunk's second set, just before the closing "Bugle Call Rag." That set had the same musicians except George Lugg took Sandy's place. The boys were really warmed up by now and Bunk's lead was amazing, strong and clear and confident. The first number was "Weary Blues" and then "High Society" with Lugg playing good tailgate in support of Bechet and Bunk. Bechet played the "High Society" chorus on soprano and then Bunk followed with a solo of incredible beauty. The next number was a Blues and Bunk really hit his stride. He can really blow the blues down and you have to hear it to appreciate it. Phrases and notes from out of the past in the real New Orleans tradition such as has never been heard in Ryan's or anywhere in N.Y. Bunk made very few mistakes and he was surprisingly strong, never faltering except in musical passages unfamiliar to him. It was funny to see his face after he thought the number was over, only to find the drummer taking the Dixieland break at the end. It only caught him once and then his sense of humor showed up in pantomimes during subsequent breaks. He's a great showman and scene stealer, Louis might have got his handkerchief tricks from Bunk.

His playing is wonderful and even the stories are a little under-stating the facts. He hasn't been playing too much recently except one record date last Saturday for Blue Note, consequently he needs some work to get his lip in shape. He'll get the work as Bechet is taking a band to Boston opening Mar. 12, for four weeks, and then he'll be back to N.Y. Bunk says he may be here to stay and I certainly hope so. Anyway, I'll be looking forward to seeing him again after the Boston job, and when you hear him then, he should be even better than last Sunday. I'll never forget the first meeting though, and until somebody else comes along, I'll agree with Bill Russell—Bunk is the best in the world.

George Lewis

It's been said that good guys don't make it to the head of the class. There may be truth to that statement. But thank goodness it doesn't always work out so. I've always thought of George Lewis as a good guy. I've never heard anything to the contrary; and no stories about the guy. Twenty years ago I spend days and weeks and hours listening to the Bunk Johnson band; I watched them in action. I was out in parties with the fellows. I can tell you from what I saw; Lewis is not a character. I come away with the feeling that there is a quiet, retiring, modest guy. And yet, after Bunk passed on, the mantle of leadership fell on George Lewis' shoulders.

Recently (June '66) there was a celebration in New Orleans. The now famous Preservation Hall, a place that furnishes some sort of employment to a number of New Orleans traditional-jazz musicians, was celebrating an anniversary. Many of New Orleans' finest (trad musicians) were there. A friend-writer, who follows this kind of jazz rather closely, writes (Harry Godwin) that "everyone who is anyone in the New Orleans jazz world was there (except Doctor Edmund Souchon)." He then goes on to mention names; clarinetist Raymond Burke, bass player Slow Drag Pavageau "83 years young, doing his little dance," Big Jim Robinson, Johnny Wiggs, a cornetist, and George Lewis. The famous Osaka Jazz Band—the Original Dixieland Jazz Band of Osaka, Japan, entertained. This last statement is what stopped me. Where did they come from? How did they learn?

George Lewis has to be honored for this one thing if for nothing else. He has been touring various parts of the globe with his band and his music; playing for the people; and evidently people everywhere have been loving his music. Wherever George had played, he and his men had been instructing; the musicians in the Osaka band had sat in with George when he played in Japan. Thus he had influenced the clarinet man. So the music is shared and musicians learn. Twenty years ago the Bunk Johnson band was playing in New York City, a time in jazz history when traditional jazz was fighting for its very life. It was Bunk Johnson, the legend come alive, that was the big draw; the attraction. But as it turned out, it was the music that continued to live. George Lewis took this music to Europe, to the East; abroad. Everywhere, the people's music, jazz, was accepted by the people. Yeh, sometimes a good guy makes out good. A.H.

Play Number Nine

by George Lewis

I always loved music since I was a little boy. My mother decided I would be a violin player, but I admired the clarinet. We lived back of Hope's Hall, a dance hall, where they had dances every night, they called them balls in those days, and on Mondays they would have what they called banquets in the afternoon, with the band playing from noon until six, and children were invited. In those days I used to hear some great clarinet players, Picou, George Baquet, Charles McCurtis and Lorenzo Tio. Sidney Bechet used to come to our home; they were family

George Lewis

friends. When I was little Sidney used to stay in the house and mind me for mother.

When I was seven years old my mother gave me twenty-five cents to go to the store and buy a toy violin. When I got there they had sold out all the violins, so I bought a fife. I learned to play on that; I never had a music lesson in my life, and still can't read music.

When I was sixteen years old I got a real clarinet. I bought it with my own earnings, and paid four dollars for it. About that time my family moved to Mandeville, and I stayed with my aunt through the summer. I learned how to play my clarinet, and in a year I joined a band. It was called the Black Eagle Band, five pieces, and we played for dances. I was with them for two years.

After that I joined another band, with Leonard Parker on trumpet and Dan Moody, trombone. That lasted for a year, and then I joined Buddy Petit's band. It was called the Black and Tan Band. Buddy was the leader and trumpeter, Ambrose on trombone, Buddy Mandy banjo, Eddie Woods drums and Chester Zardis played bass.

That band broke up and Buddy and I came back to New Orleans. We both joined the Earl Humphrey band. I played with Buddy in those two bands for two years. I think Buddy was one of the greatest trumpeters New Orleans ever had. He was never recorded. He sounded a lot like Louis, not the range but the tone. Buddy was no high note man, but fine in the middle and low registers. He has been dead fifteen years, he was about 45 when he died. He was a dark brown man and had funny eyes, gray eyes. He had a lisp in his talk and he was a really hard drinker. But a fine guy to work with. We were always friends. Any place where Buddy took his band, the other bands closed up. He could always have all the work in New Orleans if he wanted it.

I recall something that happened one summer over at Lake Pontchartrain. I was in one band then and Buddy in another. We used to come to work, or go on parades, in big horse-drawn trucks, and when two trucks met there would be a cutting contest. One day we caught Buddy drunk, and our band really wore them out. The following Saturday we drove up and we saw Buddy sitting there with his head hanging down and his hands flopping, so we got set to go after them again. And then somebody sneaked around and chained the wheel of our truck to theirs so we couldn't get away, and Buddy jumped to his feet and that Saturday they really wore *us* out.

To me, Buddy had better fingering than Louis, and a wonderful sweet tone. Outside of Louis, Buddy was better liked and better known around New Orleans than any other trumpet player. He was always reliable too, and he could take any band, any kind of musicians, and always draw a crowd.

Through those years, 1916 to 1922, I was playing with various bands around the Lake. Baquet, Sidney Bechet, and some others were around then. One band had Earl Humphrey on trombone; Buddy, trumpet; Roy Evans, drums, and Alex Scott, bass. Banjo was a little short man, an invalid, we called him Dad. Whoever was leader would handle the money, the forfeit posted by the place, and so on, and sometimes there would be trouble about how the money was divided. We had some of that trouble with Buddy, and Earl Humphrey took over the band.

After I left Humphrey I organized my own band. I had Red Allen, Ernest Kelly on trombone, Arthur Mitchell on bass, Albert Morton on drums, and Little Dad, banjo. We played lawn parties and dances, parades on Sundays, and managed to make a living. That band lasted about a year.

Then I joined Chris Kelly's band. Kelly was supposed to be a preacher, and he played everything in the sacred style. He was the first to play with a plunger and silver mute together, I remember he played "Careless Love" that way. I had heard Oliver before that, but in those days he didn't use much mute, he used a derby hat. Chris Kelly was one of the greatest blues players. The band had Chris on trumpet, Manuel Manetta on alto, Butler Rapp, banjo, Yank (Arthur) John-

son and his brother Buddy, trombones (they were first cousins of Bunk Johnson's). Roy Evans was on the drums and the bass player was a pigeon-toed fellow, we called him Duck Ernest. I stayed with that band a pretty good while.

Then I went to Kid Rena, and was with his band a long time. It was long enough for us to win two silver cups from the Tuxedo Band at Gypsy Smith's Auditorium. The Tuxedo had Celestin on trumpet, Baby Ridgely, trombone; Abbie Foster, drums; Paul Barnes, alto. One of the saxes was Sidney Carriere.

Our band played at Bull's Club every Tuesday and Economy Hall every Saturday and Sunday. We played other spots on weekdays. I was with the band until 1928, when I had a leg broken and was out for a while. Then I went to the Olympia Band under the leadership of Arnold DePas, drummer. The trumpet was Talbert, bass Thomas Copeland. Piano was Blackie Santiago, brother to Vernell, who played a boogie style, and nephew to Willie Santiago.

After I left that band I had jobs off and on, wandered from band to band. I was going around with Jim Robinson and Sam Morgan, we would sit in at different times when some man was off. I played with Punch Miller but was never a member of his band. Punch had George Boyd, clarinet; Ed Morris, trombone; Walter Preston, banjo; Joe Gabiel, bass and "Happy," drums. Once in a while I'd sit in in George Boyd's place. Punch was powerful and strong and was a good man on the blues, which he'd blow into a derby.

Well, I wanted to tell you about parades and funerals. I started playing for funerals in New Orleans about 1923. I remember the first was on St. Joseph's Day, March 19th, with the Original Eureka Band. I also played with the Tuxedo Band. I liked it better than playing dance music; I could have that clarinet singing all the time. I had never played that kind of music before but I had all the ideas and it never was hard. I would have a man alongside me like Petit to help out, and would get the time from the bass drum, always on the left foot.

The funerals were generally for some society or club. Every member would be notified where to meet. We would leave the club and march to the home of the deceased, the band playing anything they liked, any rag or march. A block away we would muffle the drum, and play something sacred, like "The Saints Go Marching In," but in rag or march tempo. When they brought the body out the bass drum would hit three beats, very slow, the snare falling in. We would play things like "The Rugged Cross," or "Flee as a Bird to the Mountain." When the body was buried the last piece we played was always "God Be With You Til We Meet Again."

After the funeral we would unmuffle the drum, take the crepe off the flag, and make a regular parade of it. The band and all the club members would march back to the hall, using other streets, so everybody could see.

There were various kinds of clubs, lodges, benevolent associations, in New Orleans in those days. It was not insurance, but they provided medicine if you were sick, relief of different kinds, and they would bury you. Even if you were poor, or had no family to make up a funeral for you, the club would take care of everything. All the club members would be notified a day ahead of time, and if they didn't come to the funeral they were fined. Nobody was allowed to leave the cemetery until the body was buried. A club officer would go around and take up the membership cards, and in that way they had a check on who was there. There would generally be one big limousine and all the club members marching behind.

If a musician would die, all the bands would get together and make a band for him. When Chris Kelly died there were nine bands in line. Some were made up of only trumpets and drums, some full-sized organized bands. When one would stop the next one would start. Chris was probably the best-liked musician in New Orleans, among both white and colored. The crowd was so big that a lot of people were arrested; they forgot it was a funeral. Different saloons sent barrels of wine to the wake, which lasted for three nights. Chris was a veteran, and he died in the Marine Hospital. People stood in line all night to view his body.

But the club parades were really the big thing. Years back they used to start at nine in the morning and last until five; we would walk all over town. Later they would last from 1 p.m. to 5.

The club I belonged to, the Square Deal, hasn't paraded since 1925. They were expensive, and during the depression members couldn't pay their dues. They used to parade

in fifteen to twenty divisions, every club with its own color for costumes and sashes. The women would carry parasols and baskets of roses. First there would be a Grand Marshal on horseback, with his sash and costume; the horse's hoofs would be gilded and a ribbon on his tail. Then about sixteen aides followed the Grand Marshal, sometimes on horseback too. The band followed the aides. Bandsmen used to wear dark pants, black shirt, white collar and black tie. But that was too hot, so later we wore blue pants and white shirts. There was always a "second line," kids and grown-ups too. After parading and playing all day, it was a relief to have somebody help carry the instruments, especially for the tuba or bass drum.

All the club members marched behind the band, wearing badges. We would march from house to house; if a member could afford it he would have drinks at his house for the whole parade.

We would play for parades every Sunday during the spring and summer. Each club would hold a parade on its anniversary each year. They still have one or two parades a week in New Orleans, but nothing to what it used to be. There are not enough musicians in the city to play; the younger fellows don't know the time or the tunes. We used to play "Bugle Boy," "Gettysburg," "Salutation," etc. The leader always carries a little black bag for the music. Now that leader has a cute trick. When he buys the music it has a title printed on the top, but he cuts the name off and puts a number on. So he calls out "Number nine," and we didn't know what we were playing. I can't read music, remember, so you see I had to have a sharp ear.

Mardi Gras starts on January 7th, King's Day. All the clubs have a big party and ball. There is a big cake, and inside the cake is a nut. Whoever gets the nut in his cake is king. The king gives a party for the girls, and there is a doll inside the cake then, and whoever gets the doll is queen. This used to be held at the French Opera House before it was destroyed by fire; now it's in some of the big hotel ballrooms. There is a party every night. On the Thursday before Carnival, Proteus Day, the parades start. The smaller clubs march on Momus Day, the Monday before Carnival, and the big clubs on Comus Day. They have fifteen to twenty big beautiful floats.

On Carnival Day first comes Rex, King of Carnival. Behind every two floats there is a band. They are mostly white bands and school bands. Last time I was with the Zulu King's float. This is decorated in primitive style, from Africa—the King has a grass suit, his face black, eyes white, shoes a couple of feet long, and as the float goes along he throws out cocoanuts for souvenirs. I played every year except one up to 1938, and in 1939 I played for a white club. I was with the Eureka Brass Band; Louis Dumaine was leader and trumpeter, with Al Landry and Kid Howard. Jim Robinson and Joe Avery played trombones. We had two drums, one sax, tuba and mellophone. Most parade bands have eight to ten men. I always played E-flat clarinet for parades, and B-flat for dances. With all that brass, it takes an E-flat to cut through so it can be heard. I also used the E-flat on some of the records we made, an old metal clarinet, all full of rubbers and things.

During the depression things were very bad in New Orleans. I played for one dollar a night and tips at a little night spot, from 8:30 to 3. We would go around with the kitty, and sometimes averaged three or four dollars. I had a family to support then, too, a wife and nine children. I worked for a while on the PWA. Then I took sick, had ulcers, and laid off a couple of months. I went back to spotting, but couldn't make a living at it, so I went on the riverfront and got work as a stevedore. I have been there as a steady job ever since.

In 1941 when Dave Stewart came down to New Orleans to make some records, I and a piano player had been stranded at a little place called Leedsville, and just got back to town the day before. In 1933 Bunk Johnson and I had played with Evan Thomas' band until Thomas got killed and the band broke up. Bunk came to New Orleans with Bill Colburn and Stewart, and looked me up. That was when we made the records for Jazz Man.

I had made some records with Lee Collins back in 1924, but they were never issued. I can't even remember who they were made for—I was drinking at the time. I remember there was Roy Evans on drums, "Tink" on piano, and Alex Scott, bass. If anybody knows what became of those records, I'd like to hear about it.

In recent years I had been playing only about once a week, and was thinking of quitting. Gene Williams came down in 1942 and we made some records, and then some for Bill Russell in 1943-44. Some of those not issued yet, funeral style, brass band records, I think are recorded better than any of the others.

When we got together to make this present trip to New York with Bunk, three of us, Lawrence Marrero, Slow Drag and I were playing together. Jim Robinson was on another job and Purnell was spotting around. Baby Dodds was in Chicago. So we all got together here, and I can say we are very much pleased by the way our music is liked here.

Jim Robinson

When I think of Jim Robinson it has to be part of a picture; the Bunk Johnson band; their engagement at the Stuyvesant Casino in New York City, 1945. That was a hot period. The war in jazz, between the "new world-a-comin'" jazz people and the "what had been and was going on" crowd was in full flower. Gene Williams, Bill Russell and Ralph Gleason were Bunk's mentors; this was the big move to bring the "missing link," the "tie" to the jazz-chain-of-events to the public's eyes and ears. Finally the day arrived and I was on hand to hear the great Bunk Johnson and his band.

Was I impressed? I'd like to answer this by saying that to the best of my recollection I didn't miss a night of their engagement; I caught this band every night. I got to know the guys; naturally, some better than others. Like the bass player, Slow Drag; he was a person aglow;

easy to like. George Lewis the clarinetist was quieter; same with Jim Robinson. Now there was a trombone player who loved the bottom land; he laid that gutty sound in there for the trumpet and clarinet to operate in. He was one of the first 'bone men that made me think that the only reason for playing trombone in this type of jazz music is to create that type of sound; Robinson was rough (and I'm talking of his playing in comparison with Ory or Brunis); much closer to jazz music as it was before it got a musical college education. Jim didn't waste words (musical words), nor did he possess an over-abundance. His musical vocabulary was short and to the point. He was where you knew you'd always find him. You must remember this was a time in jazz history when there was a definite music called jazz and the player expressed it and played it and basked in it.

So meet Jim Robinson; long, tall, a bit of weight (but not too heavy); on the quiet side (except when he blew); read on. . . .   A.H.

New Orleans Trombone

by Jim Robinson

"Jim, I'm going to show you how to play an instrument." That's what Willie Foster, who is "Pops" Foster's brother said to me in 1917 over in France, and that's when I started to play trombone. I was 25 years old at the time and had never played anything but a guitar until then.

I always had a feeling for music and wanted to play something, so when I was a kid, my dad bought me a guitar. The fellows showed me how to play it and I just fooled around with it by myself. I liked the blues and used to play the blues to myself on the guitar. But when they took me to war, they had plenty of guitar players and I figured I had to blow something to get by. My first day in France they handed us picks and shovels and put us to work. It was cold and we were building roads and working in mines and it was hard work. That lasted two days and Willie Foster told me to cut it out and try to learn something.

The next morning at reveille, we lined up for inspection and the lieutenant said, "Any-one who has the spirit and wants to play in the band, step forward." I couldn't move but Willie was in back of me and gave me a push. There were nine of us who stepped forward and we stayed behind while the rest had to go out on details. They piled us in a truck and off we went to the supply camp to get some instruments. Willie asked what I'd like to learn. He said I can teach you any instrument you want and I said I'd try the trombone. I always liked the trombone ever since us kids used to sneak down to hear Kid Ory and Joe Oliver. Ory could really play the blues. He was so smooth and he could play those low pedal notes. I liked to listen to a lot of trombone players but Ory could really drive.

Next day we had a rehearsal. We had the big band and a small jazz band. Willie was the leader of the jazz band and I played in it. I used to practice at night in my bunk. It wasn't allowed so I had to blow real soft. Willie got me playing "Till We Meet Again," and that's the first tune I learned. We played every night entertaining different outfits and for dances and we got paid extra for playing. Before I got in the band I could never make my pay last long and now I had a little money in my pocket. It didn't last long anyhow because it was all French money and we'd never get the right change in a cafe. Especially if we had any American money. They sure liked to get hold of any American dollars.

When I came back after the war, the fellows played so much trombone in New Orleans, it seemed I couldn't play anything. I lived in back of Economy Hall and I'd just sit on the back steps and listen to the band. George Washington and Morris French played there then and they sounded so good I was disgusted with myself and put my horn down. About this time my sister bought a pianola and I'd sit on the bench and work the pedals and play along with my trombone. That way I got going pretty good and John Marrero used to come around and take me out on a job now and then. One night Morris French didn't show up at Economy Hall. It was Kid Rena's band and John Marrero was his guitar player. John knew I wasn't doing anything and came over and got me. Rena didn't think much of it and I was nervous too, but when he hit the first tune, my bad feeling passed. I liked playing in front of a crowd, especially with all the pretty girls dancing, and Kid Rena always packed the hall when he played. He was powerful then and he said he didn't know I could play that much trombone.

After that I never had any trouble getting work and I played with all the bands, especially Young Morgan's, Kid Rena's and the Tuxedo Band. I worked days as a longshoreman for the Southern Pacific R. R. and played at night. We played every weekend and nights during the week too. I was blowing pretty good with all the playing and sometimes I'd practice at home with my nephew, Jim Little, who played violin, and Simon Marrero on bass. John Marrero got me into the Tuxedo Band as an extra. That was Oscar Celestin's band and he had Baby Ridgeley on trombone, Paul Barnes, sax; Emma Barrett, piano; and Simon and John Marrero on bass and guitar. Simon and John are both brothers of Lawrence and Billie Marrero is their father. Sometimes they'd have two jobs and Ridgeley would play on one and I'd play the other. After that I played

in Isaiah Morgan's band, which was called the Young Morgan Band. Isaiah was the leader the first three years I was with them until Sam Morgan, who had had a paralytic stroke, got better and came back to the band. Sam came back in 1923 and then we had two trumpets. Then in 1924 Sam made some records for Columbia. Those are my first records and the band had Earl Forsley, alto sax; Andrew Morgan, tenor sax; Johnnie Dave, banjo; Walter Decou, piano; Jim Little, bass violin, and William Nolan, drums, besides Sam and Young Morgan, trumpets, and myself.

Some of the tunes we made were "Bogalusa Strut," "Down By the Riverside," "Short Dress Gal," "Everybody's Talking About Sammy," "Over in Glory Land," "Steppin' On the Gas," and "Mobile Stomp." We had two sessions that year—both for Columbia—and the only change in the band for the second date was Roy Evans coming in on drums.

That was one of the best bands at that time in New Orleans. We were working all the time for both white and colored dances and on the road. We were very popular wherever we played and it was a tough band to handle. We didn't play together for parades and funerals because Sam couldn't do much walking with his bad feet, but I worked with somebody every Sunday. I didn't care about playing funerals—too much grief on those jobs. The priest goes in and then the drum starts out and the music gets sad. It's a wonderful thing but it's too sad. No matter how stubborn your heart is, some pieces make you full of grief.

We were on the road for weeks at a time playing places like Mobile, Montgomery, but mostly near New Orleans, except for one week in 1929 when we went to Chicago. Kid Ory was in Chicago then and he got the band to come up. We played at Warwick Hall and we burned up the town. That only lasted a week and after we went back the band broke up due to Sam's bad health. Then for seven years I played with different bands at the Levita dance hall, which was a taxi-dance place. The first band there was led by John Handy and after a while the job fell to me. I had Kid Howard on trumpet, Paul Barnes, sax; Benny Turner, piano; Sidney Flushia, banjo; and Robert Davis, drums. After that there were no steady jobs but I was playing most of the time gigging around. In 1940, I made the records with Kid Rena. The Kid and Big Eye Louis came around one day to the corner of Dumaine and Villere, where I used to hang out, and got me. My next records were made by the Jazzman people, and they remembered me from my days with Sam Morgan and the records we made, and they looked me up. The last records were made for Bill Russell and everyone should listen to the ones of the brass band. The funeral pieces we made are good too but I like the brass band best.

I sure appreciate the way everybody here in New York treats us and I hope we'll be playing a long time. I enjoy playing for people that are happy—I like to see people happy. If everyone is in a frisky spirit, the spirit gets to me and I can make my trombone sing. If my music makes people happy, I will try to do more. It is a challenge to me. I always want people around me. It gives me a warm heart and that gets into my music. When I play sweet music, I try to give my feelings to the other fellow. That's always in my mind. Everyone in the world should know this, that I try to get everybody happy and contented with my music. Then I am happy and everybody would be more friendly. If we really love our music, we would be more happy and friendly. Just keep living and loving your music and keep no evil in your heart.

"Big Eye" Louis Nelson

by Robert Goffin

Tragedy struck at Louis Nelson when he was 15 and holding down his first job. It was in July while he was playing in Peyton's band that racial uprisings took place in New Orleans. One Wednesday Louis was told that Negroes were being massacred. The band was playing a number at the time and didn't stop for what they considered to be rumors. Louis, while blowing on his clarinet, thought of his father, a butcher who was to go to the slaughter house for meat around midnight. When the piece was finished he wanted to go home and warn his father not to leave the house, but Peyton and Buddy Bolden made such fun of him that he remained. The next day he was called to identify his father's body at the hospital. He had been killed in the race riots.

Louis was born in the Ninth Section where his father had a flourishing butcher shop. He belonged to a Creole family, who, in spite of their English name spoke French. He went to an English school in the Section and he himself only spoke the French patois while out playing with other schoolkids.

When I heard the name "Big Eye" Louis Nelson, I expected to see a species of Cyclops. I was entirely mistaken. At 59, Louis Nelson looks extremely young, his face is clear and unwrinkled. He dresses to perfection, wearing a gold chain across his chest. His eyes are slightly prominent and that is what warranted the moniker of Big Eye from his schoolmates.

When he was about 12, Louis' father, who was comfortably situated, decided that his son should be a musician, so he had two clarinet teachers, Lorenzo and Louis Tio. When he was 14 the youngster went around to neighboring dances and picnics, intrigued by and loving the way the popular "faker" bands made music. Already Emmanuel

Perez was known to the younger fervent musicians who admired a master who could throw away the music score and let his heart dictate the notes.

The first one to revolutionize the young candidates before 1900 was a Creole named Armand Metayer. The boys followed him from dance to dance until he became a member of the Golden Rule Band. That was during the romantic and tragic period when colored people lived between fear and hope. At the time when kids of the Ninth Section were told the story of how Denny Boyd had killed two policemen and the same night people of the Section had sat on their doorsteps singing plaintive ballads praising the victims and damning the assassin.

The youthful musicians looked for work. Louis, who was just 15, was already substituting in certain bands, and used to hang out at the bar at St. Philippe and Clayborne, owned by a Creole gangster named Eddy Boissiere, or at St. Anne and Villere, in a place belonging to Henry Ponce, a rival of Eddy. This was where Peyton used to go to drink his double gins after having played his accordion in some hospitable house or other.

Thus it was rather natural that Louis Nelson got into the first band engaged by Club 28. It consisted of Huey Rankin, bass, Henry Peyton, accordion, Jim Gibbson, banjo, Chas McCurdy, clarinet, Buddy Bolden, trumpet and Octave Brown, trombone. Louis had hoped to take McCurdy's place. Peyton refused and instead, offered him that of Rankin. Louis accepted but soon became clarinetist where he was often replaced by Alphonse Picou.

There were no drums at any time. They only became general and popular after Robichaux had hired Deedee Chandler. But that was after Louis had lost his father.

Until about 1904, Louis Nelson was a versatile musician. He played the banjo, the bass, the accordion or the clarinet. It was only at about that time that he devoted himself entirely to the instrument which made him famous. First he played in a three man band, called the Ninth Ward Band, which finally grew to four members. They were Johnny Gould, violin, Henry Ford, bass, Albert Mitchell, banjo and Louis Nelson clarinet, which he played almost entirely in the lower register. He was on the road to success.

One could find Louis and his group in some shady cabaret such as Rochelle's or even at Joe Rice's in the District, where wild women were tamed by the color and rhythm of the band. For a while Louis was manager for the orchestra and got them an engagement from some Spaniards who lived on the Island, but transportation was difficult and they had to be content with irregular shows at St. Bernard or Plaquemines. And bit by bit the little band died a natural death.

Later Louis was hired by Alcide Frank, leader and violinist of the Golden Rule Band. They played nightly in a cabaret owned by George Fewclothes, on the corner of Liberty and Iberville Streets. Besides the leader and Louis there were Joe Brooks, banjo, James Brown, bass, Adolphe Alexander, cornet and John Vigne, drums.

Speaking of John Vigne, Louis Nelson pointed out the instability of certain foreign names in New Orleans. Vigne was a Creole of French origin, who with Deedee Chandler shared the reputation for having begun the use of drums. For the Section half Creole and half American, Vigne was written and pronounced Veine, and at Perdido, where the name Vigne was unpronounceable it was transformed into Vean, and the musician was called "Ratty" Vean. Many names have undergone this process of evolution. An excellent example of alteration is that of the Creole trumpeter Rene, whose Americanized name was written to follow the French pronunciation: Kid Rena.

In 1905 Louis left the Golden Rule to join the Imperial Band, so well remembered with Emmanuel Perez, cornet, Jimmy Palao, violin, Buddy Johnson, trombone, Jean Vigne, drummer, and Billy Murray, bass. The popularity of the Imperial Band has already been told. After playing in dance halls of the Crescent City such as Colony Hall, Hopes Hall or at the Francs Amis, his popularity spread all over Louisiana.

One of the most exciting evenings the band ever spent was when they were engaged to accompany an excursion to Shreveport. In that town there was a tough quarter frequented by shady characters, stevedores and prostitutes. In a dive of the district called St. Paul's Bottom the band was to play for the excursionists and any of the natives who happened to be present. The dancers were turbulent and noisy. Beer and gin flowed freely.

Suddenly there was a movement in the crowd. Louis nudged his neighbor Raphael Beving. Everyone was looking towards the door. What was going on? Soon they learned that a man-hunt was taking place outside. A celebrated criminal, Booker, had escaped from the chaingang and had been tracked to Shreveport. Those in the dance hall shivered at the thought of this assassin being loose. Suddenly the announcement was made that all doors from the hall to the street were closed, and for the very good reason that Booker was inside among the dancers.

The orchestra continued playing, but the audience was nervous. Suddenly, through a small window near the stage a revolver was thrust pointing towards the patrons.

"Keep quiet now, all of you. Booker, put up your hands."

It was Sheriff Cradock who had spotted the bandit among the crowd.

"No use in trying to fight it out, all exits are blocked by the police."

Booker swore, then he promised to shoot the first policeman to come near him. The band kept on playing but the musicians were getting slightly anxious. Already the crowd was backing away from the floor and women were fainting. The band started another tune. At this moment the police entered, and Booker, taken by surprise, ran towards the musicians and leapt onto the platform. In doing so he struck Raphael Beving such a blow that the latter fell, knocked out, beside his trombone. Bedlam reigned. Jimmy Brown had dropped his bass viol and scampered behind the piano. The sheriff called out:

"Give yourself up or you're a dead man."

Two minutes later the bandit was shot, right on the stage among the players. He fell screaming on the drum while Louis Nelson rolled over behind a protecting pillar.

Finally the sheriff got up on the platform but none of the musicians budged. Booker was dead, full of holes. "Go on, play!" shouted the sheriff, "You've got to make these folks feel safe." Jimmy Palao was pea green. Louis Nelson was gasping for breath. Nevertheless they attacked the "Tiger Rag" but without drums or trombone. Raphael had had to be removed and cared for and Jean Vigne was busy wiping the gory mess off his drums.

"Those were great days," said Big Eye Louis.

Suddenly a question flashed through my mind:

"Louis, you knew Buddy Bolden pretty well didn't you?"

"Sure, as well as you, that is, I mean a lot better."

"Bob Lyons contends that Buddy didn't start to play until about 1900."

"I guess that's about right."

I opened a copy of *Jazzmen* which contained the letter from Bunk Johnson in which he stated that he left Oliver's orchestra to join King Bolden in 1895. I even pointed out a certain sentence:

"When I started playing with him, Bolden was a married man, had two children. He must have been between 25 and 30 years old at that time."

Alphonse Picou had come up to us and both of them stood for a while thinking. Picou was the first to speak:

"That's impossible. Emmanuel Perez was the first jazz trumpeter in about 1898, and Bolden came after that."

"Bunk Johnson's statement is impossible" added Louis. "In 1895 there were no drummers. Deedee Chandler only began in about 1900. Besides," he added, "I have positive proof."

He pulled out his wallet and extracted an article from the *Times-Picayune* of July 1900.

"Here's a date that doesn't lie. It's the announcement of my father's death. That week I was playing at Club 28 with Buddy Bolden, and at that time he didn't even have his own orchestra. He was just a young apprentice playing the accordion and making his first attempts on the trumpet." Picou confirmed this argument which one of these days will be cleared up.

Next we spoke of ragtime and its first pianists.

"Did you know Scott Joplin?"

"Just as well as I knew Buddy Bolden. Look, here's a souvenir which dates back to 1917." And again he fished into his wallet and drew out a small calling-card which read:

Mrs. Lottie Joplin
Neatly Furnished Rooms
By Day or Week
163 W 131

And Louis, again reminiscent, added:

"When I left Freddy Keppard in Boston, the day the Creole Band broke up, I wanted to go and stay with the Joplins. I was anxious to see my old friend who had written such marvellous ragtime. A few years before he had written an operetta in ragtime from which he expected great things. It was a complete flop. To my great sorrow, when I arrived at 131st Street I heard that Joplin had just died. Lottie was in a terrible state. I remember that he was to be buried on the Wednesday before Easter, but religious neighbors interceded for the funeral not to be held on that holy day. The funeral was postponed two days and that is why Scott Joplin, the famous composer was buried on Good Friday. I can still see the funeral procession. On each side of the carriages was the name of one of his compositions, and naturally the 'Maple Leaf Rag' was in the lead."

I asked Louis Nelson something about his present musical life. He laughed.

"I'm modest. I play the clarinet whenever I can. That is to say two or three times a week. The golden age of New Orleans has passed. Picou is rich . . . I spent everything I made. I live on memories and consider myself lucky to be doorman at Perseverence Hall! There I see the youngsters and give them advice. But maybe you've never before seen a modest musician?"

We both looked at Picou who was blushing furiously. And Big Eye Nelson turned and walked off to take up his job as doorman.

4

The Second Line

As almost everybody knows, "the second line" is the name for the people who followed parade bands in New Orleans, many of them boys who would become members of the next generation of musicians. Part Four is made up of jazzmen who came along after the fathers of traditional jazz. All of them are white, and most of them were raised in the Mississippi Valley, although there are three Easterners—Danny Alvin, Eddie Lang and Max Kaminsky. For many years they provided much of the best jazz to be heard. Most of them are gone now, but a few of them are still going strong.

C.H.

George Wettling

I don't have any trouble thinking of amusing incidents that have cropped up around George Wettling, just as I don't have any trouble remembering dates we've played together that were thoroughly enjoyable. Stories? There's the one I heard where his wife said, "Georgie, I'm going out for a bit; I want you to promise me that you will only have a couple of bottles of beer while I'm gone," only to come home to find Georgie stoned. "I thought you said you'd only have a couple bottles of beer?" That's all he had, but he managed to find gallon bottles. Then there was the story about the fire. I think that was a classic. Wettling had sacked out after a tough night. He was parked in a hotel and fell asleep with a cigarette going. It happened; the fire department arrived, busted in his room and started spraying. In the midst of all this George awakes, annoyed; takes his pillow and blanket and curls up just outside his door.

How to describe a drummer; do you say "He really plays" and leave it there? or, "He puts down a beat?" Sum it up by saying its good when he's in the band. With Wettling behind the drums the band arrives at a groove (and it doesn't take till the next to the last set for it to happen). I've played my music with a select few great drummers. I've got to include George Wettling. You know there's so many drummers who could just as easily have taken up the study of the violin or harp and it wouldn't have hurt the business. Fact is, some of the cats I ran into who owned drums and appeared on gigs could just as easily (as far as I'm concerned) have been working days. You don't find many Wettlings.

George the person? I can't think of anyone who didn't get along with George Wettling. He had moments (and who am I to talk?) when he got trapped by something he drank. There will always be people in night spots who invite you to stop for a taste and most of the musicians I've played my music with will stop. So there are days when one sounds greater than other days. In spite of the hazards of our trade George Wettling played a lot of great drums for a lot of great musicians. In the last twenty years I hear he's takin' up painting. No comment; I've never seen any of his work. Usually George hangs his hat in New York City. If he leaves it's for a short jaunt. Like the gig we were on at Soldier Field (what a secluded rendezvous for jazz) in '65. Everyone sounded good; the drums were right.   A. H.

Baby Dodds Knew How

by George Wettling

Yes, it is probably pretty hard to believe, but there really was a time when a fellow had to know how to drum in order to play in a jazz band. Of course it was 'way back there, but there really was a time like that.

There was also a little fellow from New Orleans who knew how to drum in a jazz band in those days, and he was not only a great inspiration to me, but to a lot of other fellows too, including Ben Pollack and Dave Tough, who also knew and still know how to drum in a jazz band.

Well, this little fellow's name was "Baby" Dodds, and I'll never forget the thrill he gave me the first time I ever heard him play. I was still in my first year of high school (Calumet on Chicago's South Side) and I had heard talk of the great Joe Oliver band, playing at the Lincoln Gardens. Well, one night I lied to my mother and dad and said I was going downtown to a movie—but instead I met another kid that I went to school with and we both went to the Lincoln Gardens. Of course in those days it was quite a rarity to see a couple of high school kids in a cabaret, or Black and Tan as they were called at that time, but the boy I was with was much larger than I was and a couple of years older so we had no trouble getting in.

Just being inside a joint like that was thrill enough, but when I heard that wonderful band and marvelous drumming, it was just too much. I have yet to hear a band that got a beat like Joe's, and I'm still waiting to hear a drummer that could swing a band like Baby Dodds could. Dave Tough comes closer than anyone, and considering the bands he has to play in he does a remarkable job.

You must understand that what I mean by a drummer giving a band a beat is a hell of a lot different from a drummer who starts out with a bang and pounds as loud as he possibly can, forcing everything until instead of a beat the band sounds as though it is rushing—in the meantime playing every figure with the brass, besides putting in a bunch of junk of his own—and working up a hell of a sweat all over nothing at all.

Yes, Baby was a wonderful drummer for giving a band a beat—and using some ingenuity of his own. I never heard Baby play any drum solos, but he certainly was in there all the time, and the way he played behind the band was a solo in itself. I wonder if most of today's drum soloists ever lisen to their own solos? And where did they ever get the idea a drum was a solo instrument in the first place?

I have sat in with many so-called modern musicians and when it comes to playing an old chestnut like "Bugle Call Rag," the simple idea of only keeping time for four bars, with either two or four beats to a bar, is just too much for them, and they play some frantic idea that comes out all off meter and throws everybody off the beat, if any.

How well I can remember many a night when I didn't have the price to go cabareting at Kelly's Stable (the original Kelly's Stable on Rush Street in Chicago) I would stand outside the Stable across the street so I could hear Baby's drums. They would cut through the band like a razor, and I could just picture Baby in there taking over.

Yes, those were the days of originality —when most every jazz drummer had his own ideas, and the more original the better. Now every drummer gets on a pair of high-hat cymbals and stays there, until it comes time to take a solo—and then the machine-gun barrage starts.

Look out, Jack—I'm heading for the first foxhole.

The Jazz Record

15c

No. 29

February, 1945

George Wettling

Earl Wiley

When I think of Earl I think of the Liberty Inn days; the floor shows that went on and on; the bucket-of-blood fights. The "Gang That Sang" (that old gang of mine). Earl Wiley, the riverboat-drummer. Once he told me about his brother having been a hoofer; then proceeded to do a tap-dance step right at the bar. Wiley was fairly tall, and sparse. Good-humored. One thing he couldn't do, and didn't do too often. That was drink. Once he started it was "Katy, lock the door." I suppose you could say he lost interest in doing anything else. Sometimes there was humor in the situation. Like the time . . .

We were gettin' ready to go on stage for the next set (today its referred to as "the next show") when someone remarked "where was Earl?" So the search was on. Soon someone found him in his room and he'd been indulgin'. So we had to get a sub; but fast. As luck would have it Dave Tough was in the room. He'd been listening, and imbibing, but he looked O.K. So here we go. But it didn't take long into that set to realize that Dave was in no shape to play. We managed to finish that bit, but the problem of a drummer for the rest of the night was still there. I don't know who it was that went after Wiley, but whoever it was, told Earl, "Man, you better get back on stage; your sub is drunker than you are."

I've seen the best that Chicago had to offer in drummers hang around the L.I. taking lessons (so to speak) from Wiley. He had a lot to offer. Talk about cuttin' a show. He was (still is) one of the best. He'd played tent shows and carnivals up and down and to and fro; just about everywhere. To hear him play for a cootch dancer (a body-shaker) was a revelation. He had that beat. And Dixieland! That was his bag.

Earl Wiley; he was part of a jazz-yesterday that's been here and gone. A part of an era when six of today's bandleaders were all players in the band. When the jazz band was part of the atmosphere; part of the showcase. No one hit you with spot-lights. You were heard; maybe appreciated, but seldom featured. The money was short; the hours were long. But we were young; and just to play; to play something that you knew was great, was worth it all. So, shut my mouth, and you read on. . . .   A.H.

Drummer from Chicago

by Earl Wiley

I had my first job at the age of seventeen, playing drums in a picture show in Kewanee, Illinois. A trumpet player named Herman Krahn had the band. I got my first drum lessons on an army field drum that my brother bought for me. My brother, who used the name of Billy Graham, was a minstrel man, one of the last of the old-time minstrels, tap-dancer and comedian. He played a little drums himself, too. He was with William H. West, Primrose and West, Al G. Fields, Honeyboy Evans and so on, working New York and the Keith circuit —but that was before my time, of course.

I went to Aurora to work for Frank Thielen, who owned a chain of theatres, and later joined a musical show that toured the middle west, as far as Nebraska. When we came back to the Tri-Cities I met Tony Catalano, cornet player, who introduced me to the Strekfus line boats, and I was with him for several years, touring every river in the south and midwest, including the Mississippi. That was my first acquaintance with real jazz.

Fate Marable played piano on one of those riverboat bands, also played the steam calliope up on the top deck. There was never anybody as good as Fate on the calliope. He did everything from jazz tunes to "Poet and Peasant" on it. He was wonderful as a pianist too, and though I haven't seen him for years they tell me he still can play. We also had Charlie Mills from Quincy, a colored pianist—even back in those days there were mixed bands and nobody seemed to think anything of it.

We got down to New Orleans by winter time and spent the winter there. I first met Joe Oliver, Louis Armstrong, and the Dodds brothers down there. And there was Paul DeDroit, who is now playing drums in a movie studio on the west coast, and his brother Johnny, who played trumpet. I also met a white drummer named Emil Stein, now dead, who today would be rated as one of the greatest.

We used to go around the district dance halls late at night. They had a dozen places with hot colored bands, real jazz bands. It was down there that I first heard Oliver and others use a mute and a derby hat on a trumpet.

In the summertime we came north on the boats, and worked various carnivals and traveling shows; once I went out with a small circus. Some of them, such as Dodson's Carnival, carried small brass bands. It was fun, and valuable experience.

Around 1920 we came back to Chicago and Tony Catalano and I worked for Mike Fritzel at the Arsonia Cafe on West Madison. About that time the Original Dixieland Band was playing at the Casino Gardens; they left soon and came to Reisenweber's in New York. I stayed around Chicago, but Catalano went back to Davenport. Bix Beiderbecke was around then, but I never worked with him; he began coming up just a little later. In Catalano's band at that time were Roy Kramer, clarinet, now on the west coast, Don Forney, trombone, and Bill Krenz, piano, who was around New York recently but is now, I believe, out on the west coast, too.

I joined Gene Green, who had a band with Muggsy Spanier, Floyd Towne, Deacon Loyacano on bass, and Red Rowland, a clarinetist from New Orleans. We opened in Aurora and then played the Orpheum circuit, big time stuff. Gene Green was a black-face singer; he used to have a drop scene behind with song titles on it and ask the audience to pick them. Muggsy said recently that he remembers it as a good band, that it would still be a good band today. After the theatre tour we went into the Palais Royal on West Madison. We were supposed to come to New York, but after working around the West Side a while there were no more bookings and the band split up, the boys taking individual jobs. I worked a while with Elmer Schoebel.

One day I was talking to the boss of the Palace Gardens, and he was asking, "What shall I do for a little business?" I suggested a good Dixieland band. Just then Floyd O'Brien came in and said he had three good men—Ernie Prittikin, clarinet, Johnny Forton, piano—and he was really very good —and Charlie Curtis on trumpet. So I said, "We've got a band!" and we got rid of the previous banjo-fiddle combination. In two weeks the place was packed, they were standing up trying to get in. People liked the music, liked to dance to it. That particular band was only together a short time, but I worked the place several times; it was a life-saver. The boss paid on the dot, and the pay went up during the engagement. On one job there Eddie Condon worked with us.

Around that time King Oliver, with Armstrong, was in town. The New Orleans Rhythm Kings was playing at Friar's Inn. There was a lot of good music around Chicago in those days.

The next year I worked for Eddie Tancil in a band with George Brunies, Paul Mares, and Roy Kramer, clarinet. Tancil was crazy about that band. Mares is still in Chicago; he has his own business now and only comes around occasionally to play for kicks.

I went down to Florida for a winter, with a small band that we called the Tropical Jazz Band; we were in a place called the Chinese Pagoda in Miami. We brought the same band back and played theatre dates around Milwaukee and Minneapolis later that year. It was a good band, but we never made any records. We were going to do it a dozen times, but something always happened.

Back in Chicago I played at some of the dime-a-dance places in the Loop. I met Bill Davidson, Art Hodes, Bud Freeman and the others around this time. In the band were LeRoy Smith on E-flat clarinet, Earl Murphy on banjo and guitar, Hodes on piano, and Benny Moylan, tenor sax. We went into the Capitol, where they were supposed to have one hundred of the prettiest girls in the city, at State and Randolph. I remember the manager fired Bud Freeman and Tut Soper to get us in; he presented us with a bouquet of flowers the first night, but he wound up owing us a lot of money.

Later I had a job with Tom Williams, near Lake Forest. It was a very high class place; a lot of the kids who were going to college in the east lived near there, and they were crazy about our kind of music. Bud Freeman worked with us then.

Johnny Lane had the job at Liberty Inn, and I went there with him. We opened on July 4, 1933. I was there off and on until 1944; I would go out and work another job but always came back. The place was known from coast to coast as a famous joint for good music. Tut Soper worked there, and Mel Henke; Bob Zurke used to sit in every morning, Pee Wee Russell sat in many times. And Fazola, Paul Mares, Wingy Manone, Marty Marsala, and Louis Prima. Dave Tough used to sub for me, and so did Don Carter. Muggsy came in often to get his lip in shape just before he organized his Ragtime band. Some of the regulars were Johnny Bothwell, alto; Clayton Ritchie, piano, and Fritz Wleckie, trumpet, now in the armed forces overseas.

The Liberty Inn used to have a floor show, with dancing in between, so the piano got a real workout with dance, songs, dance, show, and so on. The piano never stopped. In the past year they remodeled the place and put the band in back on a stage. It is known as the home of striptease now; there is always somebody taking off clothes, as many as ten strip dancers. But in the old days it was a great place, never a lull. Three fights on week nights and five on the weekend; if there was no fight nobody had any fun.

Bob Thiele came to Chicago and made some recordings, with Bud Jacobson, clarinet, Frank Melrose on piano, Carl Rinckert, cornet, Bud Hunter, sax, Joe Rushton, bass sax, and myself on drums.

I got married while at the Liberty Inn, and my wife had a lot to do with my coming to New York. In those years I was always telling everybody else to go to New York, but never did it myself. However, I think New York is better for hot music now than Chicago —everybody has left there by now. I intend to make it my home.

Danny Alvin

Now we were headin' home; behind us was the benefit . . . Monday nite, Dec. 1st . . . a room, jam up with people . . . unimaginable; you couldn't make the front door, and through the back it was chock full of musicians . . . guys you hadn't seen for years . . . all there for one purpose . . . to benefit Danny . . . one of their own. Saturday, 9 A.M. we lost him. By now the shock that had numbed, had passed. This was Tuesday the 9th . . . same month . . . bitter cold . . . final services at 10 A.M. . . . and man it was cold. Bill and I had driven in from Park Forest . . . my daughter Janet had taken a half-day off . . . she'd remembered Danny from Greenwich Village . . . a guy a child remembered. We didn't do much talking. The church was in an out-of-the-way neighborhood . . . maybe that accounted for the sparse attendance; but we were definitely the mourners . . . those who knew him best and would miss him the most.

On the way back we got to thinkin' . . . and then to talkin'. "You knew Danny pretty well, didn't you Bill?" Yes, it turned out he did. Bill Tinkler picked up the conversation. "When Reinhardt opened Jazz Ltd. they sent for Danny . . . that place did alright from the beginning . . . but you know how it is . . . after awhile, Danny left. Just about that time, Johnny Lane was opening at Rupneck's. Jimmy James (another guy we just lost . . . a fine musician) on trombone; Grunwald on piano, myself, Lane . . . don't remember who opened with us on drums . . . but about a week later, Danny dropped in . . . sat in. Now you know, Jimmie James and me, we were new at this Dixie music. We really hadn't ever heard how it should go . . . not in any band we were in. So, the thing just wasn't jelling . . . not 'til Danny sat in. Man, when he sat in, everything fell in place! It fitted. I had never had it happen to me before. Well, after that, there was no question . . . Danny got the job.

Dear ole Chicago . . . the Windy City . . . a well-earned moniker . . . it got cold in dear old Chi . . . in more ways than one. Yep, back then, when I came in, playing was the most important thing in your life . . . and Danny was one of the first guys that gave me a job. He was the leader-man at a jernt named the 100 Club. A Rush Street production . . . Jess Stacy was pianoman on the gig and I was subbin'. Wingy Manone had just hit town and Ray Biondi was takin' him around. Wingy was organizin' and needed men. They stood directly under the bandstand, in the basement, and I got the gig . . . and many things happened for me after that, in my growth as a jazzman. Those were my school years. My teachers held class at any of the various places that furnished employment . . . a barbeque joint; a gambling den, or an after-hours flat. You went in and you listened . . . and after that, you had to have a place to play in . . . practice. There weren't many leaders then that understood . . . that furnished employment . . . Floyd Town; Wingy; just a handful . . . and Danny Alvin . . . Charles Pierce. Don't get the idea it was jazz work. We played jazz in spite of the job, not because of it. I remember in the '30s, Danny had the band at the Marigold . . . a big place . . . dancing, and some acts to play for. If memory serves me right, Johnny Bayersdorffer blew horn in the band . . . and again, if I remember correctly, he followed Jack Purvis . . . just to give you an idea of the kind of company Danny kept . . . and the guys he gave work to.

It took me 'til '38 to divorce my town and try it elsewhere. Some guys it takes a little longer; but when I lost a gig to an accordion player, I'd had it. So we dared New York City . . . the usual bit. You put in your name for transfer and for three months you're not supposed to accept any work but the most casual and irregular; if you are caught cheatin', out you go . . . back to where you came from. It's rough, but if you survive, you figure the prize is worth it . . . and I'd been told there was gold on them thar streets. We made it; and you know something? One day I became a leader. And you know something else? Yeh, you guessed it . . . I gave Danny a job . . . Jimmy Ryan's on 52nd Street . . . a trio, with Mezz on clarinet. It was a good groove, and we did good for Ryan too. Fact is, one night Ryan said, "Come on; have a drink." It was the '40s, and a war was on; brandy was hard to get. So Mezz ordered Three Star Hennessey . . . and Ryan made a special trip down the basement. Well, Danny and I were on gin, which was O.K. Ryan poured and Mezz downed it like "Here goes," which caused J. R. to come up with this gem, "It's like feedin' cream to a pig."

Yeh, we did a fast ten months together on the street . . . long enough to cut some sides and a gang of transcriptions. The latter I never did get my hands on, but some enterprising gent did, and boot-legged same; Danny told me about it, not mad-like, but more "Can you imagine, Art, somebody got hold of those sides," etc. You rarely saw Danny mad, although one time some critic go him hot. Danny and his son Teddy cornered the cat . . . as I got the story the writer admitted it was all a mistake, etc. Those were the hectic years when we were being written out of the picture. That's another tale. Right now a word about Teddy Walters.

The late T. W. . . . that was the name Danny's kid used. Kid . . . heck! . . . he was taller than Danny . . . football player type . . . actually a guitar man . . . sang too. When we were on the Street, Teddy was doing bits with Billie Holiday . . . gives you an idea of his ability. Well, he didn't make it as long as Danny . . . beat him out by months.

Carnegie Hall? Town Hall? Blue Note records? We met on many a date. We had a lot of laughs . . . and if you dig the music you must know we cut a couple of sides that have lasted. Danny lived; up to the hilt. Even at the end, with a club of his own goin' great guns (it was this year . . . '58 . . . that I had a trio Monday nights at Jazz Ltd. and Danny visited me . . . told me "Art, we're finally in the black") didn't change things . . . didn't mean that much . . . he'd always been among big people, and he played life at an up tempo. Did you ever see him work? You knew of course he'd been with Ted Lewis . . . no . . . that was Brunis . . . but he did a Ted Lewis bit that you had to watch . . . and that barber-shop routine, in which he played sticks on your head . . . vocals . . . things that never appeared on records; bits that came from those days when the booking agent asked, "What else do you do?"

Danny Alvin Viniello . . . a drummer man who came up in an era that produced Krupa, Wettling, Tough . . . all little guys . . . Baby Dodds, Kaiser Marshall, Fred Moore . . . not a one of 'em over 5′ 10″. But they were like the fighter I once knew . . . to describe him you'd say, "He only came up to here, but man, how he came up." Well sir, there you have it. You're born to die and musicians ain't any different than anyone else (I keep telling myself). But if you're like me, you collect as you go along. Some stick to gold . . . others believe in diamonds . . . then we have record collectors. Most of us collect people inside of ourselves . . . and when they go a little piece of us goes too, you can't help it. We didn't write the script. Musicians are by nature warm people . . . we play it with feeling.

I've really said very little about Danny. What can you say about a guy who was a human being . . . a warm person who had time for you . . . and an ear . . . who made it and spent it. Just let me say he played it all the way with a beat.   A.H.

Reprinted from *Jazz Report* (December 1958) 5 and 6.

Drummer Danny

by Bob Aurthur

This is a story about a jazz musician who is said to be one of the most underrated artists in the business. However, the interesting part about it is that every day one hears an everincreasing number of people make that statement. So perhaps Danny Alvin, of whom we're talking, isn't so underrated after all.

Certainly the open-mouthed fans who hang nightly over the pianos down at Nick's little tavern watching Danny's flashing sticks

The Jazz Record

15c

No. 35

August, 1945

Danny Alvin

don't think so; who are to be heard arguing whether it's Alvin or Wettling for their present-day dream band. No, it is to be happily reported that smiling and good-natured Mr. Alvin is coming into his own.

And it's certainly about time. Because here is another example of a guy who had had a tough time in his own home town. It might be hard to believe that one of the best Dixieland drummers in jazz, replete with cowbells and woodblocks, is a native New Yorker, but that is the case. For Danny was born and christened to the name Daniel Alvin Viniello two years after the turn of the present century right here on New York's east side.

Danny started playing drums when he was very young and worked his first professional job with Aunt Jemima at the Central Opera House in New York. From here on in, the story of Danny Alvin is almost the history of white jazz itself.

It was in 1919 that Danny got his first real break. He was hired by Sophie Tucker, the loudest and most buxom of them all, to work with her at the now historic Reisenweber's up in Columbus Circle. At the same time that Danny and the Red Hot Mama were working the Crystal Room, the Dixieland Band was breaking it up in the Dixie Room to the amazement and sometimes confusion of New Yorkers who were hearing jazz for the first time. It was from Tony Sbarbaro, the Original Dixielanders' drummer, that Danny got the style in which he has become so proficient. There is still to be seen the hint of hokum that Tony brought up the river from the Crescent City.

Apparently Sophie Tucker was satisifed with her choice of drummer, because Alvin worked a steady three and a half years in her company. Then came a period of slightly over a year with a vaudeville act, after which, in 1924, Danny Alvin and Chicago found each other in mutual agreement. It was an agreement that lasted for twelve years.

Some very important things were happening in Chicago in those lush days of the twenties. There were the gangsters and the Creole Band; and whiskey and the Wolverines; and Noone and Keppard and all the things that made this era one of the most exciting in our history. Danny's eyes light up when he recalls this period, but when asked with whom he was working at the time, he

has the grace to blush. "I worked with Wayne King," he says.

But Wayne King couldn't hold Mr. Alvin, who soon became associated with Charlie Straight. It was with Straight that Danny met Bix, a friendship that lasted until Bix's early death. When Danny mentions the great cornetist, he becomes slightly dewy-eyed.

"He was a good guy," he tells you. "In the summertime, after the job, we used to take some gin and a portable record-player, out to the beach and watch the sun rise, playing records and drinking like mad."

Danny will also tell you that he was with Bix on Beiderbecke's last drunk in Chicago. "It was a whizz-bang," he reports modestly.

After Straight came a stretch with the Joe Kaisar band, also in fairly good company, namely Teschemacher and Muggsy Spanier. Following this Danny became a leader. His bands held some pretty good men: Jess Stacy, Muggsy, Bud Freeman, and Ray Biondi. Another band at the Midway Garden was composed of Benny Goodman, Steve Brown, Muggsy, and Jess Stacy.

The twelve-year period in Chicago was almost up now and Danny's last job in the Windy City was with Art Hodes on piano at the Vanity Fair in 1936. Hodes tells you that it was wild. "For that matter," Art says, "any time you work with Alvin it's wild."

This was the end of the Chicago period.

Back in New York for the first stretch in twelve years, Danny remained right in the company of Chicago musicians, working the Hickory House with Joe Marsala for two years.

After Marsala, Alvin worked with Wingy Manone at Kelly's Stable on 51st Street and other New York spots. Then over two years ago Danny went to work at Nick's with Marsala. He has been there ever since, drumming complacently through the succession of leaders who have graced the stand at that famous Village spot.

A listing of recordings that Danny has played on shows that he has stayed strictly in the company of Chicago musicians. Probably the most important sides were the ones made with Bud Freeman, Pee Wee Russell, and Max Kaminsky in the "Comes Jazz" album made for Decca. He also appears with Manone on Bluebird and with Joe Marsala.

So there we have Danny Alvin, gentleman and drummer par excellence who is, to his own surprise, one of the star attractions on the present job. Since the professional demise of George Brunis it is now the lusty tenor voice of Mr. Alvin that bursts into "Sister Kate." And if coaxed he will also render such favorites as "I'm Coming Virginia" or "Sweet Lorraine." By standards set by the Metropolitan it might not be considered too good, but the spirit is there and it certainly is loud.

The same thing that was said about Bix might very aptly apply to Danny Alvin. He is a musician's musician. One has only to take the word of two great swing drummers, Davy Tough and Gene Krupa. For it was Danny who taught both Dave and Gene how to drum.

"They would come to where we were playing and watch all night long," Danny says dreamily. "Then after the joint closed down for the night they would ask questions and I would show them how it was done." Apparently Danny was a good teacher, as anyone who knows jazz will testify.

It might be a good idea the next time you are at Nick's to devote a little bit of time to watching the drumming technique of Danny Alvin. It's both a kick and an education and well worth the attention. Or get next to him between sets and hear about Chicago and the great days of jazz. You'll be listening to a guy who was there when it happened.

Jack Bland

It was during the war . . . oh yeah! Which one? I'm talkin' about the early '40s. I was on a gig in Lawrence, Mass. Man, that was a big joint we were working. Mezzrow, Jacques Butler (trumpet), Kaiser Marshall, Brunis, Bland and me. That place was so large you could get lost in there. Fact was it was used for circus acts. But with war shortages, etc., the owner was trying the small band plus vaudeville acts. That in itself was somethin' else. We were jazz players; what did we know about playing for acts? True, I could always play for singers; I'd come up in the business that way. But here we had dog acts, European dance teams; anything and everything. I recall one act, a chap who played all sorts of instruments; a show-stopper. He did everything but wave the American flag. A tough act to follow.

I think I'll skip the part of our band handling those acts. If my memory serves me we didn't lose the gig on that account. In fact we fulfilled our entire contract. But some funny things went on. We were seated on stage at one end; and there was enough room for a trapeze act on to the other end. So when it came our time to "front and center" (we also were featured in the show) a soloist would be out of reach. Our star was Butler. He'd go out there and blow 17 choruses of blues; finally having the house come down (our talk for a ringing round of applause). Usually Mezz would follow him. This one time I recall, Mezz was out there struggling and not givin' up. Chorus after chorus, and you could see people up front asking for their check; movement that makes a band nervous. You could shout at Mezz; wave at him, but he was oblivious. He went on and on. Finally it was over and he was back (when he was out there he was so far we couldn't reach him with a hook). It was Bland who barked, "Mezz, what the hell were you thinkin' of; man, you could have quit long ago." And who'll forget Mezzrow's answer. "I thought any minute I had 'em'."

That was the summer Butler showed us how well he could swim though he only had one leg. "Shark got to me." That cat played a lot of Louis (Armstrong) style; and he could sing, too. Yeh, and that was the summer we took to playing poker in our spare time. It didn't take a house to fall down on me to see I didn't belong in the same league with Bland. I believe that cat made enough bread from us (especially from Brunis; he was an unbeliever) to build his own brick house; brick by brick. He just didn't seem to be able to lose. And I remember we'd be sittin' there on stage and Jack would notice a light out, way up there on (above) the balcony. Bland would up and away, and replace it. No wonder that boss loved him.   A.H.

The Kazoo Comes On

by Jack Bland

Jack, can you remember how the Mound City Blueblowers got together?

Well, Art, to tell you the truth, I was working in a soda fountain in St. Louis and one day a fellow came in and asked for a job. He got the job . . . but he wasn't so good as a soda clerk. That night he went out with me to the place where I was staying. I had a banjo; he saw it and inquired if I could play it. I said, yes, a little, so he pulled a kazoo out of his pocket and we stomped off. It sounded pretty good, so that night we went to the Arcadia Dance Hall . . . banjo, kazoo and all.

After the dance we took a couple of girls home; they lived in North St. Louis. After leaving the girls we stopped at the Water Tower Restaurant, and we ran into Red McKenzie. We sat there and played until the Greek ran us out of the place; then we got onto the Grand Avenue streetcar with the whole gang and a donkey conductor who liked music. We played for two round-trips until Dick Sliven, the kazoo-playing soda clerk got into an argument with the conductor.

After that we played around at different places, house parties, beer parties, and finally we got a job with no money through Frank Trumbauer, playing at Alice Busch's wedding (the Anheuser-Busch beer people, that was). We set our band up in the hunting room and it wasn't long before everyone there was crowded into this one room.

Some fellow came over and wanted to know if we could play the "Merry Widow Waltz" . . . and he held up twenty dollars to Sliven. Sliven said "Sure!" and we went right into "Rose of the Rio Grande" and kept playing "Rose of the Rio Grande" all night for more twenties.

Then our next adventure was to go to Chicago to take a chorus on a record with Gene Rudermich. The night before we were supposed to make the record we went down to Mike Fritzel's place, known as the Friar's Inn, where the Brunis brothers had the band. They asked us what we were doing in Chicago. We told them that we could make some funny kind of a noise so they got us out on the floor to play.

Right in the middle of our second number a fellow walked out on the floor and said, "What kind of music is this?" It happened to be Isham Jones.

We told him that we were going to take a chorus on a rcord with Gene Rudermich the next day. He told us to go to a Turkish bath and "Get yourselves hoarsed up so you can't play those freak instruments." And he pressed some folded money into Mc-Kenzie's hand, and said, "I will get you a date on Brunswick records by yourselves."

The Jazz Record

15c

No. 33

June, 1945

Jack Bland

We didn't show up for the Rudermich records and two days later recorded what is now known as the "Arkansas Blues" and "The Blue Blues" on the Brunswick white label records known as the "Mound City Blue Blowers."

About two weeks later Ray Miller came to St. Louis and signed us up to go to New York . . . we opened in Atlantic City on Easter Sunday at the Beaux Arts. We worked there three months until the first of August and during these three months we would come into New York at least twice a month to make recordings . . . and on these recordings we added a guitarist . . . Eddie Lang . . . the greatest guitar player that ever lived, I think.

The first or second week in August we got a booking of four days at the State in Jersey City . . . this was where Eddie Lang joined us. We were supposed to meet him at the theatre at eleven o'clock in the morning; he showed up all right but he came in by the fire escape through the gallery.

Then we worked three days at Proctor's 125th Street, New York City . . . and right into the Palace Theater at 47th and Broadway.

O.K., Jack, that's all right as far as the story of the beginning of the Blue Blowers, but what do you consider the best record of all, from a collector's view-point, that you fellows made?

Well, Art, I'll tell you . . . I wake up every morning hearing "One Hour" . . . as my wife plays it continuously. This record was made for the Victor people in November 1929. On it were: Pee Wee Russell; Glen Miller; Gene Krupa; Eddie Condon; Red McKenzie; myself; and last but not least the soul of the tenor saxophone . . . Coleman Hawkins.

Are there any other records that you made that stand out in your memory?

Well, Art, I'm going to skip a couple of years . . . we put some records together with spit for the Brunswick people in 1932 under the name of "Jack Bland's Rhythm Makers" . . . "Who Stole the Lock" . . . "Margie" . . . "Mean Old Bedbug Blues" . . . "Bugle Call Rag" . . . that was the best one, there was no singing on that. And by the way, Art, Milt Gabler has a few of these records under the Commodore label.

Well, Art, I'm going to sign off now, I'm going upstairs and give the boys a few lessons in the fine art of poker.

As I Knew Eddie Lang

by Jack Bland

I first met Eddie Lang in 1924, in Atlantic City. He was playing with the Scranton Sirens—Russ Morgan, Jimmy Dorsey, Alfie Evans, Tommy Dorsey. It was in the summer, we were working the Beaux Arts; they were working on New York Avenue in a cafe.

Then in August he joined the Mound City Blue Blowers and we played the Palace Theatre after a week's break in Jersey City, the State. He was supposed to meet us backstage at the State at 10 a.m. for rehearsal. We waited about an hour, and finally from way up in the balcony we heard a voice: "Hey, are you boys down there?" He had come in through the fire escape.

He used to come from Atlantic City to New York to record. We only made two records before he joined us—"Arkansas Blues," "Blue," "Red Hot" and "San." Trumbauer was on the last two sides; "Red Hot" was his tune. After that Lang was on every record that we made.

The Blue Blowers were going big at that time, and we got an offer to play the Picadilly

Hotel in London. We had to get birth certificates to go to England, and Langie didn't know whether he was born in Philadelphia, Atlantic City or Italy.

On the way over we had a few bucks saved, and we ran into a great dice shooter, who proceeded to take everybody's money betting he could throw the dice against the wall and throw ten or four.

Finally we reached England. First thing happened when we got off the boat, Lang wanted to go back immediately. The English fog hit him and his hands turned purple and he got scared.

Before we opened at the Picadilly an agent put us out at Haggerty's Empire, out in Limehouse. We played the first number real fast—"Tiger Rag." Nobody understood or clapped or anything, and the orchestra leader looked at McKenzie, so McKenzie took a spit at the leader and said: "Which way do we go, boys?" and out we went.

We finally got through the first show and we wanted to cancel the whole thing, but the agent said, "All you have to do is play 'Red Hot Mama' and they'll learn it and sing it with you, and everything will be O.K." So we played "Red Hot Mama" the rest of the week.

Langie and I lived together. We went up to hunt an apartment on Germaine Street. We asked the price of the apartment and the attendant said, "Seven guineas," and Langie said "You wouldn't by any chance be gettin' personal?"

He was the swellest guy that ever lived, the best disposition—you couldn't make him mad. He was about five feet eight and a half inches, curly dark hair—and one of the best card players in the country. He could play any kind of cards. Lang stayed with us for four years. I'd say he was about 26 when he joined us. We used to unpack and play on a street-corner, or any bathroom, if anybody, a friend, wanted to hear us.

He had the best ear of any musician I ever knew. He could go into another room and hit "A" and come back and play cards for fifteen minutes, and then tune his instrument perfectly. I've seen that happen.

When we rode trains Langie would sleep in a lower berth with Dick Slavin. He used to let Dick have that privilege for a buck cheaper, providing he let Dick have a half hour start on him so that Dick could fall asleep before Langie started snoring.

In London, Langie took his guitar to the London Sporting Club and played, and they made him and me charter members. That really meant something, because the Sporting Club was composed of sportsmen who could bet up to a million without putting up the money.

Then, back in this country, I remember that at a theater date in Minneapolis on a Friday night they had to take the picture off three times because the crowd was clapping so hard, especially for Lang.

Maybe once every month he'd take some drinks. He didn't like to drink because he had a bad stomach and was afraid he'd get ulcers.

The Mound City Blue Blowers finally broke up. McKenzie got rich—had a lot of money, and wanted to go to St. Louis. So Langie went with Venuti as a team. I was still with him every day for a while, but then he finally went with Bing Crosby, and he was with him at the end.

He died from an operation on his tonsils. He bled to death.

He had one of the biggest funerals ever held in Philadelphia. Joe Venuti was mad because Crosby got to ride in the first car and he had to go in the second. All the guys in the pool hall liked him so much.

He was such a nice guy. I remember sometime after I'd first met him, we were playing pool in a small town for twenty dollars a game. I thought I was such a shark, but he could beat me so easy that the last show he missed purposely so that I'd win—he didn't want to take my money.

Of all the records he made I like best the ones that he made with Bessie Smith.

Eddie Condon

Eddie was talking. We were on stage at the Manassas (Va.) Jazz Festival. "I just finished an 8-week tour with Art Hodes," he said. "We covered 26 states in 8 weeks. That's over half the country. My gosh! No wonder I'm in a wheel chair."

This was in '72 (I believe). A bit later in the program Fat Cat (Johnson McCrea) who runs this shindig asked Eddie to come on stage and introduce me playing Hoagy Carmichael's "Washboard Blues." There's at least ten seconds of silence (with Condon at the mike) and then you hear him saying, "Am I talking too loud?"

I don't think Condon has ever gotten the accolades he deserves. It's my contention that when it comes to who'd done the most for jazz, Condon has got to be in the foreground. His night club, which gave jazz players a home, ran some 20 years. He was instrumental in producing jazz concerts at both Carnegie and Town Hall. He was one of the first to do a jazz program on TV. On and on; somewhere there must be data on all Condon did. But there's one funny scene I'd like to share with you. . . .

Julius's bar (just around the corner from Nick's in the Village . . . New York of course) was the hang-out for us jazz guys; and buffs. We practically "resided" there. At the time I'm remembering, Charles Edward Smith had written a book on jazz and felt good about it. It got to where it got to Eddie and he decided to take him down a peg. So he rigged this joke. He had some character with a beard drop in at Julius' and Eddie introduced C. Smith to him as a writer from Russia. Now here's how it went from there. . . .

"Mr. Nikokef, I want you to meet an American jazz writer, Charles Smith." After a handshake the so-called Russian said to Smith, "I hear you wrote a big book on jazz?" Smith acknowledged it and the Russian proceeded. "Do you play an instrument?" To which Charles answered in the negative. The Russian acted astounded. "You wrote a book on jazz music and you don't play an instrument?" Then came the crusher. "In Russia we shoot you." After that C.E.S. again became "one of the boys."   A.H.

Idyll of the Kings

by Amy Lee

Once Eddie Condon had a thousand dollars in his pocket, once in 1928.

Where he was—Chicago—didn't come on with anything to lure that one thousand out of his pocket the way where he could be—New York—could.

So Eddie gave over the banjo parts in Louis Panico's band to someone else, and came to New York just to have some fun. In the midst of that fun, he met Bea Palmer who was singing at Lou Schwartz's Chateau Madrid. Bea wanted some Chicago jazz to sing with as much as Eddie wanted New York fun. Even more: she sold him so thoroughly on the idea of Chicago jazz for the Chateau Madrid that he doubled back to Chicago,

Eddie Condon

rounded up his mob, from this band and that, and brought them east for their intended fiesta, Chicago style, at Chateau Madrid.

It's simple to think how the Chateau's manager, Lou Schwartz, should have felt when he saw Gene Krupa, Bob Freeman, Joe Sullivan, Frank Teschemacher, Jimmy McPartland, Jim Lannigan, and Eddie Condon, on the stand ready to audition. An all-star band, pre-Town Hall.

Awed should have been the word for Schwartz.

Pure jazz was right there for him.

And when they pitched it to him, instead of letting it go by once or twice, he swung at it wild and missed of course and broke up the game right there. All he could say was, "What goes? What is this noise anyway?"

Explanations couldn't change the noise, so the Chicago Rhythm Kings finished their job at the Chateau Madrid before they started.

As Condon says, "Schwartz thought we were a bunch of carpenters."

New York music was never like that!

No job and no dough in New York was no fun. The Chicago Rhythm Kings had to work somewhere, and the somewhere that came along, like out of nowhere, was as complete a surprise as if Lou Schwartz had suddenly said, "You're hired."

The Chicago Rhythm Kings got a week at the Palace.

The Palace, the final stage in the survival of showdom's fittest.

The Chicago Rhythm Kings had never been on any stage before. They came on the Palace stage and played just the way they played for the Chateau Madrid audition —with guts and spirit and freedom, despite all obstacles. Tesch and Freeman were feuding. In the middle of the week, Freeman decided he wanted to go to Paris, so he left, just like that. ("I think he stayed over there about twenty minutes," Condon says.) They had to add a fiddle to the band to put over the waltz number for the dance team on the bill, a fiddle while jazz burned unwanted. Variety commented, "The less said about the band the better."

It was a glory week, if a tough one, and the reign of the Chicago Rhythm Kings did not end altogether at the Palace, but shifted to one night of splendor at the swanky Newport Club. "We took over," Eddie says, "in real midwest style."

But New York wasn't much taken with that midwest style. It was too busy with prohibition and how to avoid it to worry about how Eddie Condon and the Chicago Rhythm Kings made music or a living. And while the living wasn't exactly easy, Condon solved part of it at Plunkett's, famous musicians' hangout, where he kept his clothes in an old unused ice-box. "Made it easy," he says. "Go in any time for a quick change."

No, New York didn't care. In a couple of months, the Chicago Rhythm Kings were dead, long live the Kings who in Chicago had recorded the inspired music New York had for the taking—and couldn't take it.

On Okeh, the Chicago Rhythm Kings made "Nobody's Sweetheart," "Sugar," "China Boy," and "Liza." The personnel was: Gene Krupa, drums; Joe Sullivan, piano; Jimmy Lannigan, bass; Eddie Condon, banjo; Jimmy McPartland, cornet; Bud Freeman, tenor; Frank Teschemacher, clarinet. For Brunswick, with Muggsy Spanier on cornet in place of McPartland, and Mezz Mezzrow on tenor in place of Freeman, they made "I Found A New Baby," and "There'll Be Some Changes Made." One other record, made by Tesch, Krupa, Sullivan, and Condon, was issued only in Australia.

Jess Stacy

I've said this before; you don't ask a piano player about a pianist. You ask his drummer, or bassist. Someone who works alongside of him night after night. Or a player in the front line. 'Course if I listen to a cat pound the keys I come away with some instant reactions. He either does somethin' to (for) me or he leaves me cool. To tell you the truth I never did get to hear Jess play except now and then on a recording. But he crossed my path and I have good vibes about him.

It may have been before that, but it certainly was one of the jobs Jess turned over to me. The Subway was advertised as "the longest bar in the world." Drummer Frank Snyder had the band and Jess fixed it for me to have the gig when he left. Man, that was an interesting joint. That was the first time I ever met anyone who wrote on jazz; Helen Oakley. That was a big place. And they kept it dim. A guy could get lost there with his chick and no one would know it. Then at certain times during the evening a bus-load of "see Chicago" tourists would gawk through. You'd hear the bus driver state "Hang on to your purse and hang on to the person in front of you." As I said, the tourists would gawk at us but for me, they were the show. The strange, curious faces; staring, like they wanted to memorize everything. Yeh, man; we'd lay for that scene.

There were several other gigs Jess gave me. Then he left the scene. Joined B. Goodman. And I didn't hear about him until one night, working the 5100 Club with Rod Cless, Jess dropped in. Latter Benny G. and John Hammond arrived and were seated. The "buzz-buzz" went around. I think I was being auditioned but I wasn't sure. Couldn't have cared less. I had no eyes for joining a big band. At one point Benny's girl singer (and if my memory serves me right it was Helen Forrest but I could be mistaken) came to the stand while we were playing the blues and tried to get into it. No way. For me the blues was somethin' you felt at the moment; not a set of lyrics. This chick hung around and listened; then went back to Goodman's table. Soon after that the whole party left. Needless to say I never got any offers from that direction. But I'm sure Jess had tried.

I never heard a disparaging word (like the song goes) about Jess Stacy. Oh I heard the usual gossip when he was married to Lee Wiley. But no one every said anything but good about J. Stacy. He was good for me . . .   A.H.

Riverboat Jess

by Mary Peart

I could tell you that Jess' whole life is bound up in music. I could rave on about how jazz has always been the only thing that mattered to him, but you know all that. Just sit down and listen to his recording of "Complainin' " or "Ec-Stacy," or any of his other compositions, and he'll tell you much better than I ever could.

Jess Stacy has the soul and technique of a great musician, but he has much more than that. He'd probably laugh if you said it to him—but he's a great humanitarian, too.

"You've got to keep in touch with people. When a guy makes too much money he gets swell-headed and forgets how ordinary people feel. I don't mean you have to get drunk every night and knock yourself out, anybody who does that is a plain fool. But you have to be down-to-earth to play jazz. You have to know how people live."

That explains somewhat the way he plays. His music is "down-to-earth," which is part of its appeal. Jess is sincere in his liking for people. He is always interested in what they think, and cares more intensely than any other musician what is said and written about his playing.

Jess hasn't always been a piano man. For the first six years of his musical career he was a drummer, and for several years he played drums in his home town band (Cape Girardeau, Missouri, where he was born August 4, 1904). I think the influence shows very plainly in his strong rhythmic drive. When he was fourteen he realized somehow that drums weren't enough. There was something in him crying for expression, something that drums couldn't satisfy. So he turned to the piano. There is an instrument that is complete in itself, with endless possibilities for rhythmic counterpoint and harmonic invention. And Jess found them all. But it wasn't easy, and it isn't easy yet. Not when you have a temperament like Jess's. Talking to him, you get the impression of restlessness and a desire for peace of mind always contending. Of a driving ambition and sureness of his ability battling pessimism and a personal feeling of inferiority.

He says he "decided to make a career of music because it was easier than driving a truck," but we know better than that. Those things are decided for you the minute you are born. If you have the guts and ambition to fulfill what's born in you, you'll do it. And Jess had. He didn't get much encouragement, even at first. His tonedeaf uncle who disliked music intensely, used to pay him not to practice. "Here's a dollar, sonny. Just run along now, and play some other time, huh?" But Jess wasn't easily discouraged. Before he

was through, he literally starved for his music.

His first job as a pianist was on the Majestic Excursion Steamer playing up and down the Mississippi, and in 1925 he worked on the *S.S. Capitol* out of St. Louis. There he learned most of his technique, and the influence of the riverboat jazz was so strong that it has lasted all through the years. You can feel it in those rugged blues, the slow, pulsating rhythm and bizarre harmonies at which he excels.

In the next ten years jobs with many bands followed, although there were plenty of times when there wasn't a job. Floyd Town, Eddie Neibaur and Maurie Stein were among the leaders for whom Jess played. During the latter part of this period he recorded with Boyce Brown and Paul Mares, old time Chicago jazz man.

This was in his Chicago days, an apprenticeship which many great jazz musicians seem to have gone through. It was in 1926 that Jess met Muggsy Spanier. This was the start of an enduring friendship which has been one of the finest things in the lives of both of them. But let Muggsy tell you about it.

"Jess and I played together in the Triangle Cafe, along with Tesch, George Wettling, Floyd O'Brien—what a band that was! The same band later went into the Midway Gardens. Jess and I used to hang around the Sunset and listen to King Oliver and Louis Armstrong. Another time when I was on vacation I rented a cottage on Lake Delavan, Wisconsin, and Jess came up—we took a boat out on the lake at night, with my victrola and some records—say, did you ever listen to music on the water? There's nothing like it—so beautiful it would drive you nuts! We played Louis and Bix records, and classical music, Delius; it was like being in another world. Well, all that ended in 1929, when I went with Ted Lewis, and Jess—he just gigged around Chicago gin mills."

"Why didn't anyone appreciate him then, Muggsy?" "Because they didn't know enough to appreciate him!" sitting up straight, with fire in his eyes. "I tried to get the Dorsey brothers interested in him when they started their band, and they wouldn't listen to me."

Finally the break came for which he had been working and hoping. John Hammond, after hearing him beat a piano in a small

The Jazz Record

15c

No. 27

December, 1944

Jess Stacy

Chicago nitery in 1935, persuaded Benny Goodman to listen to him, and to try him out in his band. Incidentally, Muggsy was there the night Hammond came in to hear Jess. The rest we all know, how he hit the top with Goodman's great band of the late 1930's, then joined Bob Crosby's band, (a band which frequently achieved some really good jazz—Muggsy was there, too) and went back to BG in 1942, with the demise of the Bobcats.

Jess doesn't feel very strongly about "atrocious commercialism." One reason, I think, is that it has never touched him very closely—he didn't have to make the choice between the way he wants and making a good living. He has successfully combined the two. Somehow, they never tried to tell Jess how to play. He never had to stick much to the arrangements—just give us a good beat, and play around in the background—and it always turned out to be much better than anything they could have written for him. Goodman says he is the greatest of all the jazz pianists and comes closest to perfection that anyone can—praise from Caesar.

But Jess does have one gripe about the public. "They want a thing to look hard. You can work up something that is very extremely difficult technically, but if it doesn't *look*

difficult, they don't pay any attention to it. But if you beat your brains out all over the stage, they think it's wonderful, and yell for more. What do they know?"

Jess plays classical music sometimes, too. He is devoted to Ravel, Delius and Debussy and pianist Walter Gieseking, other influences in his style, and practices Chopin Etudes to keep his hand supple—those marvelous hands that can reach an octave and five keys. One minor ambition was to master Ravel's "The Fountains." "Why should anyone get conceited over his playing? Now, if I could play that," holding out the music, "then I'd really think I was a good pianist." But he wouldn't. Because it's part of his nature to be over-modest about anything he can do, and if he could play the most difficult composition ever written, he'd just say, "Well, I worked on it until I had it licked. I guess anybody could play it if they practiced long enough."

No, you can't tell Jess he's good. He knows it, but he's afraid to admit it, because the years were so long when no one believed in him. "You never know about the future. I hope to be playing always, even after I retire. Oh, that won't be till I'm sixty. I ought to be a pretty good pianist by that time, don't you think?"

Frank Melrose

There were three of us; all piano-players. Melrose, George Zack and myself. If Jess Stacy and Joe Sullivan were up front in jazz circles (recognition) we were "the second line." And for a bit we were inseparable. When I had a gig you could be sure that Zack and Melrose would show up before the night was over. Once Frank sat out there and wouldn't spell me; it just sounded too good to him. Finally, he couldn't stand it so he left; came back within hours and brought a fiddle. I never knew he could play anything but the piano. Then he sat in; then I knew.

Pete Daily? Off and on; we'd meet; make some music together. He blew good lead horn. But all those guys he mentions! That brings back memories. Huh! Sleepy Kaplan. There's a cat that got a moniker that fits. I remember one job I had (or was on). We kept waiting for Kaplan to show up so we could start work. He finally did; forty-five minutes late. "Sleepy, where the hell were you?" And he answered "I ran into this guy and he wanted to talk and I couldn't interrupt him." And I'll never forget calling him for a gig, and his mother answered. "Is Sleepy there?" I asked. And her answer floored me. In a heavy Jewish accent she said, "there's no one slippin' here."

Never heard Jack Daily play anything but piano and guitar. He was soft and gentle on that string instrument. When Blue Note gave me some dates (recording) I remembered Jack. One of the tunes carries his name. And Leroy Smith! He played all styles of clarinet. Fact, if you didn't have a lead horn Leroy played fine melody. But he wandered; you saw him for a bit and he was off and gone. Lonnie Johnson; Lee Collins. Chicago names. Did get to play with Lee at the Blue Note in '50. That's another story. But he blew.

Yeh! You can read this tale and re-read it. Honest; it tells it as it was. Close your eyes and you'll get the picture. For it was a time of discovering this jazz music. And nothing else much mattered. Except getting knocked out (or high; whatever your thing was) and playing music. Making money seemed so unimportant. But to play! You never missed out on that. Never let a day (night) go by without playing music. Didn't matter where or for whom. Like the time we walked into a bar (room); and there was an upright piano. So we asked the man (boss-man) "Care if we play?" He told us to go ahead. So back to the car; unload the instruments; set up the drums and we're off and away. Play 'til we get tired. Bought our own drinks too. I guess the boss and those people (customers) thought we were crazy. Yeh! We were; crazy 'bout music. . . .   A.H.

Barrelhouse Frank Melrose

by Pete Daily

I had heard about the pianist Frank Melrose by 1930. Both of us lived near Hammond, but because he played up in Chicago or in Kansas City, he wasn't home much; I didn't meet him until later. Fellow musicians made a legend of his terrific piano style. It was in about 1932 that we worked together for the first time on a gig in Hegewisch. I started the job on bass horn, but before half the evening was over our trumpet man went blotto, so I finished the night on his instrument. Little details of that job are clear in mind. I recall as if it happened yesterday how Frank played even beyond his reputation—a solid and beautiful barrelhouse piano. He wore a brown suit; his straw hat was crown up on the upright lid. He played with his hands high over the keyboard, like a classical man, his fingers walked around like spider legs.

Afterwards we were on a lot of weekend gigs together. Whenever I got a job or could suggest personnel, Frank it was on piano. Evidently he was satisfied with my horn because he used to call me for work too,

perhaps even oftener than I called him. One night in the summer of 1933 Frank and I went to the Fair in Chicago, and then when it closed, to some spots on the South Side. At one place Frank heard a good sounding piano. He pushed a fumbling black kid off the stool and we took over for about six hours. Along about daylight five Indians arrived from one of the Fair's sideshows. I guess Frank didn't realize about Indians and firewater when he said, sure, they could use our jug. When the quart was gone, we got some more. Soon the chief went mildly nuts and insisted on marrying a dizzy frump who had come in and had started giving them the routine. Frank wanted everybody happy, so he put his coat on backwards and married the couple with a phone book. Last we saw they were blissful.

By 1935 we were pretty regularly together. There were several weeks at Johnny Nichols' in Calumet City with Owen Johnson drums and a Joe Sullivan reeds. At Nichols' we celebrated like New Year's Eve on the night when Frank's first child, Franklin Jr., was born.

In 1932 we had a pretty good stay at the Continental Club in Cal City. Nick Nicholas was on drums, Dooney Ward clarinet. During this time my eyesight failed completely for several months. The fellows had to pick me up at home to take me to the job, and then lead me to the stand and afterwards down again and home. Sometimes they came during the day and we'd talk or walk or listen to the radio.

Frank's playing had kids and young musicians packing around the stand every night. He killed them and us with his unpredictable breaks, wild solo choruses, and the piano burlesques he'd do with a straight face. One of his tricks reminded me of the drunken dance where the dancer begins to lean and then runs to catch up with himself, but finally too late. Frank would play a staggering arpeggio or chromatic chords, getting farther and farther off the beam, and finally as if "What the Hell," he crashed both arms down on the keyboard. Two beats and away he'd go again. During my blind spell I couldn't see the crowd that applauded Frank's solos, but it made me feel good inside. He was my boy. I was getting an idea like religion that everything in spiritual life was in good jazz, and that we were almost over the hill, almost we were playing perfect jazz. The joint jobs were more fun for us than anything that happened since, still there was something more we wanted.

By 1935 we had begun to shape in our minds a dream band, an outfit that would stick together until it was perfect, playing jazz ragtime, and blues. Jack Daily, who sometimes came in on piano when Frank couldn't, had the same slant. But he knew Frank was the man for piano, so he concentrated on his banjo. When we talked about the dream band we considered the fellows we had worked with. Some of them seemed consistently better than anybody on records; conceitedly perhaps we didn't bother with anybody outside the Chicago area to get exactly what we wanted. Just as any jazzman whom we had learned to know on records, our boys made mistakes, but in the dream we had cured their errors or rehearsed away their shortcomings. And honest to God, it finally worked out that way, John.

Sleepy Kaplan became our drummer (he's at a place on North Avenue now); Leroy Smith clarinet (he was last heard from on Bataan). Bill Helgert was trombone (now in Boyd Raeburn's outfit at the Band Box in Chicago). Bill Moore was on bass. All of us had the Blues and Dixieland spirit. It was Frank's library which we used, and in a short time we began to find that as well as on the Blues and two-beat jazz we were sold on Frank's versions of breakdown ragtime tunes like "Russian Rag," "The Romp," "Wild Cat," and "Roll Up The Carpets." Frank gave us the ragtime urge by showing us what could be done with it. I've listened to every ragtime band that has come out on records, and to dozens which haven't. None of them could compare with ours, I honestly believe. Maybe Frank was the only man who ever lived who knew all the secrets. Some day I hope I can get with a group that will make that kind of music again. You'll learn then what I'm talking about.

For a while we held Wednesday rehearsals at the Chelsea Hotel where a gang besides our own would collect and listen: when we were through rehearsals, everyone would sit in for jam. Fazola once told me, when playing with us on a post-rehearsal session, "Pete, if anything should happen to Leroy, remember I wanna."

It didn't occur to me until later that I had neglected to tell Fazola that our spirit stemmed from the results Frank drew out of us with the same kind of natural ease Jelly Roll had used in shaping his groups. When recently I heard Lu Watters band I recognized from their first note that their greatest deficiency was a Frank Melrose, someone who could dominate and mold the group into musical unity. Louis, Muggsy, Fats and Noone have done it.

For two reasons this was a group like nothing commercial. First, because we couldn't wait for rehearsals (we even got together on Sunday afternoons); second, we couldn't get jobs. Once when we did manage to snag an Irish picnic up on the North Side, a priest who apparently knew all things righteous asked for "Georgia Swing." That was No. 19 in our books. But you may be able to imagine how rushed for jobs we were not, playing full programs of "Georgia Swing," "Gary Blues," "Bluesiana," "Sweet Daddy," "69th and Wentworth," "Have You Ever Felt that Way," and rags. Nearly we got in the Sherman Hotel—nearly. Even though nobody hired us, there were a lot of good people who knew what we were doing and said so, and gave us confidence. "Hummer" Collette, now with Columbia's Chicago Studios, was then at Gamble's recording laboratory. After hearing us, he invited us to use Gamble's sound-treated rooms with good pianos. As we played he would often copy things down on record. Frank Lyons came over from his brokerage office on LaSalle Street to listen and to buy copies of what he liked best. When Hummer left Gamble, Frank bought all the copies we fellows in the band hadn't wheedled away. Some I have still, kind of ragged now—"Wild Cat," "Da Da Strain," and a piano solo.

In 1936 and 37 Frank and I sat in many times with Lee Collins' band at the Derby Club. Lonnie Johnson was for a time in the outfit and he gave Frank such kicks with his 12-string concert guitar that we never would quit until everybody had dropped out dead drunk or dead tired. I don't suppose Frank admired any musician more than Lonnie except Jelly.

Here are some incidental data. About the time of the Chicago Fair, Frank played with Max Miller's outfit at Club Ultra, 39th and Cottage. Frank's recording of "Whoopee Stomp" on Paramount is really "Boy In The Boat," which was always one of his favorites. Wherever a piano can be heard on the Kansas City Tin Roof Stompers sides for Brunswick race series, it is Frank. He may not have played on all sides, since I cannot hear piano at all on two of them. I am positive that Frank was a pianist on the 6 Memphis Nighthawk sides for Vocalion.

It was about 1937 that Frank and Georgie Barnes worked for the winter at the Little Club in Hammond. Georgie was about sixteen, and his father brought him to work and then called for him about midnight. Papa would sit around a while if they were really hitting the ball, or if a session had developed. No wonder Georgie has always worshiped Frank—you should have seen how, if business was dull, they would spend entire evenings on jazz rudiments. Frank enjoyed teaching earnest youngsters who showed promise.

One of the Detroit characters figuring in his reminiscences was a hoodlum who flashed a gun when Frank made like intermission. After bullying Frank for three hours, friend hood would clear up his little joke with a $10 tip.

There were some things about that Sunday before Labor Day 1941, the day before Frank's death, you left unsaid. Late on Sunday morning, Frank came to our apartment in the Windsor-Wilson. My wife, Faye, helped him fix a bite, and then I sent him to the davenport to nap for a few hours. After rolling out, he played with our kids until dinner—that was unusual for Frank. I never before saw him show such interest in any children except his own. Frank was jubilant about the prosperity his machinist's job was to bring. Faye caught the mood and celebrated by preparing a whoppin' chicken dinner. That early evening, while I played a society fray at the Sheridan Plaza, Frank went to the Espana to see Max Miller, Sleepy, and Clary Vern Joachim. (I had been playing with the boys up to the previous week or so, but because business slumped, the boss had to lay off first our singer, then the brass section; within another few weeks chronic slumping killed the spot). After short stops in several spots, he came back at 11:30 p.m., in a hurry to make the one o'clock South Shore train to Hammond. I remember Frank saying that on the Saturday night previous he had been down to the South Side looking for some of the old familiar "barbecue gang" around 48th and State. None were around. He mentioned that he wanted to try again when he had more time but tonight he had too little money left and time was short. I repeated this comment at the inquest after his death. As I said goodbye, I told him that I would stop off at the Melrose cottage on my way back from Crown Point, where I had a job the next night. I left him at Wilson Avenue.

Some of us said at the inquest that many circumstances of his death smelled fishy. Frank had no business at 135th and Oglesby, where his body was found; it was a lonely place, only indirectly on his way home. Although bruised as if a car had run over him, Frank's face had a long, clean cut below the left ear. His watch was not damaged. Nothing remained in his billfold but his Social Security card. Nobody knows.

(Thanks to John Steiner and Pete Daily for permission to reprint this article, which originally appeared in "Piano Jazz," No. 1, published by the Jazz Sociological Society of London, 1945).

Davenport Piano

by Floyd Bean

Back in 1918 I had a little jazz band, just a bunch of kids, and we got the job at Linwood Inn, on the river seven miles south of Davenport, Iowa. It was our first trip away from home. We had a nice little five-piece band, and spent the whole summer there. Bix Beiderbecke used to come out from town once in a while and sit in. He hardly ever played trumpet; used to like to sit in on piano instead. Of course we knew he was a wonderful musician, but he had only a local reputation then. We even thought of hiring him when our trumpet player left. But we needed somebody who could read well enough to carry the lead on new sheet music, and Bix couldn't read. However, we liked having him come and sit in, and he showed me a lot of new things about playing piano. Playing tenths—I'd never heard of that before, always played octaves in the bass. Bix would sit down for hours and show me tricks on the piano.

I had started out when I was just a kid playing drums for school dances when I was still in knee pants. My mother made me take piano lessons, but it was considered sissy for a boy to play piano, and I didn't like it. I used to pull down the shades so nobody could see me practicing. I borrowed the town band drum, an old thing about four feet high, with ropes to tighten the head, and a snare drum with a single head, and with a piano player I would do the town dances. Later my uncle bought me a good set of drums. My cousin, Carl Bean, still has a territory band out in Iowa. He's the one who wrote "Scatterbrain," a big hit a few years ago.

I played drums most of the way through high school, but about that time I got interested in jazz piano. There was nobody to show me how to play it, though, and I didn't know how to go about it until I got hold of George "Stick" Leins who had a small band around there, and he taught me a few chords. Then I listened to phonograph records and worked out the first step toward playing jazz by myself.

I gave up drums then, and organized a bunch of kids to go around playing. We had the all-summer date at Davenport, where we met Bix, and then the band broke up. I moved to Muscatine, about thirty miles from Davenport, when I was nineteen, and was around there for two years, playing with several territory bands through the midwest. Although I had been playing piano for several years, I was still trying by myself to figure out how to play jazz piano. I remember that while in Muscatine I first figured out augmented and diminished chords by listening to an old crystal radio set.

In 1924 I worked out of Fond du Lac, Wisconsin, in a band with Bunny Berigan. And part of another summer, about 1929, I was with a band booking out of Albert Lea, Minnesota, with Jack Jenny.

About 1932 I landed in Davenport with a staff job at the radio station, WOC. I was studying off and on then, and starting to do some arranging. I worked for a while with a band led by Jimmy Hicks. He played trumpet, and it was a very good little jazz band. Then later I had my own band. I was also arranging and playing piano at the radio station. Along about this time Bix, who was then with Whiteman, came back home for a short visit, and came around to sit in with the band once in a while.

I was listening to Rube Bloom and Lee Sims on radio and records, but when I heard Earl Hines I knew this was the real thing. At one time I even had a couple of pupils in Davenport, trying to teach them to play like Hines. However, I don't think it did any of us any harm; Hines has so much stuff that you can learn a lot from him and still have a style of your own.

Then the depression came along and things really got bad. There was only one piano job in town and another man had it. My own band—and it was a good little band, too—was working seven nights a week for $15 a man. I pulled out and went to Chicago.

I began studying hard in Chicago, both piano and arranging. I was a fairly schooled and experienced pianist and had done considerable studying, but now I settled down for a whole year of studying like mad. One of the first things I did on reaching Chicago was to go out to hear Earl Hines in person. And until I heard Paul Mares and some of the other good musicians, I didn't even know real blues, the old slow kind.

The first good thing I got in Chicago, after being there a year, was a job with Eddie Neibaur, who had the Seattle Harmony Kings, later disbanded. It was a good band for those days, ten pieces. We worked four seasons in Chicago, alternating between the Casino Moderne on the South Side and going in summer to an open air place on the North Side called the Wilshore. I was doing all the band arranging.

The next year I went in with Jimmy McPartland at the Three Deuces, Chicago, with a small band in which I had a third interest. After a few months there, the Bob Crosby band was in town, and Zurke was having some trouble, so I subbed for him for a short time. We made a few records during that time, "Sigh No More Lady," and the rest of the Shakespearian song series. The labels credit Zurke and Sterling Bose, but Billy Butterfield played trumpet and I was on piano. When Crosby's band left for Milwaukee to play a theatre engagement, they hired Pete Viera, but Pete got arthritis in his hands and couldn't play, so I went up there and took the job again. Then they left for New York, and Joe Sullivan took over.

I jobbed around with small combinations; at one time I was with Eddie Howard, a 26-week radio account making transcriptions, in which I played and also made the arrangements. I was jobbing on the side, too, on the air twice a week, and we made the week's records in one session. We also made twenty-one sides for Columbia, strictly commercial.

About five years ago I joined Boyce Brown, out Howard Street at the Silhouette Club. When that was ended I got my own little trio at the Barrel of Fun on Broadway. This was just what I wanted, guitar, bass and piano in a small spot, and I was probably playing at my peak right then. It was this trio that cut a few private recordings for John Steiner, which have never been issued publicly.

Then I joined Boyd Raeburn, and was with his band for ten months. In January of 1944 I had my own small combination at the Brass Rail, four men and a girl.

In July, a year ago, I had an offer to tour with Eddie Stone's band. He was at the Aragon in Chicago. It's a big band, commercial, and not the kind of music I want to play, but it gave me a chance to do a lot of advanced arranging. Stone is now in the Roosevelt Hotel in New York, which means that we have to try to please the crowd Lombardo plays for. We go on the air three times a week, and sometimes Stone can feature the piano and a few boogie things I wrote myself. I have been arranging for a long time, but with this band I have learned quite a lot. For a while I did all the arranging, but it was too much to do and play piano all the time; Stone now has another arranger and I do only a few numbers now and then.

I wrote a song about six years ago, but did nothing with it until recently, when Eddie Stone wrote lyrics for it and we are now using it for our closing theme. It's now being published, titled "I Never Thought I'd Sing the Blues," and Woody Herman is slated to record it. I have also written a number of other numbers, such as "Bean's Boogie," "Jumpin' Bean" and "Back Room Blues," not published.

I hope to do more composing and arranging; I am interested in going on to symphonic type arranging. As for playing, I'd much rather do it with a small and strictly jazz combination somewhere, but such things are hard to find.

George Brunis

There's going to be a lot written about George. He was that kind of guy. Out-going. Out-spoken; what came to mind came to mouth. Funny? Yes, at times very funny. Brunis was built "mid-size"; with a little weight on him (at least when I knew him in the '40s and on). George usually was quick to smile; sort of a sly grin. There was more than one side to Brunis. Like . . . Brunis was rehearsing a band; he was going into the Blue Note (Chicago). This was the very early '50s. He picked the men himself and they worked out the routines. Now then, when George isn't working he cools it. He stays cold sober. But on stage he likes a taste. After one set (half-hour or so) George picked up the mike and started telling the audience "This is the worst bunch of bums I ever worked with." Sober it didn't sound bad to him. But after a few drinks reality set in and he really heard what he had put together.

But the story I'd like to lay on you is one I knew of first hand. It was this same Blue Note that I had brought a band into on a January ('50). Pee Wee Russell, Fred Moore, Chippie Hill had come with me from N.Y.C. In Chicago we were joined by Floyd O'Brien and Lee Collins. But within a month Floyd and Lee were to be replaced by Brunis and Wild Bill Davison. The plan (as it later was unfolded to me) was to build an all-star group (Bechet was slated to join us) and as we were working for the Glaser Agency, we would be following L. Armstrong around in the various clubs he played. The clout would be "if you want Louis then take the All-Stars." It probably would have worked. Brunis did take O'Brien's place. Zutty Singleton replaced Moore. We never did get to Wild Bill; I'll tell you 'bout that sometime.

Frank Holsfiend was the club's manager, and he'd introduce the group when we hit the stage. We were called The Dixielanders. Most of us were treated to a straight intro; but not George. "Ladies and gentlemen, I want you to meet the great trombonist George Brunis. He was born at the turn of the century and there's some talk that he helped turn it."

We lasted 11 weeks. I can't recall all the name groups that appeared opposite us. I do remember Sarah Vaughn being there. Probably Errol Garner. This was the top jazz club in Chicago. The agent had a great plan and we had a beautiful opportunity but looking back I can see where it didn't have much chance to suceed. It was exciting but to tell you the truth I couldn't stand too much of that excitement. O'Brien, Brunis, Collins, Pee Wee; all gone now. But they made big music while they were here. . . .   A.H.

Portrait of George Bruni(e)s

by Amy Lee

His horn can make you happy, and that's something to be thankful for in these days of horns that too often blast, too often scream, too often say nothing, and that very loudly.

His horn speaks honestly always—and confidently, yet modestly.

From the heart of Dixieland he came with that horn. His name is George Brunis and his horn's a trombone.

He first played upright alto and drums, as a kid in New Orleans. Nor did he ever have to worry about people to play with because his whole family played: his father, fiddle; his mother, piano; his sister, guitar; three brothers, Abbie, Richie, and Merritt, trumpets; another brother, Henry, trombone.

Work was to be had from Papa Laine, the Meyer Davis of New Orleans, and in the Mardi Gras parades.

Young George first came to playing terms with a trombone the night he went on a job at the Crescent City Club with Papa Laine's son, Alfred, musically known as Pansy Laine and his Wampas Cats. The trombone player didn't show up, so Pansy said to George, "We've got to have a trombone. How about you playing trombone?" George figured what could he lose, so he faked on trombone that night, just as eloquently as the rest of the Wampas Cats were faking, and he's been faking ever since to the eternal glory of jazz and the eternal delight of everyone who gets a kick out of true harmonizing, and on-the-nose playing, never messed up with a lot of phoney tricks and useless notes.

No, George Brunis never learned to read. He didn't need to. He's blessed with an ear that tells him the right notes and the right harmony every time.

That ear and that trombone began taking him places. There were at Bucktown on Lake Pontchartrain, near New Orleans, two roadhouses—Brunning's and Martin's—across the road from each other, where George and his trombone and Leon Rappolo with his clarinet blew back and forth at each other until they saw that blowing together was a much better idea.

And not long after that, a wire came from a New Orleans drummer, Ragbaby Stevens, then in Chicago, to Abbie and George Brunis, saying the playing was fine in Chicago, come on up. The Brunis brothers didn't want to go, so Paul Mares took up his trumpet and went instead.

He soon sent for George, and this time George decided it wouldn't make sense to stay home. He joined Paul in Ragbaby's 5-piece outfit at Chicago's Campbell Garden. Next move was into the Blatz Palm Garden, with pianist Elmer Schoebel, C-melody sax-man Jack Pettis, and drummer Frank Snyder. There he met Muggsy Spanier, and first thing George knew he and Muggsy were boxing each other at an Athletic Club. "Some gangsters made us do it," says George. "I don't know why."

From the Lincoln Gardens, another famous Chicago jazz haven, Brunis and the boys boarded one of the Strekfus boats, plying the Mississippi, St. Louis to St. Paul. At Davenport, he met Rappolo again, and Bix Beiderbecke, who came to listen to this music he knew was right, the music he was soon to send singing triumphantly out of his own horn, that little cornet without an equal.

That summer's boat trip landed the band—Schoebel, "Rap," Mares, Pettis,

THE JAZZ RECORD

15c
A COPY

PUBLISHED SEMI - MONTHLY

No. 4   New York, N. Y.   April 1, 1943

George Brunis

Brunis, banjoist Louis Black, Snyder, and bassist Steve Brown—at Mike Fritzel's Friar's Inn, where they were dubbed Friar's Society Orchestra. When Schoebel left to go to the Midway Gardens, Mel Stitzel came in on piano, and Ben Pollack on drums, and the band changed its name to the New Orleans Rhythm Kings, quite more appropriate than the society tag.

Before George joined Ted Lewis in 1923, he had his own band at Valentino Inn. The 12-year stretch with Lewis included tours all over America and Europe, which Brunis liked very much.

1935 saw him back for a repeat of his pre-Lewis days, this time in a New York setting. He went into the first Famous Door on 52nd Street with Louis Prima, and then joined the short-lived group of nine girls and nine men known as Mills' Cavalcade, in the company of drummer Frankie Carlson, tenorman Herbie Haymer, bassist Sid Weiss, and Kitten-on-the-Keys Zez Confrey.

In 1936 began what might be called Brunis' Travels Through Nick's, the Greenwich Village spot which got with jazz early and has stayed late. His travels started with the band headed by Sharkey Bonano. From that time Nick's bands have come up regularly with different leaders, yet the music and the names have a sameness that's inspiring: Pee Wee Russell, Eddie Condon, Joe Sullivan, George Wettling, Dave Bowman, Jimmy McPartland, Bud Freeman, Bobby Hackett, Mary Marsala. And always George Brunis.

Brunis' first serious side-trip out of Nick's was in 1939, when he played the record-breaking five and a half months date with Muggsy Spanier's Ragtime Band at Chicago's Hotel Sherman, followed by two months —yes, at Nick's. His next detour took him, in the winter of 1940-41, to Child's Restaurant at Broadway and 103rd Street, with Art Hodes and Rod Cless. Their two-beat outfit couldn't take the Viennese waltz-rhumba requests forever, so one of the finest Dixieland combinations in New York had to check out before it had hardly checked in, and George drifted back to Nick's. And then to a shipyard in Mobile, Alabama, and back to Nick's, and out to Chicago's Brass Rail with McPartland and Joe Sullivan and Pee Wee and Condon, and back last April to Nick's, where he isn't momentarily.

His records are legion: Deccas with Sharkey Bonano, and Wingy Manone; the Muggsy Bluebirds; Vocalions with Chauncey Morehouse ("On the Alamo," "The Blues," "My Gal Sal"); Milt Gabler's Commodores—"Carnegie Jump," "Carnegie Drag," "Jada," "Love is Just Around the Corner."

This Brunis, Dixieland trombonist supreme, likes only one Dixieland tune, "Ostrich Walk," "because it has some melody to it." He loves all music that sounds pleasing to his ears. Writes beautiful tunes, words and music, which aren't published "because you've got to be a big bandleader and have your own publishing house." He'd like to have a little band that could play like Bix and Don Murray (Murray he thinks one of the greatest and least appreciated jazz clarinetists) and the others on Frank Trumbauer's "Riverboat Shuffle" record, "but where could I find men like that?"

He used to talk about writing a symphony to be titled "The Faker," and now he talks about not playing anymore because he's getting on.

When the day comes that George Brunis stops playing trombone, for any reason, that's the day jazz, and honesty, will sustain a stunning loss.

Pray that day never comes.

George Lugg

Dateline: February 1947 . . . George Lugg, my trombone man and friend from Chicago days, was fished out of Sheepshead Bay early in January. He'd been missing since Dec. 18th. Lugg was born in Chicago, Oct. 6th, 1898. He lies buried now in National Cemetery at Farmingdale, L.I.(N.Y.). . . .

Dale Curran wrote "there never were very many trombones like that, and when one is gone there is a hole in the world, a sore spot like a pulled tooth . . . and the sad part of it is that he was just beginning to be recognized, after a quarter-century of scuffling, when a meaningless accident knocked him off. Something of that strange impulsive disjointed mood that was in his music carried over into his personal life; he was not a man to push himself forward, he played his own kind of music for himself alone, and whether he had jobs or recognition didn't seem to make much difference to him. . . ."

Dateline: April 1975 . . . I don't think I can add much. . . . Certainly there's nothing to subtract. Lugg was mid-sized; sort of plump, but you couldn't call him "fatty." A quiet sort of guy who fit in but never seemed to overlap. He was a tail-gate man who had a high opinion of both Brunis and O'Brien. And he could get a sweet tone. Here was a musician that could fit in many a bag. One thing you can believe; when he played he told the truth. I'm sure what he had to say here was just as truthful. . . .   A.H.

Modest George

by Harvey Lebow

We were sitting in my parlor, listening to records and draining a couple of quarts of beer one rainy afternoon when I decided that the time was opportune to spring the trap.

"George," I said innocently, "tell us about some of your experiences as a musician."

This rendezvous at my house was the result of a prearranged plot that Art and I had devised to get George to talk.

"You don't want to write about me," he protested; "no one knows who I am."

I expected that he would be reluctant to talk about himself, for George Lugg is an extremely modest man, but armed with a big block of paper and a king-size pencil I made it obvious that I was not to be begged off this time.

"Your story, George, will be of special appeal to people interested in jazz," I encouraged, "because you were there when jazz was being created!"

"I'm just a 'Lugg'," he quipped, "that's spelled with two 'g's,' you know," he added, a grin spreading across his round, cherubic face.

I made a motion as if to write and George reticently began, "Well, I suppose you want to know when I was born?"

"Yes, that would help."

"I was born in Chicago on October 6, 1898," he continued.

"Right on *the spot!*" I interjected. "When did you first get interested in jazz?"

"Around 1916 or '17, I should say," Lugg continued. "I was taking trombone lessons, and I played some old Edison phonograph records—Earl Fuller's Jazz Band. That's when I first got really interested in jazz. I wanted to play like that."

After this early inspiration George said he played in neighborhood orchestras, kid-bands with no one of any note in them. Then later, in 1918, he played in a Navy band. After the war he played several club dates in Chicago with Benny Goodman, Harry Goodman, Murph Podolsky (piano), Jack Shargle (drums), Chuck Walker (guitar) and Harry Greenberg, who played trumpet in Ben Pollack's Chicago band of 1923-24.

A short time after this, Lugg went to St. Louis and played in a vaudeville band. "That reminds me," George said, "one night Carl Pierce, who played piano with the Friars, you know, and I walked around the corner from the theatre to the Arcadia Ballroom. On one side of the hall a big band sat, and on the other side—Wingy Manone! We got a great kick out of meeting Wingy there, and after we got through, we all went up to his house for a spaghetti dinner. I'll never forget that night."

The first job that Eddie Condon had with his banjo was with George Lugg at a dive on Clark Street in Chicago called "Camel Gardens"—a block from Liberty Inn. Lugg had replaced Floyd O'Brien on trombone. Jimmy Lord (clarinet) also left at this time. Earl Wiley played drums (still playing drums at Liberty Inn) and Harry Le Grande played piano. This was in 1923.

"My first job with Art (Hodes) was on club dates at the LaSalle Hotel; it was a good band, with Westerfield on sax and clarinet, and John Whitehead on trumpet."

In 1925 Lugg left Chicago and came to New York with Jules Alberti and his Tennesseans. The orchestra derived its name from the fact that none of the personnel came from Tennessee. On the way East the band played at Richmond, Indiana and made a couple of records there for the Gennett company.

"I remember a fellow from the record company pointed out to us where Bix had stood, also where Tommy Dorsey and Don Murray had stood. These men had already established reputations for themselves among musicians, and we were very much impressed."

The band played in New York, and after a couple of months on this job George got the opportunity to go to Europe with Gene Jones, a Canadian orchestra leader, in 1926.

"For some reason or other Athens was the spot for American bands. We had a job there, but it was a flop," George continued. "Then we went to Paris. Palmer Jones had a six piece colored band at the Chez Florence. Florence was a singer, also Jones' wife. The band was the best in Paris and I went often to listen. Also in Paris, Leon Arnaud was a great inspiration to me. Leon is now an arranger and orchestra director in Hollywood, but at that time he was the outstanding musician in France. He played trombone, 'cello and tympani. He would get a great kick if he were to read this."

In 1927 Lugg returned to New York and after playing a couple of months here he returned to his hometown, Chicago. Then began his most interesting musical period.

"I played club dates with Bud Freeman and Dave Tough. Then followed dates with hotel bands and with 'sissy' bands, which happened to be the best jobs I could get at a particular time. The next good job I had was at the Subway, located on Wabash Avenue. It had two bands and also boasted of the longest bar in the world. The leader of the band was Frank Snyder, who played drums and had been with the New Orleans Rhythm Kings when Brunis and Polo were in that band. And speaking of Brunis—one of my biggest kicks was the first time I heard him at Fox Lake, Illinois. I was with Ben Pollack, Goldberg on sax, and Joe Herman on piano. We worked on one side of the lake. On the other side of the lake was a New Orleans band that we hadn't heard but had heard about. One night they came over to our place. They were the New Orleans Rhythm Kings, who had just come up from New Orleans. They were playing at a place called Fontana Inn. When they came over to our place, Brunis really knocked me out with his playing. After hearing him play, whenever I got the chance I went to hear him at the Friars Inn.

"Coming back to the Subway," George was really warming up to his story now, "the personnel of the band was Bud Jacobson, clarinet; Carl Rinker, cornet; Jess Stacy on piano, and myself on trombone. Art Hodes replaced Stacy later. Business was so terrific that we had an hour intermission after playing a set. The boss didn't want us to play too much.

"On sightseeing tours, I remember, the conductors would take the people through the Subway and as the party entered, they would say, 'Hold on to your purse, and hold on to the person behind you.' They thought they were seeing the sights, but actually we were the ones who were seeing the sights, for whenever the sightseers came through we always stopped playing to watch them.

"It was very easy to get lost in the Subway because it was so vast, so mobbed, and so mysterious with its low ceiling and scores of catacomb-like alcoves and passageways. I can recall times when I might be talking with someone only to find the person completely engulfed and carried away by the crowd before we could finish a few words of our conversation.

"The critics, such as John Hammond and Helen Oakley, used to stop by here because we had the only Dixieland band in Chicago at the time. The place was open 24 hours a day. We were there about two years."

From that time on till 1937 when George returned to New York nothing eventful happened in Chicago, because there was no one with whom to work. All the New York bands were taking the Chicago jobs, and there was a general exodus of Chicago men from Chicago. The big outfits wanted outside talent, so that there was nothing left for the older Chicago musicians except the beer joints. Youth was taking over!

After leaving Chicago, Lugg had a number of different jobs; he worked with Bobby Hackett in Philadelphia, replacing Brad Gowans; also in the band were Pee Wee Russell, Sterling Bose, trumpet, Eddie Condon, Don Carter on drums, and Dave Bowman on piano. He worked two weeks with Charlie Barnet in Boston.

In this same period George worked with "Mezz" Mezzrow's fine band at the Harlem Uproar. The personnel consisted of Zutty Singleton, drums; Max Kaminsky, Frankie Newton, Sidney DeParis, trumpets; Vernon Brown, George Lugg, trombones; Gene Sedric, tenor sax; Eddie Apple, tenor sax; Johnny Nicolini, piano; Bernard Addison, guitar; Elmer Jones, bass. It was a sensational band.

There was a great deal of antagonistic feeling amongst racial intolerants over the fact that this was a mixed band. One night when the band reported for work, the music was found scattered all around and a big swastika painted on the dance floor.

When Art Hodes formed his new jazz band, the personnel included George Brunis, the man whom Lugg first heard at Fox Lake, Illinois and always admired. Little did he dream, however, that fate had it in store for him to take over Brunis' place in this same band to play hot Dixie trombone as he did in the old days.

But besides being a jazz musician this modest gentleman of the hot sliphorn is very fond of classical music and is also an avid reader. And if you want further proof of how modest George is, he sums up his exciting story of his encounters with the fabulously famous men of jazz with the words, "That's about all I can tell you; there isn't really much of a story."

Bud Freeman

"Are my Favorite Bands Playing or am I Dreaming!" Ever hear that record? It's on a Victor label. Must be rare. Really it's a "take-off" (spoof) on the big bands of the day (somewhere in the '40s). And it sounds to me like a bunch of musicians out of the Tommy Dorsey Band of that period. You can't mistake Bud Freeman. He does the recitation; in an English accent. Which reminds me; someone told me he's living in England now. Anyway, that's a funny bit.

I wouldn't know why Bud said you couldn't play good jazz on sax. He certainly makes a lot of sense on the instrument. Of course, at that time (10/44) the word jazz hadn't been bent out-of-shape and possibly what Bud had in mind was the jazz of the '20s and '30s that we all listened to as we were coming up. I'll have to ask him when I see him.

Bud and I go back to when he (and I) had hair; and that's way back. We both played the El Rado Club with Wingy Manone as leader. Krupa was in that band. Man, that band swung. We not only played for kicks, we kicked a floor show. Didn't last long. None of the good ones (jobs) did. Then there was the time we called on Bud to step in for Bennie Moylan (who was sick). So through the years I'd do a gig with Freeman now and then; here and there. You know he's a straight cat. In all the time I've known Bud I never knew him to indulge. Women? Yeh; he had 20-20 vision, but if he drank or smoked I never noticed it. And he always came for to play. . . .

There was a show we did on TV. Bud flew in from New York. Made time for rehearsal. No problems. We discussed a few things I had in mind. Then Bud told me, "Art, this is actually the first job I've taken since my accident." I hadn't known about it, but he told me it was a real bad one. "I'm still shaken up over it." So we picked a group of numbers we both felt at home with,

THE JAZZ RECORD

ART HODES, *Publisher*

15c
A COPY

No. 23   New York, N. Y.   August, 1944

Bud Freeman

and that was it. The people at the station told me "That was one of the best shows you did." I guess that's the way it goes. You get a pro who comes for to work, and you're on and you're off.

Someday I'd like to get him to talk. Hope so. . . .   A. H.

Bud Freeman Said It

by Jasper L. Wood

Bud Freeman was in Cleveland for a few days. He was sitting in Jimmy Watson's place behind the Statler with some of the boys and they got to talking about jazz, a little sooner than later. (You see, Bud Freeman in Cleveland was an event.) Questions were popping all around when Bud came out with the following extraordinary statement:

"You can't play good hot jazz on the saxophone. The instrument won't take it. It would be easier, I think, to do a hot jazz ballet than to do it on a tenor saxophone. It is easy enough to play changes and chords, but then that isn't jazz, is it? I mean really jazz. For real jazz you need a real tone and a fluidity of melodic expression—and on the tenor all you get most of the time is honks and squeals.

"Someday I hope that I can hear a really beautiful tone on a tenor. I've been trying to get one for years and play jazz at the same time. It has been a heart-breaking experience, fellows. I don't really think that it is possible. People complain about my honking horn. Well, I don't like to make it honk myself—it just happens that way—you lose all control of the thing and it starts honking and doing the damndest things.

"But I'm going to keep on trying and maybe someday it will happen—and then you can add a tenor to the trumpet and trombone and clarinet and have an eight piece jazz band, not just seven like it will have to be until that time comes along."

And if I remember correctly, that was what I heard Bud Freeman say in Watson's Bar behind the Statler. Do you still feel that way, Bud, or was that just talking?

Pee Wee Russell

I've always said (about Pee Wee) that he has to be the most indestructible gent I know (knew). The way he'd punished his body and how long it held together for him has to be a medical miracle. "We, the people" as Brunis would call him. He's one guy that just thinkin' about him gives me a warm feeling. Scenes come back; like . . .

We were both livin' on 10th Street in the Village. And course we'd run into one another. This one afternoon I saw Pee Wee walking his little dog (must have been some sort of poodle); and the dog was dragging behind and every once in awhile it would sit down and refuse to move. I wondered about it 'til somebody told me Pee Wee would feed the dog some of his beer; a loaded dog. What's good for the master is good for the pup.

One of my big kicks was when the (so-called) modernists discovered Russell as "one of them." Suddenly his salary zoomed. He became a high-priced (in jazz circles) act. As Bud

Freeman told me, "Pee Wee's expensive; if I get five he gets a thousand." Then I heard about him becoming a painter. Yeh! The unbelievable. See, we were towns apart. I didn't run into him daily. But when the opportunity arose for me to do educational TV in Chicago, Bob Kaiser (director) and I decided on having Russell and Jimmy McPartland as guest artists. That was a funny show. Maybe you saw it. Bob cracked up. He was in the sound room and both Jimmy and Pee Wee had mikes around their collars. The conversation went something like this. "Pee Wee, how 'bout you changing places with me?" Pee Wee liked to stand next to the piano. Some wag remarked that it gave him somethin' to lean on. May be true; but he also liked to hear the chords a piano man was layin' down. Anyway, Russell was happy where he was and said so. I still don't know why Jimmy wanted to change but he did. "I'll give you five dollars." All he got was a mutter.

A bit later Pee Wee discovered the bartender. Now that was a prop Kaiser had inserted. There was a bar and a bartender but no booze. But just seeing him made Pee Wee go into his act. "Hey bartender, I mean you; come over here." Bob K. finally had to shut off the mike. All through the show Russell would look over in that direction and seemingly he couldn't help himself. Automatically he'd call out "Mr. Bartender." But lest we forget, he and I got into a blues that I would sure like to hear again. No one; I do mean no one ever played clarinet like Pee Wee Russell. He was an original; a composer-clarinetist. Colorful? Yes, to be sure. Not a conversationalist. But then he didn't have to be. His clarinet said it all.   A. H.

Pee Wee's Soul Is Music

by Alma Hubner

He's the clarinetist who plays with the band at Nick's, in Greenwich Village. In fact, he almost belongs to the place; he's been there for so long and with so many bands that customers would complain were he to leave. Surely, you've heard of him. He never fails to give you a two-for-one show any time. Tall, thin, dark hair and inquisitive black eyes; place a clarinet in his hands, add to that the name of Pee Wee Russell and there you have him! By the way, that clarinet is approximately just about the world's eighth wonder. Held together by rubber bands, coming apart most any minute, its holes so clogged with —could we call it sediment?—yet it renders Pee Wee admirable service night after night, however hard he has to blow to achieve the results.

People say they like him. Everybody does. Jazz fans like him, musicians like him, the steak-eaters at Nick's do too, even society girls feel "magnetized" by him. (The Village is a "fashionable" place nowadays.) They say he is funny. The girls call him "cute."

Charles Ellsworth Russell has the most intriguing personality to be found amongst jazz musicians. It is both interesting and strangely spontaneous. His words are as unpredictable as the notes that flow from his instrument. Rather on the laconic side, he has a tendency to speak incoherently. I might even go so far as to say that he suffers from

March 1947

No. 53

25c

Jazz Record

Pee Wee Russell

"acute taciturnity," an illness for which very few know a cure. If you are able to make him sit down and keep up a conversation for half an hour, congratulate yourself upon having accomplished an astonishing feat. Pee Wee rarely sits down to talk for half an hour. It is against his nature to do so. He has an unusually witty and pleasant humour. He'll make you laugh any time; but only for five minutes at a time. Yet, if you are able to "pin him down" and converse with him for some length of time, you'll discover, probably to your greater astonishment, behind his frivolous good humour, a man of great spiritual restlessness, of marked philosophical tendencies and, most important of all, of a very human, sincere and honest soul. Pee Wee's soul is music. His whole existence is music. His only friend and pleasure is music. Therefore, you'll find no man more sincere about his music.

Pee Wee's good humour is forever at work. With a good audience, he'll oblige with a couple of jokes. He even jokes in his speech. Sometimes, you are able to catch a trace of extremely literate language. Thus, when he wants to invite you to a drink, he'll say: "Won't you kindly join me in a libation?" On Sunday afternoons you'll hear him say: "I'm inhibited today, make it a beer, Jack." Or, when having forgotten a promise, he'll scold himself: "Fie upon me!" Once, he disappeared from a table at Nick's. The boys went to investigate and found him playing marbles in the back room. He said he was "relaxing" his own way. Pee Wee can get away with it, he'll play marbles, quote Shakespeare and still be a great clarinetist.

One night at Nick's, after I had finally succeeded in breaking down Pee Wee's laconicism, he philosophized on his life: "I don't know what I would do without my clarinet, I'm not good for anything besides music. But what would become of me without it? I couldn't live without my music. Besides, it's my way of making a living, like anybody else. I'm married, I've got a tent, a frigidaire and a radio like everybody else. I also get paid every week like everybody else. Besides, I'm happy—don't know if everybody else is though. What am I driving at? Don't mind the way I talk, I get this way sometimes. Perhaps it's because I'm getting old." He'll be 38 this month, on the 27th, and if that isn't the prime of life, I don't know what is.

He commented on *J.R.*: "Certainly I read the *Jazz Record*, I get it up at Commodore every month. It's so different from other magazines, reading it kind of gives you a life. I like its sincere attitude towards jazz and jazz musicians. Always so honest about the truth. The majority of trade publications print so many lies—and they have to, they know nothing about us nor our music either." Rubbing his hand across his eyes, he squinted as if hating the dim lights, took a long sip of rye and continued: "You know what I mean." Indeed I did. "If there were more magazines like the *Jazz Record,* and if writers tried to understand the musicians they write about, jazz would be much better off. Don't you think?" The half hour intermission is up and Pee Wee is back on the stand again. Hearing him play you become convinced of how much good music an inspired musician can produce, with the proper stimulation. Miff Mole, Eddie Condon, Joe Grauso and Sterling Boze are Pee Wee's stimulants. They could not be better. Night after night, chorus after chorus, Pee Wee never lacks inspiration. He plays from the heart, blows his soul right out, always striving to produce something better.

"Ballin' the Jack," "Muskrat Ramble," "I Can Do Most Anything For You," and "That Da Da Strain." Pee Wee blows his soul right through every number in absolute ecstacy. You feel it present in all of his music. If you have a "wild" imagination, you could watch it emerge from the clarinet, as I did. It came out triumphant, but it had gone through a lot, that soul. Finally, the farewell theme, "Tin Roof Blues," which somehow always seems to come too soon. We are back with Charles Ellsworth. "Well, honey, where were we?" He'll nonchalantly call you "honey" and "darling," it seems his memory has trouble retaining names, girls' names especially. "You'd just been born in St. Louis, Pee Wee." His passive moustache undergoes a thorough combing, satisfying his now idle nervous hands. "Were we that far back? Let me see . . . what happens to a baby? I guess I wore diapers like the rest. Childhood is kind of blurred in my memory—everything is for that matter—as I was raised in Oklahoma and left St. Louis while still quite a 'half pint.' Then, I went to Western Military Academy in Oklahoma. I studied music there, with the military training that went along with it. It's a good thing for you, that training. It prepares you to meet the ways of life; makes a man out of you. You learn so much more about people in that way. There I go again! Excuse me, but I'm so darn tired I don't know what I'm talking about." He makes desperate gestures with his hand, twitches his moustache and squints, endeavouring to explain his philosophical vagaries.

"What musicians did you first hear that you liked?" He raises his eyebrows in helpless indignation. "Musicians? My dear girl, where did you expect me to hear musicians in Oklahoma in a town of 2,500 people? There were none. To hear one was as hard as to find a needle in a haystack. Harder." "Were you born with a clarinet in your mouth then instead of a silver spoon?" "Gosh no, honey"—softening again—"don't misunderstand me. I'm just nervous, that's all. Playing all day, sleeping little, seeing friends off to the Army. You'd think I'd reached Hell already. I've even had to be best man at two weddings this week. And they had to be at 9 in the morning! To get back to the subject, I didn't start by playing clarinet. I took piano lessons first. Then violin. Could you imagine me playing a fiddle? I didn't, so I switched to clarinet, to my advantage. That little black stick always fascinated me. At school I used to play in all the dances and parades, also in the carinivals. That was the most fun, those carnivals, something like Mardi Gras in New Orleans but in a smaller scale." He surprises me with a most abrupt change of subject: "Did you know I had Indian blood? Indeed, I've one-sixteenth of Indian blood in me, and I'm proud of it." His voice trails off to a whisper. I'm practicing super-human ear-straining not to lose a syllable of what he says.

"When did you first go to Chicago?" "Chicago? Darn it, that's a silly question. How do you expect me to remember dates? I'm too tired to think. Please don't make me think." That last phrase was uttered pleadingly. It made me feel like a tyrant, or even an extortionist. "You'll understand, won't you? I never could remember dates, anyway." All of a sudden he returns to life. "One

thing I won't ever forget is a trip I took to Mexico in 1923. I was only a kid then, but I remember Mexico very well. Mexico City is so beautiful, and, what most Americans don't suspect, it's just as modern as any of our large cities. That tequila they drink down there isn't bad either! I got a big kick out of those 'mejicanos,' I guess they got a kick out of me too. We're such opposite races. Funny, but all the Spanish I can remember is 'saludos' and 'adios.' I'll have to brush up on it if I ever go to South America." He lights a cigarette and orders another rye from the waiter. "Where to now? Chicago? Not yet. I went to the University of Missouri after returning from Mexico. I studied music there, harmony, counterpoint, and all that. Polishing up on my clarinet at the same time. I wish I'd taken up writing too. That's one thing I've always wanted to do; to write. Not poetry, it's too complicated, just straight prose writing. Something to use my imagination on. But, as it is, I can hardly spell my own name."

The boys start drifting back, another half hour is back again. Pee Wee is in no hurry, drinks his rye slowly. "You want to get to Chicago, don't you? Well, let's go then. Only that, right now, I must get back to play. And besides, I forgot to tell you I went to Europe before that." Giving his moustache several energetic twitches, he gets ready to blow his soul right out again.

Pee Wee is 38 this month. He's young, but has been playing for a long time. We all hope he'll still be blowing his clarinet in another 38 years, whether we are here to listen to him or not. Music that comes from the heart is eternal. Since Pee Wee is all one heart and a soul, maybe he's eternal too. In any case, Happy Birthday, Pee Wee!

I've done my best to describe Pee Wee Russell. The rest of him you can only comprehend through his music. Listen to him, whether at Nick's or on records. I'd suggest some of the Commodores, and you'll find yourself enjoying his music, because he enjoys playing it. Indeed, everybody likes him. I like him too, even though we never did get to Chicago.

Rod Cless

There's a side to people very few get to see. Like you'll read about Rod Cless; his travels, his music. Who he played with and when. But unless you were close to him you only see that one side. And there's more to each one of us than the cover. Yes, I remember Rod very well. Our small family were living in the Village (Greenwich) alongside of a handful of jazz players; Pee Wee (Russell) and his Mary; the Condons; Brad Gowans, Hackett, Wettling. Occasionally Thelma (my wife) would see Mrs. Roosevelt (Eleanor) walking her dog. It was fairly peaceful then (the early 40s). Rod liked to stop at our house and hold my daughter Janet (she must have been three or four then) on his lap and talk to her. Sometime later I found that Rod had been married (to Bud Freeman's sister) but they'd broken up. He was basically family oriented but somethin' happened.

Cless never did get the recognition he deserved. Let me tell you somethin'. So many clarinetists (and I'm talkin' about good; even great ones) play all over the clarinet. They don't stick to the clarinet part. They wander; a bit of melody; harmony. And believe me; I'm not talking about playing solos. I mean ensemble playing. But Rod had learned (and I do believe from Johnny Dodds) to play the clarinet part that wove around the trumpet lead but didn't get into the trombone department or suddenly became a mixture of anything that came to mind. And that was difficult to do. I really appreciated that style. It was rare.

Now I remember it was Rod who got me that recording date where the drummer (George Wettling) couldn't make it and sent us a sub. I'd never played with this chap and drums was too important to me to take a chance. So I sent the cat home and we (Marty Marsala, trumpet; Earl Murphy, bass; Jack Goss, guitar; Rod, clarinet, and myself, piano) cut the date without drums. And I remember standing in a record store, a'listening to the record when it was issued. I was joined by a well-known jazz authority and writer. We were swinging. The Chicago Rhythm Kings. No drums but we were compensating. As one track ended, the authority said to me "Who was that on drums?"

A.H.

Rod Cless as I Knew Him

by Ray Cless

My brother, Rod, was a good man, even on the violin. When he was about ten years old he sawed away on a beat-up fiddle and liked it, but it wasn't the thing that he wanted. Everyone in our family played something, so by the time you were ten or eleven, you naturally thought that you were sup-posed to be sharp on some musical instrument. Rod then tried the cornet for a brief period, but was never really inspired by that horn.

When Rod was a freshman in high school he bought a sax, along with everyone else in the neighborhood. That was the thing most

Rod Cless

interesting things come out of his sax and clarinet.

He made a pretense at going to college after graduating from high school, but I don't think his heart was really in it. He enrolled in Drake University for one year, then tried Iowa State College at Ames for another and made excellent grades, but I think the general routine was a little too corny for him. During his summer vacations he played at Lake Geneva, Wisconsin, in a Peoria hotel and at various local roadhouses here in Des Moines. During the winter he played the usual fraternity and sorority hops at school. He kept in constant practice, whether he was playing right or not.

I remember one night during this period when a bunch of guys were forming a small band. They were practicing at our house. Two notables in this group were Gil Bowers on piano—currently associated with the music of Twentieth Century Fox and long-time pianist and arranger for the Ben Pollack and Bob Crosby bands—and Carl Bean who for years played sax with Frankie Masters and composed, "You're a Sweet Little Headache," and others. This bunch got tired of their work, so hit on the idea of switching instruments. It was amazing how little difference it made who was playing what horn.

I remember so well the summer that the Wolverines came through Des Moines and played a six weeks engagement at the Riverview Park Ballroom. I think Rod went out to hear them every night. That's how he met Jimmy McPartland, Frank Teschemacher and Bud Freeman. When the Wolverines left town, Rod and Des Moines were through. He went to Chicago soon after and roomed with Tesch. There is no doubt that Tesch had a great influence on Rod's playing as did Bud Freeman, too. Rod married Bud's sister, but they were later divorced.

He recorded for the first time here with Tesch, Mezz Mezzrow, Gene Krupa, Joe Sullivan, Eddie Condon and Jim Lannigan. The tune, "Jazz Me Blues." Rod played alto sax on this date, but he was beginning to lean more toward the clarinet and kept in constant practice.

He suffered through those hungry days of the depression, jobbing around Chicago. It wasn't until Muggsy Spanier formed his Jazz Band at the Sherman that Rod began to live again. He went to New York with this group.

boys learned to play during this period. Mother made him practice in the bathroom—there's nothing quite so painful on the ears as an untamed sax! But with a few lessons and lots of practice, Rod was soon playing well enough to get himself club dates around town.

His life in Des Moines was just about the same as that of any other boy growing up in a Midwestern city after the last World War. Music was being stressed in the schools. Jazz was being played and heard and a musician in a jazz band was a very glamorous character, indeed. From the time Rod started to play his sax, there was nothing in the world he wanted to do besides play jazz. In that respect he was a lucky man, because so few people ever really know what they want to do.

By the time he was a senior in high school, he was trying to play the clarinet, too, and was squealing away in the high school band and orchestra. Anything he picked up seemed to come easily to Rod. He was good at mathematics, captain and pitcher of the baseball team and an exceptionally agile swimmer and diver. I have often thought that this combination of coordination and adaptability were the leading factors that made such

The records they made then are collectors' items, now.

I saw more of him in New York than I had for years. His playing delighted me as did his associations and his record sessions in his beatup Greenwich Village apartment. Rod's career in New York ended tragically with his death in December, 1944, but he left a host of friends and some mighty fine records to remind everyone that he was right all the way through.

I'm not very good at dates or remembering places, but I do remember how good Rod was at everything and especially at jazz. And I also like to remember that, success or failure, Rod did the thing that he wanted to do all his life and he didn't care where it took him and he did it well. So what better thing can you say about a guy, other than he was always so right?

Muggsy Spanier

It was kind of a windy day; morning. We had gathered at this Catholic Church on the Near North Side to attend a service for a jazz man. Bassist Truck Parham; drummer-man Wally Gordon; myself. We'd been close to Muggsy (Spanier), in one way or another. It was a small gathering. Muggs' wife Ruth and her son were there, as was Joe Glaser (Louis Armstrong's manager and Spanier's booker). Truck, Wally and I were to be pall-bearers. As we rode around the block we passed the Gaslight Club. Wally remarked, "Let's bare our heads, for here is where I leave a pint of my blood nitely."

I had plenty of time to think; going way back when we all were young and this "jazz" had hit Chicago. We came from every-which neighborhood, attracted to the jazz-fire. Louis Armstrong and Earl Hines were the gathering-spa's. But before that came King Oliver and Teddy Weatherford. Louis and the King were horn men; Teddy and Earl 88-ers. Then there was Baby Dodds, drums. Man, the jazz teachers were here in dear old Chi, and the pupils came from every place. Chicago was a magnet that drew 'em all. Bix Beiderbecke, Jack Teagarden, Max Kaminsky all stuck their heads in. Jess Stacy, Joe Sullivan, Frank Melrose, George Zack, Tut Soper; piano men that absorbed. Wingy Manone came up from New Orleans and lit a fire. Red McKenzie and Eddie Condon got it together. Davey Tough, Gene Krupa, George Wettling. Bud Freeman, Teschemacher, Pee Wee Russell, Floyd O'Brien, Mezz, Benny Goodman. Chicago was the jazz-classroom and the teachers had arrived. School was wherever your jazz practitioner held forth, be it a night club, a dance hall, or an after-hours flat. The admission was your tuition. You sat at the feet of the greats and you absorbed. You bought their recordings and dwelt in them. You listened 'til the music sung out in you all day. Jazz was your life.

Now it's today; reality. So many of my cohorts have been here and gone. Some left recordings that will live on. A few stopped with me and I helped gather some of their thoughts on paper. I look at words and think of lives. That was a great age we were part of. No question (in my mind) about the music and its value and worthwhile-ness. We all played a small part. Possibly you can piece it together as you read these stories.   A.H.

Muggsy Spanier

by Alma Hubner

"Oh, play that thing, Muggsy!" George Brunis yelled encouragingly at the end of Muggsy Spanier's recording of "Big Butter and Egg Man," one of the first four sides the Ragtime Band recorded for Bluebird. And Muggsy played it, all right. "Yeah, Muggsy, rip it out!" is what Louis Armstrong used to tell him in Chicago back in 1928 when Muggsy, Jess Stacy, Frank Teschemacher, Floyd O'Brien and George Wettling were playing all of Louis' repertoire at the Triangle Cafe. And Muggsy would never fail to rip it out. He'd play Louis' own solos with fire and feeling unparalleled by any white cornet player. Louis would just stare and listen and urge him on enthusiastically. Not that Muggsy needs any coaxing or urging to play but when he fronts an appreciative audience and is backed by first-rate musicians he can "play that thing" and "rip it out" anytime, again and again.

Muggsy's musical genius is boundless, unlimited. He was born a "hot" player and speaks the "hot" language as authentically as any Negro jazzman born in New Orleans during its hey-day. In fact, Muggsy is one of the few white cornet players to play a true New Orleans style and one of the very few to have succeeded in capturing the spirit of the great Negro players of New Orleans. It shows up clearly in his playing; the driving force or so-called "drive" characteristic of colored instrumentalists. Muggsy plays a direct, unaffected cornet. His use of rhythm and dynamics is something to marvel at. You might say that he plays cornet with a good drummer's beat, with the subtle taste and drive of King Oliver (limiting himself to a middle range) and the punch and "joie de vivre" of Louis Armstrong's horn. The rest is himself, so much so that you can distinguish his horn in a million. A fertile imagination,

direct attack and spontaneous feeling for true jazz make Muggsy's playing what it is.

Muggsy is a restless, deep-thinking, shy fellow. He is incessantly at work exploring the unexplored, longing to learn the unknown, never satisfied with himself. You might tell him he's the greatest, but he won't believe you. He can't believe you because he is in search of the "better" qualities he wants to achieve but which he is at a loss for words to describe. I asked him what he thought of his playing (a strange question to ask any musician), his reply was merely that he wants to play "better." His most trying duty is to have to listen to himself on records, as he was forced to not so long ago when interviewed over Station WHN by Fred Robbins. "I get sort of a frustrated feeling after listening to myself, knowing all along that I could have played better, but didn't manage to at the time. Maybe it's the recording studio that restrains you, maybe the thought that what you're playing will remain on wax for posterity, I don't know."

You like Muggsy through his playing, through his heart-felt, soulful music, and as soon as you meet him you like him too. After all, isn't a musician's music a transcription in musical terms of the man himself? There's nothing restrained about Muggsy, he'll set you at ease immediately. The friendly smile, the sparkling eyes with the mischievous almost quizzical look, yes, you know you'll get along with Muggsy right away; and you do. There's nothing in the vast greatness of his music that you don't find in him; it and he are one, an inseparable amalgam of genius, honesty, sincerity and soul—a lot of soul, a kind-hearted, unselfish soul. I use adjectives profusely, yet even the profusion doesn't do Muggsy justice, somehow he's far too big for words. You can't size him up with a couple of

THE JAZZ RECORD

ART HODES, *Publisher*

15c
A COPY

No. 19   New York, N. Y.   April, 1944

Joe Marsala, Muggsy Spanier, Bud Freeman

hundred adjectives and give a true picture of him in black and white.

Muggsy is passionate and spontaneous about everything he does, he never stops to draw out conclusions. His frantically desperate love for music has taken him through life in a constant turmoil. He isn't fickle, and being true to his love has caused him many a deep wound, many a sad moment and, on occasion, has led him to spiritual depression and confusion. At times, the confusion has been so great that he's wanted to give up. But he couldn't and can't and probably never will. He loves his music too well and too earnestly to quit. He'll endure the pain, overcome the confusion and stick by his love.

It is this determination to be sincere —because he can't be otherwise—that has directed the course of Muggsy's music. His horn is determined, like he is, and has been that way ever since he first held it in his hands when only a kid of thirteen. Muggsy was born Francis Joseph Spanier in Chicago's South Side, November 9, 1906. The Windy City was the right place for jazz; from his very early youth Muggsy grew up with it. Thus, it was always a part of his life. Though he is one of six brothers, Muggsy was the only one to be caught in the nets that jazz spread out in Chicago. There is no mistaking that jazz fished a mighty haul when it pulled Muggsy in.

At first he was torn between two loves that widely differ—sports and music. He could swim and box and was an expert baseball pitcher. Once he almost came to New York on his own to pitch for the Giants; being too young his mother managed to keep him home somehow. He attended parochial school in Chicago; has always been a Catholic. But school was only a minor worry, he never could get along with numbers or chemistry. While in high school his companions nicknamed him "Muggsy" because he played baseball like John Joseph "Muggsy" McGraw, famous baseball player and manager of the New York Giants. "McGraw knew what he wanted, he'd run right after it without considering the consequences. That's the way I played, on impulse, without figuring out the 'why' or the 'what' . . . and I didn't do so badly." Muggsy speaks of McGraw with stirring emotion, he still respects and admires the other Muggsy, the one who didn't play a cornet but who had just as important a

part in shaping his youth as did King Oliver and Louis Armstrong.

"Like most kids I started playing drums, they fascinated me. I never had a chance to do much with them but always had the beat. I could keep time perfectly. That's why out-of-time drummers exasperate me. I'd been hearing Joe Oliver so much that I decided I wanted a cornet. After six months I gave up the drums when my mother bought me my first cornet. I was only 13 at the time and kind of small. In fact, so small that it became routine to borrow my brother's long pants to go to the Royal Gardens Cafe to hear King Oliver play. Jimmie Noone was playing clarinet with the band then—they were a team, Oliver and Noone!"

Muggsy isn't an introvert, he loves to talk. With a couple of packs of cigarettes and a comfortable chair he hardly needs any encouragement. Past, present, uncertain future, the war, politics, painting, classical music or jazz, he discusses them all enthusiastically. As long as the conversation doesn't dwell on his person he'll be extremely eloquent. Muggsy enjoys exchanging ideas and knowing what others think. He lives with his two feet on the earth, is aware of what goes on around him—which is more than you can say for many a jazzman. He's even a great philosopher, although his philosophical knowledge doesn't come from books. It's within him, inherited undoubtedly from the unusual mixture of two great races—the Irish in his mother and the French in his father. Both of his parents had musical background and encouraged him in the field he chose for himself.

Muggsy first heard Oliver while still in grammar school. At first, the novelty of the new syncopated music called "jazz" (a word that was considered lowly, obscene and immoral) caught his fancy. He liked the easy flowing rhythm, the simple melodies, the straightforward, spontaneous interpretations. It's easy to understand why Muggsy said "That's for me" when first hearing Joe Oliver's cornet. Oliver played on the beat (in the New Orleans tradition), using mostly a middle register and the utmost sparsity of notes. His phrases were of a melodic simplicity and grace rarely surpassed. You'll find all that in Muggsy today. He took up cornet seriously and had some technical training at school with a teacher. More he couldn't be taught, the music was in him, there was no more to it than pressing the valves down and it would come out.

"When Joe first came up from New Orleans he didn't have a band of his own. Bill Johnson, the bass player, was manager of the band at the Royal Gardens. Joe played two jobs at the same time, the Royal Gardens and the Dreamland Ballroom and finally moved into the Dreamland with a band of his own in 1920. Lil Hardin and Johnny Dodds were in that band. I knew the owner of the Dreamland and was alllowed to sit in a dark corner in the balcony to listen to the music. I was only 14 then, still not old enough to be allowed in a public dance hall. But as long as I heard the music the conditions didn't matter. The band played from about 9:30 to 1:00 a.m. and after-hours they played the Pekin Café, one of the worst gangster hangouts in Chicago, which has now been turned into a police station. In the summer the Pekin kept its windows open, so I'd sneak from home just about every night and sit outside on a curbstone listening to the music. Sometimes the goings-on would get rough inside, the music would stop and you'd hear the flash of 45-caliber revolvers trying to fire with a beat. Before I knew it I'd be running home as fast as my feet could take me. But the next night would always find me sitting on the same curbstone. I thought the music well worth running the risk of getting shot by a stray bullet."

Jazz hit big time in Chicago by the end of the last war. New Orleans musicians, no longer able to find jobs in their home-town after the closing up of Storyville, drifted up the Mississippi to find the Windy City a profitable place. The public was there, anxious and waiting; it wanted jazz. The South Side became a jazz haven. 1917 saw Freddie Keppard and his Creole Band causing a sensation; Jimmie Noone played clarinet in that band. Then, in 1918, King Oliver arrived to astonish the already very much astonished Chicagoans.

Next were the New Orleans Rhythm Kings; the first white jazz band to dish it out "hot." The Rhythm Kings were actually organized in Chicago by cornetist Paul Mares, but they played authentic New Orleans music. George Brunis was from New Orleans, so was Leon Rapollo, they both helped give the Rhythm Kings a true New Orleans flavor. The Friar's Inn made big money with these "jazz crazy" musicians, and the "jazz crazy" kids that hung around the place eagerly absorbed all and every single "hot" note. Brunis and Rapollo became heavenly deities; the Friar's Inn, no longer a nightclub, was considered a shrine.

Louis Armstrong came up the river in 1922 to play second cornet in King Oliver's Creole Band, and Chicago's jazz fans were delighted. High school kids were the most ardent and most devoted of fans. Thus, Muggsy was but a satellite revolving around a mighty great center: King Oliver and Louis Armstrong. He got his start and inspiration from them. The Austin High School gang (Bud Freeman, Jimmy and Dick McPartland, Frank Teschemacher, Dave Tough, Jim Lannigan, etc.) were the cultists who made a shrine out of the Friar's Inn. They, in turn, were inspired by the N.O.R.K., Armstrong, Oliver and, later on, to a very great extent by Bix Beiderbecke. This was the group that gave birth to Chicago style.

By all the above it isn't hard to understand the reason for the large output of jazz talent which Chicago gave to the world. Jazz came there and the younger generation was eager and anxious to pick up where the older jazzmen left off. Similarly, it's easy to comprehend why Muggsy plays a truer, more negroid, more authentic jazz style than any other contemporary white jazz cornetist. He's based his style closely upon the pattern of Oliver's, at the same time taking a lot from Armstrong but never falling under the influence of Beiderbecke. With the exception of Sterling Bose, a truly great New Orleans player, I can think of but few white cornetists who play on the beat and who've managed to remain free of Beiderbecke's influence.

Muggsy took his music seriously from the very first; he loved it, had a yearning for it. He says that if he hadn't felt such a need for music he would probably be a surgeon today; after sports, medicine is his only weakness. In 1921 Joe Oliver left Chicago going on tour throughout the West Coast. Muggsy was left without his idol so could dedicate more time to his cornet. Up until that time he'd done more listening than actual playing. He played numerous high school jobs with other kids and nights would often find him sneaking from home playing all the back rooms on North Clark Street. His first real job was at

Blatz's Palm Garden (1921) where he improvised behind a lush, plump singer in the most perfect Oliver fashion imaginable. To this very day Muggsy is hard to beat at that sort of thing. His cornet blends almost magically with the singer's voice and actually carries on a dialogue throughout the interpretation. He'll make his cornet wail, he'll make it laugh, he'll make it melancholy, always improvising with the most impeccable taste.

In 1922 the Lincoln Gardens announced the triumphant return of King Oliver and his Creole Band. The new Lincoln Gardens was nothing but the same old Royal Gardens with slight remodeling and maybe a little dusting. A dreary-looking place, as Muggsy recalls. "As soon as Joe was back I'd be there every night, glued to the spot nearest the bandstand which was available. Louis Armstrong came up from New Orleans to join the band for its reopening, this was my first meeting with Louis. I can say that from the very first he fell right in with the boys. He played melody mostly at the time and wasn't featured on solos much, Joe would take them, however, when they'd team up on duets it would get so hot there was no telling whether the roof would hold out or not. In the band were Lil Hardin, Johnny and Baby Dodds, Honoré Dutrey, Johnny St. Cyr and Bill Johnson. I got to know Oliver quite well, both he and Louis encouraged me in my playing a lot. Joe sometimes would teach me some of his tricks with the mutes; I learned a lot from him. After a little practice I was invited to sit in with the band, I was the first one to do so ... it must have seemed strange, a little kid blowing a cornet with those two Titans! That's one thrill I'll never forget: having played with the two greatest cornetists in jazz!" Muggsy recalls Oliver and Armstrong with nostalgic enthusiasm—and the sparkle in his eye, always there, shines brighter.

"That same year, 1922, my cornet and I got our first steady job with Siggy Meyers' band at the Columbia Ballroom. There was plenty of kicks to be had there—we'd have jazz battles and that was where the fun began. Five nights a week we played the Ballroom and when the battles started the place really bounced. Sometimes Louis would play opposite us, others it was the New Orleans Rhythm Kings. It was there I met my pal George Brunis, we've been friends ever since

and I still get as many kicks from George's trombone as I did then. About this time I met some of the boys from Austin High who had a little band called The Blue Friars which was much talked about by musicians in the South Side. I got to playing with them quite often, our favorite spot for jamming was the 3 Deuces on North Clark Street, where Joe Sullivan, Eddie Condon and George Wettling frequently dropped in for a chorus or two, usually more with the lure of a bottle.

"In 1924 the Meyers band moved to the White City Ballroom and I went right along. The job wasn't bad, we worked from 8:30 'til 12 midnight. We had some fine boys in the band, Volly De Faut, the clarinetist, was one of them. From White City I'd go to the Rendezvous Café to do some after-hours jamming with Bix who played there with Charlie Straight's band. Bix's cornet could be heard all night, he stayed right on with the small band that usually got started about 1:00 a.m. It was a jam session every night and nobody knew just what would happen. We'd blow at each other until dawn sometimes and we'd just play until exhausted. The rest of the fellows dropped off to sleep little by little until only Bix and I were left, with maybe a dozing bass player supplying the four-four which we often ignored. Bix sure had some resistance! There has been so much said about him, but no matter what, you can never say enough. He was a true genius!

"By this time Oliver had moved over to the Plantation Café on 35th and Calumet. Louis had just returned from New York and had his own band across the street at the Sunset Café, with Earl Hines on piano. I had to split my time between the two of them. I really can't tell whom I like best, Louis or Joe. They are both too great for words, and though Louis has a lot of Oliver his ideas are so original that he's altogether different.

"The Meyers band finally split up and Floyd Towne, the sax player, took things in hand with the result that we organized a new group out of the old one to go into the Midway Gardens. By and by things started shaping up and before long we had a real band. Frank Teschemacher came on as clarinetist, Floyd O'Brien played trombone, George Wettling, drums, and Pat Pattison, bass. Soon we added Danny Altier on alto sax and one night got a welcome present by way of Jess Stacy who walked in asking for a job.

Jess played our kind of music and fell right in with the mood of the band. Jess and I got along fine, we always have, because we have the same tastes in music and speak the same musical language. We certainly couldn't have asked for a better piano-man in that band. That was some band we had! We were so much ahead of our time that nobody understood us, usually the customers were only perplexed at what they heard. Even in the 20's the public in Chicago went for the more commercial music. Floyd Towne's Midway Gardens Band, as we called ourselves, lasted for two glorious years ('26-'27), we could have stayed longer but one day the boss decided he wanted us to wear funny hats because the public liked it that way and 'other nice bands that played beautiful waltzes did it'; that was where we quit. Funny thing, as soon as we left business fell off. It got so bad that in no time at all the place was torn down and turned into a garage."

In 1927 Muggsy often played and recorded with Charlie Pierce's band. Pierce was a butcher and amateur sax-man who cut meat five days a week and played alto sax on week-ends. He liked good jazz and could pick the best musicians. The band was only a pick-up job put together for several Paramount recording dates. Muggsy and Tesch made the best of those dates knocking themselves out on every number. "China Boy" and "Bull Frog Blues" were recorded under Charlie Pierce's name, "Darktown Strutters Ball" and "Friar's Point Shuffle" under the name of the Jungle Kings—these were reissued by the United Hot Clubs of America a few years ago.

"What happened to the band after you left the Midway Gardens?" Muggsy is far, far away, brooding on, perhaps, some secret recollections he doesn't want to bring back to life. He suddenly re-awakens, the puzzled I-know-nothing-why-bother-about-me expression on his face: "The band? What band? Oh! yeah, we were back with Floyd Towne . . . well, nothing happened. We just moved ourselves right over to the Triangle Café, this was in '28, with the same band as it was. The Triangle put up with us for about six months and we really had a time of it. Jess, Tesch, Wettling and I used to hang around the Sunset Café more than too often. Louis' band was there, the attraction was too great and we couldn't think of not being there whenever

we weren't playing ourselves. If Louis' boys wanted a rest we'd sit in and take over for them. I'd take Louis' place, the piano would swap Father Hines for Jess, Tesch would replace Darnell Howard on clarinet and Baby Dodds had no alternative but to hand the drumsticks over to Wettling. We had most of their tunes memorized and could really swing out on them. The way it was you really couldn't tell who had more fun, Louis listening to us or ourselves playing for him. But good times aren't supposed to last long, we all split after six months of good fun and good music. It was becoming a big problem to get a good job in Chicago, hot musicians weren't wanted because the commercial bands were doing all the business the 'corny' way, which seemed the easier way to them because the public readily swallowed whatever it was fed. Most of the boys joined commercial bands. Jess and I went into Joe Kayser's band at the Merry Garden Ballroom, as long as we were together we didn't care what we played. Somehow, we'd always manage to make the best of any situation, enjoying ourselves no matter what; which proves, in a way, how valuable a good friend is at certain times. The job with Kayser lasted for four months, then we separated. Jess toured the gin mills, it was hard getting a job, and I joined Ray Miller's band at the Hotel Sherman's College Inn, which is now the Panther Room.

"While playing with Miller, Ted Lewis heard me and came up with a nice offer, contract and everything set. It didn't take me long to decide and I joined him out on the West Coast, San Francisco to be exact, in 1929. George Brunis and Don Murray were with the band at the time, it was a kick playing with George! In 1930 we went to Europe, Jimmy Dorsey was in the band also and did most of the clarinet playing for Lewis. We played some good jazz too. You'll probably hear a lot of kidding about Lewis' clarinet, but he knows what he likes, and he happens to like good jazz. On our trip abroad we played in England, France, Belgium, Holland, etc. We spent two week's vacation in Paris and were so busy having a good time that we hardly got a chance to see the city. One thing I didn't miss though was the Louvre, I love painting and would have taken it up as a hobby if I'd ever got around to it. A funny thing happened to me there: I was just standing around in the lobby of a Paris hotel when a cute little bell-boy was paging a 'Monsier Spaneeeay' at his lungs' extent. It was alright, but after half an hour of yelling it got tiresome. Finally, he actually bothered me and I was about to tell him to tone down when someone nudged me in the arm and said it was *me* the kid was paging! They never could make out my first name and the way they interpreted my last name was so authentic that I couldn't make it out. Outside of little incidents of that sort we got along smoothly without the slightest knowledge of the language."

In Europe, Muggsy really made a big name for himself. Strange as it seems, European jazz fans are quicker to grasp the true values of a great jazzman than most American enthusiasts. In England, you'll find fans who've stood by Muggsy long before anyone "discovered" him here.

After returning from Europe Muggsy joined Ben Pollack's band in 1935. In the band at the time were Harry James, Irving Fazola and Freddy Slack. He made some fine records with a small group—Pollack's Pick-a-Rib Boys—which had the Swedish pianist Bob Lane on them. The band played California for a long time and toured the country. 1938 saw the Pollack group in New Orleans and Muggsy was forced to leave it. His hectic existence and the years of endless toil and spiritual restlessness finally succeeded in overpowering his physical resistance; he was compelled to rest and had no alternative but to remain at the Touro Hospital in New Orleans. Being seriously ill, the doctors, Muggsy says, were extremely discouraging about the whole affair, saying that he'd never be able to play again. But Muggsy never, not for one moment, doubted that he'd be up and playing in no time at all. It took him a year of earnest effort to get well.

Back in his home in Chicago, now a convalescent, Muggsy was afraid for the first time in his life. The mental torment he had undergone during his long illness was gradually undermining his self-assurance. Doubts clouded his mind. Suppose his lips didn't vibrate enough? After all, a fellow's lips get soft without practice. What would he do if he couldn't play? Would he have to start all over again? Yet no sooner did he touch his horn than all the doubts were dispelled. There was the same old cornet with the same Muggsy behind it. He exercised his lip for a while, played jam sessions in Chicago's joints here

and there, regained his self-confidence and finally, in April 1939, was all set with a little band of his own and went into Chicago's Hotel Sherman.

It was Ernest Byfield, of the Sherman, who gave Muggsy the break he needed so badly. Muggsy Spanier's Ragtime Band invaded the Sherman and established a new record by remaining there for five and a half months. The band had Coast-to-Coast radio hook-ups and the crowds at the Sherman Hotel went for it in a big way. It played good jazz, which was good listening or good dancing, whichever way you were inclined. Bands like the late Bunny Berigan's and Gene Krupa's played opposite them, yet Muggsy's boys always managed to steal the show. It wasn't only Muggsy's driving, inspired cornet that proved sensational to the general public opinion, it was the band as a whole as well. George Brunis and his tail-gate trombone plus his irrepressible flair for comedy gave the Ragtimers a solid basis for good showmanship. Rod Cless' clarinet was inspired and inspiring. Then too, men like Pat Pattison, Bob Casey, George Zack, Joe Bushkin, Ray McKinstry, Nick Caiazza, Marty Greenberg, Don Carter and George Wettling added to the atmosphere of perfection.

Inspiration was always high and musicianship wasn't wanting. Everybody got big kicks out of playing and the music was almost too good to be true. Muggsy was happy, his boys were happy and the little Ragtime Band was going places. After the Sherman they played Chicago's 3 Deuces and later on played an American Legion convention at State Lake, where Muggsy was privileged with the honor of being the first jazzman to lead the Salvation Army Band. Then they came to New York. The band had recorded four sides for Bluebird in Chicago, recorded twelve more in New York. When listening to the records many of you probably wonder how Bluebird ever got around to recording such exciting, authentic, and genuinely hot examples of improvised jazz. I do too. Listen to your copy of "Dippermouth Blues" again and reconsider the greatness of that muted cornet; the fire and extreme subtlety of Muggsy's phrases are unique. I doubt the existence of a living cornetist who could surpass Muggsy's playing on "Dippermouth."

Things didn't go so well for Muggsy in New York. The great little Ragtime Band, hailed by critics as the finest jazzband since Joe

Oliver's of 1923, got a brush-off from the Big City. It lasted just about the whole of six weeks down at Nick's in Greenwich Village. Muggsy had done well financially in Chicago, used to good living, he was easily discouraged by conditions in New York. Outside of the few record dates which hardly paid enough, there was no way of keeping the band together, musicians can't play on an empty stomach any more than an Army can fight on an empty stomach. The band broke up and the boys went on their own.

When asked about his Ragtime Band, Muggsy didn't offer any comment. He murmured almost inaudibly: "Please let's not talk about it, it makes me sad." In sum, the little Ragtime Band lived for nine short months, dying a cruel death because the public let it down, because it was too great a band to last. Muggsy rejoined Ted Lewis' orchestra, leaving him after six weeks to join his old friend Jess Stacy in the Bob Crosby Band. "One of my greatest thrills was playing with the Crosby Band, I enjoyed myself immensely. Those boys have the right spirit. Jess, Eddie Miller, Bobby Haggart, Nappy Lamare, and Ray Bauduc certainly made something out of that band." Muggsy remained with Crosby for a year, recorded several numbers for Decca with the Bobcats and some with the entire band. In the early spring of 1941 he organized his first big band to go into the Arcadia Ballroom on Broadway. "That was a fine band I had . . . " Muggsy recalls sullenly. The second pack of cigarettes rapidly diminishes in quantity of contents. "It was a star-studded band. I had fellows like Irving Fazola, Dave Bowman, Vernon Brown, Nick Caiazza and Don Carter. You never heard that band? . . . you would have liked it. It was so easy-going and played so smoothly that it was really a pleasure. I like it as much as the Little Ragtime Band, which is saying a lot." He played the Arcadia for six months, then going into Jack Dempsey's Broadway nitery and returning once again to the Arcadia for another pretty successful run. In June, 1943, Muggsy made an extensive tour of U.S.O. camps with his band. "Sometimes, we'd even play two camps a day. The work

proved exhausting, in fact, I dropped 24 pounds in that tour, which I'm still trying to regain."

Back in Chicago to rest after the U.S.O. tour, Muggsy was in two dangerous car accidents. The last one (Nov. '43) almost proved fatal, both he and his mother were seriously hurt. So Muggsy went to the hospital again until he fully recovered. Last March he reappeared in jazz circles, after an absence of eight months, when he came to New York. He gigged around to get his lip back and you were bound to find him most any place. At Jimmy Ryan's he sat in with Art Hodes' Trio, and Nick's jam sessions had him often as well as Milt Gabler's. He cut eight sides for Commodore records, two of which have already been released. Then, in April, he rejoined Ted Lewis and was again together with George Brunis in the Lewis brass section. But before four months he was out again—back at Nick's in New York.

When last talking to him in New York, Muggsy seemed quite discouraged, and confused as usual. He wants to have a little band of his own but is tied up with contracts in Chicago. He yearns to play but isn't given the chance. "The trouble with me is I'm too sincere, maybe I should turn commercial and stop kidding myself. I could get fat, have a house with a swimming pool and a nice yearly income. Wouldn't that be grand? It's really a curse to think that all good jazz, and all sincere art for that matter, has to be tied down to economics."

After much talking it over and many heart-breaking revelations, Muggsy brooded silently for a while and, lighting his last cigarette, gave what he believed was a solution: "You know, I wish I were a bookkeeper. Nothing but little numbers to write down all day, from 9 to 5. Then, at 5, you close the office door and your brain with it until 9 a.m. the next day finds you at the same thing. Wouldn't that be the life? No worries, no music to suffer for, not even the shadow of the word 'commercialism.' But, Hell, why am I telling you these things anyway! Let's go out for a pack of cigarettes . . . "

Hear That Ragtime Band

by Dale Curran

"I had always wanted to come to New York," Rod Cless says reminiscently when you get him to talking about those days 'way back in 1939. "There wasn't much jazz left in Chicago then. Even in 1928, Condon, Tesch, Bud Freeman, McPartland and my other pals left the town, and I felt like a lost soul. In 1929 I worked for Charlie Pierce, with Kaminsky, O'Brien and Johnny Mendel on cornet. We didn't make any records, and before long they went to New York, too. By 1939 I was working in a band at the Silhouette Club on Howard Street, and it was pretty commercial. I was playing saxophones and flutes. That gives you the idea.

"So when Muggsy came along with his proposition for a good small band, I was glad to come along. He had a nice line-up; Brunies on trombone, Pat Pattison, Bob Casey, George Zack and Marty Greenberg. The sax man was a problem; Ray McKinstry came in a little later after the first man moved out.

"We didn't rehearse very long. Everybody in the band worked out an arrangement to use as a guide on certain tunes; we worked up our arrangements from that. Later on we had everything memorized and went on that way.

"Muggsy got a contract from Ernie Byfield, of the Sherman Hotel—this was just after he had been laid up for so long at the Touro Hospital in New Orleans (that's where we got the title for the record "Relaxin' at the Touro"). Byfield was interested in Muggsy, and wanted to give him a break, and it was his idea to organize the small band. Byfield, being a society man, had a cocktail party for us, with photographers taking pictures for the society page.

"Well, we opened at the Sherman in April, 1939. The crowds liked our music. We played opposite a lot of big bands and small combinations—Krupa, Bunny Berigan, Count Basie, and so on. Twice a week we had "tea dances." The crowds seemed to like our music best for dancing. No matter what band was playing there, they always had us play for the floor show. We were all fakers and could handle the acts without any orchestrations.

"We had all worked together before that at different times; in the old days in Chicago I had played with Muggsy in Charlie Towne's band, where Pat Pattison was playing bass. And of course Brunies and Muggsy had played together for years in Ted Lewis's outfit.

"We stayed at the Sherman most of the summer. I remember that the first night we had a coast-to-coast hookup on the radio, we were all set; the engineer said 'all ready'—and just then Muggsy stepped on an electrical floor-plug and flame shot up all around him. Muggsy jumped about ten feet, but we got calmed down and went on the air all right.

"While Berigan was playing opposite us, with his big band, we used to go into our act on "High Society," marching around the floor like a colored band coming back from a New Orleans funeral. One night John Barrymore and Mary McCormick were in and they got a big kick out of it. The first show was o.k., but the second one was a little woozy on account of the saloon across the street.

"We made our first record date in Chicago, the first four sides of the Bluebird series. They took us to the brand-new RCA studio in Chicago, which was rigged up with the finest and newest of everything for recording symphonies or something. The engineers worked on us scientifically; they put chalk marks in front of all the horns and had the drums face the corner—really very technical. They got us so confused we decided to make the record our own way, just get around the microphone and play. We certainly baffled those engineers.

"After the Sherman we went into the Three Deuces, played a week with Billie Holliday. Then we had a week at State and Lake during the American Legion convention. Fats Waller and his band played opposite; six shows daily, and a battle of music all the way. They had a big thermometer rigged up on the stage, and we kept it boiling all the time.

"Bushkin joined us about then, replacing Zack. Outside of Brunies and Muggsy, none of us had had any stage experience. That was where Fats Waller helped us out. His personality was so wonderful that he soon made everybody feel at ease on the stage. He would come over and put his arm around me while I was playing in the spotlight, and I would relax and get along fine. We did all sorts of specialty numbers during that theatre date. Fats played organ, and Brunies did his number standing on one foot and working the trombone slide with his other foot. We used to knock out "Royal Garden," "When My Baby Smiles" (with Brunies doing an imitation of Ted Lewis), and "Tin Roof," and always for a finale both bands would go to work on "Honeysuckle Rose."

"Then we came to New York. So many of the old Chicago gang were here ahead of us, it was like old home week. When we went into Nick's, there were four other bands from Chicago right around the neighborhood. Joe Sullivan was in Cafe Society Downtown, Art Hodes at the Pirate's Den, Jimmy Kennedy at the Nut Club, and Bud Freeman playing in Nick's opposite us. We used to hold reunions every night; I remember somebody celebrated so much he fell down all the subway stairs. I forget who it was.

"We made our other twelve sides for Bluebird here in the New York studios. Ray McKinstry had stayed in Chicago, with NBC.

It wasn't easy to get a tenor man who could jam along with the band; we were never satisfied until we got Nick Caiazza, who was the best man we ever had for small-band ensemble work.

"We were lucky that any of those records turned out well. It seemed that everybody else had already made recordings of our best tunes, and we had to think up new ones to record. We had played ourselves out on "Muskrat," "That's a Plenty," and some others; then Bluebird wouldn't let us record them. The record companies never did get the idea that we might do them in a completely different way from the other bands.

"We lasted about six weeks at Nick's. We had been making good money in Chicago, and Muggsy was disgusted with things in New York. We were waiting for a big booking agency that was going to make us the greatest band on earth, but they never came through, and you can't live on record dates. Like all good things, it had to come to an end. Muggsy went back to Ted Lewis, and later to Bob Crosby, and then started a big band; Brunies went into the delicatessen business; some of the boys got homesick for Chicago and went back there. The rest of us are still around."

That's a very interesting story, Mr. Cless. But how about this—how does it feel to work in a band that is tops in its field? "It was a kick," Cless says non-committally, and more than that he simply won't say. He is an intelligent man with very definite opinions and the ability to express them, but he just isn't talking. His field is music, not criticism. And maybe he is right. After all, there are plenty of others to go around beating the drum for that great and lamented little band.

This correspondent, for one—who remembers practically paying Nick for board and room during those few exciting weeks when the band held forth at Tenth and Seventh. And all the record collectors who cherish those 35¢ Bluebirds as though they were made of diamond dust. You don't have to talk when you are secure in the knowledge that for a little while you were part of an organization that made musical history.

Wild William

by Bob Aurthur

The other night while sitting in the Onyx Club listening to Bill Davison's band, a friend of mine remarked. "You know, right now I'd rather listen to Davison's horn today than any other cornet around."

After a little bit of discussion I had to admit that my friend might have had something there. And why? Well, in Bill's case it might not be so hard to analyze. In the first place the guy has more spirit and drive than any other musician in town right now with the possible exception of George Brunies. But when you talk about Brunies you are talking about something else, so let's stick to Davison.

It was a great surprise to many people about a year ago to discover that Wild Bill was really playing some inspired cornet. It seemed to happen after his return from his first trip to Boston. Why should he suddenly wake up? Well, let's take Bill's explanation.

"You've got to remember that for years I was playing with a bunch of Micky Mouse bands," he'll tell you, "and it takes quite a while to get out of that groove."

Davison is one of those musicians who played jazz for a long time without ever really hitting the top until recently. Born in Defiance, Ohio, in 1905, there is nothing much of his early life that is of interest as far as music is concerned. When I asked him why he played cornet rather than trumpet, I rather expected a complicated answer such as Bix gave. However, Bill just grinned and admitted: "It's a hell of a lot easier to blow."

For a long while in the early jazz period Bill played around the Middle West with different bands of all kinds. Early recordings were made on the Gennett label with Chubby Steinburg's band in Cincinnati. This was about the same time that Bix and his Wolverines were the "Sensations of the Na-

tion" and made those all-important waxings on the same label.

Other recordings of some historical importance were made with the Seattle Harmony Kings with Jess Stacy on piano. These were made on Victor. However, the only sides in the jazz vein were made only about three years ago on the rather obscure Collectors Item label. This was the beginning of the modern Davison period. Shortly after these sides were made Bill came to New York.

It was in 1940 that Wild Bill came to New York, and he went almost immediately into Nick's where he worked rather steadily for almost two years in the company of all those jazz immortals who have come in and out of the famous down-town spot so regularly. Now Bill is on his own, and, Uncle Sam permitting, he is determined to carve his own personal niche in jazz history.

Besides being an exciting musician to listen to, Wild Bill is a veritable gold mine for the gathering of interesting stories. And it doesn't take much to get this happy-go-lucky guy talking about the terrific prohibition days out in Chicago. Of course, the fact that Bill has, and this is by his own computation, inhaled approximately five thousand quarts of whiskey might have something to do with his many experiences. But don't get the idea that Bill brags about his drinking even though he claims proudly: "I can outdrink any drunkards I know, and I know plenty." No, Bill just enjoys life to its fullest extent.

He often thinks reverently about a job that he had at the Sportsman's Club out in Chicago where the musicians could get both gin and whiskey for a nickel.

"That was the greatest job I ever had," Bill says reminiscently, "All the customers, who were mostly gangsters, would come in just to see the musicians get drunk and fall off the stand. And we never disappointed them."

The Jazz Record

20c

No. 41

February, 1946

"Wild Bill" Davison

But out of those lush Chicago days came a break that might have meant a completely different end to our story. It was the result of the automobile crash that killed the immortal Frank Teschemacher that changes the complexion of things for Bill Davison. Bill and Tesch had just signed a year's contract in Chicago's Guyon's Paradise. That band might have been the medium for Wild Bill's becoming a great figure in jazz long before this.

However, the break said "no," and then followed several years with sweet bands ending with a five-and-a-half year stretch with Benny Meroff and his own outfit in Chicago.

But now things are different. Outside of a few mysterious disappearances into the unknown, Wild Bill has come into his own and settled down.

Let's all hope that Bill's ambitions for a fine jazz band will come true. We have seen in the last couple of months that Bill's band with Rod Cless and James P. Johnson as a nucleus can really produce the stuff. What we want and need is more stuff and a lot more Wild Bill Davison.

Talking About Boze

by Mary Peart

Some things always seem to baffle me. Particularly things about the music business. The thing that is baffling me right now is something that I guess is pretty common —and that is, why one musician becomes known and acclaimed by fans and critics, and another completely overlooked, even though he's been around just as long and played with the big boys, too.

Right now I'm talking about Sterling Boze. And I'm going to keep right on talking until some of you put away your Kaminsky and Hackett Commodores, shut off your vics, and march right down to Nick's to hear him. There stands a guy who night after night blows some of the nicest jazz you can hope to hear, a guy who has everything. He plays fast numbers with a neat drive and nice vibrato, and blues with a vibrant, husky, yet sweet tone, and just the right shade of blue.

Sterling Belmont has been around for a long, long time, and he's played with most of the Names, too, and yet how many of you can boast of having in your collection a good Boze solo? I know, not many. And why? That's what I keep telling you. It baffles me.

Sterling was brought up in New Orleans in the days when N.O. was synonymous with jazz, and every theater had its own jazz band.

As a kid he listened to Buddy Bolden playing with the Maple Leaf Jazz Band, and Joe Oliver on the *Capitol* steamer, and Louis Armstrong and Fate Marable's band. Young Sterling loved it all. Even then, jazz was a big part of his life; a most important part. It got him, finally. It was during high school that he picked up his trumpet, and another musician was caught by that thing that gets hold of you and won't let go.

"When I was fifteen," he told us, "I used to go down to the Arcadia Ballroom and sit in with a trombone player named Tom Brown, who, incidentally, is a brother of Steve Brown who played with Goldkette, and who now has his own band in Detroit. A couple of years later I played with the Crescent City Jazzers, and then headed for St. Louis. That was in 1933. There we made records for Okeh under the name of the Crescent City Jazzers. I guess those records are pretty rare now," with a wry smile. "They didn't sell very well."

From 1924 to 1926 he recorded with a band known as the "Arcadia Serenaders." (Don't you love those names?) In 1927 he joined Jean Goldkette, and from there went to Chicago. He followed the time-honored route of N.O. up the river to Chicago, and thence to New York. In Chi, he worked at WGN with the Studebaker Champions band. Vic Young conducted, but it was a Goldkette outfit. Joined Ben Pollack the latter part of 1930. With the band at that time was Charlie Spivak, Teagarden, Harry Goodman on bass, Matty Matlock, Eddie Miller, Nappy Lamare, and Gil Rodin on sax—the band that later become Bob Crosby's.

"Let's see, what did I do after that?" Jobbed around Chicago, and then came to N.Y. That was in 1931. Here he worked for Decca and Brunswick doing studio work. He took quite a few solos on these records, but can't remember the titles or artists. (Could you?) From 1935 to '37 worked with Joe Haymes band (which T. Dorsey took over in 1935), Ray Noble, B. Goodman and Glenn Miller's first big band. Then came a stint with Bob Crosby, and later about four months at Nick's. After a job with Bob Zurke he "starved for about two and a half years." Then came six months with Teagarden, back to New York and Nick's . . .

That's only the bare outline, and leaves out the hopes and disappointments, the heartbreak, the hard work, all of which he probably wouldn't tell you about, anyway. But it's there—he doesn't need to tell you in words, he just picks up his horn and blows, and there it is.

Doc Evans

I wondered about Doc. Was he a real Doctor? So I asked him; and he said, "No man; that's just a tag from my college days." Sometimes Doc kinda reminds me of an Adlai Stevenson type. Quiet, dry humor; but he blows that lead (horn; trumpet man). Never thought Doc would finally be in charge of a 100-piece symphony orchestra; but that's what he's into. Plus at this very writing he's vice-president (I do believe) of the Minneapolis Musicians Union. But you call him for a gig, and I'm talkin' about playing jazz, and he'll get away. And he still goes out with a small group of his own, to play music.

You know, there's a jazz club in (around) Minneapolis. The Emporium. Right now it's the home of a group called The Hall Brothers. And it's successful. The band (seven, eight pieces) owns and operates the club. Well, I understand Evans had it before Stan (Hall) took it over. Doc tried. But it was too much for a "one-man" job. Or the time wasn't right. Some of us are cast in that role. We appear to plow the ground for those who follow. I never heard Doc complain about his role. And anybody hip to jazz knows of Doc Evans. So he may pop up at a jazz festival in California or Florida. Then again, he gets a call to go to New Orleans. Ain't too many guys who can blow that good. Not when it comes to the real jazz. The jazz that came out of the '20s and '30s; when nobody bothered to argue about what jazz was. They either knew and dug it or they let it alone.

A. H.

Dixieland, Twin City Style

by Paul (Doc) Evans

The influences which shaped Twin City jazz were the same as those that moulded the jazzmen of Chicago and New York, and throughout the rest of the country for that matter. We learned at first hand from personal appearances, at second hand from records. The riverboats, with Fate and the rest, seldom got up this far and consequently had less effect on our playing than they had on Bix at Davenport and other Tri-City musicians. Our style is still pretty much a white one, since we took our inspiration from Dixieland veterans rather than directly from the Negro pioneers of New Orleans. Sometimes we play like the Chicago men and sometimes like those from New York, usually a cross between the two with an occasional dash of New Orleans.

Actually those three styles are all Dixieland, yet they are also distinct and different from each other. A particular type of jazz often derives its prime characteristics from the tempo and tone of the city in which it originates. The Dixieland of New Orleans before the first World War was relaxed, easy and lazy, after the fashion of the southern Negro. That of Chicago during the prohibition era was furious, frantic, frenetic, in the prevailing gangster manner and speakeasy mode. New York's, both before and after repeal, was wrapped in cellophane in response to the urbane demands of slick and sophisticated cosmopolites. Here in the Twin Cities we have always been just a bunch of guys who think right and feel it, playing to a schottische crowd.

As far as records go, during the preswing decade that began halfway through the twenties, the Original Dixieland Jazz Band and the New Orleans Rhythm Kings, and the Wolverines were minor influences. Our first idol was Nichols, with his Five Pennies. Our second was Beiderbecke, with his Gang or with Trumbauer, and later with Goldkette or even with Whiteman. It was the Austin High bunch, McKenzie and Condon's Chicagoans or the Chicago Rhythm Kings, that seemed to us most important as a group. Red's stuff we frequently took note for note. Bix wasn't so easy to copy, but the Chicagoans we imitated merely in spirit. From these sources evolved the essence of the solo and ensemble style employed by most of us here today. After 1935 three big bands recorded music in the Dixieland idiom, Pollack and Crosby and the Dorsey Brothers, so we listened and learned some more. Each of these orchestras

Doc Evans

had a small outfit within it. It was Tommy's Clambake Seven, Ben's Pick-A-Rib Boys, and Bob's Bob Cats that really appealed to us. Of the many jazz units whose records we heard, Spanier's Ragtime Band and Freeman's Summa Cum Laude Orchestra impressed us most. Condon, of course, was always a standby. Now Eddie is practically a guarantee. In our formative years we didn't know anything about Oliver or Morton, and not much about Henderson or Ellington. McKinney we knew from the radio, Moten from records and theater dates. All of us paid attention to Armstrong and Hines, but none of us played like them and few even tried.

Of the big bands we saw in person between 1925 and 1935, Paul Whiteman at the Minnesota Theater and Glen Gray at the Lowry Hotel were the best known. They didn't affect us half so much as the New Orleans Rhythm Kings and Leon Prima on trumpet and Leon Rappolo on clarinet at the Marigold Ballroom, and not one-quarter so much as Pollack. Ben had a very extensive stay, probably spending more time here than anywhere else, playing the Boulevards of Paris in Midway and the Plantation in White Bear and the Lowry in St. Paul. His band was sensational, including such star jazzmen as Boze and Jack Teagarden and Matlock and Eddie Miller and Bauduc and Harry Goodman. He went over remarkably well, even on his last trip when he brought along Cherock, James, Squires, Gates, Taylor, etc. Local musicians just about lived wherever Ben was playing, often sat in side by side with the greats. Pollack's influence was perhaps the most significant of all. With the coming of swing the Lowry Hotel presented Louis Prima on several occasions and Red Norvo with Mildred Bailey. The Nicollet Hotel in Minneapolis likewise introduced Bob Crosby and Jimmy Dorsey and Woody Herman, all at their finest, just at the beginning of their bandleading careers. Venuti, Pollack, Arnheim, Miller, Chester, and Nichols followed in rapid succession. Still, it was Dixieland we were after. We listened chiefly for Spanier with Pollack, for Dixon with Arnheim, for Fazola with Miller. Although Fuller, McShann, Waller, Henderson and Towles all played the Happy Hour, we preferred Tut Soper at the Dome or Jack Gardner at the Minnesotan.

The first good local jazz was played by the various campus bands at the University of Minnesota. Not everyone went to school, but all worked at one time or another with most of these orchestras. None of them had libraries; everything was off the elbow, by ear. The earliest location date for a local jazzband was in 1926 at the Golden Pheasant, an upstairs Chinese spot, where Red Ballard and others made music similar to the Memphis Five. My first chance for a steady Dixieland job came in 1929 with Norvy Mulligan at the Nankin Cafe, where Lute Leraan blew some of the finest tailgate I've ever heard. In 1932 Johnny Davis opened at the Lowry, backed by some of the best men in town. Vinny Bastien on trombone and Frankie Roberts on clarinet and Chief McElroy on drums. Scat left in 1933, and with that Dixieland was through in the Twin Cities for the next four years.

In 1937 there was a local Dixieland revival at Lindy's. Two years later began the best, and longest, Dixieland job of them all. This was at Mitch's Cafe in Mendota, where pianist Red Dougherty led a band built around clarinetist Harry Yblonski, drummer Eddie Tolck and myself. Don Thompson was the original trombonist, Hal Runyon his successor. 1941 was our biggest year, when Bob Zurke came in as solo pianist only to give way months later to Joe Sullivan. There had never been anything like it here before, and there's been nothing to equal it since. Mitch's closed in 1942, so we opened at the Casablanca with a revamped personnel. This was still fine jazz, but the end was plainly in sight. Soon we were out of a job and, forced to split up, went our separate ways. Early in 1945 there were four semi-Dixieland bands in town, where before there had been one real one. Vinny Bastien had made one record, "You're Driving Me Crazy," for Miracle. Some of the boys had been engaged by WCCO to form the nucleus of the Ad Lib Club. But the old Mitch days were gone. In a final effort I organized and ran off a series of four Sunday afternoon jazz concerts, but all in vain. Even here the palmy days of Dixieland had passed.

Now we are all just jobbing around, playing Dixie when we get a chance, taking anything we can get the rest of the time. Of the men I haven't mentioned, trumpeter Duke DuVall and trombonist Wally Schultz and clarinetist Guy Capman and drummer Red Maddock could form the core of one very good unit, trumpeter Larry Brakke and trombonist Jerry Mullaney and clarinetist Windy Swanson and drummer Bob Bass of still another. All of them know their jazz and long to play it again. Perhaps better times are ahead, who knows?

I've said nothing about the fine local Negro swing musicians, because that's another matter. There was Boyd Atkins at the Cotton Club, with Lester Young on tenor and Rook Gans on trumpet. There was El Herbert at Swing City. The famous Pettiford tribe worked the Harlem Breakfast Club and the Southern Barbecue. Sid Williams and other piano soloists have created a lot of excitement. Nevertheless, I think the Twin Cities have produced more fine Dixieland men than anything else. Now that they're here, what will St. Paul and Minneapolis do with them?

Max Kaminsky

Little Maxie . . . The little guy with the big sound comin' out of that trumpet. We played some scenes together. An you know somethin'? Max played different horn with me than he played with other bands. It came out black (with us). Still, on dixie-combo ensemble tunes he led that front line (clarinet, trombone, trumpet) like the book called for. When I say Max is a little guy I mean he's got to be about 5 feet (around there). Never noisy. But not un-humorous. He was one of us jazz players that could step into a big band and do the job that was called for. That wasn't my bag but I sure could see where it helped when it came to eatin' regular and payin' bills. But you know, everything has a price. I once asked Max. . . .

"Hey Max, how did you make it playin' in Artie Shaw's band?" Two stories he told me come to mind. "Art, we were on this battleship out there in and around the islands, and I wanted a cold drink, like a coke; so I asked Artie to let me have a half-dollar. Now you know you got to get this scene. There's a war goin' on and they're blasting. Well, Shaw gives me a half-buck, then calmly reaches into his pocket, takes out a notebook and marks it down."

"Max, tell me the other story." "Well Art, before we went abroad I was making a hundred-seventy-five a week with Shaw. And I spent $175 a week forgetting him."   A. H.

Gentleman of Jazz

by Fats Baker

Now that it's been Sailor Max Kaminsky for over half a year, more of us begin to realize how much it meant to have him around Nick's, Ryan's or Town Hall, and how great it will be to have him back again. Maybe "most underrated" doesn't apply, but have you ever read a tribute as glowing or good as the notes that sing out of his trumpet?

No one has yet.

Maybe it's because no records have ever caught his music at its best. Or because of his own modesty, the character that keeps him from being a "character." Or because it's not one flashy tune, but set after set, night after night, of steady goodness of playing that shows the full measure of his genius. The more you listen to Kaminsky, the more there

Max Kaminsky

is to hear; the more you see of him, the more there is to know.

He despises, more than anyone, the "Who is best?" chatter of critics. It's irrelevant to good jazz. "Great" and "success" means nothing to him; he has learned their Broadway meaning the hard way. Yet few men can attain the greatness of Kaminsky's success; none can attain greater. It upsprings not from headlines or box-office receipts, but from the hearts of those who hear the horn and know the man. It is: This guy is right and his work is right.

Max Kaminsky, Seaman 1st Class, was born in Brockton, Mass., some 33 years ago. As a kid he tagged after Beiderbecke, built a crystal set so he could hear Armstrong broadcast. (He still feels neither can do wrong.) At 14 he led his own pro band, the Six Novelty Syncopators. It wasn't until after he had joined Dorsey, years later, that he learned to read; his first training and work were pure jazz. For 20 years now he's followed and played with most of the other jazz greats in Boston, Chicago, New York and elsewhere—through the Chicago golden era, the rise of commercial swing, and the crewcut obeisance to jazz and jam sessions.

The big bands have had him serve time—T. Dorsey, Leo Reisman, Tony Pas-

tor, Goodman, Marshard's society outfits, Miller, Shaw. The twin necessities of helping his family and of having to play regularly to stay happy were usually responsible. Sometimes it was promises leaders later forgot. With some bands he just played. In other cases he rehearsed bands being whipped into shape, or gave leaders ideas on which they built their success. It was his suggestions that led commercial leaders to start using Delius effects. Once he even had to teach a leader how to give the downbeat. In return he rarely got more than scale and heartaches, though with a stronger stomach and a smaller heart he could have done well in the scramble for personal gain.

But, always a jazz man, he'd stand the commercial stuff just so long, then turn down, for instance, an Alvino Rey bid, saying "I was afraid I'd be electrocuted," and go back to the guys he knows—Art Karle, or Freeman, or Pee Wee, or Condon. His last civilian job was with Joe Marsala, when Condon was in the band, and his last appearance, at the final Town Hall jazz concert, was one to remember.

Kaminsky's ensemble playing with a Pee Wee band is the glorious thing. Usually he dislikes taking solos with a jazz band, and when you've heard some of them, with or without plunger, you could weep at this dislike. He likes drums and might have been a good drummer, and those who have heard, say he sings good jazz. There's a genius in the absolute rightness of his musical instincts.

The full glory of his playing isn't on records. The various Commodore ones come close; possibly the unreleased ones, made with Marsala last year, will have it. Best, though, are the little-known, still available ones made with Condon, Bushkin, Freeman, Waller, Wettling and others, accompanying Lee Wiley in Gershwin tunes, for Liberty Music Shops; and another Lee Wiley album, of Rodgers and Hart, for Rabson's—both from Summa Cum Laude days. Even as experienced a collector and Kaminsky listener as Pete Ehlers was amazed, when he recently heard them for the first time, at how much of Kaminsky does come through on these.

Now he's with Artie Shaw for the third time, with the U.S. Navy as sponsor. He enlisted when friends were offering an honorable way to serve while staying civilian and staying with good jazz, and when others were offering better military "deals." But joining the Navy struck him as right. With Dave Tough, John Best and the rest, including an accordion man to play in spots no piano can go, he played in and around Pearl Harbor from Christmas until recently. They ran into jazz people like Pat Condon, Don Burke, Herb Sanford, Vic Moore. A few servicemen come up to ask about Freeman or Pee Wee, but it's the Shaw music most want, and that brings home to them. Getting aboard ship and into real Navy life recently, Kaminsky says, brought them the most appreciative audience he's ever seen.

Twice-promoted, deeply bronzed, cigarette-abstaining, on a daylight schedule, newly engaged to be married, serious-minded and healthy as never before, Kaminsky seems to be finding a new maturity in Navy life. If so, it's bound to show in his playing once he can again be heard in the States and with his own boys.

In the middle of a war, from Pearl Harbor, he could stop to defend a friend, telling another friend, "I see where —— is also taking up the idea of riding Pee Wee's playing, writing about his faces and rasping sounds. What dopes they are. They have no idea how good he is. They judge him by his solos, which are not bad, but his great forte is his ensemble playing. But they don't know anything, except what someone tells them, and then only take the word of the one who makes money. What a phoney world. Well, I don't know how phoney the world is, but when it comes to music I do know about that. Of course it is useless to argue about it; the only thing is not to be misled or lose one's beliefs. They will never convince me. All they have is words. I don't blame Pee Wee for anything he does, after so many years. Eddie too. They are good guys and certainly gentlemen."

Later he wrote a friend, "We leave this place, as they say in the travelogues. I don't know where we are going or for how long or anything about it. But I know how serious this all is and I know my job . . . All the Nick's stuff sounds interesting, but I would not be happy there with this war going on. It sounds pretty good but this is the real job now. Now we will have a chance to help the war more than ever. At least we will be the only pro orch that will be doing so much. We'll be entertaining a lot of boys who need entertaining, and I feel that I am doing the best I know how. I call it a tour as I have travelled so much that to me this is similar to another tour, though of much more mileage and for a greater cause. Of course we have done some good work here in Pearl Harbor, but now we will have a chance to get to the real things of it all. The sooner everyone helps to do all he can, the sooner this war might end."

He'd laugh if you said that the greatest gentleman in jazz is Kaminsky himself.

Music Is a Business

by Fats Baker

This is the story that was ended before it could be printed. The three press releases that follow tell a story in three acts. The moral? Maybe that music and business do not mix. Maybe that Boston still hasn't a paying public for good music. But hats off to Kaminsky for trying.

ACT I

Maxie's opens Sunday, February 3, at 220 Huntington Avenue in Boston. It's four walls within which Maxie Kaminsky and his Jazz Band will rip out their music for any citizen who comes across with a buck twenty admission. A basement hall unused for years, the joint provides an acid test of the staying power of Kaminsky fans.

"I'm not nuts," says Maxie, "but I go nuts when I can't play every night. Besides, for 25 years I've worked for other men, and 25 is enough, especially after sharing foxholes with the Guadalcanal rats. Besides, this is my home town, and I want to stay here."

Guest star for the Sunday opening is Joe Bushkin, lavishly advertised by Maxie as "Direct from Tokyo" and "World's greatest jazz pianist."

"If people like our band as much as we do," Maxie says, "then we can't lose. So far here, they have."

"We've got the worst room and the best jazz band in the world. My bet's on music."

Music meant is from the clarinet of Pee Wee Rusell, drums of Buzzy Drootin, trombone of Sparky Tomasetti, and two others unset. Plus leader's trumpet. Latter is well tarnished, and Maxie says, "At last I'm in a room that for looks matches my bugle."

ACT II

Maxie's made its opening. So did Bushkin. People, too; plenty of people.

Bushkin, the ex-Tommy Dorsey boy, liked it well enough to stay all night. Pee Wee, in form, broke everything up. Maxie says it wasn't bad, and that's his highest praise for anything except Louis Armstrong. The customers left happy.

Even the cellar room was on the beam. Thanks to a couple of guys, it had abstract paintings and, unexpectedly, a becoming coat of paint on the walls. In fact, the whole thing happened because of lots of people with big hearts, as Max Kaminsky won't forget.

"I'm sorry for anyone who missed Joey," comments Maxie. "As for business, we didn't get hurt too much. In case we don't make it, I've just landed a vet's priority on the apple concession at Tremont and Boylston."

ACT III

No more Maxie's.

At 11:30 P.M., Sunday, February 17th, the door will close on the cellar room in which Bostonian Max Kaminsky has battled to keep his band together. It opened February 3, the band having been fired February 2 from the local club which it had worked since October.

At the wind-up Maxie is heavily indebted on all sides, as to gratitude; but he pulls out owing no one a cent. As he says, "This is one time that Pee Wee and I have our train fare back to New York. I've shot my savings, and it was worth it for the music the boys played. It was worth it to discover how great all kinds of people can be when some good music hits them.

"If this hasn't been the best jazz band in the world, I'd like to hear the one that is. These boys have proved themselves first-class musicians and first-class guys."

The men rating this praise are Pee Wee Russell, clarinet; Buzzy Drootin, drums; Sparky Tomasetti, trombone; Johnny Field, bass; and Harry DeAngelis, piano. Their work has set Boston jazz fans agog. On vocals with the band has been the tremendously talented and beautiful discovery, Judy Powell. Remember that name too. The staff of Maxie's has been: Steve Church, room manager; Harold Kline, financial manager; Paul Greenberg, expert liaison artist; Moe Cartoof, Bernie Chaiet, and George Poor, designers; Mary Russell, assistant to all; and Nancy on publicity and hat checks.

"We're winding up clean, the way we started," concludes Maxie. "I tried, and I learned how wonderful people are, and I'm happy.

"I figured from the start that this band was my hobby. It was a hell of a hobby while it lasted."

Village Tavern League

by George Avakian

Julius's, the place the current lost generation has been looking for to get lost in, is all agog with shop talk these days, and if you think it's the state of jazz or why the Village is going to the dogs or who owes for the next round, you can guess again, although the last is a pretty good stab and probably rates at least half a giant step.

No, the big topic today is baseball, and you're just not in it if you aren't ready to discuss squeeze plays (the back room's marvelous for that kind of stuff) and pop flies (they're bar flies who order cokes). And don't come around with the latest Red Sox and Dodger averages. It's the Village Tavern League we're talking about.

Never heard of it? Stranger in town, eh? Stick around, bud, we might wangle you a pass.

The League, which is not mentioned in Delaunay's *Discography*, has its origins in the incredibly informal softball games played by Bud Freeman's Especially Augmented Summa Cum Loudlies against the Equally Enlarged Nick's Waiters and Bartenders Brotherhood in an empty lot on Sixth Avenue at the corner of Washington Place back when Leonie the Cat, terror of all mice in Julius's, was still a twinkle in a dozen Waverly Place Toms' eyes. These games, photographically recorded on the walls of Eddie Condon's soda fountain on 3rd Street, were marred by the inability of most of the performers to grope their way from first to second in dazzling daylight without recourse to lengthy conferences with the first base coach over a magnum of Budweiser. The turnover in first basemen was terrific, too. The season came to an untimely close when the local truant officer mistook Max Kaminsky, Dave Tough, and Eddie Condon for three diminutive renegades from the Washington Progressive

School and it was fall by the time they could pass their clay modeling and backhand printing finals. However, by then there had been sunshine and good fresh air for all and skinned knees for most, none of which are ordinarily found in the lfie of a Village musician, except the skinned knees from crap games behind the garage door.

This summer things are expanding enormously, with every brewers' retail outlet represented on the diamond with a first-class ball club. If you don't believe it, ask them. The red hot favorites at the moment are Condon's Quintessential Athaletics, Julius's Five Stein Finals, and Nick Rongetti's Nonpareils. (That also means 6-point type. Ask your printer what size that is, and then don't tell Nick.)

The latest dope is that the Condon club is appealing to Commissioner Landis (when told about Happy Chandler, Condon, who had just gotten back from playing at George Morrell's Princeton Class reunion, asked "*Whom* did he ever lick?") to permit Pete Pesci to play center field despite his original allegiance to Julius's, on the grounds that Packy Andriole's presence at the 10th Street ice cream parlor has enabled Pete to establish legal residence at the Sign of the Angular Pork Chop. This, obviously, is an attempt to bolster the team's loss of its ace speedballer, Wild Bill Davison, who recently secured his waivers to the 52nd Street League, and third baseman Buddleigh Freeman, who no longer operates as Director of Talent on Relief Night. There was some question as to how shortstop Joe Bushkin, who still bears the scars of a ground ball that bashed him in the kisser during spring training, would be qualified, but the League President, Mayor Bill Kennedy, has ruled that he can be listed either as a steady customer or intermittent intermission pianist.

Condon's Athaletics, withal, shape up as strong contenders, with a couple of outstanding fly chasers (bar flies, again) in Andy Gardella (no relation to ex-Giant Danny) and Augie Cellini (positively no similarity to the great lover, the local girls assure me), both of whom also know how to handle an infield tap expertly, especially if it's behind the bar and is marked "Schaefer's." The Condon team is also graced by Johnny Mazzuco, whose fielding of buck-fifty tips is flawlessly artistic, and Bill Funaro, who doesn't hesitate to admit that he plays first base only because he's never been able to get past there.

Nick's outfit will depend mainly on the sturdy right arm of Muggsy Spanier, who used to keep in trim at the Panther Room of the Hotel Sherman by throwing a pitch at the end of the first ensemble chorus every time his Ragtime Band played "Big Butter and Egg Man." Old Soupbone works out every afternoon on 10th Street between 7th and Waverly and is looking forward to a hot summer, Chicago style. That milk diet should enhance his control at little loss of speed. Muggsy is also something of a slugger, as Cousin Lenny can tell you.

Another dangerous man on the Rongetti club is Miff Mole, whose unique batting style cost the 10th Street bookies a small fortune his first time out. Miff uses an old Conn trombone instead of a bat, and the smart operators figured on most of the pitches slipping by between the tubes of his slide. However, Miff knew what he was doing. With his eyes, he can't help but miss by several inches with a regulation bat, so this way he aims to hit the ball and one of the tubes is bound to connect. Adds Miff: "You can't beat that seventh position for going after an outside curve."

Pee Wee Russell, who once caught a fly ball on the third bounce in the early spring of 1924, is a shaky proposition in the outfield, but at bat the boys figure that any pitcher who can put across three strikes while Pee Wee fidgets at him isn't going to be worth much after the second inning. The key to the team's defense is Nick's maitre de cafe, Jack "No Relation and Twice Pee Wee's Size" Russell, who has a perfect record on put-outs of foul balls in his territory. Francis Palmer is expected to give Condon's Jack Lesberg a

swift run for the base-stealing championship of the league, although both men insist "We never stole a bass in our lives. We always buy them from Wurlitzer."

An entry that loomed in the early training days but which has been reported forced to retire due to lack of air conditioning on the home grounds was the Stuyvesant Superbas. The real story, however, has been learned only recently by tapping Gene Williams' letter box. It seems that those people you saw talking to Bunk Johnson and his boys between sets all last spring disguised as Fred Ramsey, Bill Russell, and Jan Kindler were really Jorge Pasquel and a couple of brothers. Bunk, who was the first man to stand on Canal Street and pitch a curve ball around the corner to a catcher on Rampart and denies that Buddy Bolden ever hit a home run clear across Lake Pontchartrain (Jelly Roll Morton did it in 1904 by his own admission), is said to be basking in 20-peso cigars just now and will take the field with his boys for the Chappaqualquapetl Aztecs for the first Sunday double-header in August. Phone Ralph Gleason for weekend reservations, which include a round trip on Fate Marable's new 4-motored excursion plane, Dixie Belle II. Leadbelly will provide entertainment between Newark Airport and Brownsville, Tex., and Mrs. Big Bill has signed on as stewardess, so hurry, hurry, hurry.

Some of the Village spots, like George's and Ernie's, can't decide whether to have a boys' team or a girl's team or start an inbetweeners' league of their own, but none of the clubs have the problems which beset Julius's Five Stein Finals. There is no numerical dearth of talent, but some difficulty exists in getting the boys off those barrelhead chairs, and the team's best baserunner has a severe limp brought on by continuous application of foot to bar-rail. Some deals are already in the offing; Manager Packy has offered Nick four dime beers and Sam, custodian of Julius's back room, for Benny, Nick's dispenser of gentlemen's boutonnieres. The boys are kept on their toes largely by the constant threat of being shipped to the minors, and God knows nobody wants to get sent to Jimmy Kelly's or the Nut Club, where no one can get mistaken for a bright young man of advertising or a potential Steinbeck.

The only regulars sure of their positions are Harold Fitzsimmons, the daytime bartender, because his size indicates that he's rung up an enviable record at the plate, and Tony, the sandwich man, because the meat shortage has given him so much time off that he's been able to finish *"RVLES & REGVLATIONS FOR THE CONDVCT OF BASE BALL"* by Abner Dovbleday. Jimmy McGraw, whose right elbow is constantly warmed up to a moments notice, will probably share pitching honors with Jerry Bakst, formerly of Eliot House, Harvard, who once had a no-hit game in hand until the first batter up for Lowell House singled sharply off the right bank of the Charles River, precipitating a rally which fast fielding held down to 37 runs at the end of the second inning. First-string catcher for Julius's figures to be the star boarder, Charlie Miller, although Pete Peterson, the second-string back room man has taken enough wisecracks and garbled orders without fumbling to rate high for the nod. The infield, consisting of Stan Warren, Jake Qualley, Phil Green, and Walter Tondettar, is considered rather porous, inasmuch as this crew is noted only for its "Porous another round, Joe."

For their own protection, although they have quite a record for operating together as a team, Charles Edward Smith and bartenders Joe Gallagher and Bob Earl have been placed in the outfield and been given football helmets, peach baskets, and the Extreme Unction. Smith, a serious student of old-time baseball strategy, has attempted to reintroduce Heinie Groh's famed bottle-shaped bat, but Charles's insistence on realism was not appreciated by Umpire Carlton Brown, who was injured by flying glass and could not participate in the subsequent ceremonies, which consisted of both teams gathering around Smith to wring his shirt into shot glasses for all.

The climax of the Village Tavern League season, of course, will be the Intra-City Championships against the pennant winners of the 52nd Street League, which plans to hold games, rain or shine, in the shadow of the American Air Lines flagship in the lot next to the Onyx Club. The re-bop boys have been screaming "fifth column" ever since George Brunies, Art Hodes, and Bill Davison invaded their hollow precincts (hollow, fallow, what's the difference?) and it will be a sore blow to them indeed if Ernie Anderson stages the play-offs at Town Hall with Fred Robbins at the microphone.

When's the first game scheduled? Don't be silly. Who said anything about *playing?* We're just *talking* about it. Nobody actually *plays.* You think we're crazy?

Musicians Are Independent

by G. F. Quittner

You come into our joint and sit down at a table near the stand. You see a great crowd of dancing, drinking, laughing people on the floor and at tables. Perhaps you own some sort of business, or work for one, and to you a great many drinking and dancing people look good. Good business. If they stay and buy plenty of alcohol, and return to do these things another day, that is profitable business, so you find that situation desirable. You are flabbergasted, annoyed, even hurt as though you had been insulted, to find that we on the stand are not so sure that all this is desirable. You may even recommend to the management that we be fired for some of the terrible things we say and do.

A lady comes to the stand and asks for a particular piece, and we answer that we do not know it, although you notice that on top of the piano is the music for that piece. Another customer requests a waltz, or maybe it is a rhumba or a polka, and we say "later," but never get to it. A drunken couple wobbles to the piano desiring to sing a duet over the p. a. system to a clapping crowd at a large table, a crowd you can see is spending plenty of money, and we play the piece so rapidly that even an experienced singer could not have followed, then, to your horror, we smirk at one another over the results, the embarrassment and discomposure of the couple.

You say "What the devil are you here for? To have a good time? To insult paying patrons? You are getting paid for playing, are you not? Are you crazy, you musicians?"

That is why you recommend that we be fired. Those thoughts irritate your economic sense of justice.

Now we of the orchestra are not all of one mind on these questions. It would be found upon investigation that in spite of a certain musical accord we do not all think alike in such matters. It is easy to see why this should be so: The trumpet man is very independent, even more than the rest of us, plays what he likes when he likes, all because he plays just for kicks, earns his living on a day job, accepts his musician's pay because he knows he is giving something worth paying for and not because he must do what is required of him for the sum. The fiddle man—he thinks we are crazy just as you do—we don't any of us think much of his playing, by the way—he plays because he needs money badly, and he plays with us because he has a touch, he is a relation of the proprietor's wife. The sax man is a legit artist, and does not have any opinions—we are looking for a replacement. Then, well, you can group the other four of us in a lump, because when it comes to jazz or economics we agree pretty well; you see we are the backbone of the band, the rhythm section, as well as the majority, and the boss of the band is in our camp. If you want to understand what all these crazy ideas are and where they come from, we are the ones to ask. When you have figured out exactly the things which cause us to have these attitudes which made you so angry, you will have gone most of the way into understanding why we feel as we do about a great number of things,

things about music, people, money, getting along.

Suppose you were a—say a very good wood carver. Suppose that all you could do was carve wood, and outside of your family the only thing that was very important to you was carving wood, and you had to bring up a couple of kids on your income from wood carving. In case you don't know it, you are in a swell kettle of fish! People in this country don't like wood carving, except as it is done on a lathe. They are perfectly satisfied to have their wood carvings stamped and turned and glued and painted up shiny, just like everybody else has. Oh, they tell you, if you show them a real complicated piece of work, one that is easy to see was hard to make, "you're very good," but they would not spend much money for one like that because it is different from the kind their friends have, so they do not know whether it is pretty, or well done, or worth the money you ask or not. So you can not sell directly what you know you do well, and you get a job in a little shop where they make wood carving originals to sell to furniture manufacturers who make the carvings on machines. They give you a lathe and a saw and a bunch of shiny varnish and tell you to go ahead and start designing.

Some gink comes up and wants a chair "like the one in Smith's window." You go out and get the chair from Smith's window to study, and find out that the chair you are to copy is not only a copy itself, but that it is hardly worth looking at. There are probably ten thousand chairs just like it, all turned out by the same machine, probably in the same month. You look over the chair very carefully, trying to find out what the hell the gink liked about it. You know about chairs and carving because that is your business. The gink knows nothing about chairs and carving because his business is fighting unions and selling stuff, but he likes that one. He has, it would seem, left it to you to decide what it is he likes about it. You remember distinctly his saying that he expects a slightly changed chair, a little better chair, one that the other manufacturer can't sue him for copying.

Now you have a lot of faith in human nature; in spite of having had a hard time earning a living at your carving, you think that in general people are all right, are on the beam, when you get to know them. So you figure what this guy liked was the mood, maybe the rhythmic balance of the chair. You find that in these respects it is not such a bad chair after all, and you can see that the fellow might have known something about it.

Now, as a wood carver, you are sick of all the cheap varnish, all the dead-head decorations, all the trinkets that only detract from what is good in the chair, so you go back to the shop and get busy. On paper you draw a chair having the mood and balance of that one. Then you develop the idea, throw out the baubles, add certain things which you know are appropriate, which you feel are beautiful and expressive. You kill yourself staying up nights trying to get into the spirit of the thing, to get just the right designs to add to the basic structure which is good in the chair to bring it to the utmost harmony and completion. After a couple of months you have built the chair and you call the fellow on the phone, tell him it is ready.

He looks at the chair and then at you. "Where's all the pretty shiny varnish finish that was on the other chair?" he says. "I wanted you to copy the chair. Where are all the little pretty curlycues that were on the other one? Too hard, huh? You couldn't make 'em? What's this stuff you got on here? Those ain't on the other chair. That don't look anything like the other chair. My machines won't stamp out stuff like that. I can't use that crap." Then he gets real friendly and helpful. "Look bud. You ain't gonna get anywhere doin' that kind of stuff. It's gotta be flashy, attract the public eye. You gotta make stuff that a machine can turn out 5000 a month, and every single person lays eyes on the chair that has ten bucks in the bank will buy. You'll never make any money that way." So he tells the boss and you get fired for wasting the company's time and money and materials, for disobeying orders; for being too independent. You are not worried. You are competent. You can do good work or bad, so other joints will hire you.

But you can bet that the next time a gink comes up to ask for crap, you are going to tell him that the fellow at the next bench can do that kind of work better than you, or you'll be able to get to it in six months or a year, or more likely never, or maybe, there being some other fellows in the joint who know what the score is, you throw a couple of sticks into the automatic lathes and set the levers, and while the goof is standing there, tear off what he said he wanted, in the cheapest most obvious manner you can manage, leaving him sort of disgusted with himself and you, and when he has left you smirk at the other fellows in mutual appreciation of his stupidity and discomposure. And when you get fired you find another joint.

You're crazy like us, now. Like a fox.

5

Lest We Forget

Jazz is a varied music, and *The Jazz Record* covered many aspects of it. Something of that variety is represented in Part Five.

Record collecting has been a part of jazz for a long time, and *The Jazz Record* published many record reviews and much discographical information, but in the long run it was Dale Curran's put-on of collecting and Mezz Mezzrow's account of a recording session that seemed to us most worthy of inclusion. Following these come pieces on musicians who did not seem to us, for one reason or another, really to fit into one of the earlier sections. Pigmeat Markham was primarily a comedian and dancer working the minstrel shows and the black vaudeville circuit and theatres, although he also sang the blues. Dewey Jackson, Harry Dial, Cecil Scott, Henry Goodwin, James P. Johnson, Fats Waller, and Gene Sedric had local or regional roots and associations that set them off from the musicians in Parts Three and Four. Lester Young is here because he, more than any other single musician, exemplifies the ties between traditional and modern jazz. Bob Wilber is here because, although he is a generation younger than any other musician in this anthology, his relationship with Sidney Bechet represents a continuation of the apprentice-master relationship which has been so important to jazz, for example with Louis Armstrong and King Oliver, with Fats Waller and James P. Johnson, with Art Hodes and the black pianists he followed on Chicago's South Side.

Art plays the last chorus. And that is as it should be, because while many talents have been represented here, neither the magazine nor the book could have existed without the guiding genius of Art Hodes.   C.H.

Dale Curran

Of course there'd never have been a *Jazz Record* Mag and the stories you have read if there hadn't been a Dale Curran. A kindly disposed man with a love of piano music. Fact is he wrote a book, *Piano in the Band* (also wrote *Du Pree Blues*). Yeh! It was Dale who grabbed me and talked me into us starting a jazz mag. And he stuck to it for some four years; four years in which the big load of putting out the mag fell on his shoulders. He was an average height man; average weight (would I say 5'6", 145 lbs.) and very good-humored. Convivial; I believe that's the word. Musicians liked being around him.

When we started *Jazz Record* we operated out of our homes. And each wife licked envelopes, applied stamps and addressed letters. Eventually we took over a basement-store on 10th Street (N.Y.C.). Dale was a printer by trade and an editor by inclination; so that was a big help. And of course I had my WNYC program six afternoons weekly (that was an educational radio station owned by the city) and had picked up a vast listening audience. So we had high hopes of building *JR* into a success. We did succeed as far as "the printed word." But financially; well, I know there are subscribers who were most kind. Plus we sent hundreds of mags, monthly, to England (our version of lend-lease). Again, there was this war going on, and one lad stationed in the Pacific would send his *JR* to a buddy in Europe. I felt good about what we were doing. But it never made us dime one.

Then I think of all the contributors. The people that gave of themselves. The photographers; the record reviewers, and those who did articles that needed recording. Without the help of many we wouldn't have succeeded. Yes, as a great piece of work there can be no doubt about that statement. Just reading the Cow Cow story and realizing that it no doubt was the only thing Davenport wrote. Wait; let me tell you. See, we didn't have a tape recorder. Our style was to invite a musician to the *JR* office; sit him down with a taste, and then I'd get him to talk. Dale would be writing or typing this down, word for word, as we went along. Try that if you think it isn't work.

Yeh! There'd been no *Jazz Record* mag without Curran. He did a job. But that ain't why I include this bit by him. No, I enjoyed reading it. I had become a record collector; got the bug there for a while. I think you'll dig it too.   A.H.

Gram-o-phone Days

by Dale Curran

When I am around record collectors I usually listen quietly to the conversation for a while, and then remark that I used to enjoy collecting until the companies started to put the name of the band on the label. This produces annoyed and apprehensive glances, and thereafter the collectors cross over to the other side of the street when they see me coming.

I remember very well the first trading deal I ever engaged in. The year was, I believe, 1908. My maternal aunt owned a Gram-o-phone and a lot of six-inch records. This Gram-o-phone consisted of a box about seven inches square, with a six-inch turntable and a horn about a foot long, attached directly to a sound-box. The machine you see on the Victor lable is a much modernized and stream-lined version of my aunt's Gram-o-phone, which was made by M. Berliner before there was any Victor Company.

The records themselves also carried the Berliner label, and they were marked simply and briefly "March—Band." No nonsense about who did it, and generally not even what it was they did. There was the record.

They weren't in the best of condition having been played mainly on the clipped ends of brass safety pins and North Dakota cactus spines. In fact, those records complied perfectly with the classic definition Ralph Berton gave not long ago for a true collector's item:

1. It is absolutely impossible to get hold of a copy,

2. When you get it it's so scratchy you can't hear it, and

3. If you could hear it it wouldn't be a very good record.

As I recall the deal, I was to get two of my aunt's records in exchange for two hours' weeding in the garden. After the first hour in the hot sun I began to feel I had got the worst of the deal. And my aunt, on her side, began to think that it was a shame to part with those perfectly good records which she had brought up from Nebraska on the steam cars, for only a little healthful exercise on the part of her lazy nephew. Incidentally, that is an attitude of mind that still persists; many times I have watched two collectors part after a record-trading session, each of them wearing the pained look of a man who has just been bent over a barrel.

At about that time a local grocery store, only fifteen miles away by lumber-wagon and ferryboat, was giving away a new machine called a Graphophone, or Talking Machine, for only a hundred dollars in coupons. I collected coupons over the entire Northwest and got one. It was a great improvement over my aunt's machine, being at least twice as big, with real ten-inch records, and you could actually hear what was being played over the scratching.

These new records were much better, of course, and they still didn't have any band names on the labels, which added to the interest of collecting. They were marked simply "Red Wing—Two-Step—Orchestra," or "At a Georgia Camp-Meeting—Band." My nearest neighbor and friend, Charlie, who happened to be a Sioux Indian, invested some of the Great White Father's ration money in a machine and records, and the second trading season was on.

Charlie had an instinctive love for music, and while he wanted all my good records, he didn't ever want to part with his. The trading used to be loud and argumentative. I was loaded up with "The Herd Girl's Dream —Violin, Harp and Piano" and it was strictly no sale for "Silver Heels—Band." In those days a band was a band, and who directed it was of no particular importance. You couldn't tell by listening to the record, either, like modern-day collectors who can tell after the first bar if it's Noone or Dodds. We didn't argue about which riverboat band had played on this one; in spots it sounded more like the riverboat itself.

We both preferred band records, on which you could hear nothing but the tune and a lot of brass volume. That is probably the reason I am still, to this day, a sucker for a good loud trombone. Or even a loud trombone.

The trading went on, somehow, until it reached the point where I owned all of Charlie's records and he owned all of mine. Then we started trading back.

I remember also that a young cow-puncher from somewhere went to town, got drunk, and spent his winter's wages on a new-fangled thing called the Edison Phonograph. Sober again he stuck with it, with no place to keep it, he left it with my family. For once I had all the music I wanted. But those cylinder records brought me down; there was no possibility of trading, and I didn't like them. I was a disc man first and last; I always said the cylinder record was a passing fad; by gollies I was right.

I believe it was John Philip Sousa who was responsible for the effete custom of putting names on labels. The man had a reputation and he got his name up there; it was no time at all before we had Prince's Band and the Columbia Band and dozens of others.

The day of the march, gavotte, schottische and two-step was over. There was a new beat coming into the music, and as the records improved that beat began to sound. Something called ragtime, faster, with a machine-like rhythm to it to match this coming new age of automobiles and machinery. A fellow named Art Hickman played it, with banjoes and strange instrumentation. The records were flooding out now, new labels like Columbia and Victor, with names on them. They became common; they could be bought from the mail-order house. We still bought them, but they were no longer rare treasures to be salvaged and traded. The fun had gone out of it.

Ahead of us there was the full flowering of the ragtime era, and beyond that a still newer thing called "jazz," which was a very indecent word. Just around the corner was Paul Whiteman and Ted Lewis and a rather obscure outfit called the Original Dixieland. We didn't think so much of them, at the time. We decided to retire from record collecting and let the kids take it up.

Mezz Mezzrow

I suppose our gig in Lawrence, Mass., is as good a place to start from as any, when I reminisce on "the Mezz." I have to say he was one of a kind. Facially he seemed to me to always wear a sort of sneer. He had semitic features; was medium built but not on the short side. He was one of the "most-certain" people I ever met up with. He was really self-assured. Now then, we were in Lawrence during the '40s, and there was a war going on. The town had its "southern" population. Oh, they accepted my mixed band; no problems. But Mezz never was one to hide his light under a bushel. He was married and he had a son and his wife was a Negro. Today, acceptable; yesterday, if you put their photos on your dresser you can expect to be noticed; talked about. Then Mezzrow liked to "shop" the stores. In one day of that, several storekeepers asked me to "please tell him to go elsewhere." I would say, in fight language, Mezz led with his chin.

One of the funny incidents I recall was when I had the trio at Jimmy Ryan's on 52nd Street. Danny Alvin was on drums. And one evening, again during war-times, Ryan felt so good about our performance that he invited us to have a drink. Now then, good booze was scarce; especially 3-Star Hennessey. But that was what Mezz asked for. Well, Jimmy had invited us and he wasn't going to back out. So down the cellar he went and got that rare bottle; opened it and poured. I don't have to tell you one sips brandy. Not Mezz; it was "down the hatch" style. Ryan couldn't take it. "That's like feeding cream to a pig."

Then there was the rehearsal Mezz called me for. He'd rented a studio for an hour and had gathered Dave Tough, myself, plus Goss and Murphy (guitar, bass). For at least 45 minutes Mezz stood and blew the blues. No one of us got to solo; it was all clarinet. When he was through he packed up and said "That's all." Never no mention of that supposed job we had gathered to rehearse for. Mezz just wanted to blow. Then I have to remember the gig I'd gotten at City College. I had Frankie Newton, Mezz, Tough, Condon; plus Cliff Jackson, an excellent pianist to play opposite us. After our set Cliff started playing. Mezz decided to join him, but for some unknown reason came in (musically) a beat late. And continued to play that way all through the tune; just wouldn't change. We were on a platform and as Mezz kept beating his foot the dust would rise and our unbelief mount. At the end the students gave Mezz a rousing ovation. Eddie C. and Dave and I just walked until we'd reached a saloon and had a drink in hand. Not a word was spoken until Tough uttered "Shit."

Musically? Mezz had a tremendous feeling for the blues. And he hustled gigs. He broke down the "colored" line in more than one place. He pioneered; broke the ground. And his book *Really the Blues* was one that held me; not that it was entirely factual; by no means. But so darn interesting I couldn't walk away from it until I'd finished. That in spite of the fact that he'd managed to keep my name out of it, although he was in the process of writing it at the time he worked for me. I remember calling Eddie Condon and complaining. And I recall Eddie's answer, "Hell man, you should be glad; many of us wish he'd left our names out."

Mezz finally hit pay dirt when Panassié gave him an offer to come to France. That was one time he did ask me to come along. That opened up an entirely new scene for him and he stayed

Hempstead H.S. Jam Session, January, 1943. Left to Right: "Wild Bill" Davison, trumpet; Pee Wee Russell, clarinet; Zutty Singleton, drums; Mezz Mezzrow, clarinet; Wellman Braud, Bass; Lips Page, trumpet; Joe Sullivan, piano. Eddie Condon, guitar, barely visible behind Russell.

abroad for most of the rest of his life. From time to time I'd hear that he was relaxed; money was comin' in, and he was playing concerts all over Europe. And that's where he finally ended up; passed on. He was a picturesque guy. I give him a lot of credit for having the sincerity of his convictions. I can still hear his voice on one of my recordings with Max Kaminsky and Danny Alvin. Danny says, "Hey Mezz, lets get some of this." And he answers (something about) "Let's get going."   A.H.

Recording with Panassié

by Mezz Mezzrow

Back in 1938, Hugues Panassié, the French critic and author of *Le Jazz Hot* and *The Real Jazz* wrote me that he wanted to come to the States. He had been studying jazz at long range through records and wanted to come here to get a lot of data for his new book *The Real Jazz*, along with doing recording for the French Pathé Company under a new label called "Swing."

He cabled me he was to arrive October 12, 1938. Along with Benny Carter, Zutty Singleton, and my wife, we met him at the pier in Hoboken.

Panassié came down the gang plank into the middle of the welcoming committee and kissed me on both cheeks and you can imagine the jive that followed.

Hugues is an enthusiastic Frenchman and nothing stops him from doing what he wants to do. With him came his very competent secretary Madeline Gautier, who is a very famous French poetess and writer on jazz. I didn't expect so much company and my apartment wasn't large enough to hold them both so they stayed with Zutty for a week until I got straight and then moved in with me up in Harlem. After explaining his plans to me, we contacted Eli Oberstein who was then in charge of recording for the R.C.A. Victor Co. When we told him we had money and wanted them to make some masters for

us to be released in France only, they insisted on having the rights to release them also and after cabling back and forth, it was finally decided in their favor.

Now the problem of men. As you all know, Panassié and myself both love real jazz. We had to scour the hills for the right men. After much trouble we located Tommy Ladnier, who was upstate at a swell cafe. Hugues and I were never so happy in all our lives. The day Tommy came to New York was a holiday at my home. I have always thought that next to Louis Armstrong, Tommy played more like King Joe Oliver than any other trumpet player I know. Along with this, his intelligence and sincerity will always stay imbedded in my heart, for no one knows how wonderful it was for me to play with Tommy. We had never played together in our lives before and when Hugues suggested we get our horns out and blow some, I'll never forget the look of astonishment and content on Tommy's face when we played the first eight bars of "Ain't Going To Give Nobody None of My Jelly Roll." He grabbed me and asked, "Where have you been all my life?" And immediately decided to quit his job and stay in New York with us. Panassié's face was full of glee and we went to work on the line-up for our first session which included James P. Johnson, piano; Teddy Bunn, guitar; Elmer James, bass; Zutty Singleton, drums; Sidney De Paris, trumpet, besides Tommy Ladnier and myself. Two tunes stand out in my memory although there were others. "Comin' On With the Come-on" and "Revolutionary Blues."

I wonder if you all realize that these are the first jam sessions recorded where not a note of music or an idea of what we were going to play was known until time for recording. These records are really spontaneous collective improvisation.

We all had been drinking a little and spirits were high so that by the time we were to make the fourth number James P. Johnson fell off the piano stool while making an introduction and Tommy Ladnier passed out of the picture. Little did we know then that we were going to lose him for good. I've never

been the same since he left us for the world beyond.

The Victor Co. was so enthused after hearing the tests that they sent a special delegation to my house, including Mr. Jack Williams, head of the advertising department to invite us to Camden to see how records are processed and little does one realize the things that happen before you get that whirling disc that tells you things.

It was then that we came upon the idea of getting the R.C.A. company to reissue and release recordings that have been lying dormant in the vaults for years, some never even heard.

Friends, I've got writers cramp now for you know I'm not used to writing—so, dig me in a coming issue—"no jive!"

I'm a Sweet Papa Pigmeat

by Alison Blair

For the past 26 years, "Pigmeat" Alamo Markham has been known in the theaters and vaudeville houses throughout the North and South as one of the most famous comedian-dancers. Combining his unique dancing talent with his original comic abilities, "Pigmeat" has become a figure in show business comparable in stature with that of the late Bert Williams. As a singer, Bert Williams had the advantage that came with recordings and through this medium, tens of thousands of his records found their way into homes thus establishing a memorial to his gifts and popular appeal.

The efforts of a comedian and dancer such as "Pigmeat," leave no such palpable record. "Pigmeat's" fame and popularity has been primarily based on memory impressions, as he is the sort of entertaining artist who ap-

pears perhaps once in a generation, one who seems to have equally superlative gifts in every branch of the profession. Audiences have acclaimed his creative abilities in comedy and dancing and he has been hitherto content to use these fields to establish his popularity. Only recently, under almost accidental circumstances, has it become known that "Pigmeat" has a sensational voice, one with an almost mythical grand style personified by Bessie Smith. This is the style of singing which demands *voice* with its full intensity and range gamut, a contempt for the microphone and an identity with the blues as the artistic and social manifestation of all the pathos and melodic richness of the Southern Negro.

In order to find out more about "Pigmeat" Markham and his background, I recently visited him back-stage at the Paramount Theatre where he was appearing for ten weeks in the stage show. This was his first appearance in a white theatre.

On entering his dressing-room, a tall, well-built, serious-looking man greeted me and outside of an engaging smile, there was nothing of the comedian about him. A record player was propped on his dressing-table and I caught the strains of Fats Waller's record of "I Ain't Got Nobody." "That was my boy," said Pigmeat as he took the record off. "He really played a mess of piano." I could do no more than agree with "Pigmeat" on that point. He pulled up two chairs for us to sit comfortably and to me his movements had the subtle plasticity of a dancer.

"Well, let's start from the beginning," said "Pigmeat," "which was 1905 in Durham, North Carolina where I was born." Laughingly he said, "You can see I'm no youngster. I was the only one in my whole family who ever went into show business. Just seems like I had a talent for being funny. But I really got my start when I was in school. You know how kids put on school plays—well we put on a play called 'Twenty Minutes in Hell' and I was the comedian.

"Shortly after that, a carnival came through my town looking for talent and a man named Booker must have heard about me because he asked me if I'd like to join up. I ran away with the show. I was just fourteen then." "Pigmeat" gazed thoughtfully at his hands as he spoke. His fingers were long and sensitive and he gestured with them gracefully.

"I toured the South with this carnival, dancing and telling jokes, until 1924. Then I left the carnival and joined a revue show led by Gonzales White. I remember Count Basie was playing solo piano in the show then. We toured the South for three more years and then I got an offer from 'Ma' Rainey to join her show in Columbus, Georgia, which I naturally did. We put on some fine shows then, 'Ma' singing the blues as only she could. I believe 'Ma' was the first one to sing those blues and she really sang them low-down. Almost all the other blues singers got their schooling from her. I learned a lot with 'Ma' but then I got the urge to see what 'Up North' was like and I got my chance to travel with a revue show called 'Sugar Cane.' I danced and joked all the way up to the Lafayette Theatre on 130th Street and 7th Avenue."

Our travels were suddenly interrrupted by a stentorian voice calling, "Fifteen minutes to curtain time." "That sounds like my cue," said "Pigmeat," "but I won't be gone long and then we can keep on talking." Glad of the opportunity to stay, I watched "Pigmeat" as he pulled on a pair of cowboy chaps, put on over-sized shoes and a cook's white jacket. From a shelf he produced a bottle of rye and poured us both a drink. "As long as I've been in show business," he said, "I always get nervous when I face a packed house and this is really a nerve-steadier."

"Pigmeat" returned shortly, mopping the perspiration from his face. "Man, they're really jumpin' out there," he said as he eased himself into a chair and pulled off his costume.

Attired in a dressing gown and once more at ease, we picked up the threads of our interrupted conversation. "I'd like to know how you got your name of 'Pigmeat'," I asked him as he lit a cigarette and inhaled deeply. "Well that name came about in a funny way," he said grinning. "On my early theatre dates I used to say, 'I'm a sweet papa Pigmeat with the River Jordan in my hips and all the women ran to be baptised.' When I came out of the theatre, all the people hanging around used to say, 'that's Pigmeat, there goes Pigmeat' and so the name stuck. I used to kill the house with that line."

After that more than satisfactory explanation, "Pigmeat" continued describing his experiences telling how he next appeared at the Standard Theatre in Philadelphia in 1930. "Bessie had a special pianist accompany her, Fred Longshaw, and when she sang the blues with that bright spot-light on her, the theatre was as quiet as a church. After 'Ma,' Bessie was the greatest singer and she was a terrific showman. It was a shame how she died," he added puffing on his cigarette.

"When the Apollo Theatre opened in Harlem in 1933, I was the house comedian and I starred steadily until 1937. I did my act with bands like Fletcher Henderson's, Cab Calloway's, Duke Ellington's, Jimmy Lunceford's and lots of others backing me up. All of my jokes are mostly adlib and I originate all my own dancing. Fats Waller and I worked together for three months in New

York and Fats used to take a lot of my sayings and jokes and develop them into songs. Like this one for instance," and "Pigmeat" pulled out the Fats record of "Who's Afraid of Love." He nudged me at the point where Fats says, "It's that fine lovely Arabian stuff that your dreams are made of." "That's one of my lines," said "Pigmeat." It always knocked Fats out.

"In 1936, I left the Apollo for a very short time and played a date with Don Redman in Washington, D.C., and that's where I originated the dance 'Trucking.' During rehearsal, Don and the band were playing 'Honeysuckle Rose' and I was just fooling around with some new dance steps, following the rhythm of the band. Don liked what I was doing because he told me to put that dance in the show. I called it 'Trucking' and before long it swept the country. Then I started the 'Susie-Q' which was just a different style of 'Trucking.' But the most famous dance-step I originated was the 'Boogie-Woogie.' I had a little saying. 'I'm gonna pitch a boogie-woogie,' then I'd snap my fingers. slide my feet, hop to the back, glide forward, hop to the front and slide back. That dance really caught on and stayed.

"The next few years I devoted to jumping between California and New York. I made three movies in California and I wrote two of them myself. Then I was signed up with the Andrews Sisters for a 36 week radio show on the Coast and now we're all together here at the Paramount."

Recorded recently by Alfred Lion of Blue Note, "Pigmeat" here gives us the opportunity to hear him sing in the creative role of an expressive musical artist, one who is not limited by the necessities of making people laugh.

In the course of this very exciting recording session, "Pigmeat" produced four blues sides which capture the authentic and essential blues spirit which was so prevalent in the era that gave us "Ma" Rainey and Bessie Smith. With a superb backing of six musicians "Pigmeat" waxed "How Long, How Long Blues," "Blues Before Sunrise," "See See Rider" and "You've Been a Good Old Wagon."

The band accompanying "Pigmeat" was led by Oliver "Rev." Mesheux, trumpet; Sandy Williams, trombone; Vivian Smith, piano; Israel Crosby, bass; Jimmy Shirley, guitar, and Tommy Benford, drums. Recorded here for the first time, Oliver "Rev." Mesheux gives a performance which makes one wonder where he has been hiding. His tone and style of attack have all the intensity and blues spirit which is so rare in trumpet players today. Also a novice to recording is Vivian Smith from Kansas City whose piano style has been greatly inspired by Pete Johnson. Sandy Williams on trombone plays in his inimitjble blues groove and Tommy Benford will be remembered by many for all the fine sides he made with Jelly-Roll Morton. Israel Crosby on bass and Jimmy Shirley on guitar round out this well-picked group. Hats off to Alfred Lion and Blue Note for coming up with another winner.

"Pigmeat's" enthusiasm for these records was framed in his parting words: "I hope all the people will enjoy hearing them, because we really enjoyed making them. They *are* the blues."

St. Louis Jazzman

by Ed Crowder and A. F. Niemoeller

It was a typical St. Louis winter evening, a raw chill fighting biting coal smoke for first place in the gloomy air—the sort of weather that must have helped develop St. Louis jazz by driving the boys indoors—when we met at a little saloon near Easton and Vandevanter to go over a block and around the corner to call on one of St Louis's early jazz greats, and still one of the best trumpets in the business—Dewey Jackson.

Dewey greeted us cordially. Inside all was warm, cheerful and cozy. In one corner stood an elaborate radio-phonograph combination, and we lost no time in getting going with some old records we had brought along. Some King Olivers interested Dewey very much, and he sat up alert and intent when we played him some Bix, but when we played him an old Trumbauer he could only waggle his head in wonderment and comment: "My, my, that *is* a purty record!"

Thus stimulated, Dewey began to reminisce. Yes, he was born in St. Louis at the turn of the century and spent all of his early

Dewey Jackson

life there. Reckons he must have been about 12 years old when he started playing on the horn. Started out playing with the old Odd Fellows band, a group of varying ages sponsored by the Odd Fellows that played mainly parades. It was with this group that he got his early, and only, instruction, the Odd Fellows providing group instruction for the members. "Understand, I don't mean that nobody takes me and teaches me by myself. I just get there with a whole crowd of other boys and a man he gets up there and tells us what to do, and we play and he try to tell us about our mistakes." From here on Dewey just "picked up" what he learned.

Let's see, he must have been about 16 when he played his first regular job. That was at the Future City, a little dance-hall run by one Tommy Evans on Pine Street near the Union Station. After playing at the Future City three nights a week for a couple of years, he got the trumpet spot at the old Keystone Cafe, an early variety of night-club and late spot at Compton and Lawton operated by Charlie Mills, a general promoter and politician around town. Here he played under George Reynolds.

After being at the Keystone for a little over a year he got his first big chance. This was to play with Charlie Creath's outfit when it opened its first engagement on the old river steamer *J.S.* (Incidentally, whereas most people pronounce Creath's name to rhyme with *teeth*, Dewey consistently pronounces it to rhyme with *breath* and Dewey should know as he spent many years with Charlie.) This was in 1919. At this time Dewey stayed on the *J.S.* only one day and a night, and then went back to the Keystone, Mills protesting that he wasn't being treated fairly.

"I'll never forget that job, though," added Dewey with a reflective smile. "That was the first time I ever hear Louis Armstrong play. You see, this *J.S.* was a pretty old tub, and after we get out in the river she break down near Alton. Well, there we are and can't do nothing until finally the old *St. Paul* come along. She see we're in trouble and she come alongside. Before this me and everybody think Creath's the best trumpet there is, but as that boat come near I hear a trumpet playing in the band on the *St. Paul.* Man! I never forget that trumpet! They playing 'High Society' and the trumpet takes four, five choruses, and *hot!* I never know anybody play a trumpet like that. Later on I find out it's Louis playing with Fate Marable's band. I say to Creath, 'Sorry, Charlie, but *there's* the greatest trumpet player in the world.' You know," Dewey smiled amusedly, "sometimes I think it was that trumpet that run me back to the Keystone."

Dewey stayed at the Keystone for about five months longer, and then he opened with a combination of his own at Jazzland, a dance-hall in the 2200 block on Market Street operated by Tom Turpin, the famous composer of rags. Dewey's band there had four pieces: Floyd Casey, drums; Charles Lawson, trombone; Walter Farrington, piano; and Dewey on the trumpet.

Dewey stayed at Jazzland for a couple of years, then went back to work for Charlie Mills again, this time at the Humming Bird that Mills was opening on Lucas Avenue, the most elegant colored cafe in St. Louis. Here he had a six-piece band: Jane Hemmingway, piano; Boyd Atkins, violin and alto sax; Sammy Long, tenor sax; Andrew Luper, trombone; Harry Dial, drums, and Dewey, trumpet. Harry Dial was one of the early fast drummers. "That man used to throw his sticks all over the bandstand." (Dial is now a copyist for a New York music publishing house.) It was in 1922 that Dewey went to the Humming Bird and he stayed there for about a year, after which this band played jobs around town for a while—theater dates, sorority dances, and a few club jobs. "We had plenty work them days. I remember we played as many as twenty-one jobs Christmas week, sometimes as many as five jobs in one day."

In 1925 Dewey broke up his band when he got an offer from Streckfus Steamship Lines to go to New Orleans to join Fate Marable's outfit on the *St. Paul.* He played the whole

season with Fate, closing on September 10, 1925, at Davenport, Iowa, when Streckfus gave them all notice, saying he was going to hire a white band. Three weeks later Streckfus sent for Dewey and wanted him to start the winter season out of New Orleans with a ten-piece band. Seven of these pieces Dewey took with him from St. Louis: Sammy Long, alto sax; Burroughs Lovingood, piano; Pete Robinson, banjo; Pops Foster, bass; Cecil White, tuba; Floyd Campbell, drums; and Dewey, trumpet. At New Orleans he took on: Willy Humphrey, tenor sax and clarinet; John Lindsey, trombone; and Albert Snaer, trumpet, to make up the ten. Later, he sent back to St. Louis for Thornton Blue, clarinet and alto sax, and still later he let John Lindsey go and hired Andrew Luper for the tram. This band played the '25-'26 winter season out of New Orleans as the St. Louis Peacock Charleston Orchestra. On the way back to St. Louis in the spring of '26 this band was renamed the New Orleans Cotton Pickers and dressed in fancy satin overalls. "Um, um! I never forget them overalls," observed Dewey with a wry smile. "Forty bucks they set us back for just a pants and two shirts!"

At about this time Dewey had an offer from Fletcher Henderson to join him in New York, "but I was doing better than that with Streckfus, so I stay; and besides I'd just moved my family to New Orleans." But, we objected, we seem to remember something about your going to New York at this time. We dug out the leaflet from the Brunswick Album of *Riverboat Jazz* (in which, incidentally, the only genuine example of a riverboat band is the record of Dewey) and showed him where it says: "After its excursion . . . the band returned to St. Louis . . . Soon after, the men deposed Jackson and Fate Marable, dean of riverboat jazz, took over the band." Dewey's eyes grew round in amazement. "Where that man get that stuff, anyhow? Nobody ever come ask *me* about this. I tell you how it happen. I'm playing on the boat during the summer of '26 when I get an offer to join the Missourians in New York. (This band was later taken over by Cab Calloway.) It's a good offer, so I join up with them in September. But first I give Streckfus two weeks notice. Streckfus sends for Fate and he sits in with us for those two weeks to pick up our music, then I leave and Streckfus makes Fate leader. That's how come they had two pianos for a while. People like the two pianos, so they keep them both. The men get rid of me and make Fate leader—huh! Nobody hire or fire anybody on those boats but Streckfus."

Here Dewey digressed to sing the praises of Lovingood. "That man sure was something on the piano." Though never achieving national fame, Lovingood is known the length of the Mississippi as a fine pianist. His last appearance was with Fats Pichon's band on the *Capitol* in 1942. At present he is working in the Chicago Post Office. Someone ought to "discover" him.

Dewey stayed in New York until January of '27 when he came back to St. Louis because his mother was ill. After doing nothing for a couple of months, he joined Fate's band playing on the *Capitol* out of New Orleans. This band had Charlie Creath with it as a sort of special feature. "People always seemed to like Charlie—he had a way about him." In April Fate fired Dewey, but Creath at once hired him for the summer season on the *St. Paul* out of St. Louis. Hardly had this season got under way when Creath took sick; Dewey filled in for him most of the summer. From the fall of '27 until May '29 he played "gig jobs" around town and then Streckfus put him back on the *St. Paul* with a ten-piece band.

On September 22, 1930, he opened at the old Castle Ballroom in St. Louis and played the winter season there. His was the first colored band ever to play at the Castle, and when from there he went to play the summer season at Sauter's Park his again was the first colored band at that place. From this park he used to broadcast over Station WIL. He returned to the Castle Ballroom for the winter season until March 8, 1932, when the colored local's charter was revoked over some trouble at one of the clubs, after which he played "gigs" around town until a subsidiary local was formed—of which, incidentally, Dewey was the first president.

In '34 he joined Creath's band at the Arcadia Ballroom in St. Louis (now Tune Town) where they replaced Wingy Manone's Arcadian Serenaders, and they stayed there for two seasons. "Boy! That was a *band!*" recalled Dewey. It included: Burroughs Lovingood, piano; Jimmy Jones, bass; Elijah Shaw, drums; Roosevelt Thomas, alto sax; John Young, guitar; Charlie Creath, tenor sax

and leader; and Dewey on trumpet. Creath had had to substitute the sax for his trumpet because of illness.

In '36 both Dewey and Creath were in the band on the *St. Paul* with Fate Marable. Fate was leader, but when some friction developed between him and Creath that impaired the efficiency of the band, Creath was made leader and Fate was reduced to the ranks. "Funny thing about a Streckfus band most people don't know," explained Dewey. "Being a leader for him didn't mean that was your band. Streckfus he hired the men he want and then he pick out one he think good and he say, 'You the leader.' If that man don't do good he pick out another and make him leader, and the first man just go back to playing." Creath headed the band until '39 when Fate took it to Pittsburgh for that and the following season. Dewey didn't stay with the band these two seasons, but "gigged around."

In '41 Streckfus fired Fate and got Dewey to front a band out of Pittsburgh on the S.S. *Senator*, which was simply the old *St. Paul* rechristened. "Streckfus do that a lot—a boat have one name at St. Louis, he send it down to New Orleans he give it another name, he send it up the river he give it another name." This band played one season and was the last colored band to play on boats hereabouts.

Since that time Dewey has been playing little club jobs around St. Louis. Right now he's heading a little three-piece combination that's plenty good at the Clover Club, a cozy little after-hours spot in the mid-town section. This same place, incidentally, features tall, slinky Ann Richardson, one of the best blues singers and wiggle-dancers St. Louis has ever produced. Dewey likes this kind of work very mich. The smaller crowds are more appreciative, he says, and he gets to play all kinds of music—some want the modern stuff, but a lot of them ask for the old time music.

Asked as to whom he thought best of the old New Orleans musicians, he was hard put to answer. Plenty of them were good, he thought, but he did confess a special liking for Kid Rena and Kidy Ory. "But it's them New Orleans drummers that do something to you! They don't just hit that pedal with their foot like most drummers—they kind of put their foot down and *draw* it out. Zutty Singleton could really send me." Piano? Art Tatum plays so much piano it's a shame!" When it came to the trumpet he had trouble answering. He knew that Louis Armstrong once had the best trumpet ever, but he didn't know about today. His biggest kick? Oh, that was back once at the old St. Louis Coliseum when Sidney De Paris blew out everybody in a trumpet "cutting session" against Freddy Jenkins and Rex Stewart when Fletcher Henderson's band was alternating with Duke Ellington and McKinney's Cotton Pickers. "That man played so much trumpet nobody else had a chance. I just stood up there in front of the stand and couldn't believe it."

Dewey did most of his recording with Creath, though for some reason discographies fail to list him amongst the personnel. He made only two records with his own Capitol Band back in '26. These are: Vo 1239 "Goin' To Town"/"What Do You Want Poor Me To Do?" and Vo 1040 "Capitol Blues"/

"She's Cryin' For Me," which latter has recently been re-issued in the Brunswick *Riverboat Jazz* album.

Dewey is still very much alive to jazz and its meanings. He is an ardent radio and record listener and through them tries to keep up on all modern trumpet trends. "I figure they all got something I can use, and when I hear something good I see if I can do it. I don't play the same trumpet I did back when I made those records, but I can still do it if anybody want to hear it. I feel just as strong on the horn as I ever did. And I just can't understand when trumpeters complain about their lip. My lip *never* bothers me. I can play all day and all night if I have to. I remember a jam once at a joint across the river on the East Side. Man takes 118 choruses and everybody go crazy. I step up and take 136 choruses, and of the *blues!*"

Drums on the Mississippi

by Harry Dial

I was very much let down when I first saw New Orleans, because I'd always heard about those beautiful Creole women, but I was there for about a month before I saw one that looked like anything. Now I've been married for twenty years, a New Orleans gal, too, and she's head and shoulders above all the rest of them.

I was born in Birmingham, Alabama, February 17, 1907. My family moved to St. Louis when I was two years old, and eight brothers and sisters were born right there in St. Louis. I was the first of my family to take up music, which I did when I was fourteen. I took a few lessons on trombone but my arm was too short, so they gave me a drum. We used to follow a brass band around, mostly on Sun-

days, until they stopped. I used to see players that I used to mark, like Dewey Jackson, R. Q. Dickerson, Ham Davis, and Irving Randoph, who was himself just a kid. The fellow who's playing piano with me now gave me my first professional job in August of 1921, in St. Louis. I can't think of the name of the place, but it was run by some fellows named Harry and Sam Panagatopoulos. I never will forget that. I still was only fourteen years old. Well, I worked there August to January, when I went to school to finish a half year of elementary training which I needed pretty badly. After going to school about a month, I got a job at the Manhattan Cafe, and worked there from 9 to 3 a.m., and attended school from 9 a.m. to 3 p.m.

I got a great deal of my experience from Fate Marable, working the riverboats from New Orleans to Davenport, Iowa. The season in St. Louis we worked the *St. Paul*, and the winter season we worked from New Orleans on the steamer *Capitol*. It was a year round job. The first year I worked with Fate was in 1923, on the steamer *J. S.* on the day trips, because they used to bring a name band from Chicago for the night trips on the *J. S.*, such bands as Ralph Williams, Don Bestor and Louis Panico. At that time Fate called his band the Metropolitan Jazz Band. It was a pretty hot band, and any man who played with Fate always made a name for himself. We played all those old New Orleans standard tunes like "Tin Roof Blues" and "Muskrat Ramble." The white bands that they used at night were strictly melody bands. We played pop tunes, too, but they had a different personification. Dewey Jackson was one of the most famous men that Fate ever had in his band, and there was Boyd Atkins and Eugene Kennedy, a sax player, and Norman Mason, also a sax player. At that time Fate used a ten piece band. I worked with Fate for five seasons, about two and a half years. In the fall of 1923 I went to work with Dewey Jackson. We were in the field, playing club dates.

The next summer I took a band of my own to work at Denny Colbeck's roadhouse. Burroughs T. Lovingood, Boyd Atkins, Andrew (Big Babe) Webb, trumpet, Eugene Kennedy, sax, Jonas Walker, trombone, and myself, that was the combination. I worked there until January of the next year, 1925. Then I rejoined Fate Marable's band in New Orleans in March of that year. I was seventeen years old at that time, and it was the first time I'd ever been away from home. The bands weren't very good from a theoretical standpoint, and often played out of tune, but the rhythm was terrific, mostly because of the drummers. You couldn't beat it. I had heard Louis when I was about twelve years old, in the summer of 1919. I used to help to unload packing boats on the levee, and Fate's band was rehearsing. He really sounded as great to me then as he does now. Baby Dodds was marvelous. So was his brother Johnny. It was a great band, no kidding, no ifs and ands about it.

After having played with bands around there like Dewey Jackson, Charlie Creath,

Willie Austin and Norman Mason, I left my last job which was at Chauffeur's Club, and settled down for the next five and a half years in Chicago. Nobody knew I was coming, it was ten below zero on February 1, 1928. I think that in three weeks' time I was working one of the swellest jobs on the Gold Coast, the Ambassador Club. It was a five piece combination, a hot band. I stayed there about five months and then went to work for Clifford (Clarinet) King. We only worked there about fifteen hours a week. I worked there fifteen months. I was doubling at the 70 Club for about eight of those months I was working there. After that I went back to the Ambassador Club with Jerome Pasquale. I worked there a year this time. That's where my record career started.

I think I made those Vocalion records about 1929 or 1930. I went to Brunswick and talked to Jack Kapp, head of the Brunswick firm in Chicago, and he referred me to Mayo Williams. The tunes were of my own composition. One tune was named "I Like What I Like Like I Like It," and another was "It Must Be Love," another was "Funny Fumble," another was "When My Baby Starts To Shake That Thing," another was "Poison," another was "Don't Give It Away" and that's all that was released. There was another one, I forget what, but it wasn't released. What stopped us from making more records was that they started this session business, and we were using Earl Hines' band, with the exception of Earl himself. Shirley Clay made the first two records, he played trumpet. Later Boone and Cecil Irwin were on saxes. The last two records Omer Simeon replaced Lester Boone. Bill Culbreath played piano on one session and Zinky Cohn on another. The bass was played by Hayes Alvis and Walter Wright, the banjo on all of them was played by Eustern Woodfork. They were not made later than 1930 in Chicago.

That was the first date I made under my own name. I had made some records with Junie Cobb and His Grains of Corn in Chicago the same year, 1930. We had Earl Fuller playing piano, Junie Cobb playing trumpet. I made some other dates with Jabbo Smith, that's how they got his name mixed up as a trumpet player on my records. I made one or two dates in a pinch for Jimmie Noone, pinch-hitting for Johnny Wells. I thought what everybody else thought about

Earl Hines, I thought he was great.

Jasper Taylor was the originator of the washboard idea. He played washboard and wooden spoons long before I even thought about playing music. One of the greatest of all-time all-around drummers was Jimmy Bertrand. He was Lionel Hampton's teacher, my teacher, and a lot of other guys' teacher. Lionel Hampton isn't playing a thing today that he didn't learn from Jimmy Bertrand on xylophone. He was the greatest xylophone player I ever saw in my life. The rhythm never stopped when he got up to play xylophone, and he played his bass drum right along with it. I've yet to hear him play a bad note. He's still alive to my knowledge.

I left Chicago in the fall of 1933, when Louis Armstrong broke up the band he had before going to Europe for the last time. I recorded with Louis and he made a couple of my numbers. "Don't Play Me Cheap" was one of my numbers.

I came to Camden, New Jersey, and played at a walkathon in Ira Coffey's band. The show included the now famous Red Skelton. We stayed there fourteen weeks, after which I came to New York January 17, 1934. It was fourteen below zero there. Cold weather seems to follow my change of towns. It was kind of hard to get around here. I didn't have the luck I had in Chicago. Union restrictions were terrif on transfer men. After a couple of weeks here I began playing club dates with Sam Wooding, which kept me alive for a while. Then in April that same year, through a lucky break, I was able to get work at Small's Paradise with Ferman Tapp's band. Joe Thomas joined the band a few weeks later.

I began making records with Fats Waller while I was working at Small's. I had met Fats in Cincinnati, when he was on tour with Louis Armstrong, but I got to really be friends with Fats through Alexander Hill, pianist, who was a good friend of mine. We had worked together at the Ambassador Club in Pasquale's band. In fact, Sidney Catlett came to New York with Sammy Stewart's band because I didn't want to come at that time. We made records there for months and months, sometimes two dates a month. Fats would send me a telegram telling me to get the guys together. He had explicit confidence in my judgment. I liked Fats very much, he was always clowning, but underneath he had a wonderful musical education.

Along with all of Fats' drinking, he was an enormous eater. He used to walk into a restaurant and holler "Waiter, bring me two steaks, and bring them on one plate." Then he'd eat them. In spite of all of his drinking, I never saw him drunk. Fats was kind of a carefree leader, and too generous. If he passed out an arrangement and the band didn't play it the way he thought they should, he'd say "Pass that in," and you'd never see that no more. I remember once we were playing a broadcast over WLW in Cincinnati. Fats had a bottle of whiskey on the piano. No one was in the studio. The announcer, thinking perhaps that the whiskey might be turned over on the piano, walked over and took it away. Fats stopped playing, got up, and went over and got his whiskey back.

I left Fats Waller's band and went to work in a dancing school and stayed there for three and a half years. In April, 1940, I left the dancing school and didn't play music any more until 1944. Those four years, I spent three years as a music autographer and copyist, and after the war started I spent one year in a machine shop. In 1944, after being advised by my doctor that the work was too hard for me, I went back to playing music.

In my present band, Erris Prince is playing piano, Reuben Reeves, trumpet, Henry (Moon) Jones, sax and clarinet, and myself on drums. We're playing now at the Swing Rendezvous in the Village. Well, I'm trying to have a band like I wanted back in 1930, a small band that plays classy, doesn't play by ear all night, but plays arrangements, and I'm featuring a lot of my old songs. I hope the public will be able to hear me again on wax soon. I think I have a great band.

I've seen the business come and go at least twice and I still think it's a great business and a great trade. It's the only other profession, outside of sports, where an uneducated man can earn a swell living. And of all the towns I've lived in and worked in, New York is at the top of the world.

Cecil Scott

I'll never forget the day Baby Dodds and I visited Cecil at his home in Harlem (N.Y.C.). He had what we referred to as "a railroad flat." It was a first floor apartment with a long hallway running through the length of the apartment. Cecil took us into the kitchen for a taste; then called in the family. He had 11 children, from the baby to the oldest going on seventeen. I had to ask, "Man, how do you guys operate?" To which he answered, "We eat in shifts and we sleep in tiers."

One of the warmest people I knew; Cecil Scott. His smile was contagious. Here's a guy, operating on one leg (and I won't go into how he lost the other; the only story I heard was hearsay); always jolly and passing it on. Pupils running in and out of his home; all day. Plus a few cats and a dog. Life all around him. And the spirit of that home; unbelievable.

I had a trio at Jimmy Ryan's on 52nd Street that consisted of Cecil (sax and clarinet) and Baby Dodds (drums); plus Chippie Hill (Bertha) doing the vocals. There was a performer. She'd go out, a'singing, to the end of the room, and start from there. And by the time she'd hit the bandstand she'd have "gathered her children" in; that whole audience was like in the palm of her hand. No mike. And Cecil could charm her. For when she came to work she could be in a mood; but Scott would look at her, and then say, "Chippie, where did you get that hat; you look beautiful." And she'd wilt; and beam. And we'd be together. They were the beautiful people.

There was a style of clarinet playing we used to call "dirty." Then there was a way of playing it that would make me think of someone a'talkin' to a chicken. Cecil knew all about that. It was later that I learned that the recording by Clarence Williams that I loved to listen to, especially because of the clarinet playing on it, was something Cecil had done. Yeh! And when my boy Bob was born, Cecil sent his oldest daughter over to my home to take care of things while my wife was hospitalized. Man, don't mention money; what do you wanna do? Insult me? I'm your friend. And then one scene that keeps comin' back.

I'd gone out to Harlem to do a benefit with Scott and others. It was a warm affair, and I partook of the goodies. In fact I "over" partook. Now we had to get to our gig (J. Ryan's). I drove and Cecil sat beside me. It seemed bouncey, beautiful, with lights flashing on; most enjoyable. Even sirens. Eventually I got the message and stopped. I had been "bouncing" up and down on the snow covered street, and the lights and sirens were the po-lice. I was "in a cast." The one-legged man had to get out and talk to the gendarmes. He must have sounded convincing for I got off with a lecture. You know I'll never forget Cecil.   A.H.

Everybody Loves Cecil

by H. B. M.

Cecil Scott was sitting on the stool before the piano, his elbow on the keys and his right leg thrust stiffly forward. I sat across from him on a metal framed settee that looked a little like a double seat on a bus. There were several similar chairs in the room, a few music stands, and a tenor sax case on top of the piano. On the walls were several posters and many photographs showing Cecil at various times in his career. His weight varied with each picture, for his hobby is food and he eats until he weighs 210, diets until he weighs 160, and starts all over again. He is about 170 now, going down.

Almost as soon as I had met him, I liked Cecil. He is as warm and companionable as a fireplace. He is an energetic man, too, despite that awkward, unwieldy, artificial right leg. He'd suddenly lunge across the room to show me something, and lunge back again. It was more like an idiosyncrasy than a handicap.

"I suppose you want to know about the children," he said. "There are thirteen of them, and I've got three grandchildren, with one more on the way. They're from my oldest daughter, the one that deserted me. She's the only one of my girls to get married." He seemed to be peeved about that. "I'll bet that's her in the hallway now. She's in this house most of the day."

It was the prodigal daughter. She entered the room very spryly.

"Has he been tellin' you 'bout my children?" she asked. "They call him 'Big Brother.' You trying to keep young, Daddy?"

Actually Cecil looked very young, more like a man of thirty than a grandfather, and his wife, who entered then, didn't look old enough to be a grandparent either. A little girl, about nine years old was with her. She looked timidly about the room. There was a large white bandage about her ankle.

"This is Elaine," said Cecil. "She's always wearing bandages. This morning it was her head. Now it's her ankle. You run along, Elaine, and don't you come back with no bandage 'round your nose.

"But, let's see now. About the music. I started when I was eleven years old out in Springfield, Ohio. I wanted to be a surgical doctor; spent all my time in doctors' offices, and I figured I could make money with music. For two years I took lessons in clarinet and theory three times a week, and never missed a day. Started playin' home dates with my brother Lloyd's band. When I was seventeen I got married."

"Eating is our big problem," Cecil informed me. "Everybody has to eat in shifts. The little ones eat first shift, the middle ones second shift, and the big ones last shift. Those dogs eat every shift."

The house was full of children now. I could hear them moving everywhere. I met some more of the family, and Cecil continued. He had come to New York and played with Lloyd's band at the Saratoga Club. By 1928 he had his own band, and by 1930 was quite famous, playing at the Renaissance Ball Room with a band that had Roy Eldridge, Chu Berry, Dicky Wells, Frankie Newton, and Don Frye. Then he moved to the Savoy and trouble started.

"There was a girl at the Savoy," said Cecil. "She had a man who was takin' care of her, but she was makin' quite a play for me. I didn't pay her no mind until one night she asked me to a 'rent party' that her landlord was giving. It was one of those places where they sold pigmeat and 'white mule.' There was a crap game going on and I started to win. I began buying everybody big pitchers of that white mule. Then her boy friend came in. There was some kind of misunderstanding right away. He slapped her, and she slapped him, and a fight started. Pitchers of white mule started flying through the air. Well, I had a big name, I had a reputation, I had to get out of there. I ran to the front door, but it had six locks that I couldn't open, so I ran to the back door. That had six locks too.

"Well, I was a very active man in those days, so I jumped out the window, but it was a three story drop and I broke my ankle real bad.

"Gangrene set in and they had to amputate several times. For a while the doctors didn't have much hope. Chu Berry, my pupil, held the band together for me. Everyone was real nice. But, when I got out I didn't feel like playin'. I was a very active man, used to jump off the piano with my saxophone and do a split on the floor, and things like that. I didn't feel right standing with that band, a cripple. So I disbanded it, although the boys sure didn't want me to.

"Then the neighbors started doing things for me. They brought me soup and stew, and stuff like that, and started sending me their

kids to teach. First one, then two, then seven, eight, ten, I soon forgot about playing. For four and a half years I taught twelve to eighteen kids a day, and never had to advertise. At the same time I studied theory with Clarence Hall three times a week and took up weight lifting. I was too busy, and liked it that way.

"It wasn't until Albert Soccorrass, a flute player with a Latin band, came to see me that I started playing again. He needed a sax player real bad. I didn't want to go, but he and my wife finally persuaded me. I played three days, and they gave me leader's pay. I've been playin' off and on ever since.

"I think that my wife is the real reason for most of my success. When I lost my leg and became sensitive, afraid to face people, she was the one who revived me and gave me confidence again. She's always encouraged me. We were born in the same town, in the same month, in the same year. We went to the same school together. Why, she's been with me all my life!"

Music Is My Business

by Henry Goodwin

I was born in Washington, D. C. and spent the early part of my life there. My family wasn't especially musically inclined, although mother played piano for her own amusement, and she didn't even make me take piano lessons. The way I started playing, my uncle gave me a trumpet. It had been given to him by a musician, but my uncle didn't play it and it was just a relic hanging on the wall, so he gave it to me. After that I started taking lessons. I was just thirteen and going to high school, but one day, when I was playing hookey, my mother came down to see how I was making out. I wasn't doing so good so she said she'd better go 'round and see my music teacher. Before I got a chance to "hip" him, he yelled, "Boy, where've you

been." That was the end of cutting classes, because that was the first, and the last, whipping I ever got.

I played with the high school band, but at first I was just a handy man in the band. I first played drums, then bass and alto sax and finally trumpet. Wherever they needed a man, that's where I played. But when I finally got to playing trumpet, I found I liked it.

While still going to high school, I played with Sam Taylor's Band, which was one of the best jazz bands around Washington at that time. It was a seven piece band with Sam on piano and I replaced Sidney De Paris on trumpet. Sidney was the first man I heard playing a "growl" style and I played a lot of

Art Hodes and his Blue Note Jazz Men at Stuyvesant Casino, New York. Left to right: George Lugg, trombone; Henry Goodwin, trumpet; Albert Nicholas, clarinet; Kaiser Marshall, drums; Pops Foster, bass; Art Hodes, piano.

that style too. Because of that, I had two offers from Duke Ellington about that time, while he was playing in Washington before he went to New York. I didn't take them then because I was only seventeen and doubted my ability at the time. I also had offers from Duke in 1944 and 1945 but turned them down too.

I played with Sam Taylor for a year and a half after graduating from high school and then had an offer from Claude Hopkins, who was playing the Belmont Cabaret in Atlantic City. Besides myself on trumpet and Claude on piano, the band had Joe Haymer, alto sax; Daniel Doy, trombone; "Bass" Hill, bass; and Percy Johnson, drums. After one and a half months, the joint was padlocked and the band was stranded. One of the fellows—Bass Hill—had a car, and we heard a rumor of a job in Asbury Park at the Smile-A-While Inn, so we all piled in the car and took the chance of getting the job. When we got there, the whole band sat in for a couple of sets and we were hired three days later.

After we were there a while, we made up a special arrangement on the "St. Louis Blues," which featured trumpet. I would put on a long frock coat, high hat and white spectacles, and preach on my trumpet, using a telephone book for a bible. I have heard preaching on a trumpet since, but I think I was the first to start that style. I got a lot of my ideas from listening to Johnny Dunn's records, as he was my idol at the time.

Caroline Regan, scouting for a band for a trip to Europe with Josephine Baker's Review, heard our arrangement of the "St. Louis Blues," and that was it. We were signed up just before closing the season at Asbury Park and sailed in the middle of September, 1924, with the Review, which also featured Sidney Bechet. I was only eighteen at the time so Claude Hopkins had to get my mother's permission before I could go.

That was my first trip abroad and I stayed eighteen months all together, the first seven with the Review. Part of the Review featured an act by Sidney Bechet. He would come out on the stage wheeling a fruit cart, with imitation fruit piled in it, and dressed in a long duster. He'd come out shuffling along slow, and then he'd leave the cart and start to play the blues. I learned a lot from Bechet about the blues and I could play those things too. Sometimes Bechet wouldn't be there for his act, and I used to take his place. Bechet kept asking me to come with him, but I didn't do it then. I remember a poker game Bechet and I were in in Berlin, just before I left Hopkins and the Review. We were playing deuces wild, and when Bechet turned up with five deuces, that broke up the game.

Daniel Doy and I both left Hopkins in Berlin, after seven months. We played in Dresden, Germany and Brussels before getting back to Paris. While there, we played a benefit at the Opera Theater. The Review was in Paris then too, and one number featured the Claude Hopkins band and Sidney Bechet on a piece called "Prince Of Wails," and that stopped the show. How that man can play!

One night we were jamming in the Palermo Cabaret and were approached by a band leader with an offer to go to South America. It was a five months contract with a five month option and I took it. I only worked five months and wouldn't accept the option because my friend Doy became very ill and I brought him home. He only lived two months after that before he died.

Back in the States, I formed my own band, which was called the Bellhop Band, and kept that together about a year. The next four or five years was spent gigging around the East, including several trips to New York, where I decided to make my home. In 1932 I had the opportunity to go to Europe again, this time with Lucky Millinder's band. In the summer of '32 we played the Monte Carlo Casino, then the Rex Theater in Paris for a month and back to New York.

Between 1932 and 1938, I worked with many bands, including Edgar Hayes, Sidney Bechet, Ralph Cooper, who was a bandleader then, Charlie Johnson, Cab Calloway and many others. I was working with Edgar Hayes in 1938, when we made another trip to Europe, this time touring the Scandinavian countries on a ten-week tour of one-nighters. After we came back, I continued to play with Hayes until his band broke up in 1939. While with him, I played on a couple of record dates, the first in 1937 and again in 1938, all for Decca.

After another period of gigging around with many bands, I went with Cecil Scott, from 1943 to 1946. We played around New York, including the Ubangi Club, relief band at the Zanzibar, and the Savoy Ballroom, and then joined Art Hodes at the Stuyvesant Casino on January 13, 1946. I play a different kind of music with Art's band than I used to play but I like the style and think it's great. I think it's the best band of its kind, barring none, and I believe we're really going places.

James P.; Mr. Jimmy Johnson

In any list of great jazz pianists one name should always appear, James P. Johnson. I believe it was Bessie Smith who called out on a recording, "Play it, Mr. Jimmy Johnson." He sure did. This is a cat I heard a long time before I met. Somehow I had gotten my hands on a Columbia recording, "Snowy Morning Blues" and (on the flip side) "All That I Had Is Gone" and believe me, I heard me some piano. And as old as I've become and as far as I've traveled, there's something Jimmy did on that recording that I'd still like to arrive at. James P. was just too much. He was what I'd choose to call a two-fisted piano player. If you could dig this short, stumpy-built type of husky man (he carried plenty of beef) a-sittin' down at a piano. . . . I'll tell you somethin'; after I got around New York a bit to the point where I was gettin' dates and deliverin' bodies (arriving with a band), anytime I could bring an extra player you can bet on it that player was James P. One thing was for sure; I'd hear me some piano; the evening wouldn't be wasted.

After I got to know Jimmy pretty well he told me about him being Fats' (Waller's) teacher an' really, I could hear it if I'd stopped. Then, as I got a program (WNYC) of my own and so began collecting le jazz hot records I discovered more and more things Jimmy had played; accompaniments behind vocalists such as Bessie's "Backwater Blues," etc. That man taught me so much about jazz piano. And what a gentleman; never a word about anyone. And there's one recollection I'd like to share with you.

I'd called Jimmy at his home. Now I knew he'd been ailing, so, naturally I asked his wife "How is Jimmy?" And she says, "Aw, I don't know; he'll be sittin' in a chair an' I'll be talkin' to him, talkin' to him, and' goin' 'bout my business, you know how it is in the kitchen. An' after awhile I'll turn aroun' to look at him and don't you know he's sound asleep?" A. H.

Fats Waller and James P.

by James McGraw

". . . **a**nd with Fats and me at those two pianos, it was the drinkinest band ever put together." James P. Johnson gave his knee a resounding slap and the walls of the dressing room trembled with the roar of his rich laughter as he ended another of the many stories about his protege and closest friend, Fats Waller.

In a few minutes James P. was to play a requiem before a Town Hall audience in memory of the fabulous Fats. "Blues for Fats" James P. called it, and as we sat in the seemingly tiny room, dwarfed by his hugeness, the great jazz pianist reminisced about Fats, his pal for twenty-five years and the man whom he had influenced to become one of the greatest jazz musicians of our time.

James P. was in no laughing mood at the beginning. The death of Fats had been one of the most serious shocks in his life. He hadn't gone near the piano since learning of the terrible tragedy.

It was only when Eddie Condon asked him to play a requiem in honor of Fats, that James P. stirred. Nothing could be more fitting than to make music for the soul that was all music and happiness. Fats brimmed over with

music and the overflow came out in the form of laughter and happiness as contagious as his tunes. James P. would play those tunes today as he had never played them before.

And now, sitting here in the dressing room, Fats was with us in spirit and James P. warmed up to the occasion and told his stories the way Fats would have wanted them told, and we laughed without restraint, from our hearts, the way Fats always laughed.

It was only on the previous Monday when James P. was cutting some records with Yank Lawson, Rod Cless and some of the other boys for Bob Thiele, that he and Rod had gotten some big kicks going over the Chicago days when Rod worked a band with Fats. "Come and git your ham and eggs, Rod," Fats would say and Rod would have his nip of gin from Fats' jug before going on the stand.

But James P. never tired of telling tales of the adventures, fun and hell-raising he and his pupil and collaborator had been through together. There had been bad times, too, and as James P. put it, "We met the Blues in person." But this pair joked over adversity just as they welcomed good fortune. All they asked was to be let at a piano, any piano, be it

The Jazz Record

15c

No. 32   May, 1945

James P. Johnson

an ancient, broken-down box in a smoky cellar "speak" or the most perfect Chickering or Steinway on the stage of Carnegie Hall, and they were as happy as two big kids under a tree on Christmas morning.

James P. first met Fats in 1919. The roly-poly kid of 15 was brought to his home on 133rd Street by Daniel Brook, a mutual friend. Fats had heard the playing of the master in neighborhood ice-cream parlors on nickelodeon player piano rolls, for which James P., the only Negro artist recording for Q.R.S. at the time, was cutting such tunes as Spencer Williams' "Blues" and the music from *Shuffle Along*, which he had written. Fats had been playing hymns for a church on the organ, but when he heard James P.'s playing he knew that here was the music he wanted to play and this was the way he wanted to play it.

He practiced the tunes on the organ and at a battered piano at Brook's home and hounded his host daily to be introduced to James P. Finally the meeting took place and James P. instantly recognized that the boy had all the requirements which could be developed into great jazz musicianship. Unhesitatingly, he took Fats on for lessons without charge.

The rest is history. How these two, tutor and pupil, grew up together, experimented with forms, collaborated on some of the biggest hit tunes of our time and played some of the sweetest music ever to come out of a piano either together or separately, is legendary.

"The drinkinest band" referred to by James P., played on stage at the Lafayette Theatre in Harlem in 1928. Some of the musicians in that band were Teddy Hill, Jack White and Otto Hardwicke among the six altos and tenors, Bass Edwards on bass horn, Garvin Bushell, clarinet, Harry Hall, bass fiddle and Teaward, Harry White and Big Charlie Green, trombones, whom James P. called, "The three trombones who could consume a saloon." Together with Fats and James P. in this lineup the curtain never did raise on time.

While working this job, Fats and James P. used to meet in a nearby bar before going on. One day they met as usual, and, it being two days before pay day, each expected the other to be broke. But to Fats' astonishment, James P. whipped out $75 in cash and told Fats how he'd drawn it on the pretext he had to pay union dues. Fats was not to be outdone. He rushed around the corner to the theatre and told the boss if he didn't get $150 for union dues he wouldn't be allowed to go on that night. How come, he was asked, that James P. paid $75 dues and he had to pay $150. "Well you see," Fats explained, "this union charges by weight and you know I'm twice as heavy as James P." He got the money, went back to lord it over his pal and the curtain was later than usual that night.

During the depression they were hit pretty hard and James P. was forced to give up the home in which they had been accustomed to practicing and composing daily. Everything but James P.'s piano was put in storage and it was sent to his sister's home. She put it, together with her own piano, in a small extra room. Here these two musical giants would sit, side by side, hours on end, smoking endless cigarettes, talking music, laughing over music, tinkling and banging music, playing duets for their own pleasure and composing the tunes that are now famous throughout the world.

Shortly before the Lafayette Theatre band broke up, the management had provided the musicians with new outfits to be worn on stage. These consisted of high hats, white gloves, ties and fancy plungers for the horns and various other paraphernalia. When the show closed, Fats fell heir to all this junk and stored it in his cellar. For some time after that, whenever he needed pocket money, Fats would dig out some of the stuff and take it to the Rhythm Club or one of the other uptown night spots and auction it off to the highest bidder.

Fats played at Tillies' Clam House during prohibition. One slow night, Walter Donaldson, the composer of hit tunes, came in. Being quick to satisfy his customer, Fats went right into "My Blue Heaven" whereupon Donaldson bought him a drink. Before the evening was over Fats had played the tune 25 times, never twice the same way, and Donaldson had stood him a drink each time he played the number.

Another time, pianist Joe Sullivan was having a party in his Hollywood bungalow and Fats was handling the piano. Neighbors complained of the noise and a cop was sent over to make inquiries. Joe came to the door and asked, "And what is your name, officer?"

"O'Shea," answered the cop, "And yours?"

"O'Sullivan," said Joe, giving his right name.

The cop looked in through the open door and regarded Fats, still banging away unmolested by the intrusion. He recognized the famous swaying, broad back and bobbing round head. Turning to Joe, he said, "And I suppose now you're going to tell me that's O'Waller at the piano!" He was invited in and the party continued noisier than before.

Fats left many good things behind for remembrance. His words and music we will hear wherever there is good jazz being played. The recordings of his brilliant playing and inimitable singing and of the wonderful bands he organized and led, we have and will cherish. His fine work in the movies will be shown to us again. But nothing can ever replace the radiance he possessed and transmitted to others wherever he went, his uninhibited laughter and his quick and brilliant wit. He lived only to be happy and to make others happy. Musicians everywhere will long remember Fats dropping by to sit in on a set and knock them out with his playing. He was every inch a musician's musician. His death is an inestimable loss to the world and particularly to lovers of real jazz everywhere.

James P. summed him up in these words, "Some little people has music in them, some big people has a lot of music in them, but Fats, he was all music and you know how big he was."

Gene Sedric

To tell you the truth I don't know a hell-of-a-lot about Gene S. Yes I worked with him in N.Y.C. We did some things together. So this bit I'm writing is really about Fats Waller. Again, I never worked with Fats! We play the same instrument; piano. But I heard him; oh how I heard him. You know the song, "Please Give Me Something To Remember You By?" Well, Fats laid it on me but good, one evening. Him I'll always remember. . . . It went somethin' like this.

Nick's (in the Village) was *the* place to play if your music was the jazz I call jazz. Nick Rongetti (the late) was a pianist turned nite-club owner. And he certainly knew his jazz music; and musicians. The players he employed looked like a "who's who in jazz" if you scanned it on paper. If you were fortunate enough to work there, you had some recognition. Pay? Well, so-so. But it was the spot to play, and even if you weren't working there you'd drop in and give-a-listen.

This particular evening I'll never forget, I was sittin' at the bar, a'listening. There was a bandstand and an extra piano out on the floor (Nick wasn't a dance-fan; rarely did anyone venture to use that floor for dancing). That music made me focus my eyes on the man at the piano. I didn't believe it; Fats Waller. Certainly he wasn't working there; so Rongetti must have got him to sit in. Man, those sounds comin' at me were great. Fats carrying that band like kitty-land. Big smile, and all that music comin' out so good together. I was in the clouds. Could have sat there, listening, all evening.

Suddenly Fats catches my eye and waves at me. So naturally I wave back. But now his wave turns into a "come-on-over-here" signal. So I do that. And when I get to the piano Waller gets up and hands me the seat. I had no idea; nor desire. Man, I wouldn't have interrupted that goings-on for anything. But now it was mine. And immediately, as we started playing, I knew I was in trouble. For that band didn't have it together. That beat that I heard from up front wasn't there. Just to keep it together got me wet-sweat in a minute. No big smile on my face. And playing a chorus when it came my turn was a chore. Boy, did I appreciate how great Fats was. By sheer effort he made that rhythm join him in "where-it's-at." And controlling it;

keeping it right there, he still managed to say (musically) what he had to say. That was the mark of a giant.

I was to see, and hear, Sidney Bechet do that at a recording date I was on. But I haven't met too many others (I'm tryin' to think if I've ever met any) that could whip a band in shape while in action, and do your thing, and have it all come out great. No doubt in my book; Fats Waller was a jazz giant. . . . A. H.

Trouping with Fats Waller

by Gene Sedric

I first met Fats shortly after I came back from Europe with the Sam Wooding band. He was playing on the Early Bird program over WABC. Of course I had always been familiar with his work from the time I was a kid; at home we had had player piano rolls by him and James P. Johnson.

Then one morning I got into a jam session with Fats; we jammed all night and then he asked me to come on down to Victor with him and make some records. We made some that turned out very good—"Don't Let It Bother You" was the first, and some of the others were "Baby Brown," "Night Winds," and "Georgia May." It was a small band, with Billy Taylor, Coleman Johnson, and Harry Dial on drums. Those records turned out to be such a success that Fats' manager talked him into organizing a permanent band, because the public was beginning to demand him and his band in person. He had had bands before but never took it very seriously. That was really the beginning of Fats Waller as a band leader.

I was working with Henderson and Redman at that time, and also doing some recording with Fats. When he formed his own band he asked me to come along, and I did.

Altogether I think I must have made about 300 records with Fats. Many times we would

stay in the Victor studio practically all day and all night recording. And once in a while some of us would go out with various other

Fats Waller and Hugues Panassié

groups, or make records under fictitious names. We made quite a few records we didn't even know the titles of. Often some of the boys would hear a record played, and say: "Is that us? Sounds like us."

Among my favorites in all those records are "Baby Brown," "Bye Bye Baby," "Big Chief De Soto," "Clarinet Marmalade," "I've Got My Fingers Crossed," "West Winds," "Cabin in the Sky," "Honeysuckle Rose" (of course), "Christopher Columbus," "Yacht Club Swing," and "Spreadin' Rhythm Around." I made the last set with him that was made before he died. It was a big band, fifteen pieces, with men like Joe Thomas and Johnny "Bugs" Hamilton on trumpets, Scoville Brown, reeds, Al Casey, guitar, Fred Robinson on trombone. We made "Your Socks Don't Match" and the "Jitterbug Waltz." That last one was one of Fats' biggest sellers, a really great record, in waltz time but a killer.

It was a funny thing that out of the hundreds of great hits Fats made on records, most all the largest hits were numbers he didn't care about making, but we'd just go into it spontaneously and some of the ones we didn't like and thought would be no good turned out to be the greatest hits.

From the time he first gave me a contract to work with him, in 1937, I was associated with Fats to the end. From 1939 to 1942 we travelled all over the country, always on the move, travelling all the time, playing theatres, one-nighters, clubs and concerts. There was such demand for Waller through his records that he was one of the greatest box office attractions of all time. One of our greatest thrills was when we played the Victor Music Hall on the radio four times in succession. In 1942 we gave a concert in Seattle with the orchestra, which was a great success. The largest crowd we ever played to was at the musical fete held every year in Chicago at Soldier Field. It holds 120,000 people, capacity, and that time, in 1940, it was packed. It was only the small band, and each one of us had his own microphone to amplify it enough for that big crowd. The largest dance crowd we ever played to was 20,000 in New Orleans at the race track.

Nobody who was a personal fan of Waller ever forgot his playing, but very few got a chance to really hear the finer things he could do on piano. Through his recordings and picture success the public went for his jive and singing, which to the general public really overshadowed his ability as one of the world's greatest swing pianists. Many times we would be on the job and Waller playing great piano, modern stuff with technique and fine chords, and people would say, "Come on, Fats, you're laying down, give us some jive." This at times would be a great drag to him; he would look at us and say, "You see these people, they won't let me play anything real fine, want to hear all that jive!" But it was the jive instead of fine playing that made him a wealthy man. He was a great comedian, but his only love was music. He loved to study and practice. I personally believe he would have been much happier had his jive not overshadowed his great musical ability.

Everybody knows Fats was a man who drank, but he was always able to do his job, and I have never seen him late at a job, or unable to play. He was the greatest and most likable leader I ever worked with. He was always good to the boys in the band, gave them expensive gifts, pleasure trips, the best of everything. Once in Chicago we had Monday off, and Fats was going to New York on business and one of the boys wanted to go with him, so Fats got two reservations and brought him to New York on the plane. And once when we were playing an engagement in Milwaukee we had to be in Boston the next morning to open a theatre engagement. The only way was by plane, so he chartered a whole plane and carried the band in it, instruments and all. That trip was so rough that when we got there we were all so nervous we could hardly make the show, and we all took a good drink to get our nerves together.

It was nothing for Fats to eat ten or twelve hamburgers or hot dogs. Working with no time to eat, we used to go to a White Tower for hamburgers after the job, but we always arranged to get there to beat Fats' valet because if he got there first there would be no hamburgers left.

Working in Chicago one year, he stayed at the Dusable Hotel, and had an organ put in his suite of rooms. After an all-night job Fats would rush home and play the organ. All the other tenants of the hotel would be in the room, and he would play all night. It was one of the greatest treats any music lover or musician would want to have. He only played his best when you could catch him without an audience and just let him sit down and play for you, organ or piano.

He could play boogie woogie but didn't think much of it—but still he was better than most you year. He liked the blues, he was crazy about the blues. He used to say I was God's gift to the tenor sax. Among pianists I often heard him mention James P. Johnson and Art Tatum. He said James P. was his inspiration, the man who gave him the foundation. He could appreciate any kind of music, and had a thorough knowledge of the classics, and the largest collection of records of anybody I know. He was also a very religious man, with a thorough knowledge of the Bible, and often said that some day he might become a preacher, and go out and give sermons with a big band behind him.

He made more money than any colored band leader in the business. The year he died he paid tax on $71,000. He could always go out and get $3,000 a week as a single. Of course he didn't have the expenses of Ellington and others who always carry big bands. And he had relatives, and was very generous to them.

He was a great man. He lived every day. I heard him say that when he died the world would owe him nothing.

"You Got To Be Original, Man"

by Allan Morrison

Lester Young, whose many adherents will tell you is far and away the greatest contemporary jazz tenor saxophonist, passionately believes originality should be the highest goal of art and life. Without it, he says, art or anything else worth while, stagnates, eventually degenerates. He maintains, furthermore, that musicians wishing to say something really vital must learn to express their inner feelings with a minimum of outside influence.

These views were expressed just the other day by the famous tenor artist during an informal conversation between jazz musicians that was held under the best possible circumstances for such talk—a smoky hotel room lighted by a single pale-green bulb.

Outside the skies were gray and a fine rain sprayed gently through the open window. From a disc spinning on a tiny turntable on the floor the husky, sensuous voice of Billie Holiday flowed all around the room and did soothing things to the ears of the men who listened.

Lester lay across the bed, his belt unbuckled, his half-closed eyes looking up at the ceiling. Every so often he would follow the solos on the records by making funny little humming sounds always in perfect tempo with the music. Sometimes Vic Dickenson's bold trombone choruses shook him out of a luxurious lethargy and made him write crazy patterns in space with his forefingers. No one else moved. No one else spoke. Billie Holiday was insinuatingly saying, "You Go To My Head."

Finally someone broke the long silence and asked Lester wasn't he born in California?" Lester said no and there was a pause. "I was born in Mississippi," he confessed, and there was a tinge of embarrassment in the way he said it.

"But I was raised in the carnivals," he went on. There was real pride in his tone this time.

"The carnivals?" someone asked.

"Yeah, travelin' carnivals, minstrel shows, y'know." The words now began to tumble easily out of Lester's mouth. He was reaching

THE JAZZ RECORD

ART HODES, *Publisher*

15c
A COPY

No. 15   New York, N. Y.   December, 1943

Lester Young

back into the past and remembering things he seldom talked about. His eyes opened wider as he spoke and he gestured slightly with his hands. He spoke of one-night stands in Southern towns and of the peculiar impermanence that characterizes the life of the itinerant musician.

He spoke too of the musical prowess of his father, Billie Young, a very remarkable man, who "played all instruments" and gave him the only music lessons he ever received.

Papa Young led a family band that toured with minstrel shows. Lester started playing with the band as a drummer when he was 10. Then he shifted to alto sax.

What made him change instruments? someone wanted to know.

"Bein' lazy, y'know," he replied. "Carryin' all them drums got to be a real grind. I decided I'd better get me a lighter instrument. That's all there was to it, man."

An alto saxophone having been duly obtained, he set about mastering that instrument with the aid of his father. But Papa Young was too busy a man, and after a few weeks the lessons stopped.

He hates to talk in terms of influences because he feels that a real musician doesn't need influence outside of his own imagination and responsiveness to life. So when someone asked who was the biggest single influence in his career, Lester arched his brows and said, "Nobody, really."

Frankie Trumbauer, a white alto player who gained some fame during the twenties, impressed him quite a lot, he said. One record in particular left a mark on his musical mind, "Singin' The Blues" on which was also featured the great Bix Beiderbecke, the poetic trumpeter of jazz's golden age, who died in 1931. Lester carried a copy of "Singin' The Blues" around with him and played it over and over again.

Bix, he remembers, sounded "just like a colored boy sometimes. He was fine." Beiderbecke's lyrical beauty of line and tone moved him. Trumbauer's startling technique made him conscious of how little he knew. He plugged away at alto for five years, covering a lot of territory but always managing to come back to Kansas City where he did a considerable amount of free-lance jobbing.

In 1931 he ran away from the family band. "I just wanted to be grown," he said in explanation. That left but seven playing

Youngs. Lester drifted into a barnstorming life, starved a little but learned a lot.

While playing with an aggregation styling themselves Art Bronson's Bostonians he changed instruments again, this time taking up the tenor saxophone. The Bronson band had its headquarters in Salinas, Kansas, but got around a lot of the Southwest area.

"What made you change this time?" the bass player, who had been standing in the corner, asked.

"Well, it was a funny deal. There was a tenor player in the band but he'd get high and never show up for dates. He just kept messin' up till one day the leader got mad and said he'd buy me a tenor if I would play it. I said I'd play it. When I saw the beat-up tenor he bought, though, I almost changed my mind. It was an old Pan-American job. But I played it and liked it, what's more."

He went on to say that he experienced no difficulty transferring his easy fluency on the alto to the heavier-toned tenor. His approach to tenor playing was essentially an alto approach, he said. Before he knew it he was playing tenor, alto style. It was unique, new, exciting to musicians who heard it.

"What about Hawkins?" some one asked him.

Lester looked up without changing expression and said: "What about Hawkins?"

"Didn't he give you any ideas?"

"There you go again," Lester said, showing some slight impatience. "Must a musician always get his ideas from another musician? I don't think so. I never did have a favorite tenor. I never heard much of Hawk except an occasional record. Everybody was copyin' him. The whole jazz world was on a Hawkins kick."

He lay back on the bed and closed his eyes. He continued talking about Coleman Hawkins, of his importance to jazz and the tremendous influence he has exerted on tenor players the world over. One got the impression very quickly that Lester is no devotee of the Hawk's, that the two greatest tenor men in jazz are worlds apart temperamentally and musically. Noticeable too in his voice was a slight trace of contempt for tenor players who slavishly followed the Coleman Hawkins pattern.

"I couldn't see copyin' The Hawk or any of the others," he said, shaking his head from side to side. "You got to have a style that's all your own. A man can only be a stylist if he makes up his mind not to copy anybody."

Lester made up his mind a long time ago that he was going to play music the way he felt it and not the way other musicians played it.

He started experimenting with tone colors and eccentricities of line and rhythm while he was with Walter Page's 13 Original Oklahoma Blue Devils, one of the most exciting combinations in jazz history. Apart from Page, now Count Basie's bassist, the Blue Devils' other distinguished alumnus is Hot Lips Page, the gutty trumpet man.

"We got around everywhere," Lester recalled, "But we starved to death, you know what I mean. We had no capital, no bookings, no nothing. But it was one great band that played some fine music."

For two years, 1934-35, Lester "scuffled" with the Blue Devils. Musically there were kicks in abundance. Financially, he was broke most of the time. When the band finally broke up Lester hung around Kansas City earning a thin living from one-night jobs.

"Life in K. C. in them days was hard, man. We were all scufflin' like mad. Saturday and Sunday we'd get a gig or two, but Monday, Tuesday, Wednesday, Thursday, Friday there was nothin' much to be had."

A brief period in Minneapolis was followed by his joining the original Count Basie band that opened in the Reno Club in Kansas City and wound up as one of the top money-makers in the orchestra industry.

"I had a lot of fun with the Basie band," he said slowly, staring out of the window. "There were plenty kicks." The coming to the band of Herschel Evans, the brilliant, deep-toned tenor star whom death cut down in 1939, brought him a new kind of thrill, he admitted. He "dug" him hard, but it wasn't until Hersch died that he realized what a stimulating force he had been not only to himself, but the whole band. He quickly qualified this appraisal by saying that Herschel was at heart and in style essentially a Hawkins man.

"Most of the time Hersch sounded just like Hawk to me," he said. There was no softness in his voice as he said it. It was a coldly critical statement. A Hawkins man. There were Hawkins men in the room and one of them asked why had he resisted the Hawkins trend so vigorously.

" 'Cause I wanted to be original. Originality's the thing. You can have tone and technique and a lot of other things but without originality you ain't really nowhere. Gotta be original."

In 1941 he parted company with the Basie group when the Count dropped him for failing to make a recording session. That closed an era. Reverses followed. For a time he found himself drifting downward, his morale sagging, his inspiration ebbing. The small combination he formed with his brother, Lee, gave him kicks but played unevenly at the outset, and suffered ups and downs right out to the coast. By the time of his induction the band had begun to play with the old fire of the Young family band.

"What was the Army like?" asked the drummer, who had just come in.

"A nightmare, man, one mad nightmare," Lester murmured, shaking his head sadly. "They sent me down South, Georgia. That was enough to make me blow my top. It was a drag, Jack."

He found it hard to reconstruct the nightmare. All he remembers was hating the army with a furious intensity, hating the brass, reveille, injustice to Negroes and the caste system in the South. He ended up in a disciplinary center in Savannah. That was sheer hell, he said.

Someone shut the window. Lester sat down on the bed, looked up at the drummer who had just changed the record, and smiled.

The record was "D. B. Blues," a Lester original.

Bob Wilber

I run into Bob every now and then. Bechet didn't hurt him (musically); but Wilber goes his own way. Still the S. B. influence is there. You can't hang around a giant and come away poorer. Sidney enriched everyone he touched; he was that kind of player. There was the State College date we did in Pennsylvania. It was my date. I'd booked it; but with Sidney on it, it became Bechet's date. He worked that hard to make it good. Anything that came to mind that needed doing he'd step in and do. You see . . .

We'd driven some 8 hours (starting like 5 a.m., immediately after finishing up on a gig) and we arrived in not the greatest of shape. In fact a couple of my guys were feeling no pain (if you know what I mean). Sidney got them both to take a cold bath, plus some aspirins; then walked them for blocks, just to get 'em straight. Then he played the gig; and knocked everybody out.

Did I ever tell you how we'd met? We were both on staff for Blue Note records. One time the date was named after Bechet; another it was Art Hodes' Hot Five. But no matter; Sidney worked those dates as if they were all his dates. Yeh; now I recall our meeting. It hadn't come about on a good note. He was supposed to play a session for me and for some reason never showed. But he did make it the following week. When the union advised me not to pay him, and to bring charges against him, I decided that wasn't for me. So we became friends.

Bechet didn't stand for no nonsense. For some reason he took a dislike to a certain drummer's playing. He only discussed it once with me. I couldn't bring myself to let this cat go. Well, the next date Bechet got, he used Wettling on drums and James P. Johnson on piano. Couldn't blame him for that; that was in good taste. Two very fine players. But dig this. Bechet, of course, was colored. So was the drummer I couldn't bear to part with. But Wettling was white. With Sidney color didn't count. If you couldn't please him musically, forget it.

The '40s (when I ran with Bechet) weren't the best of times materially; financially. Sidney tried various businesses to make things go, but never successfully, or for long. And he liked to sail; take to the water. For a bit I heard he dug photography. Finally, he left the U.S. scene and landed in France. I'd heard he married some wealthy woman (titled). They must have loved him over there. When he passed on they re-named a street after Sidney Bechet.   A. H.

Sidney Bechet, Musical Father to Bob Wilber

by Al Avakian

There is a natural drive in a man to perpetuate himself. The biologists, psychologists, sociologists and philosophers all have their own way of explaining and expressing this drive, but it all adds up to a desire to continue something worth while that one has started. The basic, physical perpetuation is simple enough. It is the foundation of that all-important institution, the family.

With the artist, the problem is more complicated. He must find a willing pupil with the proper temperament, ability, capacity for learning, and feeling to carry on his own creation. In nineteen-year-old Bob Wilber, Sidney Bechet has found that pupil and, what's more, a spiritual son.

When Sidney and Bob are on the stand at Jimmy Ryan's they sound like the Bechet soprano sax of 1947 and the Bechet clarinet of 1912. "High Society," Panama," "When the Saints Go Marching In" are typical numbers played with complete sympathy between the two instrumentalists.

How did the 'teen-age son of a Scarsdale businessman and the aging veteran of the high and low roads of jazz ever get together? How did this green, bespectacled high school student learn and absorb the style of one of the creators of jazz in less than two years and to such a point that a standard gag today on hearing Sidney play is: "Gee, plays just like Bob Wilber, doesn't he?"

Bob has not only absorbed Sidney's full tone and sensitive phrasing, but he has also inherited Sidney's natural leadership. Among veteran musicians of many times his own experience, Wilber holds his own. As the leader of the Bob Wilber Wildcats (the Scarsdale High School Gang), he is a standout performer among several promising youngsters who have performed as a group at Jimmy Ryan's jam sessions and won an award presented at the Press Photographers' Ball. The names of these youngsters will perhaps someday eclipse those of the group's 1920's counterpart, the Austin High Gang. Bob Wilber, soprano and clarinet; Ed Hubble, trombone; Johnny Glasel, cornet; Denny Strong, drums; Dick Wellstood, piano, and Charlie Traeger, bass.

Sidney is proud of this boy, but doesn't discount his own part in molding this artist of tomorrow. Sidney will readily admit that Bob couldn't play a thing when he first came to him. "He wanted to play, but he couldn't. Laura—she's my wife—she says, 'You're drivin' that boy too hard, he ain't gonna come back.'" Sidney laughed to himself quietly in recollection.

"Yas, she says, 'You're drivin' that poor boy too hard. He's too young.' But he come back. I had to tell him a lie—I said, 'That's it Bobby, that's it, now you're comin'.' I had to tell him a lie, but he come back."

"You told me lots of lies, Pops, or you'd never have seen me again."

"Yas, I did. But you come back. This boy, when he first come over to me, he thought that old clarinet would blow itself. He says, 'I can't play all that without breathin'!' But I gave him a little sherrry to build himself up.

JAZZ RECORD

25¢

JUNE, 1947
No. 56

Sidney Bechet and Bob Wilber

You know, he was anaemic then. And my wife says, 'Now he's just a young boy—you take it easy—he shouldn't be takin' that stuff. You're rushin' him too hard.' But I says, 'I got to build him up or he'll never blow.' And then I tell Bobby another lie, 'That's it Bobby, now you got it.' Yas, he kept comin' back and he can really blow now. Man, he can blow.

"And then there was the time when they wouldn't let Bobby practice at home." Sidney was now sitting on the edge of the Ryan's bandstand, sitting on his hands as his eyes narrowed.

Bob broke in, "Now I live up on 111th Street. Dick Wellstood, Denny Strong and I live in a closet together. We moved the brooms and pails out and moved ourselves in. You should see that place now. Books all over. E. E. Cummings, Joyce, Huxley —Wellstood wants to be a writer."

Someone said, "Plays piano like that and he wants to write?"

"Yeah and he plays awful good."

Sidney shook his head bent down about waist level and chuckled to himself, "Just listen to that Bob Wilber—but he can blow awful good now."

Selections from the Gutter

by Art Hodes

"Night has fallen; Darkness settles down on me.

Blues keep callin'; Callin' everywhere I see . . .

Pull myself together . . . Bottom ain't no place for me."

I wrote these words to a blues I composed. It represented a feeling. "I've been down so long 'til down don't worry me." To understand, you have to go back; way back. Lets retire to the '20s. . . .

I remember being in the union hall, and someone I knew would point at another musician, saying "There's a legit man." It seemed the highest compliment; like we were in awe. It almost followed that we who weren't were illegitimate. Certainly, if you played jazz, you were on the bottom of the social heap. A body to be pulled out of the musical background, and given a few bars to feature in (actually to pep up the proceedings; to "get hot").

"Hey, do you read or fake?" How often we were to hear that expression. There's a story of two musicians meeting and chatting. One says, "I heard this Sidney Bechet play. Man, he really can blow. But he's not a musician; he don't read." I don't know if it's true (that Sidney didn't read music). But it shows how the jazz player was rated.

You could say we were consigned to the gutter. Certainly, for years, jazz didn't get top billing. A few there were that raised their heads. But the many played the bottom-land. Cow Cow Davenport wrote some 300 tunes, but it practically took an act of Congress to get him his ASCAP rating and some sort of income. Big Bill Broonzy composed about as many blues but he never scratched the material-financial surface. On and on. Jelly Roll Morton and Muggsy Spanier had great jazz bands; it never led to bread; just a taste. Jimmy Noone! One of the all-time greats. Edmond Hall. Buster Bailey. You talk about clarinet players; but did any one of them ever rate tops? How many of our greats could have made it at least 10 years longer than they did, had they got the acclaim and fame and money their jazz ability deserved? No tellin'; but I do believe these very lacks ate into them.

Yeh: Jazz came out of the feelings of people; their lives. It's not something you think; it's something you are. It's your make-up. It's the greatest but it exacts a high price. As one critic said, "Art would just as soon play in a basement." Well, the smarter the setting, the less chance you had of hearing jazz played there. I've heard it at a barbeque joint. I heard it at rent parties, and a few "out-of-the-ordinary" nite clubs. In my day the best night club in Chicago was the Chez Paree. I never heard jazz played there. The Bucket-of-Blood, the Upholstered Sewer (or as more than one player states it, the Shit-Houses) that's where you heard it.

That's the way it was. That's what most of the stories in this book bring out. The background; the way it was. But don't shed no tears; for the real jazz player had something money couldn't buy; the feeling you got from the music itself. One critic said "I don't un-derstand why Art didn't pick up the ball and run." Run where? Where could you take the music that was in you? Top-land was a phony-baloney (still is, if you look keenly). Work whatever you can get, and then go out somewhere and play for kicks? Well, why can't you play for kicks? That's somethin' we all tried. But always compromised.

I hope you feel why I call this collection of tales *Selections from the Gutter;* for like jazz itself, its something you dig by feel. You know you can learn to read (music) an' run them scales ragged. But if you ain't got anything to say, forget it brother. Again, as Duke (Ellington) put it, "It don't mean a thing if it ain't got that swing." Man, I'm cuttin' out. I just feel like sittin' down an' playing me some jazz. Probably start with the blues. Come to think of it I did record "Selection from the Gutter." Just the blues. I told my story. A 3-minute track; and I had somethin' down I could live with. I exposed part of me. And today when I hear it I can live with it. And that's how I feel about these *Selections from the Gutter.* . . .